"A HOUSE DIVIDED CANNOT STAND."

ABRAHAM LINCOLN

PREVIOUS PAGE: *The 33-star United States flag was flown over Fort Sumter during the bombardment of April 14, 1861. After the fort's capitulation it was replaced by a Confederate flag like the one shown at top, featuring a star for each of the seven states that had seceded by that date.*

THIS PAGE: *Few mementos of the Civil War were more treasured than photographs of soldiers in uniform or images of loved ones back home. The photographs shown above offer a cross section of Americans caught up in the epic struggle. From left to right: Captain James Holeman, 24th North Carolina; Hispanic Confederate from Houston, Texas; photograph of a young girl found on the battlefield of Port Republic, Virginia; Confederate officer from the western theater; Private Benjamin Franklin Ammons, 1st Tennessee Heavy Artillery; wedding portrait from North Carolina; trooper of the 5th Massachusetts Cavalry (Colored); unidentified Union soldier.*

FOLLOWING PAGE: *President Lincoln meets with Allan Pinkerton, head of the Federal Secret Service (left), and Major General John A. McClernand near the battlefield at Antietam in early October 1862. Pinkerton, celebrated as a detective, flopped as a spy.*

EYEWITNESS TO THE

CIVIL WAR

THE COMPLETE HISTORY
FROM SECESSION TO RECONSTRUCTION

EDITED BY **NEIL KAGAN** NARRATIVE BY **STEPHEN G. HYSLOP**
INTRODUCTION BY **HARRIS J. ANDREWS**

NATIONAL GEOGRAPHIC
WASHINGTON, D.C.

CONTENTS

ABOUT THIS BOOK

THE CIVIL WAR IN THE DIGITAL AGE

Through high-resolution scans, researchers now have access to all of the fragile original glass plate Civil War negatives in the Library of Congress collections. Some of the 7,000 images lack corresponding prints and have not been widely seen before. Because the high-resolution scans used throughout this book are of such superb quality, many surprising details are revealed for the first time, allowing readers to examine anew everything from facial expressions to buttons on uniforms to building signs. In addition, many photographs are examined as artifacts, taking the reader behind the scenes to explore the photographer's original notations scratched into the glass plates on the battlefields of the Civil War.

NARRATIVE

The opening spread of each chapter is distinguished by a dramatic black background containing a text block that sums up the major themes of the period or year. The narrative that follows, based on first-person accounts and the work of eminent historians, is divided into chronological sections devoted to a critical battle or campaign. Time lines of key events, superb National Geographic maps, and quotes throughout the text and in the margins add both clarity and texture to the story and help convey the powerful emotional history of the Civil War.

ON THE SECOND DAY OF THE BATTLE OF GETTYSBURG, WITH LITTLE more than an hour of daylight remaining, Colonel Isaac E. Avery of the 6th North Carolina was mortally wounded as he led a brigade up the slope of Cemetery Hill. As he lost consciousness he scrawled a final message: "Tell my father I died with my face to the enemy."

In *Eyewitness to the Civil War,* National Geographic offers you an opportunity to experience the emotional history of this tragic era through the eyes and words of those who were there. A compelling narrative tells the complete history chronologically, starting with a prologue on secession, followed by five chapters organized by year and an epilogue on the difficult period of Reconstruction.

To add to the eyewitness experience we pored over thousands of photographs, battle sketches, letters, maps, and artifacts from public and private collections around the country, carefully selecting more than 450 and placing them within the text exactly where key events unfold. Hundreds of quotes further define each critical event. Thirty "Eyewitness" boxes that feature an original letter, first-person account, or diary entry appear chronologically and provide an in-depth view of what life was like for soldiers and citizens. In addition, rare historical maps by Union cartographer Private Robert Knox Sneden are combined with period photographs and art in specially designed "Mapping the War" spreads to give the reader an eyewitness perspective on 11 major battles. Finally, we created sidebars and photo essays on significant topics such as slavery, soldier life, heavy artillery and other equipment, the cavalry, medicine, the role of music, and the assassination of Lincoln.

When viewed together, these features, artfully designed and interwoven, add depth to the book, making it ideal to read from cover to cover or just to browse, experiencing a surprise on every page.

NEIL KAGAN
Editor

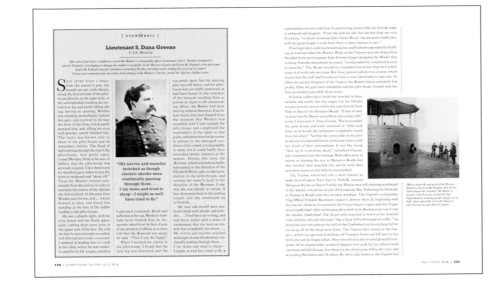

EYEWITNESS ACCOUNTS

Thirty eyewitness accounts are placed in gray boxes and appear chronologically as events unfold. Each account contains the name of the eyewitness, a photo, and a brief introductory note that puts the account into perspective. For example, during the famous naval battle between the ironclads *Monitor* and *Merrimac*, Lieutenant S. Dana Greene had to take control of the *Monitor* after his commander was blinded in battle. This account, like all the others we've chosen, puts the reader in the battle alongside the brave soldiers who were there.

MAPPING THE WAR

Specially designed spreads featuring historical maps by soldier, artist, and cartographer Robert Knox Sneden give us an eyewitness perspective on 11 major battles. Designed with a red background to set them apart, these "Mapping the War" features combine Sneden's rare maps with period photographs and artwork. The accompanying text tells the story of the battle, directing the reader to points on the map identified with leader lines, while the photographs and artwork show you exactly what some of these key locations looked like.

PICTURE ESSAYS

Six four-spread photographic essays, designed with a parchment-colored background, are located between each chapter. These essays combine documentary photographs with artifacts and text to focus on a specific theme, such as "The Cavalryman's Flair," or a specific event, such as "The Assassination of Lincoln." Smaller essays and sidebars, also identified by a parchment-colored background, are located throughout the text and illuminate a variety of rich topics, from field music to heavy artillery to the plight of Federal prisoners at Andersonville.

EYEWITNESS TO HISTORY

BEGINNING IN THE SPRING OF 1861, THE UNITED STATES SPLIT INTO TWO WAR-ring nations, North and South, set apart by cultural differences and the bitter and divisive issue of slavery. Many Northerners, particularly New England men, marched south on a crusade to put an end to the Confederacy's "peculiar institution," a slave system that they had come to view as an intolerable blight on the republic, while others fought to preserve the 85-year-old union of states that they cherished as the world's great beacon of liberty.

Their opponents in the seceding states fought to preserve a way of life they had inherited from their ancestors. Whether they viewed slavery as good or evil, few could conceive of accepting any change imposed from the outside. While some people on both sides decried the violent breakup of the American Republic, many felt a bit relieved that this long-simmering sectional rivalry, which had troubled the nation since its inception, would finally be settled.

The resulting Civil War, fought through four Aprils between 1861 and 1865, would become a defining event in American history. Innovations in military technology and the willingness of armies on both sides to withstand terrible punishment resulted in ruinous battles, and casualties reached staggering proportions, with more than 600,000 soldiers dying of battlefield wounds or the devastating epidemic diseases and infections that stalked camps and hospitals. The war convulsed society and government, uprooted families, and scattered populations.

In spite of the carnage and misery, many who took part in the conflict believed that their struggle was necessary and worthwhile. On Memorial Day, May 30, 1884, Oliver Wendell Holmes, Jr., Massachusetts Supreme Court Justice and Civil War veteran, gave an address in the town hall at Keene, New Hampshire, before members of the Grand Army of the Republic. In his speech Holmes argued that his generation had been compelled by the challenges of the Civil War to better themselves and their world and called upon his fellow veterans to bear witness to the tremendous ordeal they had undergone. "The generation that carried on the war," Holmes proclaimed, had "been set apart by its experience. Through our great good fortune, in our youth our hearts were touched with fire. It was given to us to learn at the outset that life is a profound and passionate thing. While we are permitted to scorn nothing but indifference, and do not pretend to undervalue the worldly rewards of ambition, we have seen with our own eyes, beyond and above the gold fields, the snowy heights of honor, and it is for us to bear the report to those who come after us."

In fact, the urge to "bear the report" of those great events had already been acted on by many participants while the war still raged. Soldiers and civilians who were caught up in the struggle heeded the inborn desire to record what they experienced. They witnessed history in the making and found many ways to convey their testimony to contemporaries and leave a record for posterity.

Soldiers wrote letters to loved ones at home and kept diaries and journals under arduous conditions. War correspondents and artists from the major newspapers and journals of the day followed the armies, intent on satisfying the public's insatiable demand for news and images from the front. "Photographic artists" journeyed to the battle zones, employing cumbersome equipment to document the conflict on a scale unprecedented in the relatively short history of photography. Military cartographers and engineers prepared maps that recorded the movement of armies and preserved a vital record of the American landscape during the Civil War. And soldiers and civilians alike preserved relics—treasured mementos of the great events they had witnessed.

Surviving correspondence from soldiers can offer historians key insight into the lives and emotions of participants in the Civil War. Many of the letters shown above are written on stationery printed with patriotic artwork and slogans.

FIRST-PERSON ACCOUNTS

THE URGE TO TELL TALES AND SHARE EXPERIENCES SEEMS INGRAINED IN THE HUMAN psyche, and the men and women who endured the four long years of the Civil War were no exception. Correspondence with friends and loved ones at home occupied much of the free time of soldiers. "Everybody is writing who can raise a pencil or a

The twin images above, showing Federal artillery-men in position near Fair Oaks, Virginia, in 1862, were taken using a double-lens stereo camera. Prints from the glass plate negative could be viewed through a special device to produce a three-dimensional effect. Below, a cameraman sets up his bulky glass plate apparatus near a Virginia railroad trestle.

sheet of paper," a Virginia soldier reported in the summer of 1861. Letters from home were vital to morale, and the exchange of news, good or bad, continued despite interruptions in mail service and the unpredictable circumstances of campaigns. Soldier's letters were not censored and often contain graphic, first-hand accounts of battle and life in camp, along with moving insights into the hearts and minds of men living under the most trying circumstances.

For thousands of veterans, written memories of the war were an indelible personal legacy. Many recorded their experiences not only in letters but also in diaries and journals. Some of those accounts were intensely personal, but others formed the basis for published memoirs. In the decades after the war, hundreds of these memoirs, by well-known commanders as well as common soldiers, found their way into print . Soldiers also contributed brief accounts to veteran's journals and local historical societies, which published collections of articles and reminiscences. As veterans and others who had lived through the war grew old and passed on, many of their diaries and letters were preserved in local archives for the benefit of future historians.

The surviving writings offer an intimate look into the first-hand experiences of soldiers and civilians seldom found in formal histories. Ohio veteran John Beatty, in his 1879 memoir, *The Citizen Soldier*, wrote that his record consisted "merely of matters which came under his own observation, and of camp gossip, rumors, trifling incidents, idle speculations, and the numberless items, small and great, which, in one way or another, enter into and affect the life of a soldier." In his narrative, Beatty says that he sought "simply to gather up the scraps which fell his way, leaving to others . . . the weightier matters of the great civil war."

AMERICA'S FIRST PHOTOJOURNALISTS

AT THE OUTBREAK OF THE CIVIL WAR, THE SCIENCE OF PHOTOGRAPHY WAS IN FLUX. THE new wet plate process, which produced negative images on glass plates and allowed multiple paper prints to be produced, was vying with the older daguerreotype, ambrotype, and tintype techniques, all of which produced a one-of-a-kind, mirror image (meaning that the initials U.S. on a belt buckle, for example, would appear reversed). While many portrait photographers continued to use the older techniques, particularly in the South, the wet plate process, while still somewhat cumbersome, allowed photographers to leave the studio and take to the field. To do so, they needed a wagon that served as a processing laboratory and a dark room, but for the first time, there was a real opportunity for cameramen to follow armies on campaign and record the ravages of battle.

Only two large fragments remain of the glass plate negative used to make this print of Federal Brigadier General J. Warner Keifer. Many of the glass negatives preserved in the Library of Congress and National Archives have suffered damage due to their fragile nature.

Photographic entrepreneur Mathew Brady is widely regarded as the conflict's master chronicler, and his name has become synonymous with the pictorial legacy of the Civil War. Brady, already established as one of America's most prestigious photographers when the war began, believed he had a responsibility to document the conflict. He took to the field himself and sent teams of "operators" to cover campaigns. He also purchased photos and plates from rival photographers, amassing one of the nation's premier collections of Civil War images.

Other photographers played an equally important role in recording the conflict. Scottish-born Alexander Gardner, manager of Brady's Washington, D.C., studio, covered several campaigns for his employer, including the Second Battle of Bull

Run (Manassas) and Antietam. In 1862 he left Brady's employ to establish his own galleries in Washington, D.C., and New York City. Gardner created regular images as well as stereo views, taken with double-lens stereographic cameras that produced a negative with two images side by side. Prints from these negatives produced a three-dimensional image when seen through a stereographic viewer.

In 1863 soldier-photographer Andrew J. Russell organized a team of cameramen under the auspices of the U.S. Military Railways. Russell's mandate was to record the operations of the Railway Construction Corps, but he was allowed a free hand in choosing his subject matter, and by war's end, Russell and his team had amassed an extraordinary collection of images.

Hundreds of lesser-known individuals recorded the war as well. Samuel Cooley chronicled Federal armies in the West, and James F. Gibson portrayed Union forces as they campaigned in Virginia under George McClellan and John Pope. The partnership of Haas & Peale recorded Federal batteries in action before Charleston, and George N. Barnard captured the carnage on battlefields around Chattanooga and Knoxville and later produced an extraordinary collection of landscapes documenting William Sherman's Atlanta Campaign.

Above, Harper's Weekly artist Alfred R. Waud sketches Little Roundtop on the Gettysburg battlefield in July 1863. One of the many drawings that Waud dispatched to his New York publisher included the sketch at right, portraying the death of General John Reynolds, a Federal corps commander, on the first day of the Battle of Gettysburg.

In the South, the Federal blockade meant that many of the chemicals necessary for photography were in short supply. To make a living, most southern photographers turned to the more lucrative business of portraits. Photographers such as George S. Cook of Charleston and Julian Vannerson and Thomas B. Rees of Richmond amassed impressive portrait galleries, including both Confederate notables and ordinary Rebel soldiers. Despite hardships, Cook worked under enemy fire to record the Federal siege of his home city in 1863.

In the 1870s the War Department purchased several thousand Civil War glass plate negatives from a cash-strapped Mathew Brady, and in 1875 the Federal government paid Brady $25,000 for full title to his Civil War images. During the war, Brady had transferred many of his negatives to the photographic supply firm of E. & H.T. Anthony & Company to pay his debts, and in 1879 approximately 2,000 of Brady's negatives were purchased by two former Civil War officers. After passing through several hands, the collection was purchased in 1943 by the Library of Congress. Around the same time, the National Archives acquired the War Department's collection of Brady negatives.

This carefully rendered pencil sketch of Sergeant Major William J. Jackson of the 12th New York Infantry was created in January 1863, near Fredericksburg, Virginia, by artist Edwin Forbes, employed by the New York-based Frank Leslie's Illustrated Newspaper.

BATTLEFIELD ARTISTS

THE EMERGENCE OF ILLUSTRATED NEWSPAPERS AND JOURNALS DURING THE MID-19TH century fostered the rise of a new type of journalist, the sketch artist. Journals like *Frank Leslie's Illustrated Newspaper*, *Harper's Weekly*, the *Southern Illustrated News*, and the *Illustrated London News* dispatched sketch artists to travel with the armies and make quick drawings on the spot. Among the talented artists who took to the field to sketch the war were the brothers Alfred and William Waud, Edwin Forbes, Arthur Lumley, and Englishman Frank Vizetelli.

In an era when the exposure time of cameras was too long to capture soldiers in action and photographs could not be directly translated into print, the public's only glimpses of men in battle came from these sketch artists. Rough drawings, often covered with instructions and notes for the engravers, were sent by express to the home

Soldier, artist, and cartographer Robert Knox Sneden, a private in the 40th New York Infantry, kept a diary of his wartime experiences that he illustrated with detailed watercolors. After the war, Sneden, debilitated by his ordeal as a prisoner of war at Andersonville, completed a series of watercolor maps of Civil War battles and locales.

office, where woodblock engravers translated the sketches into finished plates for printing. In many cases the resulting engravings were stiff and stylized, but the original works, where they survive, offer a fresh and vital look at the war.

Aside from the professional artists, many soldiers with an artistic bent kept illustrated journals and notebooks. One such soldier-artist, Robert Knox Sneden, a mapmaker serving in the Army of the Potomac, kept a meticulous sketchbook of his surroundings. Captured in 1863 and held at the notorious Andersonville prison, Sneden returned to his home in Brooklyn severely disabled and worked to turn his pencil sketches into watercolors and prepare maps of other campaigns using official sources. A few of his illustrations appeared in the 1880s in *Battles and Leaders of the Civil War*, a classic anthology of accounts by prominent figures involved in the conflict, but the remainder were lost from public view until 1994, when the Virginia Historical Society rediscovered Sneden's album of 400 ink and watercolor sketches.

PERIOD MAPS

FEDERAL AND CONFEDERATE AUTHORITIES WERE ALL TOO AWARE THAT ANY successful campaign demanded good maps, based on reliable data. In the North, Federal planners were able to call on trained personnel from existing organizations, including the Army Corps of Engineers and Corps of Topographical Engineers. Federal topographers prepared tens of thousands of maps and charts, many of which were printed for distribution to officers. In 1864 the superintendent of the Coast Survey reported that more than 22,000 military maps and sketches had been printed, and the following year the Union Army's chief engineer calculated that 24,591 map sheets had been distributed to forces in the field.

Their Confederate counterparts faced considerable difficulties in supplying field officers with satisfactory maps due to the lack of established mapping agencies and adequate printing facilities. Nevertheless, Confederate authorities acted quickly when war broke out, dispatching survey parties to map Virginia counties where fighting was likely to occur. Confederate engineers such as Jedediah Hotchkiss prepared detailed maps, drawn in ink on tracing linen.

Some of those maps were then reproduced in print, and others were copied by hand, in ink, either on paper or cloth.

RELICS AND MEMENTOS

TO MEMORIALIZE THIS GREAT CONFLICT, SOLDIERS AND civilians carefully preserved relics that symbolized the struggle and the sacrifices they had made. Veterans cherished the uniforms they had worn, and families carefully preserved the bloodstained effects of lost husbands and sons. State governments enshrined war-torn battle flags, and towns and villages honored their old soldiers by placing captured enemy cannon and memorial statuary on countless courthouse lawns.

The entire lower third of this Confederate battle flag, now lost to decay, was soaked in the blood of its bearer. The flag was captured in March 1865 during a cavalry action at Waynesboro, Virginia, by Private Michael Crowley of the 23rd New York Cavalry.

These symbols of devotion and sacrifice lost none of their power over the years. Writing after the war, Union veteran Frederick Hitchcock recalled the emotional impact of watching the battle flags of his division pass in review. As he watched "those battle-scarred flags kissed by the loving breeze," he wrote, "my blood tingled to my very fingertips, my hair seemed almost to rise straight up." Now as then, these inanimate objects, mute things given life by association with extraordinary events, act as talismans of times past, tangible reminders of an era when millions of Americans on both sides were "touched with fire" and willing to die for their cause. They also impart information that otherwise was not recorded in the historical record.

Thanks to all the compelling testimony handed down to us by those who witnessed this epic struggle—relics, diaries, letters, memoirs, photographs, and sketches—we too can experience the extraordinary events of the American Civil War.

HARRIS J. ANDREWS
Annandale, Virginia, July 2006

"COTTON IS KING,
AND THE AFRICAN MUST BE A SLAVE."

SOUTHERN PLANTATION OWNER
JAMES HENRY HAMMOND

A NATION DIVIDED

"THE TWO HALVES OF THIS UNION WERE MADE FOR EACH OTHER AS much as Adam and Eve," declared Senator Thomas Hart Benton of Missouri. Benton died in 1858, three years before the Union between North and South, which he considered a match made in heaven, ended in violent discord. For decades, the two regions had been growing apart. By mid-century, the contrasts were glaring between the increasingly urban and industrialized North and the largely rural South with its plantation economy. But many Americans still hoped this marriage could be saved. Northerners and Southerners studied and trained together cordially as cadets and midshipmen at West Point and Annapolis and commingled peacefully in border states such as Kentucky.

To be sure, many Southerners differed with Northerners in favoring states' rights over the claims of the federal government. But that issue in itself was not enough to shatter the Union until it mixed explosively with the controversy over slavery. Southerners felt they had as much right to own slaves and profit by them as Northerners did to exploit the cheap labor of servants or factory workers. Many Northerners disapproved of slavery and opposed extending it to the nation's western territories. Some in the North favored the abolition of slavery throughout the United States. To abolitionists, slavery was the nation's original sin—a disgrace that poisoned relations between North and South and had to be done away with if the Union was to be saved. ■

A plantation owner mounts his carriage with help from a slave in a rare photograph of life in the rural South before the Civil War.

> **"God forgive us, but ours is a monstrous system and wrong and iniquity."**
>
> DIARIST MARY BOYKIN CHESNUT OF SOUTH CAROLINA

TWO AMERICAS

O N MAY 19, 1856, CHARLES SUMNER OF MASSACHUSETTS ROSE IN THE Senate Chamber to deliver a defiant speech that exposed him to violent retribution. An outspoken opponent of slavery, Senator Sumner stood over six feet tall and made a formidable impression on the floor, blasting away at his political foes in a booming voice. As he pressed home his arguments with forceful gestures, remarked his friend and admirer, poet Henry Wadsworth Longfellow, he looked like a cannoneer, "ramming down cartridges."

The target of Sumner's fury on this occasion was the Kansas-Nebraska Act of 1854, which left the issue of slavery in those newly formed territories to be decided by the settlers and their local legislators. This "Crime Against Kansas," as Sumner put it, was championed by Stephen Douglas of Illinois and backed by Andrew Butler of South Carolina and other Southern senators. The legislation overturned the time-honored Missouri Compromise of 1820, which admitted Missouri as a slave state but banned slavery from all other territories north of latitude 36° 30'—the line formed by Missouri's southern border. Sumner blamed Douglas and those who supported his act for unleashing a bloody contest for control of Kansas in which proslavery forces from Missouri and other slave states clashed with antislavery settlers from free states.

When Sumner delivered his much-anticipated speech on Kansas, it was

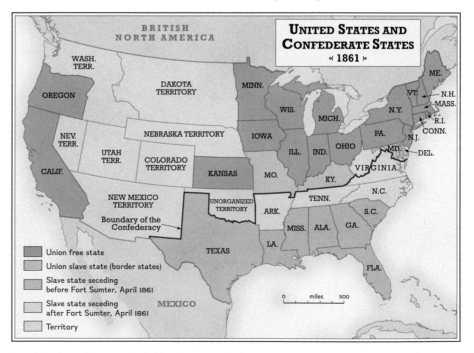

UNITED STATES AND CONFEDERATE STATES ❉ 1861 ❈

- ■ Union free state
- ■ Union slave state (border states)
- ■ Slave state seceding before Fort Sumter, April 1861
- ☐ Slave state seceding after Fort Sumter, April 1861
- ☐ Territory

By 1860, the 18 free states in the North and West had the potential to dominate the 15 slave states in the South politically. Southerners feared that slavery would be prohibited in western territories and might be abolished throughout the nation.

standing room only in the Senate. "Not only were the galleries thronged to their utmost capacity with ladies and gentleman," observed one reporter, "but all the doorways were completely blocked up with listeners." Many from the House of Representatives came over to hear Sumner, among them Congressman Preston Brooks of South Carolina, a relative of Andrew Butler, one of the few senators absent.

Sumner accused Butler, Douglas, and other proponents of the Kansas-Nebraska Act of trying to force Kansas into the "hateful embrace of slavery." They were responsible for the "rape of a virgin territory," he charged, and were raising themselves "to eminence on this floor in championship of human wrongs." Senator Butler, he added venomously, "has chosen a mistress to whom he has made his vows, and who, though ugly to others, is always lovely to him . . . the harlot, Slavery." Sumner's scathing language appalled Stephen Douglas, who remarked ominously, "That damn fool will get himself killed by some other damn fool."

No one was angrier at Sumner than Congressman Brooks, who felt the speech maligned both his kinsman Butler and the state they represented. It would be no great loss to civilization, Sumner railed at one point, were "the whole history of South Carolina blotted out of existence." Sumner's lurid references to rape, mistresses, and harlots echoed accusations that Southern planters routinely forced themselves on female slaves and impregnated them. Such incidents were common enough to make Southerners highly sensitive to charges of impropriety. Diarist Mary Boykin Chesnut of South Carolina trusted that her husband, Senator James Chesnut, abstained from affairs with slave women but saw evidence that other planters were less scrupulous. "Like the patriarchs of old our men live all in one house with their wives and their concubines," she wrote, "and the mulattoes one sees in every family exactly resemble the white children." Privately, she agreed with Sumner that slavery was corrupt and degrading. "Sumner said not one word of this hated institution which is not true," she confided to her diary. "God forgive us, but ours is a monstrous system and wrong and iniquity."

Far more typical of Southern attitudes was the defiant response of Congressman Brooks to Sumner's words. As Northerners escalated their attacks on slavery, proud Southerners like Brooks defended their way of life with ever-greater fervor. Many who once regarded slavery as a necessary evil now hailed it as noble and virtuous and saw attacks on the slave system as assaults on their honor. For Brooks, Sumner's "Crime Against Kansas" was itself a crime because it libeled Senator Butler in particular and Southerners in general.

According to the code of chivalry that many prominent Southerners adhered to, gentlemen were supposed to settle points of honor by dueling with pistols or swords. But Brooks regarded Sumner as too ill-mannered and ill-bred (his mother had once been a seamstress) to be treated as an equal. When insulted by an inferior, the Southern gentleman responded by beating the culprit with a whip or cane. Such was the punishment Congressman Brooks had in mind for Senator Sumner.

Passengers and pedestrians throng Broadway in New York City, which by 1860 was home to a million people, or nearly twice the population of Texas. Southerners feared losing out to the fast-growing North economically as well as politically.

Charles Sumner

MASSACHUSETTS SENATOR AND ABOLITIONIST

A graduate of Harvard Law School, Boston lawyer Charles Sumner was elected to the Senate in 1851 with the support of Democrats and Free Staters. A confirmed abolitionist, Sumner attacked the Fugitive Slave Law and denounced the 1854 Kansas-Nebraska Act. On May 19, 1856, he delivered a powerful antislavery speech—"The Crime Against Kansas." Two days later he was assaulted and beaten on the Senate floor by Congressman Preston S. Brooks, who was incensed by Sumner's virulent attacks on his uncle, Senator Andrew Pickens Butler of South Carolina.

BUT THE WICKEDNESS WHICH I now begin to expose is immeasurably aggravated by the motive which prompted it. Not in any common lust for power did this uncommon tragedy have its origin. It is the rape of a virgin territory, compelling it to the hateful embrace of slavery; and it may be clearly traced to a depraved longing for a new slave State, the hideous offspring of such a crime, in the hope of adding to the power of slavery in the national government. Yes, sir, when the whole world, alike Christian and Turk, is rising up to condemn this wrong, and to make it a hissing to the nations, here in our Republic, force, ay, sir, *force* has been openly employed in compelling Kansas to this pollution, and all for the sake of political power. There is the simple fact, which you will in vain attempt to deny, but which in itself presents an essential wickedness that makes other public crimes seem like public virtues.

But this enormity, vast beyond comparison, swells to dimensions of wickedness which the imagination toils in vain to grasp, when it is understood that for this purpose are hazarded the horrors of intestine feud not only in this distant territory, but everywhere throughout the country. Already the muster has begun. The strife is no longer local, but national. Even now, while I speak, portents hang on all the

"It is the rape of a virgin territory, compelling it to the hateful embrace of Slavery."

arches of the horizon threatening to darken the broad land, which already yawns with the mutterings of civil war.

But it is against the people of Kansas that the sensibilities of the senator are particularly aroused. Coming, as he announces, "from a state"ay, sir, from South Carolina he turns with lordly disgust from this newly-formed community, which he will not recognize even as a "body politic." Pray, sir, by what title does he indulge in this ego-

tism? Has he read the history of "the state" which he represents? He cannot surely have forgotten its shameful imbecility from slavery, confessed throughout the Revolution, followed by its more shameful assumptions for slavery since. He cannot have forgotten its wretched persistence in the slave trade as the very apple of its eye, and the condition of its participation in the Union. He cannot have forgotten its constitution, which is Republican only in name . . . And yet the senator, to whom that "state" has in part committed the guardianship of its good name, instead of moving, with backward treading steps, to cover its nakedness, rushes forward in the very ecstasy of madness, to expose it by provoking a comparison with Kansas. South Carolina is old; Kansas is young. South Carolina counts by centuries; where Kansas counts by years. But a beneficent example may be born in a day; and I venture to say, that against the two centuries of the older "state," may be already set the two years of trial, evolving corresponding virtue, in the younger community. In the one, is the long wail of slavery; in the other, the hymns of freedom. Were the whole history of South Carolina blotted out of existence, . . . civilization might lose— I do not say how little; but surely less than it has already gained by the example of Kansas. ∎

Before acting, Brooks revealed his plans to colleagues, including Congressman Lawrence Keitt of South Carolina. Far from discouraging Brooks, Keitt took his part and accompanied him to the Senate Chamber. Brooks approached Sumner as he was sitting at his desk after the Senate adjourned and beat him with a cane repeatedly on the head and shoulders. "Every lick went where I intended it," Brooks wrote his brother afterward. "For about the first five or six licks he offered to make a fight but I plied him so rapidly that he did not touch me. Towards the last he bellowed like a calf. I wore my cane out completely but saved the head which is gold."

Senator John Crittenden of Kentucky, who often served as a mediator in political disputes between North and South, witnessed the attack and tried to restrain Brooks. "Don't kill him," he said. Furious at Crittenden for intervening, Congressman Keitt raised his own cane menacingly and shouted, "Let them alone, God damn you." By his own reckoning, Brooks gave Sumner "about 30 first rate stripes," holding him up by the lapel of his coat until he collapsed. Sumner lay on the Senate floor "as senseless as a corpse for several minutes," an onlooker reported, "his head bleeding copiously from the frightful wounds, and the blood saturating his clothes." Three years would pass before he felt strong enough to resume his Senate duties.

Brooks was charged with assault and fined $300 in a Baltimore court. The House censured Keitt and voted 121 to 95 to expel Brooks, but the measure fell short of the required two-thirds majority. Brooks and Keitt then resigned their seats and returned to South Carolina, where they were reelected to Congress by wide margins. Merchants in Charleston gave Brooks a new cane inscribed with the motto, "Hit him again." Some newspaper editors in the South criticized Brooks for attacking his opponent while he was seated and not in a position to defend himself, but others argued that Sumner got just what he deserved—the same sort of beating administered to unruly slaves.

> **"I wore my cane out completely but saved the head which is gold."**
>
> CONGRESSMAN PRESTON BROOKS
> OF SOUTH CAROLINA

SOUTHERN CHIVALRY _ ARGUMENT versus CLUB'S.

As Southern senators look on approvingly, Congressman Preston Brooks of South Carolina beats Senator Charles Sumner of Massachusetts with a cane in a Northern cartoon mocking the idea that Brooks was defending Southern honor.

"These vulgar abolitionists in the Senate," proclaimed the *Richmond Enquirer*; "must be lashed into submission. Sumner, in particular, ought to have nine-and-thirty early every morning. He is a great strapping fellow, and could stand the cowhide beautifully."

Northerners, for their part, largely overlooked the verbal assaults by Sumner that prompted the beating. A few editors in Boston, where Sumner had angered political rivals with intemperate remarks over the years, faulted him for "vulgarity of language" and for being "excessively insulting and provoking." But most Northerners saw him as a martyr, struck down for defending "human rights and free territory." As one pundit wrote, it was time for Northerners to put aside partisan wrangling and unite against the "villainous acts of the South." To the philosopher and orator Ralph Waldo Emerson, the attack on Sumner was proof of the barbarism of slavery and slave owners. "I do not see how a barbarous community and a civilized community can constitute one state," he concluded. "I think we must get rid of slavery, or we must get rid of freedom."

A PECULIAR INSTITUTION

AMERICANS WITH LONG MEMORIES COULD RECALL A TIME WHEN NO Mason-Dixon Line separated slave states from free states. All 13 colonies that declared independence in 1776 permitted slavery, and it remained legal in some Northern states into the early 1800s. Several of the nation's Founding Fathers once owned slaves or traded in them, including John Hancock of Massachusetts, Benjamin Franklin of Pennsylvania, and Thomas Jefferson of Virginia. Like other prominent Northerners, Hancock and Franklin renounced slavery and hired servants to run their households. Jefferson, by contrast, was so dependent on the many slaves who worked his estate at Monticello that he freed only a few of them, despite his conviction that slavery was immoral. "The whole commerce between master and slave is a perpetual exercise of the most boisterous passions," he wrote, "the most unremitting despotism on the one part, and degrading submissions on the other. . . . Indeed I tremble for my country when I reflect that God is just: that his justice cannot sleep forever. . . . The Almighty has no attribute which can take side with us in such a contest."

Many in the South harbored similar misgivings about slavery but found it no easier than Jefferson did to part with their slaves. Slavery persisted in Virginia and other Southern states because the region came to depend on the labor of millions of African Americans held in bondage there and could not free them without risking economic and social turmoil. White Southerners called slavery their "peculiar institution," meaning that it distinguished them as a society, for better or worse, and proved indispensable to their way of life.

Nothing did more to perpetuate slavery in the South than the introduction of the cotton gin, devised in the 1790s by Eli Whitney. The machine separated out the fibers of short-staple cotton, which grew well in the Southern interior and provided an alternative to the long-staple cotton that grew only in

Above, a slave woman in the South holds a white child placed under her care. Some slave families like the one pictured at left in Beaufort, South Carolina, remained intact for several generations, but others were broken up when their masters died or chose to sell family members separately.

coastal areas. Planters employing slave labor could now raise cotton profitably across much of the Deep South, from Georgia to Texas. Between 1820 and 1850, cotton production in the region increased sixfold, and the South became the world's leading supplier of cotton fiber, shipping millions of bales to textile plants in New England and Great Britain. "Cotton is King," declared planter and politician James Henry Hammond, "and the African must be a slave."

Despite the rise of the cotton kingdom, slaveholders remained a minority in the South. Only about one family in four owned slaves, but many Southerners benefited indirectly from slavery through commercial ties with slave owners and took pride in the fact that they were free whites, spared the degradations heaped on black slaves. "No white man in a slaveholding community is the menial servant of any one," declared Jefferson Davis, the future Confederate president. In the South, he added, the only class distinction that really mattered was the "distinction of color." White men in the South shared not only a sense of racial superiority—a bias harbored by most white Northerners as well—but also a fondness for riding, shooting, hunting, and other tests of skill and strength. In this militant South, some of the brightest and most ambitious young men went not to universities but to military academies. Southerners distinguished themselves at West Point and played a commanding role in the Mexican-American War that broke out in 1846 and greatly enlarged the nation at Mexico's expense.

By the late 1840s, Southerners were keenly aware that they were falling behind the North economically and politically and might soon lose control of their own destiny. While the South remained a largely agricultural society, the North was fast industrializing and attracting European immigrants, who provided cheap labor for factories and helped build canals and railroads that linked the cities of the Northeast to midwestern boomtowns like Chicago. Southern propagandists such as George Fitzhugh of Virginia charged that Northern capitalists were engaged in a white slave trade that was "far more cruel than the black slave trade, because it exacts more of its slaves, and neither protects nor governs them."

Unlike black slaves on plantations, however, the so-called wage slaves of the North could not be forcibly separated from their families and sold to other employers. They were free to leave their bosses and seek work elsewhere and had reason to hope their children would fare better than they did. Most farmers and factory workers in the North did not want to compete with slave labor and opposed slavery in the nation's territories. Southerners took solace in the admission of Florida and Texas as slave states in 1845, but that was soon offset by the admission of Iowa (1846), Wisconsin (1848), and California (1850) as free states. Anxious Southerners could foresee a day when a political party dominated by Northerners might seize control of the House, the Senate, and the presidency by sweeping the states of the populous Northeast and Midwest and defying the interests of the South.

As of 1850, the two main parties—the Democrats and the Whigs—still drew considerable support from both the North and the South and sought to compromise on the divisive issue of slavery. That year, Senator Stephen Douglas pushed through Congress an elaborate compromise involving territories

---

"The Negro, when a 'slave' to a Caucasian, is vastly higher in the scale of humanity, than when in his native state."

SOUTHERNER CHARLES CHAUNCEY BURR

"I appear this evening as a thief and robber. I stole this head, these limbs, this body from my master, and ran off with them."

ESCAPED SLAVE AND ABOLITIONIST FREDERICK DOUGLASS

SOJOURNER TRUTH

FREDERICK DOUGLASS

WILLIAM LLOYD GARRISON

HARRIET BEECHER STOWE

Editor William Lloyd Garrison, who once burned a copy of the U.S. Constitution in public because it provided legal protection for slavery, was one of the founders of a diverse abolitionist movement that included former slaves Sojourner Truth and Frederick Douglass and novelist Harriet Beecher Stowe, author of Uncle Tom's Cabin.

> **"Here, before God, in the presence of these witnesses . . . I consecrate my life to the destruction of slavery!"**
>
> ABOLITIONIST JOHN BROWN

Holding an abolitionist banner, John Brown swears allegiance to the cause in the earliest known photograph of the antislavery agitator, taken in 1846.

recently won in the Mexican-American War. In exchange for admitting California as a free state and abolishing the slave trade in the District of Columbia, the deal appeased Southerners by enacting a stronger Fugitive Slave Law—which allowed masters to reclaim slaves who sought freedom in the North—and by letting settlers in the newly formed territories of New Mexico and Utah decide for themselves the issue of slavery there. That concept, known as popular sovereignty, raised a firestorm when it was applied to Kansas in 1854.

Efforts to reach a lasting compromise on slavery collapsed in the 1850s because both sides in the longstanding debate were hardening their positions. In response to criticism from abolitionists—whom Southerners blamed for inciting slaves to rebel against their masters—apologists for slavery portrayed it as good for blacks as well as whites. "The Negro, when a 'slave' to a Caucasian, is vastly higher in the scale of humanity, than when in his native state," wrote Southerner Charles Chauncey Burr. "Many in the South once believed that slavery was a moral and political evil," Senator John Calhoun of South Carolina remarked. "We see it now in its true light, and regard it as the most safe and stable basis for free institutions in the world." If abolitionists had their way, he warned his fellow white Southerners, Negroes and their Northern allies "would be the masters and we the slaves."

Abolitionists were no less fervent in their attacks on the institution of slavery. Although opponents scorned them as traitors to the white race, some of the most eloquent abolitionists were in fact African Americans like Frederick Douglass, an escaped slave who mocked the Fugitive Slave Law by declaring to audiences: "I appear this evening as a thief and robber. I stole this head, these limbs, this body from my master, and ran off with them." Women also figured prominently in the abolitionist movement, among them the escaped slaves Sojourner Truth and Harriet Tubman and New Englander Harriet Beecher Stowe, whose novel *Uncle Tom's Cabin* did as much to turn Northern sentiment against the South's peculiar institution as all the speeches ever delivered on the subject combined. It took more than sentiment, however, to transform the controversy over slavery into a cause for war. Not until abolitionists stepped forward who were prepared to shed blood for their convictions did slavery become the wedge that split the Union.

JOHN BROWN'S WAR

ON MAY 23, 1856, NEWS OF THE ATTACK ON SENATOR SUMNER BY CONGRESSMAN Brooks reached abolitionist John Brown at his homestead near Osawatomie, Kansas. Brown, born in Connecticut in 1800 and raised in Ohio, had settled here recently with his six surviving sons and their kin to help keep Kansas free of slavery. He was alarmed by recent attacks by proslavery forces on those who shared his views in Kansas and was planning to retaliate. When he and his followers learned that Sumner had been caned in the Senate after denouncing the "Crime Against Kansas," recalled Brown's son Jason, they "went crazy—*crazy*. It seemed to be the finishing, decisive touch." One acquaintance tried to calm Brown and counseled caution, but he would not be appeased. "I am eternally tired of hearing that word caution," he said. "It is nothing but the word of cowardice."

Brown and others in his camp feared that settlers from free states would lose the political struggle for control of Kansas unless they threw caution to the wind and battled proslavery forces. As one New Englander observed, "the peaceable and industrious people of the free-labor States were not familiar with the use of the bowie-knife and revolver, and therefore not likely to place themselves in any dangerous proximity to the armed champions of Slavery." But John Brown was different. He had taken a solemn oath to fight for his cause. "Here, before God, in the presence of these witnesses, from this time," he vowed at a prayer meeting in 1837, "I consecrate my life to the destruction of slavery!" Any assault on slaves or on fellow abolitionists like Sumner was a personal affront to Brown. He was "in sympathy a black man," wrote Frederick Douglass, who knew him well, "and as deeply interested in our cause, as though his own soul had been pierced by the iron of slavery."

On the night of May 24, Brown led a party of seven vigilantes, including four of his sons, in attacks on proslavery men living along Pottawatomie Creek. We must "fight fire with fire," he told his followers; "better that a score of bad men should die than that one man who came here to make Kansas a free state should be driven out." Most of those targeted had been involved in recent court proceedings against John Brown and his sons for advocating abolitionism, which had been declared a crime by the proslavery Kansas legislature. James Doyle, a grand juror in that case and an ardent foe of abolitionists, was seized in his cabin along with two of his sons and dragged into the woods, where they were hacked to death with swords at John Brown's order. Two other men died by his command that night: Allen Wilkinson, the acting district attorney; and William Sherman, whose brother Henry owned the tavern where the court convened. Jason Brown, who took no part in this murderous vendetta, denounced it as a "wicked act," but his father offered no apologies. "God is my judge," he said. "It was absolutely necessary as a measure of self-defense, and for the defense of others."

John Brown was indicted for murder but never brought to justice. Amid the chaos of "Bleeding Kansas," many such attacks by proslavery and antislavery men went unpunished. Brown led followers in battle against proslavery forces in Kansas before leaving the territory. His attacks contributed little to the ultimate victory of antislavery forces in Kansas, who prevailed by sheer force of numbers as more and more settlers flocked there from free states. Free Kansas was no sanctuary for free blacks, who were barred from the

This revolver was among hundreds of weapons purchased by John Brown, using funds contributed by wealthy abolitionists, to arm opponents of slavery in Kansas. One arms manufacturer in Massachusetts sold Brown 200 revolvers at half price for the purpose of "protecting the free state settlers of Kansas and securing their rights."

territory along with black slaves by a Negro Exclusion Act passed by anti-slavery legislators eager to distance themselves from radical abolitionists like Brown. Yet Northerners celebrated the defeat of slavery in Kansas and gave Brown more credit for the outcome than he deserved. Press accounts ignored or excused his bloodbath at Pottawatomie Creek and hailed him for standing up to proslavery Border Ruffians from Missouri. The *New York Times* called him the "terror of all Missouri."

John Brown's newfound celebrity allowed him to pursue a long-cherished goal. Since the 1840s, he had dreamed of invading the South with an aboli-

---

[EYEWITNESS]

James Townsley
MEMBER OF JOHN BROWN'S MILITIA, THE POTTAWATOMIE RIFLES

Born in Maryland and a veteran of the U.S. Regular Army in the Seminole Wars, James Townsley moved to Kansas with his family in the fall of 1855 and settled along Pottawatomie Creek. In 1856, as tensions between pro- and antislavery factions in Kansas flared into open warfare, Townsley enlisted in the Pottawatomie Rifles, a militia company commanded by Captain John Brown. On May 21, 1856, the Pottawatomie Rifles were called into action to defend the town of Lawrence from attack by proslavery forces. When word that Lawrence had been sacked reached the militiamen, their commander led them in an act of biblical vengeance.

AFTER MY TEAM WAS FED AND the party had taken supper, John Brown told me for the first time what he proposed to do. He said he wanted me to pilot the company up to the forks of the creek some five or six miles above, into the neighborhood in which I lived, and show them where all the proslavery men resided; that he proposed to sweep the creek as he came down of all the proslavery men living on it. . . .

We started, the whole company, in a northerly direction, crossing Mosquito Creek above the residence of the Doyles. Soon after crossing the creek someone of the party knocked at the door of a cabin but received no reply. I have forgotten whose cabin it was if I knew at the time. The next place we came to was the residence of the Doyles. John Brown, three of his sons and son-in-law went to the door, leaving Frederick Brown, Winer and myself a short distance from the house. About this time a

"He was slain with swords by Brown's two youngest sons, and left lying in the road."

large dog attacked us. Frederick Brown struck the dog a blow with his short two-edged sword, after which I dealt him a blow on the head with my sabre and heard no more from him. The old man Doyle and two sons were called out and marched some distance from the house toward Dutch Henry's in the road, where a halt was made. Old John Brown drew his revolver and shot the old man Doyle in the forehead, and the two youngest sons immediately fell upon the younger Doyles with their short two-edged swords. One of the young Doyles was stricken down in an instant, but the other attempted to escape, and was pursued a short distance by his assailant and cut down. The company then proceeded down Mosquito creek to the house of Allen

Wilkinson. Here the old man Brown, three of his sons and son-in-law . . . ordered Wilkinson to come out, leaving Frederick Brown, Winer and myself standing in the road east of the house. Wilkinson was taken, marched some distance south of the house, and slain in the road with a short sword by one of the younger Browns. . . .

We then crossed the Pottawatomie and came to the house of Henry Sherman, generally known as Dutch Henry. Here John Brown and the party, excepting Frederick Brown, Winer and myself, who were left outside a short distance from the door, went into the house and brought out one or two persons, talked with them some, and then took them in again. They afterward brought out Wm. Sherman, Dutch Henry's brother, and marched him into Pottawatomie creek, where he was slain with swords by Brown's two youngest sons, and left lying in the road. ∎

tionist force that would raid plantations, liberate slaves, and arm them for guerrilla warfare against slave owners. When he revealed his plan to a skeptical Frederick Douglass in 1847, he insisted that it would take only a small contingent of freedom fighters, harbored in mountain hideaways, to destroy the South's peculiar institution. "Twenty men in the Alleghenies could break slavery to pieces in two years," he predicted. But before setting any such scheme in motion, he needed funds to purchase weapons and train his recruits. Brown, who was chronically in debt, could not strike at the slaveholding South until his exploits in Kansas made him a hero and enabled him to solicit donations from wealthy abolitionists for what he described as "the most important undertaking of my whole life."

By 1859, Brown had evolved a plan of breathtaking audacity. He and his recruits would seize the federal armory at Harpers Ferry, Virginia. That in itself would cause slaves in the area to rise up against their masters and flock to him, he believed, and he would then arm them with pikes and firearms and launch them on a guerrilla war against slavery. Some people close to Brown thought the scheme suicidal and suspected he wanted to die for his cause. Frederick Douglass, for one, refused to take part in the raid because he considered Harpers Ferry, a town hemmed in by rivers and mountains, a trap from which

Free Staters such as these volunteers, manning an antiquated cannon, fought for control of Kansas against proslavery settlers and Border Ruffians from neighboring Missouri, a slave state. With antislavery warriors like John Brown matching proslavery men blow for blow, the territory became known as Bleeding Kansas.

"Twenty men in the Alleghenies could break slavery to pieces in two years."
JOHN BROWN

Brown and his men would never escape. Brown's own son Salmon, who had shed blood at Pottawatomie Creek, saw it as a doomed venture and also declined to participate. "You know father," he told his brothers; "he will dally till he is trapped." Three of Brown's sons—Owen, Oliver, and Watson—nonetheless joined their 59-year-old father in this reckless undertaking, which Brown did not expect to survive. "Save this letter to remember your father by," he wrote his daughter Anne in September 1859, shortly before launching his raid.

RECKONING AT HARPERS FERRY

"MEN, GET ON YOUR ARMS," JOHN BROWN TOLD HIS FOLLOWERS ON SUNDAY evening, October 16. "We will proceed to the Ferry." For several months, Brown's force of 21 men—16 whites, four free blacks, and one fugitive slave— had been preparing for their raid at a farm in Maryland five miles north of Harpers Ferry. Locals learned of their intentions, but authorities ignored warnings. Aside from a few night watchmen who were easily overpowered, Brown and his men encountered no opposition as they seized bridges leading into Harpers Ferry and occupied the armory. They also took several prominent men in the area hostage, including Colonel Lewis Washington, a descendant of George Washington, and enlisted their slaves in Brown's cause. Those slaves were confused and fearful. Some thought they were being stolen and would be sold to other masters. Their reluctance to join in Brown's scheme did not bode well for the spontaneous slave uprising he anticipated.

> **"You know father . . . he will dally till he is trapped."**
>
> SALMON BROWN

After seizing the U.S. armory in Harpers Ferry, John Brown—shown above around the time of the raid—took refuge with his men in the fire-engine house. U.S. Marines led by Lieutenant Colonel Robert E. Lee stormed the site, as depicted in this illustration from Frank Leslie's Illustrated Newspaper.

He and his men could have left Harpers Ferry that night unscathed with a large cache of weapons, but he clung to his precarious position, still hoping to galvanize slaves into action. "I could not help thinking that at times he appeared somewhat puzzled," said one of his men later. "Hold on a little longer, boys," he told them, but they could not hold Harpers Ferry indefinitely and saw his lingering there as "an omen of evil."

Before dawn on October 17, two of Brown's men shot and mortally wounded Shephard Hayward, a free black man who worked as a baggage handler for the Baltimore & Ohio Railroad and refused their orders to halt as he neared the railroad bridge. He became the first casualty of the raid. Militia units were summoned from nearby towns, and a company of U.S. Marines under Lieutenant Colonel Robert E. Lee, the future Confederate commander, left Washington, D.C., by train that afternoon to reclaim the armory. Civilians in Harpers Ferry, meanwhile, organized for their own defense and traded shots with the raiders. The first of Brown's men to die was Dangerfield Newby, a former slave from Virginia who had hoped to free his wife and children, enslaved on a plantation some 30 miles south of Harpers Ferry. He carried with him a letter from his wife: "Oh dear Dangerfield, com this fall without fail," she wrote, "I want to see you so much that is the one bright hope I have before me." Angry townspeople mutilated Newby's corpse and left it to be eaten by hogs.

Robert E. Lee offered John Brown and his men no terms except surrender and warned that if they resisted arrest, he could not "answer for their safety."

As militiamen poured into Harpers Ferry and pressure mounted, Brown and most of his men abandoned the armory and took refuge in the nearby fire-engine house, a small brick building with heavy oak doors. He sent his son Watson out with another man to negotiate a deal that would allow the raiders to leave Harpers Ferry, but their foes ignored the white flag they carried and shot them down. Watson crawled back to the fire-engine house, where his brother Oliver tried to comfort him until he too was mortally wounded by incoming fire. Oliver was in such pain that he begged his father to put him out of his misery, to no avail. "If you must die," Brown said sternly, "die like a man."

Robert E. Lee reached Harpers Ferry with his Marines that evening. Early the next morning, October 18, he sent his aide and fellow Virginian, Lieutenant James Ewell Brown (Jeb) Stuart, to demand the surrender of Brown and his surviving raiders. Stuart had served in Bleeding Kansas with U.S. cavalry assigned to pacify the territory and recognized Brown as the man "who had given us so much trouble." Lee did not expect Brown to yield peacefully. If he refused to surrender, Stuart had orders to step aside and wave his cap, "at which signal the storming party was to advance, batter open the doors, and capture the insurgents at the point of the bayonet." One Marine died in the ensuing assault, and two raiders who resisted were bayoneted. Brown himself was knocked to the ground with a sword and arrested. "The whole was over in a few minutes," Lee reported. Stuart could not resist claiming a trophy from the man who had bedeviled him in Kansas. "I got his bowie-knife from his person," Stuart wrote, "and have it yet."

Although Owen Brown and several other raiders escaped, their leader John Brown stoically accepted captivity and looked forward to his trial and execution as if his fate were preordained. A strict Calvinist, he believed that everything that befell him was part of God's plan and saw his impending martyrdom as an opportunity to focus the nation's attention on the dreadful consequences of slavery. Many in the North, including some who had aided Brown financially, distanced themselves from his botched raid by calling him insane. The raiders were "fanatics," concluded one Chicago newspaper, "commanded by a man who has for years been as mad as a March hare." But Virginia Governor Henry Wise, who spoke with Brown in prison and brought him to trial, disagreed. "They are themselves mistaken who take him to be a madman," Wise wrote. "He is a man of clear head, of courage, fortitude, and simple ingenuousness." Brown's sanity, Wise believed, made him all the more dangerous and culpable.

Brown rejected efforts by his lawyers to mount an insanity defense and was found guilty of inciting a slave rebellion, murder, and treason against the state of Virginia. He saw no shame in being condemned as an enemy of Virginia and its slave owners and spoke defiantly after the verdict was announced: "Now, if it is deemed necessary that I should forfeit my life for the furtherance of the ends of justice, and mingle my blood further with the blood of millions in this slave country whose rights are disregarded by wicked, cruel, and unjust enactments, I say, let it be done."

On December 2, 1859, he was led to the gallows, after handing a note to a guard that served as his last testament: "I John Brown am now quite certain that the crimes of this guilty land will never be purged away but with blood." Among those who witnessed Brown's execution was a militiaman from Maryland named John Wilkes Booth, who wrote afterward: "I looked at the traitor and terrorizer with unlimited, undeniable contempt."

THE IRREPRESSIBLE CONFLICT

IN OCTOBER 1858, A YEAR BEFORE JOHN BROWN LAUNCHED HIS raid, New York Senator William Seward warned that the nation faced an "irrepressible conflict." Sooner or later, he said, the United States would undergo a crisis and emerge "entirely a slave-holding nation or entirely a free-labor nation." The shocking events at Harpers Ferry a year later seemingly confirmed that prediction and left little hope for compromise. As the *Richmond Enquirer* put it: "The 'irrepressible conflict' was initiated at Harper's Ferry, and though there, for the time suppressed, yet no man is able to say when or where it will begin again or where it will end." In Charleston, South Carolina, long a bas-

Senator Stephen Douglas of Illinois, while debating Abraham Lincoln in 1858, accused his opponent of advocating "a war of the North against the South, of the free states against the slave states."

tion for those defending slavery and the right of states to secede from the Union, one editorialist wrote that the "time has arrived in our history for a separation from the North." Otherwise, he warned, Northern abolitionists like Brown would continue to wreak havoc in the South by inciting slaves to commit unspeakable atrocities: "We must separate, unless we are willing to see our daughters and wives become the victims of a barbarous passion. . . . Better civil war than injustice and oppression."

Many in the South believed that leaders of the recently formed Republican Party—whose members came largely from the Northern wing of the defunct Whig Party and opposed the extension of slavery to western territories—were behind John Brown's raid. Rival Democrats called them "Black Republicans," an epithet with racial overtones, implying that they cared more for black slaves than for free whites. No Republican had a blacker reputation in the South than William Seward, the favorite for his party's presidential nomination in 1860. One Richmond paper branded him a traitor for allegedly encouraging Brown and offered a reward of $50,000 for his head. Seward denied aiding Brown in any way and denounced the Harpers Ferry raid as an "act of sedition and treason." But the swirling controversy hurt Seward's candidacy. Although he feared civil war and favored political compromises to preserve the Union, he was seen as a radical abolitionist who eagerly awaited the "irrepressible conflict." Party leaders began looking for a candidate with less baggage, a dark horse who might be more appealing to the many Northerners who were not abolitionists and dreaded disunion.

Republicans found their dark horse in Abraham Lincoln of Illinois, an eloquent lawyer who had served one term in Congress and had nearly unseated Democratic Senator Stephen Douglas, the champion of popular sovereignty and architect of the Kansas-Nebraska Act. In a series of debates in 1858 with the "Little Giant," as Douglas was known, the gangly Lincoln argued against extending slavery to western territories through popular sovereignty or any other means, while countering charges that he and his fellow Republicans were "negro-lovers" who believed in racial equality. "Douglas will have it that I want a negro wife," he quipped. "He never can be brought to understand there is any middle ground on this subject." Blacks were not the equals of whites, Lincoln argued, but they had an equal right to life, liberty, and the pursuit of happiness apart from whites: "As God made us separate, we can leave one another alone, and do one another much good thereby."

Lincoln's most memorable address during his campaign against Douglas was similar in spirit to Seward's "irrepressible conflict" speech, but Lincoln expressed himself with a clarity and simplicity that none of his Republican rivals could match and that helped propel him to his party's nomination in 1860. "A house divided against itself cannot stand," he declared. "I believe this government cannot endure, permanently half slave and half free. I do not expect the Union to be dissolved—I do not expect the house to fall—but I do expect

"Douglas will have it that I want a negro wife."
ABRAHAM LINCOLN

Lincoln, pictured here at the time of the debates, denied Douglas's charge that he was seeking to divide the nation. "To the best of my judgment," he stated, "I have labored for, and not against the Union."

THE DRED SCOTT DECISION

BEFORE THE U.S. SUPREME COURT handed down its decision in *Dred Scott* v. *Sandford*, president-elect James Buchanan confidently predicted that the ruling would end agitation about slavery in the territories once and for all. Buchanan guessed right about the case's historical importance, but he was spectacularly wrong about the consequences.

The landmark 1857 decision was the end of an 11-year court battle for Dred Scott, a Missouri slave who had belonged to army surgeon John Emerson. When Emerson died, Scott sued for his freedom on the basis that Emerson had once taken him to live at military posts in Illinois, a free state, and Wisconsin, a free territory per the Missouri Compromise. Scott lost his initial case in state court, then won on appeal, only to have the Missouri supreme court reverse that decision and return him to slavery. When all seemed lost, Scott's lawyers found a legal angle that allowed Scott to sue in federal court. Scott lost his federal case in 1854. However, the U.S. Supreme Court agreed to hear the appeal, thus setting up a momentous confrontation between pro- and antislavery factions.

The opinion delivered by Chief Justice Roger Taney on March 6, 1857, was tortuous and legally suspect. Taney held that Scott, as a slave, was not a citizen and had no right to sue. Furthermore, slaves were property, and as such, their owners were protected by the Fifth Amend-

> **"We shall lie down pleasantly dreaming that the people of Missouri are on the verge of making their State free; and we shall awake to the reality, instead, that the Supreme Court has made Illinois a slave State."**
>
> ABRAHAM LINCOLN
> *to Illinois Republicans in 1858*

ment's guarantee that no person shall be "deprived of life, liberty or property without due process of law." In other words, slaveholders had an absolute right to take their slaves into free states and territories. This part of the ruling was devastating for abolitionists. The Missouri Compromise of 1820 had banned slavery in territories north of 36° 30'. Taney's ruling, tainted by his background as the scion of wealthy Maryland slaveholders, made the Missouri Compromise unconstitutional, as any attempt by Congress to ban slavery would violate slaveholders' Fifth Amendment rights.

Legally, there was now nothing standing in the way of the Supreme Court ruling that slavery could not be prohibited anywhere; that there could be no such thing as a free state or territory. If this ruling "shall stand for law," wrote newspaper editor William Cullen Bryant, slavery would go from being the "peculiar institution" of the South to "a Federal institution, the common shame of all the States." Republicans began fanning fears of "the next Dred Scott" decision that would do exactly that. The issue ultimately drove a deep wedge between Northern and Southern Democrats, opening the way for the election of Abraham Lincoln in 1860.

As for Dred Scott, he died a little more than a year after losing his final court battle. But he died a free man. His new master had freed him, his wife, and his two daughters ten weeks after the court's decision. ■

Dred Scott is pictured with his wife, Harriet, and his two daughters (top), in the June 27, 1857, edition of Frank Leslie's Illustrated Newspaper, one of the country's first illustrated periodicals.

it will cease to be divided. It will become all one thing, or all the other." Lincoln denied any intention to interfere with slavery in states where it was already established. "Wrong as we think slavery is," he said, "we can yet afford to let it alone where it is, because that much is due to the necessity of its actual presence in the nation; but can we, when our actual votes will prevent it, allow it to spread into the national territories, and to overrun us here in these free states? If our sense of duty forbids this, then let us stand by our duty, fearlessly and effectively."

Southerners were not soothed by such remarks. Lincoln's statement that "we can yet afford" to tolerate slavery in the South suggested to skeptics that Republicans, once in power, might soon find they could no longer afford to be so tolerant. Lincoln's nomination at the Republican convention in Chicago in May 1860 struck many Southerners as calamitous. He was as black a Republican as Seward, they believed, and would be a more formidable candidate than Seward in the Midwest, a region Democrats hoped to carry by nominating Stephen Douglas of Illinois.

The best chance Southern Democrats had to defeat Lincoln was to unite behind Douglas, but Democrats, like Whigs earlier, were breaking apart over slavery. Southern extremists called fire-eaters, who favored secession if their political demands were not met, were no longer content with compromises such as Douglas's Kansas-Nebraska Act. Emboldened by a controversial Supreme Court ruling in 1857 that the slave Dred Scott had no right to sue for freedom because slaves were "articles of merchandise" owned by their masters, fire-eaters argued that any act by the federal government that barred slaveholders from settling in western territories with their slaves was an unconstitutional infringement on property rights. Douglas and his supporters rejected that argument and endorsed popular sovereignty. Led by fire-eater William Yancey of Alabama, many Southern delegates then bolted the party's convention and backed their own candidate, John Breckinridge of Kentucky, while the remaining Democrats nominated Douglas.

The fracturing of the Democratic Party improved prospects for Republicans by so weakening Douglas that many Northerners saw Lincoln as their only hope against Southerners who defied the Democratic establishment and backed Breckinridge. Would-be secessionists who bolted to Breckinridge felt they had nothing to lose. If their candidate fell short and Lincoln won, they reckoned, Southern states would leave the Union in disgust. Southerners, Yancey warned, would not abide a Black Republican administration that let abolitionists invade their homeland and fan the "flames of midnight arson." Slavery would be destroyed under Lincoln, he prophesied, and white Southerners would be reduced to menials: "hewers of wood and drawers of water."

Another fire-eater, Edmund Ruffin of Virginia, wrote that the election of 1860 would decide "whether these Southern states are to remain free, or to be politically enslaved." Ruffin kept alive bitter memories of John Brown's raid in the South by carrying with him one of the pikes Brown's raiders had intended for the use of rebellious slaves. Attached to the pike was a label that read: "Samples of the favors designed for us by our Northern Brethren." On Election Day in November, Ruffin voted for Breckinridge, whose candidacy helped

> "I believe this government cannot endure, permanently half slave and half free. I do not expect the Union to be dissolved—I do not expect the house to fall—but I do expect it will cease to be divided. It will become all one thing, or all the other."
>
> ABRAHAM LINCOLN

At right, a bareheaded Lincoln, standing at the door to his house in Springfield, Illinois, towers over supporters attending a rally held in August 1860 during his run for president. Aside from such local appearances, Lincoln did not campaign actively. Most Americans knew him only through books, articles, political cartoons, or party banners like the one above.

"Well, boys, your troubles are over now, mine have just begun."

ABRAHAM LINCOLN,
the day after the presidential election of 1860

spur Lincoln to victory. Then he left at once for South Carolina, "to forward the secession of the state & consequently of the whole South."

The presidential election of 1860 was symptomatic of a nation on the verge of fracturing. Besides Lincoln and the two Democratic candidates, John Bell of Tennessee ran as the nominee of the newly formed Constitutional Union party, which took no position on slavery but simply pledged to support the Union and the Constitution. Three states of the Upper South—Tennessee, Kentucky, and Virginia—went for Bell. The rest of the South went for the breakaway Democrat, Breckinridge. Stephen Douglas, the best-known candidate, captured only one state, Missouri, and split New Jersey with Lincoln, who swept the Northeast, the Midwest, and the Pacific states of California and Oregon, claiming less than 40 percent of the popular vote but nearly 60 percent of the electoral vote. He was the first American president elected without any help from the South and knew what that foretold. "Well, boys, your troubles are over now," he told reporters the day after his election; "mine have just begun."

On December 20, 1860, delegates meeting in Charleston, South Carolina, adopted an ordinance of secession and withdrew their state from the Union. Church bells pealed and secessionists danced in the streets, but not everyone was pleased. "We shall be envied by posterity for the privilege that we have enjoyed of living under the benign rule of the United States," lamented James Petigru, a South Carolina Unionist. Henceforth, he warned, "we shall have no more peace forever."

Within six weeks, it would be followed by Mississippi, Florida, Alabama, Georgia, Louisiana, and Texas. For Northerners, who had heard so much idle talk of secession by the South over the years, it was hard to believe that the nation was truly breaking apart. Difficulties facing the seceders "are so great that I fear we shall not get rid of them long enough," wrote Charles Sumner, now back in the Senate and arguing against compromise with the seceding states. "My desire is that four or five should go out long enough to be completely humbled and chastened and to leave us in control of the government."

Lincoln, who would not be inaugurated until March, knew that the secessionists meant business and would not easily be coaxed back into the Union. Southerners were driven to defiance by the fear that they would lose their own freedom and independence if Northerners gained power over them and abolished slavery. That was Lincoln's goal, they believed, however much he denied it. "The fortunes of war may be averse to our arms," declared Louisiana Senator Judah P. Benjamin on December 31, 1860, not long before his state left the Union; "you may carry desolation into our peaceful land, and with torch and fire you may set our cities in flames . . . but you never can subjugate us; you never can convert the free sons of the soil into vassals, paying tribute to your power; and you never, never can degrade them to the level of an inferior and servile race."

Moderates in Congress hoped a political deal might yet be reached that would avert civil war. But Lincoln would accept no compromise that extended slavery beyond its present limits. "On that point hold firm, as with a chain of steel," he wrote Republicans in Washington. "The tug has to come, & better now, than any time hereafter."

THE BRUTAL LIFE OF SLAVES

IN A REGION RENOWNED FOR ITS storytellers, Southerners began to cultivate a mythology before the Civil War that slavery, far from being immoral, was a benevolent institution that elevated the former African above his natural state. "God bless you massa!" read the caption of one proslavery illustration showing a slaveholder and his family surrounded by his grateful slaves. "You feed and clothe us. When we are sick you nurse us and when too old to work, you provide for us!"

In truth, many plantation masters neglected even these most basic responsibilities, sometimes due to their own dire economic circumstances, other times out of sheer cruelty. In 1813 a white citizen of Alexandria, Virginia, wrote the mayor of her city on behalf of a slave who had been badly burned in the service of her master, who then refused her treatment. "She is now loathsome to every beholder, without change of clothing, or one single necessary of life, or comfort. Can you not compel the savage creature who owns her to do something for her?"

While not every slave owner was a Simon Legree (the inhumane overseer of *Uncle Tom's Cabin*), the lot of virtually every slave, man or woman, in the South was the same—absolute servility maintained by brute force. No punishment by a white against a black was unlawful except murder. And as late as the mid-19th century, killing a slave was usually punished with a fine.

One of the most profound rebuttals to the idyllic white version of slave life was the narrative by

> **"Don't done you task, driver wave that whip, put you over the barrel, beat you so blood run down."**
>
> HAGAR BROWN,
> *slave on the Oaks plantation,
> Georgetown County, South Carolina*

Braided leather whips often left permanent scars, such as the gruesome relief carved on the back of a former slave (right) who was photographed after he escaped north during the Civil War and served in the Union Army.

escaped slave Harriet Jacobs. Published in 1861 under the pseudonym Linda Brent, *Incidents in the Life of a Slave Girl* described scenes of abuse even toward the house servants, who were considered far more privileged than field slaves. "The cook never set a dinner to [the master's] table without fear and trembling; for if there happened to be a dish not to his liking, he would either order her to be whipped, or compel her to eat every mouthful of it in his presence."

What made Jacobs's book especially provocative, though, was her frankness about an uncomfortable and unspoken truth of master-slave relations: sexual debasement, which in some cases went as far as rape. Jacobs herself was spared this ultimate crime, but she tells us that upon turning 15, "My master began to whisper foul words in my ear. Young as I was, I could not remain ignorant of their import. The master's age, my extreme youth, and the fear that his conduct would be reported to my grandmother, made him bear this treatment for many months. He peopled my young mind with unclean images, such as only a vile monster could think of. I turned from him with disgust and hatred. But he was my master. I was compelled to live under the same roof with him—where I saw a man forty years my senior daily violating the most sacred commandments of nature. He told me I was his property; that I must be subject to his will in all things. My soul revolted against the mean tyranny. But where could I turn for protection? No matter whether the slave girl be as black as ebony or as fair as her mistress. In either case, there is no shadow of law to protect

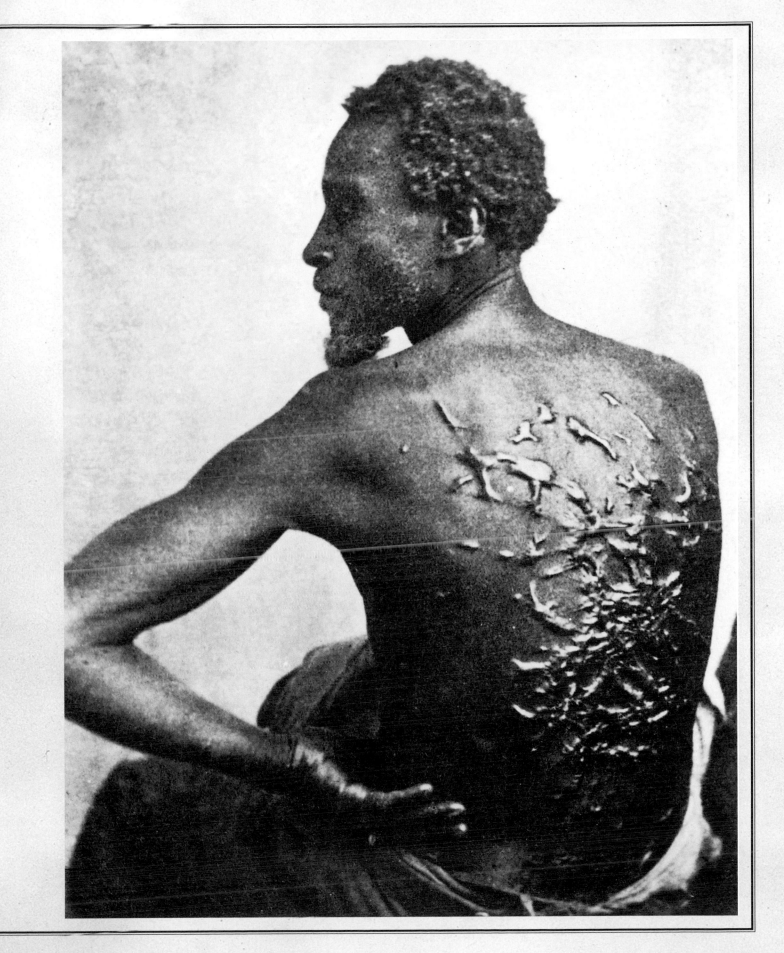

Between 1700 and 1850, raw materials such as tobacco, cotton, and sugar went from the Americas to Europe, to be exchanged for finished goods. Some of those goods were shipped to West Africa as payment for slaves who were then brought to the Americas—the so-called Middle Passage of this lucrative trade triangle. Even after the end of the Atlantic slave trade, captives such as those shown below continued to be sold into slavery in the African interior.

her from insult, from violence, or even from death; all these are inflicted by fiends who bear the shape of men. The mistress, who ought to protect the helpless victim, has no other feelings towards her but those of jealousy and rage. The degradation, the wrongs, the vices, that grow out of slavery, are more than I can describe. They are greater than you would willingly believe. Surely, if you credited one half the truths that are told you concerning the helpless millions suffering in this cruel bondage, you at the north would not help to tighten the yoke. You surely would refuse to do for the master, on your own soil, the mean and cruel work which trained bloodhounds and the lowest class of whites do for him at the south."

THE TRADE IN HUMAN FLESH

THE PRECIOUS NATURAL RESOURCES OF West Africa led to the rise of mighty trading empires between the 8th and 16th centuries. Once these fell, Europeans and Americans made West Africa the hub of their own lucrative trade empire, with Africans the main commodity.

The horrors of the Middle Passage— the forced migration from Africa to the Americas—began long before the ships were actually loaded. African slave hunters from coastal tribes sometimes captured their cargo hundreds of miles into the interior of the continent, then lashed their captives together and marched them in slave processions called coffles to the Atlantic coast. There, most captives were held in barracoons—military slave barracks—until enough could be accumulated to fill a

This deck plan of a British slaver diagrams the inhumane way captives were packed for their transatlantic journey. Disease spread rapidly through such "tight-packing"; smallpox and dysentery were leading causes of death on slave ships.

"The financial genius of Africa . . . has from time immemorial declared that a human creature . . . is the most valuable article on earth."
SLAVE TRADER THEODORE CANOT

Slave Room   *Slave Room*

ship that for many slaves proved to be their coffin.

The ship was "so crowded that each of us had scarcely room to turn himself," wrote Gustavus Vassa (born Olaudah Equiano in Nigeria) of his 1756 transatlantic crossing. "The air soon became unfit for respiration . . . and brought on sickness among the slaves, of which many died. . . . This wretched situation was again aggravated by the galling of the chains, now become insupportable, and the filth of the necessary [toilets], into which the children often fell, and were almost suffocated."

More than 11 million Africans crossed the Middle Passage to North and South America between the 16th and 19th centuries. Early on, mortality rates were higher than 50 percent. By the early 1800s, the figure was down to around 10 percent as profit motivated slave traders to improve the living conditions of their investments. Those that did die en route might be considered fortunate. For at the end of the 6- to 12-week journey lay the shock of a whole new world and the brutality of plantation life.

A ban on the importation of slaves to the United States after 1807 did not extinguish the international slave trade. Right up until the Civil War smugglers dodged naval patrols and blockades to satisfy a burgeoning demand for slave labor in the Deep South.

The most famous scofflaw was a refitted sporting yacht called the *Wanderer*, owned by wealthy Georgian Charles Lamar. In 1858 the *Wanderer* captured around 500 slaves from the Congo and brought the 400 survivors to Jekyll Island, Georgia. Lamar was arrested and his ship seized. But a jury acquitted him, and he immediately repurchased his ship and continued to use it for illegal slaving until the war began, when he was killed in battle.

LIFE AND DEATH IN AMERICA

FROM THEIR HOLDING PENS ON THE AFRICAN COAST TO the hold of a ship, slaves brought to the Americas commonly ended up in yet another cell—what slave traders called "nigger jails." Here slaves could be kept until auction and examined or inspected like any other livestock. Prospective white buyers were willing to pay almost $3,000 for a healthy black male, or $250 for a child.

The idea of family, such an integral part of African culture, was from this point on something only grasped at, and if obtained, was always in jeopardy. If by chance families were still intact after being brought to America, they would likely be sold to different masters. New families of a kind formed on plantations—slaves were not allowed to marry, but they did live together and have children, and women often bore their masters' children. The women were also forced to breed after the ban on slave imports took effect in 1808, or they were given incentive to do so. "Women with six children alive at any one time are allowed all Saturday to themselves," wrote one plantation overseer.

But the ban on international trade only served to increase the slave trade within America, and also encouraged the practice of hiring out slaves to other plantations, which meant parents and children were never safe from separation. Charles Ball remembered his mother pleading with her owner not to sell her son: "He gave her two or three heavy blows on the shoulders with his raw-hide, snatched me from her arms, handed me to my master, and . . . dragged her back to the place of sale. My master then quickened the pace of his horse . . . the cries of my poor parent became more and more indistinct . . . and I never again heard the voice of my poor mother."

Plantations generated so much

> **"I'd ruther be dead than be a nigger on one of these big plantations."**
>
> *White Mississippian to a Northern visitor*

wealth because most of the jobs were performed by slaves. Field slaves worked the land, dug ditches and repaired fences, harvested crops, and tended livestock, usually from sunup to sundown, sometimes seven days a week. Pregnant women were not exempt from hard labor, nor were new mothers. "The cotton planters generally, never allow a slave mother time to go to the house, or quarter during the day to nurse her child," wrote former slave Henry Bibb. House slaves cooked, cleaned, took care of the mistress's children, and generally kept the household running smoothly, while skilled slaves performed carpentry, blacksmithing, and other artisan jobs. On smaller farms slaves worked both the field and the house, which required rising as early as three in the morning to tend livestock and then prepare breakfast.

The days of both field slaves and house slaves and artisans were heavily regimented and long. Former North Carolina slave Sarah Gudger later wrote, "I never knowed what it was to rest. I just work all de time from mornin' till late at night. I had to do everythin' dey was to do on de outside. Work in de field, chop wood, hoe corn." In the house, "I had to card and spin till ten o'clock; . . . get up at four de next mornin' and start again." Nights were spent mainly confined to bedchambers (if they lived in the house) or small cabins on the grounds, which were furnished like livestock pens and usually housed at least 12 slaves of both sexes, with no privacy.

In addition to all the other hazards of slave life, either from the malice of the owner or the stress of the working conditions, the slaves' diet was woefully insufficient. Before Frederick Douglass escaped from Maryland, "there were four slaves of us in the kitchen—my sister Eliza, my aunt Priscilla, Henny, and myself; and we were

Price, Birch, and Co. of Alexandria, Virginia, was one of the South's most notorious "Dealers in Slaves." (Opposite): The invention of the cotton gin in 1793 sped up cotton production and made the crop hugely profitable, spiking the demand for field hands. The slave population in the South grew from less than 700,000 in 1790 to four million in 1860, a third of the South's population.

allowed less than a half a bushel of corn-meal per week, and very little else, either in the shape of meat or vegetables. It was not enough to subsist upon. We were therefore reduced to the wretched necessity of . . . begging or stealing." Diets heavy on rice, fatback, and salt pork left slaves vulnerable to everything from malnutrition to blindness. The life expectancy for a black male in Louisiana in 1850 was 29 years; for a black female, just 34 years.

While death meant deliverance, it often happened without dignity. Runaway slave turned abolitionist Sojourner Truth told how she was not allowed to care for or even visit her father on his deathbed in New York State. He died "lone, blind, and helpless." Eventually, "this deserted wreck of humanity was found on his miserable pallet, frozen and stiff."

THE URGE TO ESCAPE

THE GENTEEL SOUTHERNER'S WORST NIGHTMARE CAME to life, ironically, in the figure of a charismatic preacher who, like John Brown a few years later, channeled religious fervor for justice into violent revolt.

Nat Turner, called "the Prophet" by some of his followers because he claimed to receive visions, began planning his 1831 slave rebellion after taking a February solar eclipse as a sign from God. Armed with knives, axes, and clubs, Turner and six other Virginia slaves went to the plantation of Turner's master the morning of August 22 and killed the entire family. By the following morning the rebel force was more than 60 strong and had moved through Southampton County, killing at least 55 white men, women, and children.

The insurgency was short-lived. Dozens of blacks were killed in retaliation, whether they were involved in the rebellion or not, and after finally being captured, the 31-year-old Turner was hanged. However, the panic that was brought on by Nat Turner's 48-hour rampage led to even harsher slave codes

> **"O, that I were free!**
> **God save me,**
> **I will run away.**
> **Get caught or get clear.**
> **I had as well be killed**
> **running as die standing."**
>
> *Escaped slave*

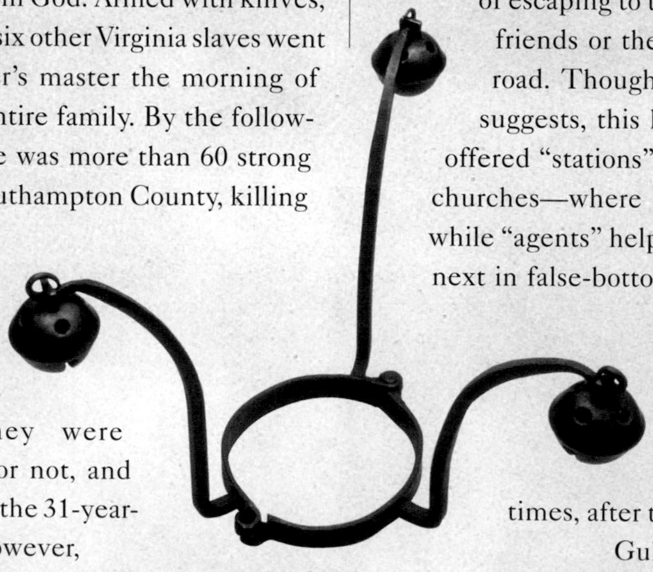

A heavy metal collar fitted with bells was one form of punishment for runaways. The bells kept the slave within earshot and the prongs made running through the woods difficult.

in the South and crippled organized abolition there.

Though Nat Turner's rebellion was the last slave revolt of major consequence in the United States, the urge to resist and escape bondage was constant and undiminished. But the odds of success were remote, in no small part because the color of their skin made slaves easy targets. From the Deep South it was almost impossible to successfully flee north, so runaways escaped into the wilderness, even forming communities of "outlyers" known as maroons (a corruption of the Spanish word for "wild"). The most famous of these was the Great Dismal Swamp on the border of Virginia and North Carolina, which by the year 1800 was the country's largest permanent sanctuary for fugitives, with some 2,000 runaways living there. They supported themselves by farming or trading illegally with nearby whites or Indians, and sometimes by raiding plantations. So inhospitable was the swamp that an abolitionist newspaper boasted in 1852 that "the chivalry of Virginia was never yet ventured on a slave hunt in the Dismal Swamp." But in the years leading up to the Civil War, slaveholders did in fact launch several assaults that all but exterminated the community.

Slaves in the Upper South had a much better chance of escaping to the North and Canada, aided by friends or the legendary Underground Railroad. Though not as organized as the name suggests, this loose network of escape routes offered "stations"—usually abolitionist homes or churches—where fugitives could find sanctuary, while "agents" helped them from one station to the next in false-bottom carts, shipping crates, boats, disguises, and other forms of subterfuge. Though no one is sure exactly how many escapees rode the Railroad, the 1840s and 50s were boom times, after the removal of Indians from the Gulf states opened up new land to cotton farming and helped increase the demand for slaves sold from the Upper to the Deep South. Some of

the era's most famous abolitionists—Frederick Douglass, John Brown, Harriet Tubman—helped operate the Railroad.

Resistance to slavery took more subtle forms than outright rebellion. When their overseers were elsewhere, field slaves often slackened their pace or deliberately did their jobs poorly in order to lower their master's expectations for them. Others broke their tools, destroyed crops, or even killed their master's livestock. Escape took another form as well, in the form of self-destruction. Slaves were known to throw themselves overboard during the Middle Passage, or kill themselves on the plantation by drowning, suffocating, or poisoning themselves. Some slaves were even driven to self-mutilation to avoid their forced labor. In one especially gruesome example, a slave carpenter used an axe to chop off one hand, then held the axe under the wounded arm to chop off the ends of his fingers on the other hand. He had been distraught about being sold away from his family and friends. ■

$100 REWARD!
RANAWAY

From the undersigned, living on Current River, about twelve miles above Doniphan, in Ripley County, Mo., on 2nd of March, 1860, A NEGRO MAN, about 30 years old, weighs about 160 pounds; high forehead, with a scar on it; had on brown pants and coat very much worn, and an old black wool hat; shoes size No. 11.

The above reward will be given to any person who may apprehend this said negro out. of the State; and fifty dollars if apprehended in this State outside of Ripley county, or $25 if taken in Ripley county.

APOS TUCKER.

A reward poster for a "Negro man, about 30 years old," who had escaped his Missouri master. The fine print reveals that the reward shrinks the closer to home the slave is caught. (Top): The most famous of the Underground Railroad's conductors, Harriet Tubman (far left, holding a pan) helped more than 300 slaves to freedom between 1850 and 1860. "Moses," as she was called, at one time had a bounty of $40,000 on her head.

CHAPTER 1

1861
FIRST BLOOD

DESPITE WORRIES THAT WAR WAS IMMINENT, PRESIDENT JAMES Buchanan observed New Year's Day in 1861 in traditional fashion by hosting members of Congress and his Cabinet at the White House. Buchanan hoped to preserve peace until he left in March, but he faced a deepening crisis at Fort Sumter in Charleston Harbor, where Federal forces were besieged by hostile South Carolinians. Some of the guests at his reception would soon leave office to join the secessionist movement in the Deep South, an effort fueled by the fears of whites living in slave-holding states that Buchanan's successor, Abraham Lincoln, would restrict or abolish slavery. Among those in Washington about to depart was Senator Robert Toombs of Georgia, whose wife shared his views. "I have despaired of the Union," she wrote, "and will begin to pack up."

The crisis at Charleston was inherited by President Lincoln and his Confederate counterpart, Jefferson Davis, who ordered Fort Sumter attacked in April. Once blood was spilled there, the conflict gathered momentum. Lincoln's call for volunteers to put down what he saw as a rebellion—and Davis viewed as a war for independence—led to secession by states of the Upper South, fierce strife within uncommitted border states, and a costly battle at Bull Run in July that left the two sides unalterably opposed. As one Yankee said of that hard loss to the Rebels: "We shall flog these scoundrels and traitors all the more bitterly for it before we are done with them." ■

Determined recruits in Virginia prepare for war after their state joined the Confederacy in defiance of President Lincoln, who summoned troops to fight for the Union when Fort Sumter fell. "There is a spirit abroad in Virginia which cannot be crushed until the life of the last man is trampled out," declared secessionist John Tyler.

FALL OF FORT SUMTER

FOR 35 YEARS, MAJOR ROBERT ANDERSON HAD SERVED WITH QUIET DIStinction in the U.S. Army, earning praise from superiors but doing nothing to attract public notice. Then, in the few days between Christmas of 1860 and New Year's Day, 1861, he became one of the Union's brightest stars. The action that made him famous was deceptively simple. As commander of Federal troops holding Charleston Harbor in South Carolina against secessionists who hoped to oust them, he moved his garrison at night from vulnerable Fort Moultrie to Fort Sumter, a stronger bastion at the entrance to the harbor. Governor Francis Pickens saw this as an aggressive act, since Sumter's big guns could be used to close the harbor to shipping, and demanded that the Federals return to Fort Moultrie. Anderson replied that his sole object in occupying Sumter was to prevent bloodshed by discouraging an attack on his forces. He had no intention of reverting to a weaker position. "I cannot and will not go back," he vowed.

Anderson was hailed in the North for standing firm. The Union desperately needed someone to "take command and crystallize this chaos into order," wrote the poet James Russell Lowell. "God bless Major Anderson for setting us a good example!" Chaos was indeed rampant in Washington, D.C., where the outgoing president, Democrat James Buchanan, exercised little control over a Cabinet containing both Northern loyalists and Southerners sympathetic to secessionists in South Carolina and other states.

Among those suspected of favoring secession was Secretary of War John Floyd of Virginia. Floyd sent Anderson to Charleston believing that as a Kentuckian and former slave owner, he would avoid provoking defiant South Carolinians. But Anderson's devotion to the Union was paramount. He once told a fellow officer from the South that they had no choice as infants where they were born, "but when we took the oath of allegiance to our government, it was an act of our manhood, and that oath we cannot break." He signaled his loyalty by raising a huge American flag at Sumter that was plainly visible to secessionists in Charleston. By acting firmly, Anderson forced the lame-duck Buchanan to take a stand. Showing uncommon resolve, the president asked Floyd to resign and pledged to defend Fort Sumter "against hostile attacks from whatever quarter."

On January 5, 1861, the merchant ship *Star of the West* left New York with 200 Federal troops below decks on a secret mission to reinforce Sumter. A merchant ship had a better chance than a warship of reaching the fort without drawing hostile fire, but it would be a defenseless target if the South Carolinians knew what was coming. The relief mission did not long remain secret. Reports soon appeared in the press, and Senator Louis Wigfall of Texas made sure Governor Pickens had ample warning by sending him a telegram. "The

Star of the West sailed from New York on Sunday with government troops and provisions," Wigfall disclosed. "It is said her destination is Charleston."

When the relief ship approached Fort Sumter around dawn on January 9, it came under fire from alert South Carolinians manning guns at Fort Moultrie and nearby Morris Island. Anderson had read in a newspaper that the ship was on its way, but he dismissed the story as rumor until the *Star of the West* appeared out of the gloom, flying the American flag and presenting him with an agonizing decision. He had orders to act "strictly on the defensive" and hesitated to fire on the opposing batteries and ignite a war when Sumter itself was not under attack. Consulting his officers did not make his decision any easier. Lieutenant R. K. Meade of Virginia advised against firing, warning that it would "bring civil war on us," while Captain Abner Doubleday of New York was all for blasting Fort Moultrie to protect the ship. The gunners at Moultrie expected the worst. "Now, boys, we'll give 'em a shot or two," their commander told them as they targeted the *Star of the West*, "and then we'll catch the devil from Sumter!" But while Anderson deliberated, the ship's captain lost heart and turned about, retreating before his vessel sustained any serious damage and ending the confrontation.

No blood had been spilled, and war had been postponed—a reprieve welcomed by both sides. Anderson hoped to complete repairs that would bolster Sumter against attack and arrange for the removal of officers' wives from the fort before a real battle erupted. Governor Pickens, for his part, needed to strengthen his batteries substantially before he could feel confident of pounding Sumter into submission. Politically, the Union would not be ready to wage war before the man whose election brought this crisis to a head, Abraham Lincoln, took the oath of office in March. And secessionists in South Carolina and elsewhere needed a president and constitution of their own to hold them together after the thrill of declaring independence faded and the struggle to remain independent began. "The separation is perfect, complete, and perpetual," declared Howell Cobb of Georgia after his state left the Union on January 19 and joined with others in the Deep South to constitute a new nation. "The great duty is now imposed upon us of providing for those states a government for their future security and protection."

Major Robert Anderson of Kentucky, who was saluted in the North and scorned in the South for defending the Union at Fort Sumter, had no desire to see the two regions come to blows. "I think an appeal to arms and to brute force is unbecoming to the age in which we live," he wrote.

THE NEWS REACHED JEFFERSON DAVIS BY TELEGRAM ON FEBRUARY 10 AT BRIER-field, his plantation near Vicksburg, Mississippi. As he read the message, his wife Varina recalled, "he looked so grieved that I feared some evil had befall-en our family." Davis, a former secretary of war who had commanded troops in the Mexican-American War, hoped to be named general in chief of secession-ist forces. Instead, the telegram told him, delegates meeting in Montgomery, Alabama, to form the Confederate States of America had chosen him as their provisional president, an appointment to be ratified later by general election.

He told his wife the news "as a man might speak of a sentence of death," and she too felt it was a great misfortune. "I thought his genius was military, but that as a party manager he would not succeed," she wrote. "He did not know the arts of the politician and would not practice them if understood." Davis's recent tenure as a U.S. senator, which ended when Mississippi seceded

---

[EYEWITNESS]

William Tecumseh Sherman
SUPERINTENDENT, LOUISIANA STATE SEMINARY AND MILITARY ACADEMY

An 1840 graduate of West Point, Sherman served during the Mexico-American War. He later resigned, working as a banker before becom-ing superintendent of the military academy in Louisiana. One of his fellow professors, David Boyd, recalled a conversation he had with him in late 1860. After reading a pro-secession article in a Virginia newspaper, Sherman took Boyd, a Virginian by birth, to task about saber rattling in the Southern press. The two men would encounter one another on opposite sides of the upcoming conflict. Boyd, an officer of a Louisiana regiment, was captured in the fighting in Virginia, and Sherman, then an engineer officer, helped secure his exchange.

"This country will be drenched in blood, and God only knows how it will end."

YOU PEOPLE OF THE SOUTH don't know what you are doing. This country will be drenched in blood, and God only knows how it will end. It is all folly, madness, a crime against civiliza-tion! You people speak so lightly of war; you don't know what you're talking about. War is a terrible thing! You mistake, too, the people of the North. They are a peaceable people but an earnest people, and they will fight, too. They are not going to let this country be destroyed without a mighty effort to save it. . . . Besides, where are

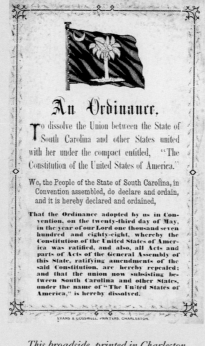

This broadside, printed in Charleston in 1860, proclaims the withdrawal of South Carolina from the Union.

your men and appliances of war to contend against them? The North can make a steam engine, loco-motive or railway car; hardly a yard of cloth or a pair of shoes can you make. You are rushing into war with one of the most power-ful, ingeniously mechanical and determined people on earth—right at your doors. You are bound to fail. Only in your spirit and determination are you prepared for war. In all else you are totally unprepared, with a bad cause to start with. At first you will make headway, but as your limited resources begin to fail, shut out from the markets of Europe as you will be, your cause will begin to wane. If your people will but stop and think, they must see that in the end you will surely fail. ■

In a sketch made on the scene by artist William Waud, slaves help hoist a cannon into place at a battery on Morris Island in Charleston Harbor during preparations in early 1861 for the bombardment of Fort Sumter. The use of slaves by Confederates for military purposes increased support among Unionists for emancipation as the war progressed.

in January, proved as much. "I make no terms," he told a colleague who tried to bargain with him; "I accept no compromises." Unlike Lincoln, who would humor and cajole strong-willed Cabinet members, Davis was proud and overbearing. He knew he was better suited by temperament for military command than for political leadership but he gave no thought to declining the presidency. It was the highest tribute the Confederacy could bestow on him, and like other prominent Southerners, he placed public honor above his personal inclinations.

Davis's vice-president, Alexander Hamilton Stephens of Georgia, seemed even more at odds with his new position. Long opposed to secession, he had recently received a conciliatory letter from Lincoln. "Do the people of the South really entertain fears that a Republican administration would, directly, or indirectly, interfere with their slaves?" Lincoln wrote him. "I wish to assure you, as once a friend, and still, I hope, not an enemy, that there is no cause for such fears." The underlying problem, Lincoln suspected, was one of conflicting values: "You think slavery is right and ought to be extended; while we think it is wrong and ought to be restricted. That I suppose is the rub."

Lincoln's diagnosis was confirmed by a speech Stephens delivered soon after his inauguration. Blacks were inferior to whites, and slavery was their "natural and normal condition," Stephens argued. "This great physical, philosophical, and moral truth" was now enshrined in the Confederate constitution, which upheld slavery in the new Southern nation and any territories it might acquire. The constitution drawn up at Montgomery also gave Southern states greater power in relation to the central government than Northern states had. But in other respects, the by-laws of this new union were much like those of the old Union. States of the Deep South hoped to enlist in their Confederacy states of the Upper South, where many people still prized the old American Republic

and its constitutional guarantees and had doubts about secession. As Robert E. Lee of Virginia said in early 1861, the Founding Fathers never meant for their compact to be broken up by members at will: "It is idle to talk of secession."

To win over skeptics like Lee, Confederates had to do more than adopt a democratic system of government consistent with American traditions. They had to challenge the Yankees militarily and force uncommitted Southerners to choose between their home state and the United States. State loyalty was stronger in the largely rural South than in the increasingly urban North, where people born hundreds or thousands of miles apart intermingled in towns and cities. To many Southerners, their own state was a beloved homeland that meant far more to them than the nation. If Confederates could pressure Federals into taking actions hostile to states and their rights, then Southerners who were holding back would join the secessionist movement. Jefferson Davis struck a defiant tone for the Confederacy when he told delegates at Montgomery: "The South is determined to maintain her position, and make all who oppose her smell Southern powder and feel Southern steel."

By the time Davis spoke, officials in the seceding states had seized most of the Federal forts and arsenals within their borders, sometimes with the help of Federal officers raised in the South. In Texas, Major General David Twiggs of Georgia freely offered to surrender Federal posts and armaments. "If an old woman with a broomstick should come with full authority from the state of Texas to demand the public property," he announced, "I would give it to her." Among the few Federal forts in Confederate territory that resisted confiscation were coastal strongholds such as Fort Sumter and Fort Pickens, in Pensacola Bay, which was reinforced by ship and would remain in Union hands. The confrontation at Fort Sumter in early January had already enlarged the Confederacy by encouraging several states to secede in sympathy with South Carolina. An all-out battle there might force the rest of the South into the Confederate camp. Was defending the American flag at Sumter worth such a risk? That was a question the Union's new commander in chief would have to answer.

LINCOLN TAKES CHARGE

NO INAUGURAL ADDRESS EVER MEANT MORE TO THE NATION. Lincoln knew how much was at stake and weighed his words carefully in advance, submitting a draft of the speech to William Seward, his former rival for the Republican nomination and soon to be secretary of state. Seward considered himself far better qualified than Lincoln to run the country and hoped to keep this rough-hewn "rail-splitter" from blundering into a ruinous civil war. Lincoln, who was never too proud to heed wise counsel from condescending advisers, agreed with Seward that parts of his address were too strident and might offend Southerners. If he alienated people in nearby slave states such as Virginia and Maryland and drove them into the Confederacy, the nation's capital would be surrounded by enemies. Secessionist sentiment was already

"I thought his genius was military, but that as a party manager he would not succeed."
VARINA DAVIS

"I make no terms, I accept no compromises."
JEFFERSON DAVIS

Neither Jefferson Davis nor his wife, Varina (above), were thrilled when Confederates chose him as their leader and summoned him to the state house in Montgomery, Alabama, for his inauguration on February 18, 1861 (left). "Mrs. Davis does not like her husband being made president," commented diarist Mary Chesnut. "She says general of all the armies would have suited his temperament better."

so strong in Baltimore that aides feared Lincoln would be attacked there as he traveled south by train from Philadelphia to Washington for the inauguration. At their insistence, he left ahead of schedule on another train, wearing a hat and overcoat that disguised him. When his car stopped in Baltimore that night, Lincoln could hear a boisterous drunk on the platform singing "Dixie," the minstrel song that would become the Confederate anthem.

On March 4, Inauguration Day, Lincoln stood beneath the unfinished dome of the Capitol and spoke beyond the assembled dignitaries to a divided America. The Constitution was the supreme law of the land, he pointed out, and those who wished to alter the government established under that Constitution had two choices: "They can exercise their constitutional right of amending it, or their revolutionary right to dismember, or overthrow it." To avoid revolution, he would accept a proposed constitutional amendment upholding slavery in states where it already existed. But if Southerners were not content with that guarantee, if they insisted on dismembering the Union, then they were acting as rebels. He had authority as president to wage war on those in rebellion against the United States, but he would not do so while there was any chance of preserving peace. He would use the powers confided in him only "to hold, occupy, and possess the property and places belonging to the government," meaning Fort Sumter and other posts. Beyond that, he promised Southerners, there would be no invasion, no use of force: "You can have no conflict, without being yourselves the aggressors."

At Seward's urging, Lincoln had eliminated from his speech a pledge to recapture Federal forts and arsenals seized by secessionists. And in conclusion, he took another cue from Seward, who urged Lincoln to soothe his opponents with "words of affection," and addressed disaffected Southerners as fellow Americans: "We must not be enemies. Though passion may have strained, it must not break our bonds of affection. The mystic chords of memory, stretching from every battle-field, and patriot grave, to every living heart and hearthstone, all over this broad land, will yet swell the chorus of the Union, when again touched, as surely they will be, by the better angels of our nature."

If Seward concluded from this speech that Lincoln would do as he advised and make further concessions to Southerners, he was mistaken. Lincoln offered kind words in his inaugural address not simply to placate Southerners but to make Northerners more inclined to blame secessionists and wage war on them if they spurned his efforts at reconciliation. The necessity of putting Confederates at fault guided his thinking in the weeks to come as he and his Cabinet debated what to do about Sumter. Federal forces there were running short of food and could not hold out much longer without fresh supplies. Seward offered Confederate emissaries private assurances that Anderson would soon surrender, but the president was not about to let his secretary of state call the shots. In late March, Lincoln ordered Fort Sumter resupplied but not reinforced, to avoid any appearance that he was inviting conflict. He informed Governor Pickens that the Federal fleet would deliver "provisions only" to Sumter and that "no effort to throw in men, arms, or ammunition" would be made unless the Confederates interfered or attacked.

Pickens promptly notified Jefferson Davis, who met with his Cabinet in

---

"The mystic chords of memory, stretching from every battle-field, and patriot grave, to every living heart and hearthstone, all over this broad land, will yet swell the chorus of the Union. . . ."

ABRAHAM LINCOLN

Abraham Lincoln, shown here around the time of his inauguration, grew a beard while running for president in 1860 and credited a young admirer in Westfield, New York, named Grace Bedell with proposing the idea: "She wrote me that she thought I would be better looking if I wore whiskers."

Montgomery on April 9 to decide whether to seize Fort Sumter before the fleet arrived. Firing first would allow Lincoln to blame Confederates for starting the war, but Davis suspected that angry South Carolinians would soon bombard Sumter with or without his orders. "No one now doubts that Lincoln intends war," Louis Wigfall of Texas wrote Davis. "Let us take Fort Sumter, before we have to fight the fleet and the fort." The only Cabinet member opposed to that course of action was Secretary of State Robert Toombs of Georgia, "It is suicide, murder, and will lose us every friend at the North," he warned. "You will wantonly strike a hornet's nest . . . and legions, now quiet, will swarm out and sting us to death." Davis decided that he would rather enrage the North than lose what might be his only chance to rally the South to arms. As one of his advisers put it: "Unless you sprinkle blood in the face of the Southern people they will be back in the old Union in less than ten days."

A crowd gathers below the unfinished Capitol in Washington for Lincoln's inauguration on March 4, 1861. Fears that secessionists might target Lincoln prompted tight security, with plainclothes detectives interspersed among the audience and riflemen stationed on rooftops.

> ### "If we never meet in this world again, God grant that we may meet in the next."
>
> MAJOR ROBERT ANDERSON

STORM OVER SUMTER

MARY CHESNUT WAS STEELING HERSELF FOR WAR. HER HUSBAND, JAMES, HAD resigned from the Senate when South Carolina seceded and was serving now as a Confederate colonel in Charleston. She believed in his cause, despite her aversion to slavery. After watching a slave woman sold at auction, she noted in her diary, "I felt faint—seasick." Slavery was not worth fighting for, she believed, but independence was. Her father, as governor of South Carolina, had agitated against a despised Federal tariff law and insisted his state had the right to nullify it. "So I was of necessity a rebel born," she wrote. It was a fearful task, defying "so great a power as the U.S.A.," but she was "ready and willing."

On April 11, James Chesnut delivered an ultimatum from his commander, Brigadier General Pierre Gustave Toutant Beauregard of Louisiana, to Major Anderson at Sumter. In demanding that Anderson surrender the fort, Beauregard offered his former artillery instructor at West Point generous terms. The flag Anderson had defended "with so much fortitude" could be saluted by Sumter's guns when lowered. And he and his men were assured safe conduct to the North. Anderson, whose rations were running out, countered with an offer to evacuate the fort on April 15 unless he received opposing orders "or additional supplies." Chesnut could not accept those conditions, for the fleet sent to resupply Sumter might arrive at any time. Around 3:30 in the morning on April 12, he handed Anderson a note informing him that Beauregard would open fire on Fort Sumter "in one hour." Anderson escorted Chesnut and his fellow officers to their boat and bid them a somber farewell: "If we never meet in this world again, God grant that we may meet in the next."

With Confederates in Charleston were two fire-eaters from Virginia, Edmund Ruffin and Roger Pryor, the latter an ex-congressman on Beauregard's staff. "Strike a blow!" Pryor had urged South Carolinians recently. "The very moment that blood is shed, old Virginia will make common cause with her sisters of the South." But when offered the chance to launch the assault on Sumter from a battery on James Island, he held back. "I could not fire the first gun of the war," he said. The 66-year-old Ruffin had no such qualms and fired a shot from a battery on Morris Island that, if not the first blast, was only seconds behind. Among those at Sumter jarred by the cannon fire was Captain Doubleday, who felt a projectile "bury itself in the masonry about a foot from my head, in very unpleasant proximity to my

Smoke billows from flaming Fort Sumter as Federal gunners there duel with Confederate batteries in the distance. By the morning of April 13, the smoke was so thick that the fort's defenders could barely function.

Mary Boykin Miller Chesnut

SOUTH CAROLINA DIARIST

The daughter of Stephen Decatur Miller, a former U.S. senator, South Carolina governor, and prosperous cotton planter, Mary Boykin Miller was educated at the French boarding school in Charleston and in 1840 married James Chesnut, a planter and major landowner. Chesnut was elected to the Senate in 1858 but in 1860 he returned home to help draft the South Carolina ordinance of secession. While staying in Charleston, 38-year-old Mary recorded the events surrounding the bombardment of Fort Sumter in her diary.

April 15th

I DID NOT KNOW THAT ONE COULD live such days of excitement. Someone called: "Come out! There is a crowd coming." A mob it was, indeed, but it was headed by Colonels Chesnut and Manning. The crowd was shouting and showing these two as messengers of good news. They were escorted to Beauregard's headquarters. Fort Sumter had surrendered! Those upon the housetops shouted to us "The fort is on fire."

. . . When we had calmed down, Colonel Chesnut, who had taken it all quietly enough, if anything more unruffled than usual in his serenity, told us how the surrender came about. Wigfall was with them on Morris Island when they saw the fire in the fort; he jumped in a little boat, and with his handkerchief as a white flag, rowed over. Wigfall went in through a porthole. When Colonel Chesnut arrived shortly after, and was received at the regular entrance, Colonel Anderson told him he had need to pick his way warily, for the place was all mined. As far as I can make out the fort surrendered to Wigfall. But it is all confusion. Our flag is flying there. Fire-engines have been sent for to put out the fire. Everybody tells you half of something and then rushes off to tell something else or to hear the last news.

In the afternoon, Mrs. Preston,

"I did not know that one could live such days of excitement."

Mrs. Joe Heyward, and I drove around the Battery. We were in an open carriage. What a changed scene—the very liveliest crowd I think I ever saw, everybody talking at once. All glasses were still turned on the grim old fort.

Russell, the correspondent of the *London Times*, was there. They took him everywhere. One man got out Thackeray to converse with him on equal terms. Poor Russell was awfully bored, they say. He only wanted to see the fort and to get

news suitable to make up into an interesting article. Thackeray had become stale over the water.

Mrs. Frank Hampton and I went to see the camp of the Richland troops. South Carolina College had volunteered to a boy. Professor Venable (the mathematical), intends to raise a company from among them for the war, a permanent company. This is a grand frolic no more for the students, at least. Even the staid and severe of aspect, Clingman, is here. He says Virginia and North Carolina are arming to come to our rescue, for now the North will swoop down on us. Of that we may be sure. We have burned our ships. We are obliged to go on now. He calls us a poor, little, hot-blooded, headlong, rash, and troublesome sister State. General McQueen is in a rage because we are to send troops to Virginia.

Preston Hampton is in all the flush of his youth and beauty, six feet in stature; and after all only in his teens; he appeared in fine clothes and lemon-colored kid gloves to grace the scene. The camp in a fit of horse-play seized him and rubbed him in the mud. He fought manfully, but took it all naturally as a good joke. . . . Good stories there may be and to spare for Russell, the man of the *London Times*, who has come over here to find out our weakness and our strength and to tell all the rest of the world about us. ■

right ear. This is the one that probably came with Mr. Ruffin's compliments."

When Mary Chesnut heard the guns booming, she sprang out of bed and fell on her knees, praying "as I never prayed before." Then she ran to the rooftop and looked out over the harbor, where shells were bursting. For all she knew, her husband "was rowing about in a boat somewhere in that dark bay." Later, she learned to her relief that he had come through unscathed and was "asleep on the sofa in General Beauregard's room."

Anderson had to conserve ammunition and did not return fire until around seven that morning. His heaviest guns were on the ramparts atop the fort, where crews manning them would have no protection from enemy fire. Unwilling to expose his men to that risk, he relied instead on lighter cannon sheltered in casemates at a lower level. Shots fired there did little damage to the Confederate batteries, whose guns—many of them confiscated from Federal forts elsewhere in the South—were shielded by iron plating, log breastworks, and sandbags. One frustrated Federal, Private John Carmody, defied orders and raced up onto the parapet, where he fired off several big guns that were already loaded. It was "Carmody against the Confederate States," wrote Sergeant James Chester, "and Carmody had to back down, not because he was beaten, but because he was unable, single-handed, to reload his guns."

Despite such heroics, Fort Sumter was doomed unless the fleet came to its relief. That afternoon, the Federals spotted a few of their ships approaching the harbor. But other vessels sent to aid Sumter lagged far behind, and the fleet's commander, Captain Gustavus Fox, was not prepared to defy enemy batteries until he had more firepower at hand. He was unaware that his strongest asset, the warship *Powhatan*, had been diverted to Fort Pickens.

As night fell with no help forthcoming, Anderson and company faced the grim prospect of going it alone. Sumter's walls were crumbling, and Confederates were firing hot shots that sparked fires. By dawn on April 13, the barracks were burning and the fort was draped in smoke. Men covered their faces with handkerchiefs and gasped for breath. "It seemed impossible to escape suffocation," wrote Doubleday. "The roaring and crackling of the flames, the dense masses of whirling smoke, the bursting of the enemy's shells, and our own which were exploding in the burning rooms, the crashing of the shot, and the sound of masonry falling in every direction, made the fort a pandemonium." Anderson ordered all but a few barrels of powder tossed into the sea to keep them from igniting. At 2 p.m., Beauregard sent a triumphant message to President Davis: "Quarters in Sumter all burned down. White flag up. Have sent a boat to receive surrender."

Remarkably, only four of Anderson's men were injured in the relentless bombardment before he surrendered on the same terms Beauregard had offered earlier. As Federals lowered their flag and saluted it with cannon fire, however, a gun exploded, injuring several and killing Private Daniel Hough, the only soldier on either side to die in action at Charleston. Here as elsewhere in the South, wild victory celebrations gave way to a sobering realization: Americans were now engaged in "that fiercest of human strifes," as Jefferson Davis put it, "a civil war." After the firestorm at Sumter, Mary Chesnut recognized, there would be no turning back: "We have burned our ships. We are obliged to go on now."

> **"It seemed impossible to escape suffocation. The roaring and crackling of the flames, the dense masses of whirling smoke, the bursting of the enemy's shells, and our own which were exploding in the burning rooms, the crashing of the shot, and the sound of masonry falling in every direction, made the fort a pandemonium."**
>
> FEDERAL CAPTAIN ABNER DOUBLEDAY

The map by Federal cartographer Robert Knox Sneden shows the Union flag flying over Fort Sumter for the last time until 1865. The first shot fired against the fort allegedly came from Edmund Ruffin (below), a Virginia fire-eater who sat for this photo six days after Sumter fell, dressed as a member of the Palmetto Guard, a South Carolina militia unit. Years later, in his diary for June 17, 1865, he wrote: "And now with my latest writing and utterance, and with what will be near my latest breath, I here repeat . . . my unmitigated hatred to Yankee rule . . . and the perfidious, malignant and vile Yankee race"—just before shooting himself.

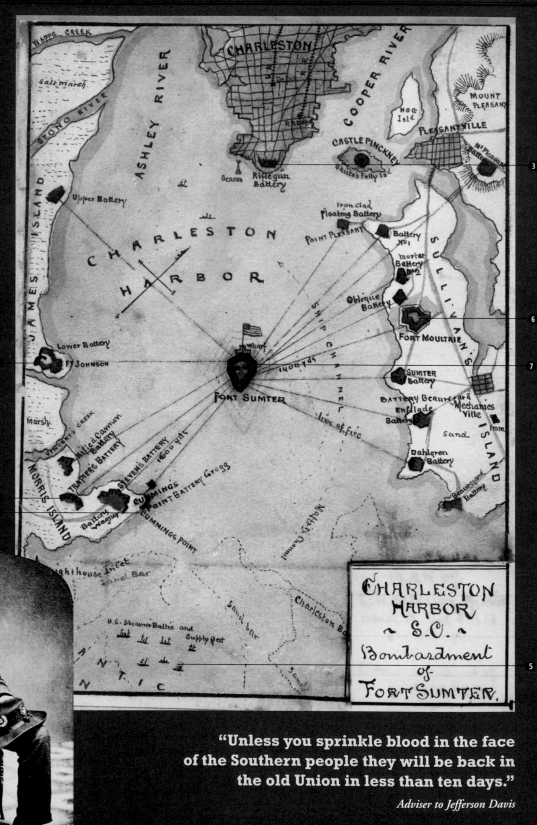

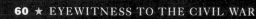

"Unless you sprinkle blood in the face
of the Southern people they will be back in
the old Union in less than ten days."

Adviser to Jefferson Davis

A CHANGE OF FLAGS

FROM THE DAY SOUTH CAROLINA SECEDED ON December 20, 1860, ownership of Fort Sumter became an increasingly bitter bone of contention between the Union and the Confederacy. Blocking the mouth of Charleston Harbor and ringed by batteries, the fort under normal circumstances was perfectly placed. But for Major Robert Anderson and his two companies of the 1st U.S. Artillery, Sumter was a lone outpost hopelessly surrounded by 6,000 enemy forces.

When a supply ship was fired upon and retreated in early January, Anderson and his men were left to hold out on existing rations for months. Unwilling to allow either surrender or starvation, President Lincoln announced plans on April 6 to resupply the fort. Jefferson Davis decided to capture the fort before that could happen. At 4:30 a.m. on April 12, a single mortar round was fired from Fort Johnson 2, the signal round for the other batteries. As the bombardment began, Charleston residents at the tip of the peninsula 3, according to Mary Chesnut, stood on their balconies drinking toasts to the much-anticipated attack.

The Union finally returned fire at 7:00 a.m. when Captain Abner Doubleday fired on the battery at Cummings Point 4, but Anderson was able to use only about ten of Fort Sumter's guns, and by noon only six of those were still operational. Later in the afternoon, the U.S. supply fleet 5 commanded by Gustavus Fox finally reached the mouth of the harbor after being scattered by a gale, but without the Federal warship *Powhatan*, which had been diverted to Fort Pickens, the fleet was useless.

The 43 guns and mortars of Fort Moultrie and Fort Johnson and the batteries of Sullivan's Island and Cummings Point bombarded Fort Sumter for 36 straight hours, until Anderson called for a truce on the afternoon of April 13. General Beauregard allowed Anderson and his men safe passage back North and let Anderson take the surrendered Union flag with him, where it was used to rally support for the war. It would take Sherman's triumphant march through the South four years later before the Union flag was once again raised over the fort. ■

1 TRAPIER MORTAR BATTERY *Confederates of the Trapier Mortar Battery on Morris Island await orders to fire the first shots of the war.*

6 DAMAGE AT FORT MOULTRIE *Shots fired by Union forces blew holes in the fort's western barracks, but did little other damage.*

7 FORT SUMTER FALLS *Seven stars, representing the seven states that had seceded, adorn the Confederate flag that flies over the captured fort.*

> **"Oh to think that I should have lived to see the day when brother should rise against brother."**
>
> *Elderly Indiana woman, upon hearing of the fall of Fort Sumter*

TRIAL AT BULL RUN

FEW AMERICANS WOULD EVER FORGET WHERE THEY WERE OR WHAT THEY were doing when they learned their country was at war. Fifteen-year-old Theodore Upson and his father, Jonathan, were husking corn on their farm in Indiana when a neighbor brought word of a distant battle that would transform their lives. "The Rebels have fired upon and taken Fort Sumter," he told them. At that, Theodore related, "Father got white and couldn't say a word." Jonathan Upson had in-laws down South and dreaded a conflict that might set him and his son against their kin. It did not soothe him to learn from his neighbor that Lincoln was preparing to fight the secessionists: "The President will soon fix them. He has called for 75,000 men and is going to blockade their ports."

When Theodore next saw his father at dinner, he "looked ten years older." He could not keep the bad news from his mother-in-law, who lived with the family. "Oh my poor children in the South!" she cried. "Now they will suffer! God knows how they will suffer!" She knew they would never seek safety with their relatives in Indiana and abandon the South: "There is their home. There they will stay. Oh to think that I should have lived to see the day when brother should rise against brother."

Several young men in Theodore's neighborhood answered Lincoln's call by enlisting, and he felt left out: "I said I would go but they laughed at me and said they wanted men not boys for this job; that it would all be over soon; that those fellows down South are big bluffers and would rather talk than fight." Theodore was not so sure about that. He had relatives who were enlisting with the Confederates and reckoned they would fight just as hard as he would, if he was given the chance. "If I were in our army and they should meet me would they shoot me," he wondered. "I suppose they would."

A CAPITAL BESIEGED

ON APRIL 14, 1861, THE DAY AFTER FORT SUMTER FELL, LINCOLN MET AT THE White House with his old political foe, Stephen Douglas, and showed him a proclamation he was about to issue, asking the governors of all loyal states to provide a total of 75,000 militiamen to serve the Union for three months. "I would make it 200,000," advised Douglas, who blamed secessionists for spoiling his bid to defeat Lincoln in 1860 and did not take them lightly. Like Douglas, Lincoln suspected it would take more than 75,000 men and three months to win this war. He would soon call for 42,000 three-year volunteers to bolster the army. But his proclamation was designed to boost the morale of citizens shocked by the fall of Sumter, not to frighten them with the prospect of a prolonged struggle involving hundreds of thousands of men.

Lincoln's call for volunteers met with a rousing reception in the North,

At the start of the war, neither side had regular uniforms, and recruits dressed much as they pleased, ranging from the stylish outfits of the New Yorkers above—Zouaves who modeled themselves after French North African troops— to the casual attire of the Mississippians at left, who went to war in their street clothes.

"Virginia has severed her connection with
the Northern hive of abolitionists."

FORMER U.S. PRESIDENT JOHN TYLER OF VIRGINIA

where news that Old Glory had come under fire at Sumter triggered a frenzy of flag waving. "Men walk the streets with badges of red, white, and blue on their breasts," one New Yorker reported. "Flags float from every public edifice, from every newspaper office, from every hotel, from every church spire, from almost every store, and from thousands of private dwellings." Democrats as well as Republicans rushed to enlist, and the *New York World* gave thanks that "we have at last, a united North." Douglas backed Lincoln in his efforts to preserve the Union and said the capital "must be defended at all hazards."

The threat to Washington came from secessionists in Maryland and Virginia, where delegates meeting in Richmond responded to Lincoln's call for troops by resolving to leave the Union. "Virginia has severed her connection with the Northern hive of abolitionists, and takes her stand as a sovereign and independent State," exulted former president John Tyler, a native Virginian. Secession would not be official until a statewide referendum was held in May, but Governor John Letcher did not wait for that vote. He ordered Virginia militia to oust Federals from Harpers Ferry and seize the armory there, site of John Brown's raid. Other Virginia troops advanced on the Gosport Navy Yard near Norfolk, where Federal ships that were not fit to put out to sea were scuttled or burned. Among the assets Virginians salvaged there was the hulk of the U.S.S. *Merrimack*, which would be converted to the ironclad *Virginia* and used in an effort to break the naval blockade that Lincoln imposed on the Confederacy on April 19.

Arkansas, Tennessee, and North Carolina also joined the Confederacy after the fall of Fort Sumter, but Virginia was the biggest prize because it was the wealthiest and most populous Southern state and adjoined Washington. Jefferson Davis and his Cabinet would soon move their capital from Montgomery, Alabama, to Richmond, only about 100 miles south of Washington. They felt confident in doing so, for Davis had called up volunteers a month earlier than Lincoln and had nearly 60,000 troops in training, many of whom were sent to Virginia. "In independence we seek no conquest," he insisted. "All we ask is to be let alone."

Lincoln doubted that Confederate troops in Virginia would remain on the defensive. To make matters worse, some of the best officers in the regular U.S. Army, which then contained fewer than 15,000 men dispersed around the country, were resigning to serve their states in the Confederacy. Among those to depart was Robert E. Lee, to whom Lincoln had

Armed civilians in top hats guard the White House in April 1861. Lincoln knew these volunteers could not withstand a Confederate attack and anxiously awaited regiments from the North.

REFLECTIONS OF GLORY

THE CIVIL WAR HAS BEEN called a war between brothers, but it was also a war between amateurs. Young men who had no notion of the horrors of war eagerly answered the call to service after the fall of Fort Sumter, ready to beat the Yanks or punish the Rebs in what both sides expected to be a quick fight. "I believe that J. D. Walker's Brigade can whip 25,000 Yankees," boasted an Alabama volunteer. "I think I can whip 25 myself."

This enthusiasm created a ready new market in the growing field of portrait-style photography: soldiers going off to battle. Volunteers proudly posed in their new uniforms, which were often homespun and highly individualistic, such as Private David Schull's fanciful plumed "shako" hat (facing page, top row middle), or an unidentified Georgian's red and white "Corsican cap" (facing page, bottom row left). These unique cased images all too often became cherished final mementos for families. Pvt. Schull died of pneumonia shortly after reporting to camp in 1861, his Pennsylvania hometown's first casualty.

Glass-plate ambrotypes and enameled metal tintypes, like those shown here, along with the cheaper, mass-

> **"I have got the best suit of clothes that I [ever] had in my life."**
>
> PRIVATE PETER WILSON
> 1ST IOWA VOLUNTEERS

produced *cartes de visite*, represented an improvement over the daguerreotype photo process, which was labor-intensive and expensive. The appeal of ambrotypes and tintypes over cartes de visite was their glossier images, which were often mounted in decorative metal frames or lockets. Ambrotypes could even be hand tinted to produce a strikingly lifelike image. Especially fine examples are those of Confederate Alexander "Long Whiskers" Price (facing page, bottom row right) and Tennessee Private Thomas Holman (below left), who would be wounded at the Battle of Shiloh.

The new technology also greatly reduced exposure times—5 to 10 seconds versus 60 to 90 seconds—but smiling was still discouraged to prevent the images from blurring. As with daguerreotypes, the image produced was reversed, and soldiers sometimes compensated for this by posing with their weapons in their opposite hand. Though the term "ambrotype" comes from the Greek word for immortal, the photographs were in fact quite fragile. And neither ambrotypes nor tintypes left a negative that could be reproduced, which made these one-of-a-kind images especially precious. ■

PRIVATE THOMAS HOLMAN
Co. C, 13th Tennessee Volunteer Infantry

PRIVATE JAMES OR SAMUEL STRICKLAND
Georgia Volunteer Infantry

PRIVATE JAMES O. SMITH
Co. A, 6th New Hampshire Volunteer Infantry

PRIVATE JOHN HOFFMAN
Co. B, 5th Ohio Volunteer Cavalry

PRIVATE DAVID SCHULL
Pennsylvania militia

UNIDENTIFIED UNION SAILOR

UNIDENTIFIED CONFEDERATE
INFANTRYMAN—CORPORAL

UNIDENTIFIED DRUMMER BOY
Georgia

UNIDENTIFIED UNION INFANTRYMAN

UNIDENTIFIED CONFEDERATE SOLDIER
Georgia Volunteer Infantry

UNIDENTIFIED UNION ZOUAVE SOLDIER
114th Pennsylvania Volunteer Infantry

CONFEDERATE INFANTRYMAN
Probably Alexander "Long Whiskers" Price

An unidentified cadet from the Georgia Military Institute wears a dress shako with a brass eagle above the Georgia state seal insignia. Shakos like this and the one pictured at bottom were popular with the showy militia units from which both sides drew recruits.

offered field command of the Union Army before Virginia officially seceded. Lee politely declined. Although he opposed secession, he explained, he could not defy his native Virginia and "raise my hand against my relatives, my children, my home." Indeed, Lee had grown sons who would soon enlist in the Confederate Army.

After losing Virginia, Lincoln feared that Maryland too might slip from his grasp. On April 19, secessionists in Baltimore mobbed the 6th Massachusetts Regiment as it was transferring by horse-drawn cars from one station to another on its way to Washington. Colonel Edward Jones then had his men disembark and advance on foot. At that point, journalist Frederic Emory related, "a man appeared bearing a Confederate flag at the head of about one hundred rioters." A few Unionists standing by tried to seize the flag from him, but they were beaten back and took refuge among the troops. That further incited the rioters, who pelted the soldiers with stones and other missiles. Finally, Colonel Jones ordered his men to fire on the crowd. "A hoarse yell of fear and rage went up from the mob, but it did not give way," wrote Emory. "Some of the rioters fought like madmen." Three soldiers and 12 civilians died before Jones and his men reached the station and left for Washington, where Lincoln awaited them. "Thank God you have come," he told Jones.

In response to such disturbances, President Lincoln suspended the writ of habeas corpus for suspected subversives rounded up in Baltimore and other areas of unrest, thus denying the suspects their right to a prompt judicial hearing. It was better to suspend one law, Lincoln argued, than to let others "go unexecuted and the government itself go to pieces." But there was now little to stop authorities from jailing people indefinitely for lawful dissent. Some of those arrested and held without trial were guilty of nothing more than cursing Lincoln or praising Jefferson Davis.

Lincoln denounced secessionists as rebels acting outside the law, but he himself was taking revolutionary steps and assuming extraordinary powers. His strong measures helped keep Maryland from seceding and prevented agitators in Baltimore from severing lines of communication to Washington. By late April, Federal troops were arriving there by the thousands, and fears of a Confederate attack on the capital receded. But Lincoln did not relent. He would eventually suspend the writ of habeas corpus throughout the Union, and Davis would do the same in the Confederacy. The Civil War would prove costly not just in lives but in liberty. Among those who would pay the price were two Northern newspaper editors who assailed Lincoln's war policies in print and were seized by troops and jailed without a hearing. When friends appealed on their behalf, they received a chilling reply from Assistant Secretary of War Peter Watson: "Let them prove themselves innocent and they will be discharged."

INVADING VIRGINIA

MAJOR GENERAL WINFIELD SCOTT DID NOT MINCE WORDS when fellow Virginians suggested that he defect to the Confederate Army. "I have served my country, under the flag of the Union, for more than 50 years," he told them, "and so long as God permits me to live, I will defend that flag with my sword, even if my own native state assails it." With that declaration, this hero of the Mexican-American War threw his considerable weight behind the Union. At 300 pounds and 74 years of age, Scott was no longer capable of riding a horse or commanding troops in the field. But as general in chief he helped shape Federal strategy by proposing that the army take control of the Mississippi River while the navy tightened its blockade on the Atlantic and Gulf coasts. The bulk of the Confederacy would then be caught in a stranglehold and squeezed until it surrendered or expired. The main obstacle to this slow-developing Anaconda Plan, Scott recognized, was the demand in Washington for "instant and vigorous action, regardless, I fear, of the consequences."

Chief among those demanding action was President Lincoln, who hoped that before the terms of the 90-day volunteers expired, they would advance into Virginia and take on Confederate forces barring the way to Richmond. That could mean a quick end to the war—or an agonizing setback for Federal troops, who were ill-prepared for battle. Simply learning to load and fire the cumbersome muskets of the day was a complex operation that required endless repetition. Some recruits fumbled with that task for months, after first waiting for weeks to be issued firearms. Warren Goss, who enlisted in Massachusetts in 1861, recalled that unlike other units he saw drilling without weapons, he and his mates received muskets soon after joining up, "but we would willingly have resigned them after carrying them for a few hours. The musket, after an hour's drill, seemed heavier and less ornamental than it had looked to be." The hardest thing for Goss and other volunteers to master was not musketry or parade-ground evolutions such as "Right, oblique, march" but unquestioning obedience to orders. "It takes a raw recruit some time to learn that he is not to think or suggest, but obey," Goss observed. "Some never do learn. I acquired it at last, in humility and mud, but it was tough."

Ready or not, Federal recruits would soon see action. On May 23, Virginians voted to secede. A day later, their state was invaded by Union troops, who crossed bridges over the Potomac and occupied the towns of Alexandria and Arlington, where Lee's handsome home overlooking the river became a Federal headquarters. Confederate troops in the area were badly outnumbered and hastily withdrew, leaving behind a populace hostile to the occupiers. James Jackson of Alexandria defied Federal troops by flying the Confederate

> **"So long as God permits me to live, I will defend that flag with my sword, even if my own native state assails it."**
>
> FEDERAL MAJOR GENERAL WINFIELD SCOTT

As shown in this rare photograph, Major General Winfield Scott remained a formidable figure in 1861 when Lincoln retained him as general in chief. If secessionists raised so much as a finger against the president, Scott vowed, "I'll blow them to hell."

flag from his inn, the Marshall House. The sight infuriated Colonel Elmer Ellsworth, an avid young drillmaster who had raised a regiment of New York City fire fighters and clad them as Zouaves, French North African troops noted for their baggy red trousers and other regalia. Ellsworth barged into the Marshall House, raced upstairs, and cut down the Confederate flag. As he came down the staircase, Jackson met him at the landing with shotgun in hand and took his life. The first officer to die in the Civil War, he was mourned throughout the Union. His bereft Fire Zouaves were in a rage. "I honestly believe that had precaution not been taken, and guards placed around the regiment," one of them wrote, "Alexandria would have been razed to the ground."

Union troops gained another foothold in Virginia in late May when they advanced from Fort Monroe, one of the few coastal bastions in the South still in Federal hands, and seized nearby Newport News, on Hampton Roads, the strategic strait between the James River and Chesapeake Bay. The Federal commander there, Major General Benjamin F. Butler, made history when he allowed slaves from nearby plantations who sought refuge with his forces to remain in camp as laborers. "I shall hold these Negroes as contraband of war," he announced, and Lincoln backed him up. But the politically astute Butler

> ## "I shall hold these Negroes as contraband of war."
>
> FEDERAL MAJOR GENERAL
> BENJAMIN F. BUTLER

These fugitive slaves in southeastern Virginia were among many who sought refuge in Federal-occupied territory after General Benjamin Butler pioneered the practice of harboring them as contraband of war and employing them as laborers. By July 1861, 900 escaped slaves, including entire families, had taken refuge under Butler's authority at Fort Monroe, known to fugitives as "freedom fort."

proved militarily inept. On June 10, his raw troops were routed when he sent them against well-fortified Confederates at Big Bethel, not far from Newport News. One soldier who lived through that debacle complained that Butler, a well-connected lawyer from Massachusetts, "had been fledged in the foul nest of party politics, without the least military merit."

No one could say that about Major General George B. McClellan, a West Point graduate who had served with distinction as an engineer during the Mexican-American War before resigning to run a railroad. In early July, McClellan campaigned successfully in western Virginia—a mountainous area whose inhabitants were largely Unionists and would later form their own state, West Virginia—by outmaneuvering Confederates and fighting them sparingly. Some felt he took too much credit for what he called this "brief and brilliant campaign." But the Union was hungry for heroes and found one in "Little Mac," who preferred the title "Young Napoleon."

Jefferson Davis and his top military adviser, Robert E. Lee, had bigger worries than McClellan's forays. Their chief concerns were to prevent the Federals from occupying the fertile Shenandoah Valley west of the Blue Ridge Mountains or advancing along the Orange & Alexandria Railroad east of the Blue Ridge and descending on Richmond. One army led by Confederate Major General Joseph E. Johnston held Winchester, at the northern end of the Shenandoah Valley. Another army, under Brigadier General P. G. T. Beauregard, of Fort Sumter fame, held Manassas Junction, where the Manassas Gap Railroad from the Shenandoah joined the Orange & Alexandria line. This strategic positioning allowed reinforcements from either army to move quickly by rail to aid the other, if called upon.

Beauregard was concerned that his 20,000-man force at Manassas, located some 30 miles from a much larger army of Federal troops that were preparing to advance from Washington, might bear the brunt of the fighting. Yet his troops felt sure the general who whipped the Yanks at Charleston would whip them again here. "They seem to have the most unbounded confidence in me," Beauregard wrote on July 8. "Oh, that I had the genius of a Napoleon, to be more worthy of our cause and of their confidence!"

BATTLE FOR MANASSAS

LINCOLN'S GENERALS WANTED MORE TIME, BUT HE HAD NONE TO SPARE. HE WAS under pressure to smash Confederates in Virginia before they inaugurated their new capital on July 20. "Forward to Richmond!" urged Horace Greeley, the influential editor of the *New York Tribune*. Lincoln feared that if his 90-day volunteers returned home without doing battle, public support for the war effort would sag. He insisted that Federal troops advance soon against Beauregard's army at Manassas. Major General Irvin McDowell, chosen by

In a sketch by battlefield artist Alfred Waud, Zouaves of the 5th New York Infantry charge a Confederate battery at Big Bethel on June 10. "Their batteries received us warmly," wrote one of the Zouaves, who blamed General Butler for bungling the attack.

Major Sullivan Ballou

2D RHODE ISLAND INFANTRY, BURNSIDE'S BRIGADE

Sullivan Ballou, a 32-year-old Providence lawyer and former Speaker of the Rhode Island House of Representatives, obtained a commission as a major in the 2nd Rhode Island Infantry. While awaiting marching orders in camp near Washington on July 14, 1861, Ballou penned this poignant letter to his wife Sarah along with a similar letter to his two young sons. He placed the letters in his trunk to be delivered in the event of his death in battle. At First Manassas a week later, he fell, mortally wounded.

MY VERY DEAR SARAH: The indications are very strong that we shall move in a few days—perhaps tomorrow. Lest I should not be able to write again, I feel impelled to write a few lines that may fall under your eye when I shall be no more. Our movements may be of a few days duration and full of pleasure—and it may be one of some conflict and death to me. "Not my will, but thine, O God be done." If it is necessary that I should fall on the battle field for my Country, I am ready.

I have no misgivings about, or lack of confidence in the cause in which I am engaged, and my courage does not halt or falter. I know how strongly American Civilization now leans on the triumph of the Government, and how great a debt we owe to those who went before us through the blood and sufferings of the Revolution. And I am willing—perfectly willing—to lay down all my joys in this life, to help maintain this Government, and to pay that debt. . . .

I cannot describe to you my feelings on this calm Summer Sabbath night, when two-thousand men are sleeping around me, many of them enjoying perhaps the last sleep before that of death, while I am suspicious that death is creeping around me with his fatal dart, as I sit communing with God, my Country and thee. I

"When my last breath escapes me on the battle field, it will whisper your name."

have sought most closely and diligently and often in my heart for a wrong motive in thus hazarding the happiness of those I love, and I could find none. A pure love of my Country and of the principles I had so often advocated before the people—another name of Honor that I love more than I fear death, has called upon me and I have obeyed.

Sarah my love for you is deathless, it seems to bind me with mighty cables that nothing but Omnipotence could break; and yet my love of Country comes over me like a strong wind and burns me unresistably on with all these chains to the battle field. . . . I have, I know, but few and small claims upon Divine Providence,

but something whispers to me—perhaps it is the wafted prayer of my little Edgar, that I shall return to my loved ones unharmed. If I do not my dear Sarah, never forget how much I love you, and when my last breath escapes me on the battle field, it will whisper your name. . . .

But, O Sarah! if the dead can come back to this earth and flit unseen around those they loved, I shall always be near you; in the gladest days and in the darkest nights, advised to your happiest scenes and gloomiest hours, always, always, and if there be a soft breeze upon your cheek, it shall be my breath, as the cool air fans your throbbing temple, it shall be my spirit passing by. Sarah do not mourn me dead; think I am gone and wait for thee, for we shall meet again.

As for my little boys—they will grow up as I have done, and never know a father's love and care. Little Willie is too young to remember me long—and my blue eyed Edgar will keep my frolics with him among the dim memories of childhood. Sarah I have unlimited confidence in your maternal care and your development of their characters, and feel that God will bless you in your holy work.

Tell my two Mothers I call God's blessing upon them. O! Sarah I wait for you there; come to me and lead thither my children. ■

Winfield Scott to mount that campaign, worried that his 35,000 men—the largest army ever assembled on American soil—were too green to challenge the waiting Confederates. "You are green, it is true, but they are green also," Lincoln told him; "you are all green alike."

McDowell prepared to set out for Manassas with his army after being assured by Scott that Johnston's Confederates would be pinned down in the Shenandoah Valley by Federal troops descending from Maryland under Major General Robert Patterson, an old friend of Scott's. But Patterson wavered and held back, allowing Johnston to begin sending reinforcements by rail to Beauregard, who had spies in Washington and knew the Federals were coming. Among his informants there was Rose O'Neal Greenhow, a prominent socialite whose coded messages were delivered by a charming young accomplice, Bettie Duval, who had no trouble passing through the lines. "McDowell has been ordered to advance," Greenhow wrote as the Federals got under way on July 16. Her warning reached Beauregard that same night.

McDowell's march was slow and disorderly. Not until the 18th did his lead units approach Bull Run, a stream meandering down from hills to the west. To reach Manassas Junction to the south, the Federals would have to cross Bull Run on a stone bridge or at one of several fords nearby, where troops could wade across. The stream's high banks made it a strong defensive barrier for Beauregard. McDowell ordered Brigadier General Daniel Tyler to test those defenses by feigning an attack at Blackburn's Ford, which offered a shorter route to Manassas than the Stone Bridge upstream. "Do not bring on an engagement," McDowell insisted, but officers as well as enlisted men were still learning to obey commands. When Tyler's skirmishers came under heavy fire from Confederates lurking in the trees on the far side of the ford, he summoned a full brigade—four regiments in all—and blundered into battle against heavy opposition, losing more than 50 men killed or wounded.

McDowell gave Tyler a tongue-lashing afterward but learned something from this sharp clash at Blackburn's Ford. Beauregard expected the Federals to advance directly on Manassas Junction by crossing Blackburn's Ford or nearby Mitchell's Ford, and he had placed most of his forces in that area—his right wing—hoping to thwart the onslaught and then mount a counterattack. This plan left the crossings farther upstream, on Beauregard's left, lightly defended.

McDowell, who was intent on outflanking Beauregard, now knew which flank to assault. While part of his army engaged Beauregard's right in a head-on assault, he would send 15,000 men far upstream to Sudley Ford, which lay undefended, and swing around Beauregard's left to catch his foe in a vise. It was a bold plan but difficult to execute. It took McDowell two days to prepare for battle and bring up men and supplies, and the delay allowed thou-

"McDowell has been ordered to advance."

ROSE O'NEAL GREENHOW,
Confederate spy and prominent socialite

Confederate spy Rose O'Neal Greenhow embraces her daughter at the Old Capitol, a former boardinghouse in Washington converted into a jail. A seductive widow, Greenhow was intimate with Massachusetts Senator Henry Wilson, chairman of the Military Affairs Committee, before she was arrested for spying in August 1861. Confined with her daughter for nine months, she was sent south in 1862 and took pride in her work for the Confederacy: "I employed every capacity with which God had endowed me."

THE HIERARCHY OF WAR

Both sides during the Civil War organized their armies in similar fashion, following the pattern of the prewar U.S. Army. Soldiers knew where they stood in the hierarchy of rank and where their units stood in the organizational hierarchy. A private belonged to a company led by a captain, and a company belonged to a regiment led by a colonel. In theory, an infantry regiment consisted of ten companies of around 100 men each, but some regiments entered service with far fewer than 1,000 men, and many were greatly reduced in number during the war by casualties, or losses—terms used interchangeably to refer to those killed, wounded, or missing in action. (Among the missing were soldiers who were captured or whose bodies were never recovered.) Three or four regiments combined to form a brigade, commanded by a brigadier general or an accomplished colonel. A few brigades made up a division, a few divisions made up a corps, and a few corps made up an army, commanded by a general of top rank. The largest Civil War armies contained more than 100,000 soldiers, but the term "army" also applied to much smaller forces, operating independently under a general of lower rank.

RANK (in descending order)
Lieutenant General
Major General
Brigadier General
Colonel
Lieutenant Colonel
Major
Captain
First Lieutenant
Second Lieutenant
Sergeant Major
First Sergeant
Sergeant
Corporal
Private

ORGANIZATION
Army
Corps
Division
Brigade
Regiment
Battalion
Company

sands of Confederates from the Shenandoah Valley to reach Manassas Junction by rail. Congressman Elihu Washburne of Illinois visited McDowell at his tent on the evening of July 20. "He seemed discouraged and in low spirits," Washburne commented, "and appeared very doubtful of the result of the approaching conflict."

It was a lovely night, and soldiers wondered if it would be their last. "The moon is full and bright," one Federal wrote, "and the air is as still as if it were not within a few hours to be disturbed by the roar of cannon and the shouts of contending men." At 2 a.m. on Sunday, July 21, Federals were roused for what was meant to be a dawn attack. But it was 9 a.m. before the lead troops sent to outflank Beauregard found their way to remote Sudley Ford. "What a toilsome march it was through the woods!" recalled Chaplain Augustus Woodbury of Rhode Island. As they crossed Bull Run and emerged from the trees, he added, they encountered startled civilians in their Sunday best bound for Sudley Church, soon to be taken over as a hospital and "filled with wounded and dying men."

Thousands of Federals were now bearing down on Beauregard's flank. Holding the far left was a hard-drinking, hard-driving South Carolinian, Colonel Nathan "Shanks" Evans, who placed his outnumbered Confederates atop Matthews Hill and attacked before even more Federals could emerge from the woods below. Supporting Evans's regiment was a battalion from Louisiana led by Major Roberdeau Wheat, a giant of a man whose men entered battle wearing red shirts and armed with bowie knives. As they charged down the slope, some cast aside their muskets and went at the Yankees with knives raised. Their major fell with a bullet through the chest, and a surgeon later pronounced the wound fatal. "I don't feel like dying yet," Wheat responded, and he managed to pull through.

The furious charge stunned the Federals and slowed their advance,

General P. G. T. Beauregard (left) was in command of Confederates at Manassas when Federals surged across Bull Run on July 21, but General Joseph Johnston (right) had seniority and took charge when the Confederate left fell. "The battle is there," said Johnston, moving to stem the Federal tide. "I am going."

allowing brigades led by Colonel Francis Bartow of Georgia and Brigadier General Barnard Bee of South Carolina to come to Evans's aid. Bartow steadied his men by riding calmly up and down their line on a white horse as enemy batteries opened up. One incoming shell gouged a hole in the ground near Private George Barnsley, who wished for a moment that he was "a ground-squirrel, or a possum so I could get into that hole." Nevertheless, he and his mates soon summoned the courage to charge the Federal batteries as ordered, coming under fire from supporting infantrymen, who unleashed a "whirlwind of bullets," one Georgian recalled. The Confederate troops suffered heavy casualties and were forced back as Federal forces led by Colonel William Tecumseh Sherman—a keen West Pointer from Ohio who had turned down Lincoln's offer of a higher command, preferring to work his way up—surged across the Stone Bridge and joined the battle. By noon, Beauregard's left had collapsed, and his men were retreating in droves toward Manassas Junction. "The day is ours!" cheered McDowell prematurely.

Beauregard was shaken, but General Johnston, who had arrived from the Shenandoah Valley the day before, held firm and hurried reinforcements still detraining at Manassas into a new defensive line near Henry House Hill, named for a farmhouse near its crest where Judith Henry, a bedridden widow, died after a shell fired during the battle smashed into her home and severed her foot. Crucial to Confederate hopes of staving off defeat was Brigadier General Thomas Jonathan Jackson, waiting in reserve with five Virginia

General Irvin McDowell, standing at center with four staff officers on either side, was credited by William Sherman, who served under him, with conceiving "one of the best-planned battles of the war." Unfortunately for the Federals, Sherman added, it was also "one of the worst-fought."

"The day is ours!"
FEDERAL MAJOR GENERAL IRVIN MCDOWELL

Drillmaster Charles C. Wight

27TH VIRGINIA INFANTRY, 1ST BRIGADE, ARMY OF THE SHENANDOAH

Charles Wight, a 19-year-old cadet from Virginia Military Institute, had been assigned along with several of his classmates to drill the untrained volunteers of a number of recently organized Virginia regiments. Assigned to the 27th Virginia, a unit raised in the lower Shenandoah Valley, Wight accompanied his charges into battle at Manassas as part of a brigade commanded by Brigadier General Thomas J. Jackson. Posted on the rear slope of Henry House Hill to support Confederate artillery batteries, Wight recalled his impressions of his first experience in battle.

As SOON AS OUR BATTERY COMmences to fire, a perfect storm of shot passes over us. It seems as if the enemy had just found out where we are. A caisson standing near us is blown up and startles us so that good many spring for their feet, but Major Grigsby of the 27th Regt. draws his sword and orders all to lie down. We lie here a long while flat on our faces in the broiling hot sun, the firing seeming to approach rather than recede. Many men were killed and wounded while we are here. The wounded cry out every moment, and are borne to the rear by their friends. Some are killed so instantly that those who were nearest to them would not know it. We begin to think that a battle is not so nice as some had imagined. We have plenty of time to think, and the constant scream of the shell & the occasional whistle of a bullet impress upon us the danger of our situation. At last guns in front of us are moved back. The fire of the enemy's batteries slackens; but the musketry increases in volume. At this moment we are ordered to rise and though we feel that our part is not done; still it is a relief to stand up. As we rise we leave many bodies of our comrades lying, as if

> **"As we rise we leave many bodies of our comrades lying, as if asleep."**

asleep, and so hard is it to realize that they are no longer of us that we felt like calling on them to take their places in ranks. We are ordered forward, and as the long line moves toward the crest of the hill that conceals the enemy, the sight rekindles our enthusiasm. I can never forget the sight that bursts upon us as we reach the summit of the slope. Opposite to us was a hill partly wooded, partly cleared. The open portion of this was black with men and along the edge of the wood we can see the glistening of muskets. ∎

Union troops stand by the ruins of the Henry House after Confederates withdrew from Manassas in early 1862 and abandoned the site of their first great victory.

regiments. As a professor at the Virginia Military Institute in peacetime, Jackson had been an obscure and eccentric figure, but he was a warrior of the first order, and his time had come.

Without waiting for orders, he hurried his fresh Virginians into line behind the crest of Henry House Hill, where his artillery could blast oncoming Federals while his infantry lay low. Weapons such as canister—shells that disgorged scores of lethal shots and tore holes in enemy ranks—and rifled muskets with grooved barrels that spun out bullets at high velocity, killing men more than a quarter mile away, allowed commanders holding strong defensive positions like Jackson's to shatter assaults by numerically superior foes. "There stands Jackson like a stone wall," General Bee told his beleaguered troops, according to one account. "Rally behind the Virginians!" Bee and Georgia's Colonel Bartow were among many officers on both sides who would be mortally wounded before the day was out.

McDowell played into Jackson's hands by ordering two batteries under Captain James Ricketts and Captain Charles Griffin to advance to an exposed position near the Virginians, where the Federals came under heavy fire. One colonel under Jackson then got carried away and ordered his men to charge the big guns. The Virginians were wearing blue uniforms, and they were not recognized as enemies until it was too late for the Federals to halt their advance. Fire Zouaves of the late Colonel Ellsworth's regiment rushed in to save the batteries but wilted in the heat of battle and gave way. Jackson then sent more men forward, while a revived General Beauregard urged them on, shouting, "Give them the bayonet!" Soon the Confederates were advancing all along the line.

For Federals who had been fighting under a blistering sun for hours, this was too much. Some retreated in good order, but others threw down their guns and ran, spreading panic among troops to their rear. Federals stampeded back across Sudley Ford and the Stone Bridge and clogged the roads to Washington. Civilians who had come out in carriages to witness a great Union victory were caught up in an ignominious retreat. Poet Walt Whitman watched the defeated troops return to the capital: "They come along in disorderly mobs, some in squads, stragglers, companies. Occasionally, a rare regiment, in perfect order . . . marching in silence, with lowered faces, stern, weary to sinking, all black and dirty, but every man with his musket."

More than 2,500 Federals and nearly 2,000 Confederates were reported dead, wounded, or missing (including those captured or killed but never identified). The battle "was lost by us," William Sherman concluded, "because our army was as green as grass." The Confederates were nearly as green, but their officers proved more daring, and the Southern forces as a whole, fighting for their home ground, showed greater determination at Manassas than their Northern opponents did. As Colonel J. B. Jones of Alabama said to Federals who found him dying on the battlefield: "Gentlemen, you have got me, but a hundred thousand more await you!"

The Union Army had failed its first great test, but to Sherman this

"There stands Jackson like a stone wall."
CONFEDERATE BRIGADIER GENERAL BARNARD BEE

Thomas Jackson, who earned the name Stonewall by standing firm at Manassas, sat for this photographic portrait at the Virginia Military Institute in 1857, when he was 33. Ill at ease as a professor at VMI, where cadets called him "fool Tom," Jackson proved a commanding figure on the battlefield, where his only fear was that "I should not meet danger enough to make my conduct conspicuous."

2 BLACKBURN'S FORD *Two photographers break near the site where Union and Confederate troops first engaged each other.*

5 SUDLEY FORD *Watched by local children, Federal cavalry pose on the same banks where, months earlier, they were able to successfully cross Bull Run.*

6 STONE HOUSE *Retreating south past the Stone House, Rebels met Sherman's Brigade surging across Stone Bridge.*

ANATOMY OF A BATTLEFIELD

U NION PHOTOGRAPHERS FROM THE MATHEW BRADY Studio were sent to Manassas, Virginia, after First Bull Run to document the historic site. Together with the map (facing page) drawn by Union cartographer Robert Knox Sneden, they illustrate key landmarks that dictated strategy and troop movement in the war's first major land battle.

In preparation for their attack, McDowell's Union Army concentrated at Centerville 1, about three miles from Manassas, where they had to wait a day for new rations to arrive, having eaten everything in their meandering march from Washington. When they approached Bull Run on July 18, Union Brigadier General Daniel Tyler, against orders, started the fighting at Blackburn's Ford 2, a clash that completely altered Union strategy.

The concentration of Beauregard's Brigades on his right flank, near the railroad, forced McDowell to scout a new attack point miles upstream. The delay gave Joseph Johnston's army time to entrain from the Shenandoah Valley to Manassas Junction 3. But the reinforced Confederates never expected an attack to come as far to their left as it did. With Rebel artillery entrenched at Matthews Hill 4 to repel advances across Stone Bridge, the Union Army marched two miles farther upstream and crossed unmolested at Sudley Springs 5 the morning of July 21.

The Yanks had a two-to-one advantage in manpower after their surprise crossing and easily collapsed Beauregard's left flank, held by Colonel "Shanks" Evans. The Rebels retreated down the southern slope of Matthews Hill, past the Stone House 6, and up the northern slope of Henry House Hill 7 by noon. There, Stonewall Jackson's Virginians earned everlasting fame by stemming the attack, suffering the most casualties of any Southern brigade in the day's fighting. ∎

Robert Knox Sneden's watercolor map shows troop positions after the battle of Blackburn's Ford, where the Union lost more than 50 men in what was supposed to be a feigned attack.

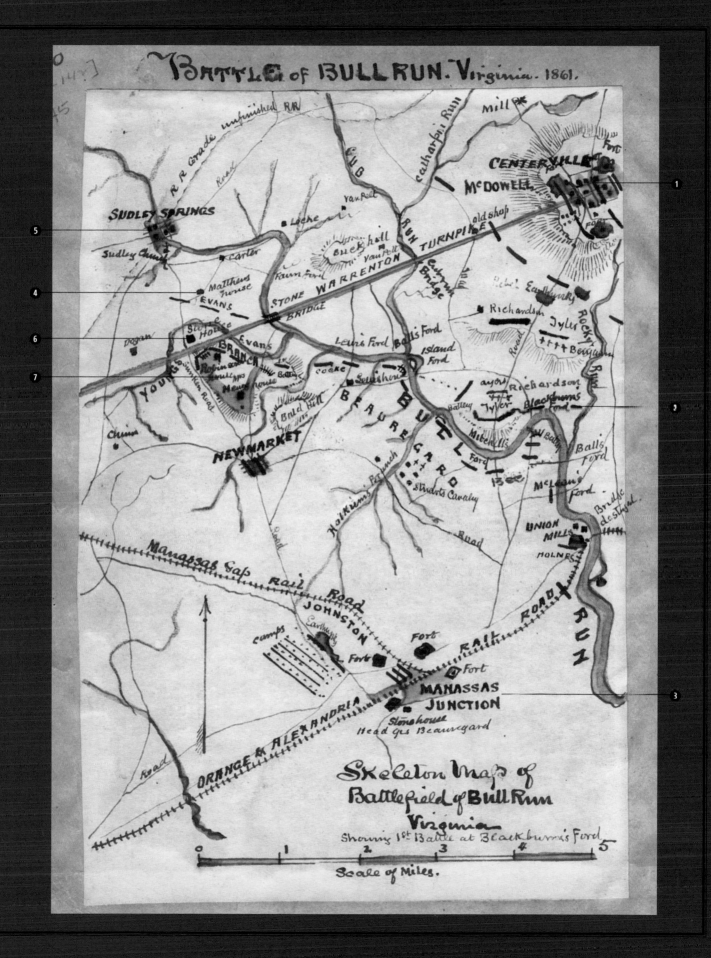

Federal captives taken at Bull Run stand in the courtyard of Castle Pinckney in Charleston Harbor, watched over by Confederates lounging on the parapet. Confinement near fallen Fort Sumter served as a grim reminder to these prisoners that the Union was powerless to help them.

disgrace served a purpose, "for we then realised that organization & discipline were necessary." Within days of the defeat, Lincoln summoned a master organizer, General George McClellan, to command Federal forces around Washington. Although the news reassured disheartened Northerners, it signaled that this war had a long way to go, for Little Mac was a meticulous planner who would not be rushed into battle. Southerners, for their part, vowed to strengthen their defenses against a renewed assault on Richmond. As one Virginian wrote: "Well, let them come—We shall be still better prepared for them."

[EYEWITNESS]

Walt Whitman
POET AND WAR CORRESPONDENT

A resident of Brooklyn, New York, and a former printer, teacher, and newspaper editor, Whitman was already well known for his powerful and controversial collection of poetry, Leaves of Grass, *when he arrived in Washington in 1861 as a correspondent for the Brooklyn Standard. In 1861, he recorded the return of McDowell's broken Federal army from Manassas. Whitman spent the later war years as a volunteer nurse in Washington and in 1865 he was appointed to a clerkship in the Interior Department on the recommendation of a friend, Ralph Waldo Emerson.*

"They say nothing; but the devil snickers in their faces."

THE SUN RISES, BUT SHINES not. The men appear, at first sparsely and shamefaced enough, then thicker, in the streets of Washington—appear in Pennsylvania Avenue, and on the steps and basement entrances. They come along in disorderly mobs, some in squads, stragglers, companies. Occasionally, a rare regiment, in perfect order, with its officers (some gaps, dead, the true braves,) marching in silence, with lowered faces, stern, weary to sinking, all black and dirty, but every man with his musket. . . .

The sidewalks of Pennsylvania Avenue, Fourteenth Street, &c, were jammed with citizens, darkies, clerks, everybody, lookers-on; women in the windows, curious expressions from faces, as those swarms of dirt-cover'd return'd soldiers there (will they never end?) move by; but nothing said, no comments; (half our lookers-on secesh of the most venomous kind—they say nothing; but the devil snickers

in their faces.) During the forenoon Washington gets all over motley with these defeated soldiers—queer-looking objects, strange eyes and faces, drench'd (the steady rain drizzles on all day) and fearfully worn, hungry, haggard, blister'd in the feet. Good people (but not over-

many of them either) hurry up something for their grub. They put wash-kettles on the fire, for soup, for coffee. They set tables on the sidewalks—wagon-loads of bread are purchased, swiftly cut in stout chunks. Here are two aged ladies, beautiful, the first in the city for culture and charm, they stand with store of eating and drink at an improvis'd table of rough plank, and give food, and have the store replenish'd from their house every half-hour all that day; and there in the rain they stand, active, silent, white-hair'd and give food, though the tears stream down their cheeks, almost without intermission the whole time. Amid the deep excitement, crowds and motion, and desperate eagerness, it seems strange to see many, very many of the soldiers sleeping—in the midst of all, sleeping sound. They drop down anywhere, on the steps of houses, up close by the basements or fences, on the sidewalks, aside on some vacant lot, and deeply sleep. ■

BATTLE FOR THE BORDER LANDS

O N JULY 25, 1861, MAJOR GENERAL JOHN CHARLES FRÉMONT ARRIVED in St. Louis to take charge of the Union Army's sprawling Western Department. Hailed as the "Pathfinder" for his explorations of the West, Frémont had campaigned for president in 1856 as the Republican nominee, but some considered him unfit for command. He had resigned from the U.S. Army in 1848 after a court-martial found him guilty of defying a superior officer to the point of mutiny. Obedience did not come easily to Frémont, and he would soon find himself at odds with his commander in chief in Washington. Yet President Lincoln was willing to tolerate a head-strong general in St. Louis so long as he held on to Missouri, where secessionism was on the rise. "I will neither lose the state nor permit the enemy a foot of advantage," Frémont promised Lincoln.

Frémont had many other worries besides securing Missouri for the Union.

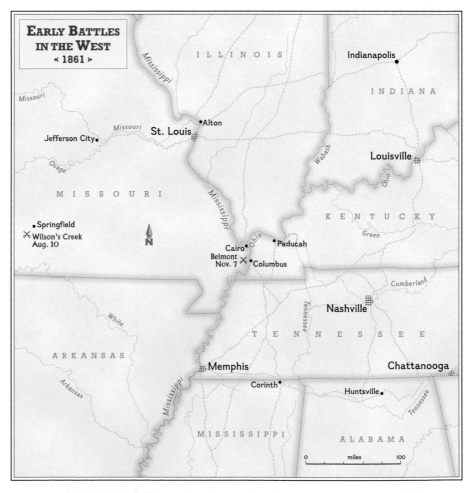

Early on, the Civil War in the West was largely a struggle for control of the region's navigable rivers, including the Mississippi, the Missouri, the Ohio, the Cumberland, and the Tennessee.

His department embraced a vast area west of the Mississippi River as well as Illinois and would soon include Kentucky, whose neutrality would not long be respected by either side. Southern forces were on the move in the West and hoped to expand beyond the 11 states now within the Confederacy: Texas, Arkansas, Louisiana, Mississippi, Alabama, Tennessee, Georgia, Florida, Virginia, and the Carolinas. Expansion was crucial, for the Confederacy had less than half the population of the Union and far less industry and mineral resources. There were more factories in New York alone than in the entire South. An editorial in the *Richmond Examiner* on July 4, 1861, warned that unless Southerners won economic independence and produced enough goods to sustain their war effort, they would soon be back under Northern control and "flooded with Yankee goods, Yankee manufactures, Yankee teachers, preachers, pedlers and drummers."

The Union's strategic advantage would be much diminished, however, if it lost control of the uncommitted slave states of Missouri and Kentucky. Whoever claimed those borderlands would dominate the upper Mississippi River and its major tributaries, the Missouri and Ohio Rivers, and would, in Frémont's words, "hold the country by the heart." St. Louis and Louisville, Kentucky, were thriving centers of commerce, and Missouri had large deposits of iron. In securing this prosperous heartland and the great rivers that served as arteries for the movement of troops and supplies, Frémont faced a hard choice. He had only enough troops at hand to respond to one of two emergencies. In southwestern Missouri, Federals under Brigadier General Nathaniel Lyon were approaching a much larger enemy force and needed reinforcements. Meanwhile, 6,000 Confederates were advancing up the Mississippi and threatening to drive Federals from Cairo, Illinois, strategically situated at the junction of the Mississippi and Ohio Rivers. Wisely, Frémont used his scarce resources to bolster Cairo and advised Lyon to retreat.

Frémont's advice did not stop the impetuous Lyon from forging ahead. Fiercely opposed to slavery and secessionists, the Connecticut-born Lyon was the Union Army's John Brown, an uncompromising crusader who showed little concern for his own life or the safety of others. "I do not think he knew the meaning of fear," one reporter remarked. As commander in St. Louis before Frémont arrived there, Lyon responded forcefully when Missouri's secessionist governor, Clairborne Jackson, encamped hundreds of state militia near the Federal arsenal. Lyon stealthily conveyed most of the arsenal's guns and ammunition across the Mississippi to Illinois for safekeeping, then summoned the city's Home Guard, which included many staunchly Unionist German immigrants, and broke up the militia camp. That led to rioting, and Lyon's men opened fire on angry civilians, killing more than two dozen people. Lyon later brought peace talks between Unionists and secessionists to an abrupt end by telling Governor Jackson and others in his party: "Rather than concede to the State of Missouri for one single instant the right to dictate to my government in any matter however unim-

Former Republican standard bearer John C. Frémont owed his position as Union commander in the West more to his political clout than his military acumen.

"I will neither lose the state nor permit the enemy a foot of advantage."

MAJOR GENERAL JOHN CHARLES FRÉMONT

portant, I would see you, and you, and you, and every man, woman, and child in the state, dead and buried. . . . This means war."

Lyon then sent troops to occupy the state capital, Jefferson City, forcing into exile Jackson and his secessionist ally Brigadier General Stirling Price, commander of the Missouri State Guard. On July 29, Price and his recruits linked up in southwestern Missouri with better-trained Confederates from Arkansas, Louisiana, and Texas led by Brigadier General Ben McCulloch. A prickly Texan, McCulloch took a dim view of the raw Missourians and agreed to join forces with them only after Price offered him overall command. Together, they had some 13,000 men, or more than twice the number in Lyon's force, which included many 90-day volunteers whose terms would soon expire. Although Frémont could spare Lyon no reinforcements, he stopped short of ordering him to retreat. "If he fights," Frémont told a messenger carrying instructions to Lyon at his headquarters in Springfield, Missouri, "it will be upon his own responsibility." Lyon felt betrayed. "God damn General Frémont!" he exclaimed. "He is a worse enemy to me than Price and McCulloch and the whole damned tribe of Rebels in this part of the state!"

Confederates of the 3rd Arkansas Infantry parade through the town of Arkadelphia shortly before entering Missouri under General Ben McCulloch and fighting at Wilson's Creek. The regiment suffered so many casualties there that it disbanded, with the survivors assigned to other units.

RECKONING AT WILSON'S CREEK

ON AUGUST 9, LYON DECIDED AGAINST retreating and prepared to attack the Confederates encamped along Wilson's Creek, southwest of Springfield. It was a big gamble, made even riskier by Lyon's decision to divide his small army. He would lead some 3,600 men in an assault on the enemy from the north while a 1,200-man brigade under Colonel Franz Sigel, a hero to his fellow German immigrants in St. Louis, would swing around to the south and attack the Confederate rear. "Men, we are going to have a fight," Lyon told his troops. "Don't get scared; it's no part of a man's duty to get scared." One listener found such advice to troops entering their first big battle "tactless and chilling," and another wrote pointedly: "How is a man to help being skeered when he is skeered?"

On the opposing side, men were no better prepared for the ordeal. Many of those in Price's Missouri State Guard had not been issued uniforms or firearms and would fight in civilian clothes with their own shotguns or hunting rifles. In the days leading up to the battle, volunteers continued to enter the Confederate camp on Wilson's Creek and offer their services. As one soldier recalled: "Old, gray-headed men came in, armed with their old squirrel rifles . . . to help the boys whip the yankees when the fight came off."

Lyon attacked at dawn on August 10, catching Price's ill-equipped Missourians by surprise and forcing them back. But Price soon rallied his men and held Lyon at bay in chaotic fighting around the aptly named Bloody Hill while McCulloch dealt with the threat to the south, where Sigel's forces opened fire with artillery. The presence of two strong-willed generals in camp had caused friction earlier, but now it worked to the Confederates' advantage. McCulloch called on some of his best units, including the Pelican Rifles from Louisiana, and directed them against Sigel's gunners. "Come, my brave lads," he urged them, "I have a battery for you to charge, and the day is ours!" With ample support from their own artillery, his men took that battery by storm and routed Sigel's Brigade. Then McCulloch threw his forces into the fray alongside Price's men at Bloody Hill. The fighting there grew "almost inconceivably fierce," wrote Lyon's chief of staff, Major John Schofield. Lyon suffered two grazing wounds, and his face was covered with blood. "Major, I am afraid the day is lost," he said to Schofield as his outnumbered forces began to give way. But Schofield urged him to keep up the fight.

Rising to the challenge, Lyon mounted his horse and summoned troops to plug a gap in his line, "Come on my brave boys, I will lead you forward!" he shouted. Moments later, a bullet pierced his heart and he fell dead. Having lost their general and many of their comrades, the battered Federals abandoned the field to their foes and retreated beyond Springfield, which was soon filled with wounded and dying men from both sides. As one surgeon reported, "There is not sufficient medical aid here—a hundred doctors could be employed constantly." The stench from the dead and dying was "so offensive as to be almost intolerable," a wounded man wrote. Each side had suffered around 1,300 casualties. For the Federals, that amounted to losses of over 25 percent, making Wilson's Creek a costlier setback for the Union proportionally than Bull Run. Among those killed was Lieutenant Levant Jones of the 1st Kansas Regiment. "My life now belongs to my country," he had written his wife before the battle. "My love belongs to you, and Dearest you have it all, all the legacy, unfortunately, I can leave to you in case I should fall."

Lyon, for his part, left a mixed legacy to loyalists in Missouri. His aggressive moves held St. Louis for the Federals and allowed Unionists to install their own governor in Jefferson City in place of Clairborne Jackson. At the same time, the abrasive Lyon pushed neutrals in Missouri into the Confederate camp and drove secessionists to violent extremes. Proslavery Border Ruffians, who had clashed with abolitionists in "Bloody Kansas" in the 1850s, renewed their assaults with a vengeance on either side of the Kansas-Missouri border. Alarmed by the violence, Frémont declared martial law in Missouri on August 30. Anyone who took up arms against the government would be executed, he declared, and all who supported the rebellion would forfeit their property, including their slaves, who would be set free. President Lincoln opposed Frémont's emancipation proclamation, fearing it would pro-

"Men, we are going to have a fight, don't get scared; it's no part of a man's duty to get scared."

FEDERAL BRIGADIER GENERAL NATHANIEL LYON TO HIS TROOPS AT WILSON'S CREEK

"How is a man to help being skeered when he is skeered?"

A Federal soldier before the battle at Wilson's Creek

voke further resistance in Missouri and turn neutrals in Kentucky against the Union. He sent Frémont a cautionary letter, but the general refused to modify his decree. "I acted with full deliberation," he wrote Lincoln defiantly, "and upon the certain conviction that it was a measure right and necessary." Lincoln then overruled him and modified the proclamation to apply only to slaves used by their masters for insurrectionary purposes, in keeping with a recent act of Congress.

By challenging Lincoln and clashing with other powerful politicians, Frémont risked dismissal. His wife, Jesse Benton Frémont, from one of Missouri's leading families, tried to restore him to grace by visiting Washington and appealing to Lincoln on his behalf. Lincoln told her firmly that this war was being fought "for a great national idea, the Union, and that General Frémont should not have dragged the negro into it." At odds with Frémont over this vital issue and his handling of troops, Lincoln fired him in early November. Yet in proclaiming emancipation, Frémont had blazed a trail that Lincoln himself would later follow. And Frémont did something else as commander that altered the Union's course. In late August, he chose a 39-year-old brigadier general from Ohio named Ulysses S. Grant over older and more experienced officers to command troops at Cairo. It was an inspired choice and a surprising one, for Grant was quite unlike Frémont in some ways. He was known for "obeying orders without question or hesitation," Frémont noted, and had "an unassuming character." But he was also a man "of dogged persistence, and of iron will," and in that sense Grant and the Pathfinder who set him on the road to greatness had much in common.

GRANT'S DANGEROUS DEBUT

GRANT'S MAIN ASSIGNMENT FROM FRÉMONT WAS TO HOLD IN CHECK CONfederate forces led by Major General Leonidas Polk, who occupied Columbus, Kentucky, in violation of that state's neutrality in early September and placed artillery there on high ground commanding the Mississippi some 20 miles south of Cairo. Polk also planned to occupy Paducah, Kentucky, where the Tennessee River enters the Ohio, but Grant hurried troops there by riverboat from Cairo and beat Polk to that strategic town. Grant's orders were to distract Polk by demonstrating against his forces without attacking them. But Grant wanted to hit Polk hard where he least expected it—at Belmont, Missouri, a steamboat landing across from Columbus. Between the time Frémont stepped down and his successor arrived in St.

A riverboat packed with Federals arrives at Cairo, Illinois, to bolster forces under Ulysses Grant. Steamboats helped Grant apply his guiding principle, which was to advance swiftly and attack before "the advantages of prompt movement are lost."

Louis, Grant launched that assault on his own authority. It was a big risk for a little-known general who had resigned from the U.S. Army in 1854 after a superior officer found him "too much under the influence of liquor to properly perform his duties," as one of Grant's friends put it. But the responsibilities of command made him a new man—disciplined, determined, and always prepared to fight.

On November 7, after journeying down the Mississippi from Cairo by steamboat with two Federal gunboats leading the way, Grant disembarked with some 3,000 troops north of Belmont and swept down on a Confederate force of roughly equal strength. After hard fighting, the Federals seized the enemy camp, but then began looting and celebrating wildly. "Some of the higher officers were little better than the privates," Grant wrote afterward. One officer mounted a captured gun and led his troops in song as a regimental band blared

Grant was just 39 years old when a photographer at Cairo, Illinois, captured him here with his aides, including Captain John Rawlins (upper right), who became his chief of staff. Rawlins "bossed everything at Grant's headquarters," wrote one observer, and challenged the general so freely that a fellow officer reckoned he was guilty of insubordination "20 times a day."

triumphantly. For General Polk—who continued to serve as the Episcopal bishop of Louisiana while commanding Confederate troops—this premature celebration was like a gift from heaven, enabling him to ferry reinforcements across the river uncontested and block Grant's escape route. When Polk counterattacked, jubilation gave way to panic in the Federal ranks, but Grant remained cool and restored order. "We cut our way in and we can cut our way out," he told his officers. In the end, they did just that, but the struggle cost Grant 600 casualties and nearly nipped his promising career in the bud.

Although the Confederates suffered comparable losses at Belmont and missed the chance to crush Grant, they claimed victory because they held their ground while he withdrew. The battle came on the heels of a more decisive Confederate triumph in Virginia at Ball's Bluff, where on October 21 troops led by Colonel Nathan Evans, a hero at Manassas, routed Federals who crossed the Potomac from Maryland above Washington. More than 500 Union soldiers were captured, and another 100 or so drowned as they fled back across the river. "Screams of pain and terror filled the air," wrote one Confederate, who saw Federals hurl themselves into the Potomac encumbered by heavy gear and sink "to the bottom like lead." Lincoln suffered a personal loss when his close friend and ally, Colonel Edward Baker, a U.S. Senator from Oregon, died in the fighting. In Richmond, Jefferson Davis saw the recent battles as highly encouraging. Northerners who had hoped to conquer the South before the year was out had been repulsed, he declared, and "the Confederate States are relatively much stronger now than when the struggle commenced."

Hoping for recognition and aid from Great Britain, which relied on Southern exports of cotton to keep its textile mills running, Davis sent two envoys to Europe aboard the British steamship *Trent*. When a Federal warship intercepted the *Trent* in November and seized the envoys, the British protested and threatened hostilities. "You may stand for this but damned if I will!" Prime Minister Lord Palmerston told his Cabinet. Unwilling to risk a confrontation with Britain and its powerful navy, Lincoln backed down, releasing the envoys on Christmas Day.

Northerners breathed a sigh of relief, but the year ended with victory seemingly more remote than ever. "Washington is beleaguered and Richmond is not," complained one Northern Congressman. Beneath the wintry gloom, however, lay seeds of hope for the Union. Losses on the battlefield had not kept Unionists from enlisting in droves or discouraged Federal commanders from pursuing plans of conquest. As Grant said to aide John Rawlins when he resumed offensive operations in the new year: "We will succeed, Rawlins; we must succeed."

Known as the Fighting Bishop, Leonidas Polk studied war at West Point before entering the seminary and taking orders as an Episcopal priest. As a Confederate general, he repulsed Grant at Belmont and opposed him again at the Battle of Shiloh, while continuing to perform religious services when possible.

OUTFITTING THE CONFEDERATE INFANTRY

THE ENTHUSIASM FOR WAR AT THE OUTBREAK WAS not matched by a readiness for it. The surge of volunteers on both sides created the problem of clothing and equipping these new armies. In the South, the job was often left to the soldiers themselves, so that until "cadet gray" became the official color in 1862, each regiment was outfitted in a confusing variety of uniforms. Each state supplied equipment to its own regiments, and cavalry brought their own horses.

The Confederacy would never fully overcome its inherent disadvantage in industrial capacity. But thanks to the remarkable ingenuity of ordnance chief Josiah Gorgas, the South did have arms and ammunition. Gorgas exploited every resource, mining saltpeter from Appalachian caves and leaching niter from chamber pots to make gunpowder, seizing stills to use the copper for rifles, melting down church bells for cannon, and remolding lead found on the battlefield for bullets. The quartermaster general's office was far less resourceful. At times during the war Rebel soldiers were marching without shoes, sleeping without blankets or tents, and fighting in threadbare uniforms. ■

SLOUCH HAT

The two most popular styles of Rebel hat were the comfortable, wide-brimmed slouch hat and the kepi, a less structured version of the famous French Army headgear.

KEPI

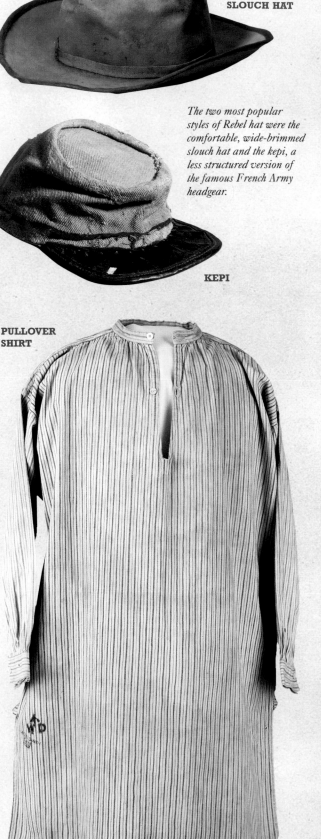

PULLOVER SHIRT

HOMEMADE SOCKS

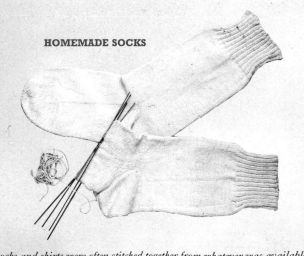

Socks and shirts were often stitched together from whatever was available, including bedspreads and tablecloths. These cotton socks were being knitted from unraveled Union tents when abandoned, needles still attached.

The Fincher brothers of the 43rd Georgia Volunteer Infantry pose in typical outfits for the Confederate rank and file—dress that included shell jackets. Made of gray or butternut wool, these waist-length coats fastened with brass buttons adorned with the seals of the Confederate states. Richmond Private John Blair Royal's jacket bears the hole left by the Union shell that wounded him at Chancellorsville.

SHELL JACKET

BRASS BUTTONS WITH SEALS OF VIRGINIA, TEXAS, AND SOUTH CAROLINA

LOW-HEELED BROGANS

WOOL PANTS

These bloodstained pants of an Alabama infantryman were made from light brown wool and cotton homespun. Other Confederates wore blue or gray pants; bone buttons and a linen watch pocket were common details. Most shoes began to wear out after a month of hard campaigning, despite being made of sturdy leather. Throughout the war, good shoes were a rarity.

REBEL WEAPONS AND ACCOUTREMENTS

Almost an exact replica of the Model 1855 U.S. Rifle Musket, the .58-caliber "C.S. Richmond" was manufactured at the Richmond Armory and Arsenal, using machinery seized from Harpers Ferry. Shoulder-fired muskets, especially the popular Springfield and Enfield models, accounted for 85 percent of all battlefield casualties in the Civil War. Around four and a half feet long, the muskets were accurate up to 600 yards.

RICHMOND RIFLED MUSKET

BACKPACK

M.C.P
G.G

CANTEEN

This tin canteen belonged to a Confederate surgeon; heavy wooden canteens were more common. A backpack or a haversack was essential for carrying rations, toiletries, and other personal items.

Socket bayonets slipped over the end of a musket barrel and locked into place on the front site. The 18-inch metal blade allowed the rifle to be used in hand-to-hand combat.

SOCKET BAYONET

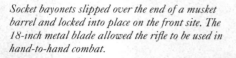

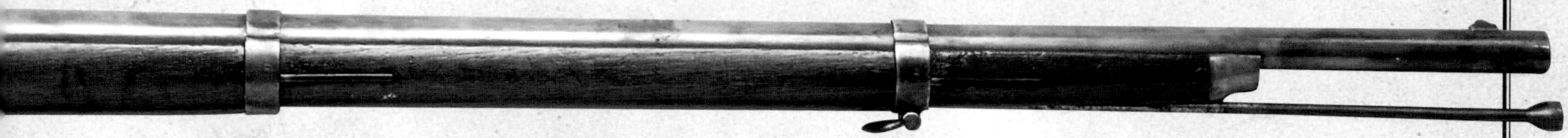

Volunteers usually brought their own bowie knives, which proved handy for skinning rabbits or scaling fish, but were rarely used as weapons. A forceful blow from the heavy knife, though, could sever a man's arm.

TOBACCO POUCH

Retta Patton made this tobacco pouch for Colonel James P. Coleman, who carried it throughout the war.

BIBLE STRUCK BY BULLET

CONFEDERATE CURRENCY

Robert Hunter, Judah Benjamin, and Jefferson Davis adorned the $10, $2, and $50 bank notes of the Confederacy. Overcirculation and counterfeiting led to severe inflation. The pocket-sized New Testament at right stopped the bullet intended for Private A. P. Hubbard of the 4th South Carolina at Bull Run.

BOWIE KNIFE

UNION INFANTRYMEN DRESSED FOR WAR

FORAGE CAP

THE NORTH, DESPITE HAVING AN ESTABLISHED WAR Department and army, also started the war unprepared. The South claimed about a third of the U.S. Army's officers and seized more than 150,000 arms. Commanding the Union base at Cairo, Illinois, Ulysses S. Grant complained, "The clothing received has been almost universally of an inferior quality and deficient in quantity. The arms . . . are mostly the old flintlock repaired."

Tragic mix-ups on the battlefield convinced the Union to make light blue trousers and dark blue tops standard. Textile manufacturers cut corners to meet the sudden demand, using compressed fibers of recycled woolen goods to make a material called "shoddy," which would enter the lexicon as a new adjective for poor workmanship.

But the North had a huge inherent advantage in industrial capacity. In 1860, Northern states manufactured 97 percent of the firearms, 94 percent of the cloth, 93 percent of the pig iron, and 90 percent of the boots and shoes in the United States. It was eventually able to feed and supply its army in a way the South never could, meeting the logistical demands of an army that was usually fighting far from its supply sources. ∎

Private Jacob Musbach's forage cap bears his Pennsylvania company's letter and his regimental number. Name tags, such as the starred badge of Sergeant William Smalley of the 150th New York Infantry and the pin of Private Sylvester Duboyce of the 26th Pennsylvania Infantry, allowed casualties to be identified.

I.D. BADGES

SACK COAT

Also called a fatigue jacket, Federal enlisted men were issued a hip-length dark blue coat that was made of flannel and fit loosely, hence the term "sack." In winter, a soldier might wear the longer, more tailored frock coat.

ZOUAVE FEZ

DRESS HAT

This distinctive red fez was worn by a member of Duryee's Zouaves of the 5th New York Volunteer Infantry. The Union dress hat at right borrowed its design from flashy European models, but was unpopular because of its bulk and stiffness.

A shortage of regulation sky-blue kersey wool overcoats led the U.S. to issue overcoats produced by private contractors, such as this model made of blue jean cloth, worn by Private Edmund Starrett of the 24th Maine Volunteer Infantry.

OVERCOAT

A private of the New York Engineers exemplifies the typically dressed Union soldier in his sack coat and forage cap. He also likely wore a belt buckle stamped "U.S." The one shown here has a bullet from Fredericksburg still lodged in it.

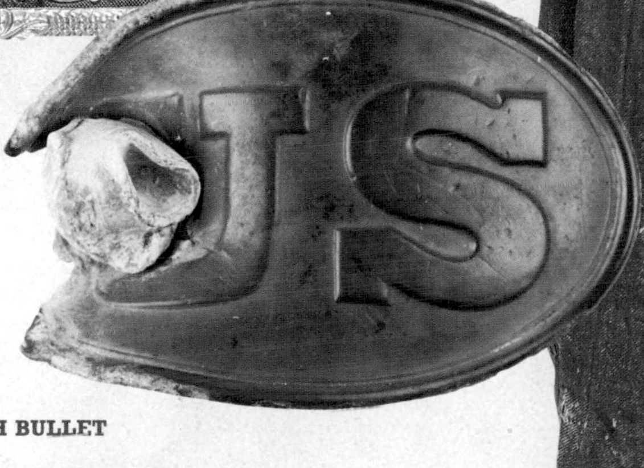

BELT BUCKLE WITH BULLET

Yankee Arms and Equipment

MODEL 1861 RIFLED MUSKET

Pennsylvania Corporal James Royer carried this wool blanket through some of the war's greatest battles, including Gettysburg.

BLANKET

The regulation firearm of the U.S. infantry, the 1861 Springfield Rifled Musket was used in every major battle. Other early weapons, like the 1841 rifled muskets of these infantrymen, also saw service.

LEATHER CARTRIDGE BOX WITH STRAP

Tin compartments inside the cartridge box held 40 rounds of ammunition.

KNIFE

Like many weapons, this silver-handled knife used by Lieutenant Everson Hurlburt, 29th Ohio Volunteer Infantry, was a personal item, not government issued.

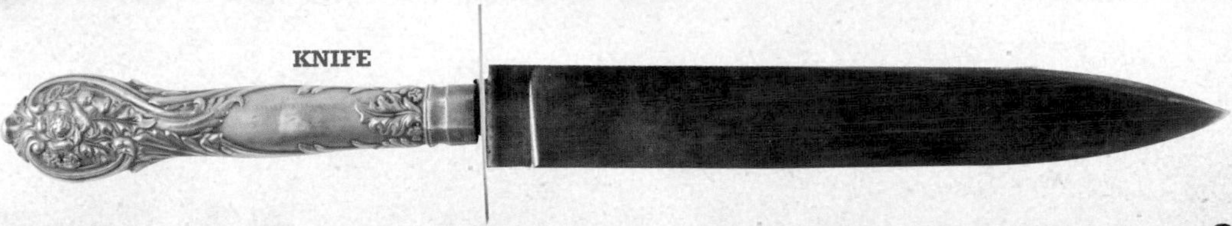

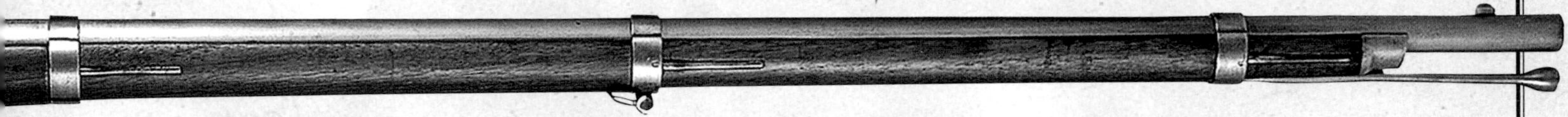

Slung over one shoulder, the haversack, like this black example with knotted strap owned by Private John Saunders of the 23rd Maine Volunteer Infantry, was a carryall for everything from rations and eating utensils to personal accoutrements.

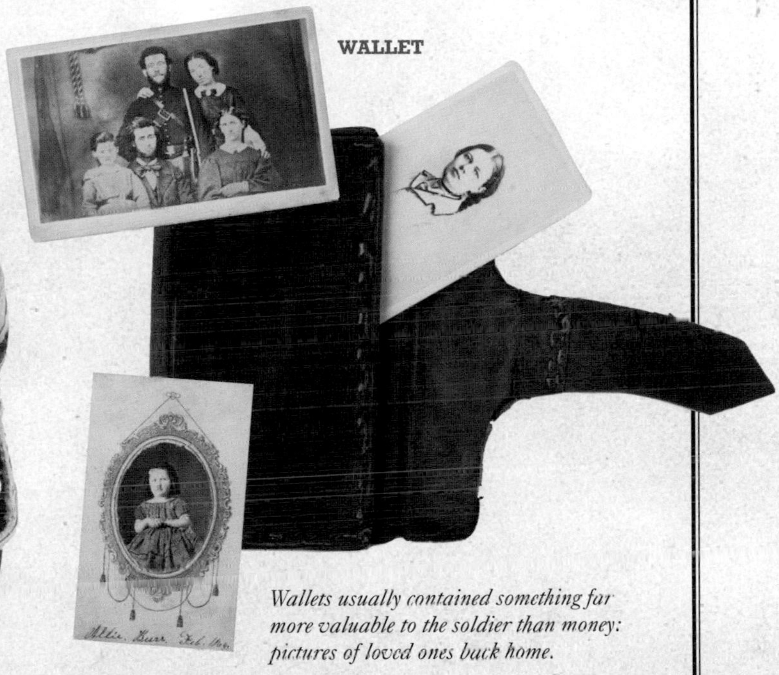

WALLET

Wallets usually contained something far more valuable to the soldier than money: pictures of loved ones back home.

HAVERSACK

HOUSEWIFE

The Brooks' Patent Toilet and Writing Kit, also known as a housewife, contained just about everything a soldier needed. This example, owned by a Massachusetts cavalry sergeant, includes scissors, thread, buttons, pen, pencil, ink, shaving brush, toothbrush, writing paper, and a checkerboard with checkers.

CHAPTER 2

1862
TOTAL WAR

IN FEBRUARY 1862, WORD REACHED ST. LOUIS THAT TROOPS LED BY Ulysses Grant had seized the Confederate stronghold of Fort Donelson and were advancing deep into Tennessee. "The city went wild with excitement and rejoicing," wrote Sarah Jane Hill, the wife of a Union soldier. "But soon the steamboats came with their loads of maimed and wounded," she added, "and we had the dread side of war." Here as elsewhere, Americans were confronting the harsh realities of a fast-expanding conflict—total war that engulfed soldiers and civilians alike. The fall of Fort Donelson left over 12,000 Confederates in captivity and caused panic in Nashville as Federals approached and residents fled. In one day, a journalist reported, seven trains left the city, "loaded with women and children inside and crowded with frightened men on the top."

Even greater shocks lay ahead for both sides. In April, far more Americans were killed or wounded in two days of fighting at Shiloh than had fallen in battle during the entire Revolutionary War. In the months to come, Federals would occupy New Orleans and besiege Richmond, and Confederates would invade Maryland, triggering a battle of unparalleled fury at Antietam. When photographs of the carnage there were taken by Alexander Gardner and exhibited by Mathew Brady in New York, the horrors of war hit home as never before. One viewer wrote of Brady's exhibit: "If he has not brought bodies and laid them in our dooryards and along streets, he has done something very like it." ∎

In this chilling photograph by Alexander Gardner, Confederate dead at Antietam offer mute testimony to the savagery of the fighting there on September 17, 1862, America's bloodiest day. One soldier at Antietam, Samuel Fiske of the 14th Connecticut Infantry, wrote of the carnage: "The excitement of the battle comes in the day of it, but the horrors of it two or three days after."

SOUTH TO SHILOH

T EXAS HAS MADE ME A REBEL TWICE," SAID CONFEDERATE COMMANDER Albert Sidney Johnston. Born in Kentucky in 1803, Johnston moved to Texas in the 1830s and joined other settlers there in rebelling against Mexico. Then after Texas seceded in 1861, he resigned as chief of the U.S. Army's Pacific Department and trekked across the country to Richmond to offer his services to his old friend Jefferson Davis. Sick in bed when Johnston called, Davis rallied when he heard him stride confidently into the parlor. "That is Sidney Johnston's step," he said. "Bring him up." The two had served together in the Mexican War, and no other officer in the South, not even Robert E. Lee, stood higher in Davis's estimation. As he wrote later: "I hoped and expected that I had others who would prove generals, but I knew I had one, and that was Sidney Johnston."

Davis made Johnston the Confederacy's highest-ranking general in the field and gave him a daunting assignment—command of a vast area west of the Appalachians that included Confederate Tennessee and Arkansas and the uncommitted states of Kentucky and Missouri. Greatly outnumbered by opposing forces in the region, Johnston did all he could to make Federal commanders believe he was stronger than they were. One of his first moves was to send Confederate troops north from Nashville, Tennessee, to occupy Bowling Green, Kentucky. Meanwhile, his trusted subordinate Leonidas Polk solidified his hold on Columbus, Kentucky, by fortifying that town overlooking the Mississippi with so many big guns it became known as the "Gibraltar of the West."

Johnston's brave show fooled many of his foes, including newly promoted Brigadier General William Sherman, who estimated it would take 200,000 troops to drive Confederates from Kentucky, where Johnston had only about 20,000 men. Unnerved by his cunning opponent, Sherman was relieved as commander of the Army of the Ohio and ended up serving under the unflappable Ulysses Grant, whose setback at Belmont, across from Columbus, in November 1861 did not deter him from calling Johnston's bluff. By January 1862, Grant was massing forces at Paducah, Kentucky, and planning to advance southward up the Tennessee River deep into Confederate territory. Both the Tennessee and nearby Cumberland Rivers were navigable for much of their length and offered Federal forces swift access by steamboat to the Southern interior.

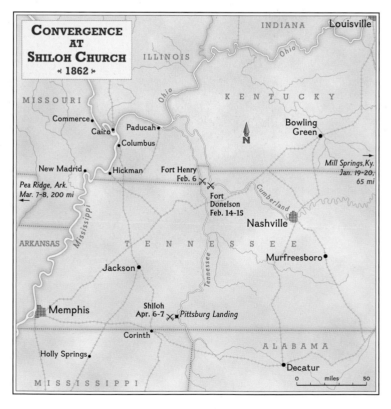

CONVERGENCE AT SHILOH CHURCH * 1862 *

In early 1862, Federals led by Grant moved southward up the Tennessee River, capturing Fort Henry and nearby Fort Donelson in February before advancing to Pittsburg Landing, where Confederates marching northward from Corinth attacked them on April 6 at their encampments near a church called Shiloh.

To meet that and other looming threats, Johnston hoped to enlist large numbers of Confederate sympathizers in Kentucky, but he misjudged his native state. Many uncommitted Kentuckians resented Confederates for occupying their territory and leaned toward the Union. Desperate for help, Johnston strained his friendship with Davis by dispatching an aide, Colonel John Liddell, to Richmond to beg for troops and weapons. Davis was taken aback. "My God! Why did General Johnston send you to me for arms and reinforcements, when he must know that I have neither," Davis told Liddell. "He has plenty of men in Tennessee, and they must have arms of some kind—shotguns, rifles, even pikes could be used."

Davis knew better than to expect men armed with pikes to win battles, but he was irked by this painful reminder from Johnston that the Confederacy's ambitions exceeded its resources. Support for the Rebel cause was solid in the Deep South, but states of the Upper South had large numbers of Unionists, concentrated in the mountainous areas of western Virginia and North Carolina, eastern Tennessee, and northwestern Arkansas. Far from having "plenty of men" in Tennessee, Johnston was disappointed by the rate of enlistment. And the shotguns some recruits brought with them when they joined up were a poor substitute for muskets or rifles, which the Confederate government had to purchase abroad to supplement the modest output of Southern arms makers. As the war dragged on, the limited manpower and manufacturing capacity of the Confederacy placed it at an ever greater disadvantage in relation to the more populous and productive Union. Davis's parting words to Colonel Liddell summed up his plight: "Tell my friend, General Johnston, that I can do nothing for him; that he must rely on his own resources."

GRANT BREAKS THROUGH

BEFORE HE COULD ADVANCE AGAINST JOHNSTON'S CONFEDERATES, GRANT first had to overcome resistance from his superior, Major General Henry W. Halleck, who had succeeded Frémont as Union commander in the West. Known as Old Brains, Halleck was a gifted administrator but lacked Grant's drive and daring and considered him reckless. In late January, Grant traveled from his headquarters at Cairo, Illinois, to meet with Halleck in St. Louis, where he sought permission to advance with more than 15,000 troops up the Tennessee River behind a flotilla of ironclad gunboats produced in St. Louis by naval engineer James Eads. With those heavily armed ironclads, Grant planned to breach Johnston's defenses by taking Fort Henry, newly constructed Confederate earthworks on the Tennessee just below the Kentucky border. That would clear the way for an assault on Fort Donelson, 12 miles east of Fort Henry on the Cumberland River. If Donelson fell, there would be little to prevent Federals from sweeping up the Cumberland and seizing Nashville, Tennessee's capital and a major manufacturing center.

Grant's thinking was too ambitious for Halleck. "I had not uttered many sentences before I was cut short as if my plan was preposterous," Grant wrote. "I returned to Cairo very much crestfallen." Soon afterward, however, Hal-

> **"Texas has made me a Rebel twice."**
> ALBERT SIDNEY JOHNSTON
> *Confederate commander in the West*

When Albert Sidney Johnston took charge of Confederate forces in the West, his troops were so few, so inexperienced, and so poorly armed that one aide said with little exaggeration, "He had no army."

Eads's Ironclads

"Of the mud-turtle school of architecture . . . [but] they struck terror into every guilty soul as they floated down the river."

Crewman of one of "Pook's turtles"

To win the war in the West, the Union gambled on an ad hoc freshwater navy that could execute a successful riverborne invasion. In the Federal scheme, all inland operations, even those on water, were designated to the army, not the navy. But the War Department picked the right man for the job: James B. Eads, an Indiana-born engineer and inventor. Awarded the contract in August of 1861, the prolific Eads produced a flotilla of two converted steamboats and seven original ironclads before the year was out.

Perhaps it's fitting that a navy built under the army's supervision should end up looking like floating forts. These wide, flat-bottomed gunboats skimmed the water with 13 cannon aimed out of an armored casemate shaped like a flat-topped pyramid *(see page 106)*. Based on plans by naval constructor Samuel Pook, the ships earned the nickname "Pook's turtles" because of their thick iron shells, but the odd design allowed them to navigate shallow waters and carry heavy artillery in spite of their draft.

Between August and December of 1861, construction crews totaling 4,000 men under Eads's supervision worked day and night to finish the ironclads. The workers were urged on by bonuses paid by Eads himself. The resulting squadron of freshwater turtles was not without flaws, however. At 175 feet in length and just over 50 feet wide, the bargelike battleships were slow moving and hard to maneuver. The decks were unarmored and vulnerable to plunging shot from forts above. Yet this hastily assembled fleet proved remarkably resilient and successful once the river wars began. ■

Works rapidly in progress: Two of Eads's ironclads, stern-to-stern, are constructed simultaneously at the Carondelet shipyard near St. Louis.

With ironclads in the lead, Federal gunboats attack smoke-shrouded Fort Henry on February 6. The gunboats were firing so rapidly, Confederate Captain Jesse Taylor wrote, that they disgorged "one broad and leaping sheet of flame."

"The fort with her few remaining guns was sullenly hurling her harmless shot against the sides of the gunboats."

CAPTAIN JESSE TAYLOR,
Confederate gunner at Fort Henry

leck was prodded by President Lincoln, who issued a general order for advances against the enemy on all fronts. Recently, Brigadier General George H. Thomas, a Unionist from Virginia, had defeated Confederates in battle at Mill Springs in eastern Kentucky and claimed the life of their commander, Felix Zollicoffer. Under pressure from Washington to make similar gains in his sector, Halleck found new merit in Grant's scheme. "Fort Henry should be taken and held at all hazards," he ordered on January 30. "You will move with the least possible delay." Within a few days, Grant had his men loaded on steamboats at Paducah and ready to follow the ironclads into battle.

Awaiting Grant at Fort Henry were Confederate gunners led by Captain Jesse Taylor, a recent graduate of the U.S. Naval Academy. On February 4, Taylor related, "the Federal fleet of gun-boats, followed by countless transports, appeared below the fort. Far as eye could see, the course of the river could be traced by the dense volumes of smoke issuing from the flotilla—indicating that the long-threatened attempt to break our lines was to be made in earnest." Taylor and his men were in a tight spot. Their fort was at water level, offering them little protection from the floodwaters of the fast-rising Tennessee and no high ground from which to command the river and fire down on opposing gunboats. Taylor's superior, Brigadier General Lloyd Tilghman, considered Fort Henry doomed and hoped the artillery could buy time for his 2,500 troops to withdraw to nearby Fort Donelson. "Can you hold out for one hour against a determined attack?" he asked Taylor, who replied that he could. Grant's troops, meanwhile, disembarked north of Fort Henry and prepared to besiege the fort if the ironclads failed to pound it into submission.

On February 6, the commander of the Federal naval force, Flag Officer Andrew H. Foote, moved in for the kill. "It must be victory or death," he declared. Foote's flagship, *Cincinnati*, and three other ironclads led the attack, advancing to within a few hundred yards of the fort and blasting away at the earthworks with devastating effect. The gunboats resembled huge turtles with iron shells, but there were chinks in their armor. One Confederate shot burst the boiler of the ironclad *Essex*, scalding its commander and crew and disabling the vessel. By then, however, most of Taylor's cannon had been knocked out of action or lost to floodwaters. "The fort with her few remaining guns was sullenly hurling her harmless shot against the sides of the gunboats," Taylor observed, while the ironclads pounded the earthworks at close range "with the coolness and precision of target practice." Taylor and company held out for over two hours before General Tilghman directed them to lower their flag and surrender.

When Johnston learned that Fort Henry had fallen, he concluded that his forces would have to abandon Kentucky and would be hard-pressed to hold Tennessee. Although he doubted that Fort Donelson would long withstand assault, he sent reinforcements there to deter a Federal advance up the Cumberland toward Nashville. As he wrote to Jefferson Davis: "I determined to fight for Nashville at Donelson, and gave the best part of my army to do it." But Johnston did not do all he could to hold the fort. His second-in-command, General P. G. T. Beauregard, later said he advised him to concentrate most of his 50,000 or so troops against Grant at Fort Donelson, located on high ground that made it a stronger position than Fort Henry. Instead, Johnston committed roughly 17,000 men to Donelson's defense. It was a poor compromise between abandoning the fort and defending it to the hilt, and Johnston made matters worse by leaving it in unsure hands. The senior officer there was a political appointee, Brigadier General John Floyd, former governor of Virginia and secretary of war under President Buchanan. Two other brigadier generals with whom he shared command, Gideon Pillow and Simon Bolivar Buckner, despised each other and disagreed over whether Donelson could be successfully defended, as Pillow believed. "I will never surrender the position," he vowed, "and with God's help I mean to maintain it."

Grant did not wait for permission from Halleck to attack Fort Donelson. On February 12, he led his troops overland from Henry to Donelson while Foote guided the gunboats back to Paducah and up the Ohio to the mouth of the Cumberland. Many in Grant's army were Midwesterners new to the South, and some thought that winter was safely behind them when the day of the march dawned sunny and mild. "The air was balmy and betokened

Flag Officer Andrew Foote, who led the naval assault on Fort Henry, was a devout Christian who preached sermons to his men and imposed temperance on them.

Commander Henry Walke

U.S.S. *CARONDELET*

A Virginian by birth, Henry Walke remained loyal to the Union after 35 years service as a U.S. naval officer. He commanded the gunboat Tyler during early operations on the western rivers and then was posted as captain of the ironclad Carondelet in January 1862. The following month he took his vessel into action against the formidable Confederate batteries at Fort Donelson.

THE *LOUISVILLE* WAS FOLlowed next by the flag steamer and then by the *Pittsburg*. The latter, in attempting to turn, struck the *Carondelet* starboard quarter and rudder, breaking off its hinges, thus compelling the *Carondelet* to retire after having nearly flanked the enemy's batteries. She was terribly cut up, not a mast or spar was standing... In this condition the *Carondelet* drifted slowly out of battle without turning; and her bow guns were playing on

> **"Our decks were so slippery with the blood of the brave men who had fallen, that we could hardly stand until we covered them with sand."**

the enemy as long as our shell could reach him. Our decks were so slippery with the blood of the brave men who had fallen, that we could hardly stand until we covered them

with sand. While thus drifting we received a 32-pounder from the enemy on a ricochet in the starboard bow port, which beheaded two seamen and cut another in two, sending blood and brains over the captain, officers and men who were standing near them. The *Carondelet* with broken rudder, wheel and wheel ropes, was drifting on a point of the shore just below the fort and ... receiving its concentrated fire, was obliged to steam ... away from it, in the rapid current. ■

The ironclad river gunboat Carondelet was built at St. Louis, Missouri, and commissioned on January 15, 1862. The 512-foot warship's superstructure was protected by 2.5 inches of armor plate, and her armament consisted of six 32-pounder guns, four 42-pounders, and two 8-inch shell guns.

spring," wrote Lieutenant Henry Hicks of the 2nd Illinois Cavalry. "Before noon of that day many an overcoat was thrown away as a useless burden, which two days later would have prevented suffering and preserved life." The Confederates digging in at Fort Donelson, which consisted of earthworks like Fort Henry, knew that conditions here could be fickle in February, but they too suffered greatly in the days ahead when cold winds swept down from the north with sleet and snow. Some commanders chose not to campaign in winter, but Grant pressed his men forward relentlessly, come fair weather or foul.

Grant hoped that Foote's flotilla would smash Fort Donelson as it had Fort Henry and spare the army a prolonged siege. But the artillerists at Donelson were better armed and better positioned to duel with ironclads. As the gunboats entered battle on the afternoon of February 14, Confederates manning batteries above the river met them with plunging fire that ripped through their iron plating and wreaked havoc. As one Confederate observed, "They could not elevate their guns properly to do effective work, but we were throwing balls into the hulls of the boats." Aboard the ironclad *Carondelet*, Commander Henry Walke watched in dismay as shots rained down on his vessel, "tearing off the side armor as lightning tears the bark from a tree." One ball "struck the pilot house," he related, "knocked the plating to pieces, and sent fragments of iron and splinters into the pilots, one of whom fell mortally wounded." Foote himself was wounded in the battle, and all four of his ironclads were badly damaged and forced out of action without inflicting a single casualty on the fort's defenders. "The taking of Fort Donelson bids fair to be a long job," Grant wrote his wife afterward.

The fort's defenders, for their part, were not content to let Grant besiege them until their supplies were exhausted and they had to surrender. "If you lose the fort," Johnston wired Floyd, "bring your troops to Nashville if possible." With that in mind, Floyd and his fellow commanders at Donelson convened on the night of the 14th and decided to attempt a breakout in the direction of Nashville the next day, with troops under Gideon Pillow leading the way. That concerted attack on Grant's right wing, which barred the way to Nashville along the Cumberland, caught the Federals by surprise and nearly succeeded. Grant had no inkling the Confederates would leave their snow-covered entrenchments and fight their way out and was off conferring with Foote when the battle began. By the time he returned, around noon, his right wing had all but collapsed, but he remained calm and saw the crisis as an opportunity. To bring so much pressure to bear on his right, he reckoned, the Confederates must have weakened their lines to his left and would be vulnerable there. As he told his staff, "The one who attacks first now will be victorious, and the enemy will have to be in a hurry if he gets ahead of me."

Surprisingly, the Confederates were in no hurry to exploit their opening. Pillow, who had vowed never to abandon the fort, seemed reluctant to leave now that he had the chance. He ordered his battle-weary men to fall back and regroup. Buckner was aghast when he learned of Pillow's about-face and urged Floyd to overrule him and proceed with the breakout as planned. But Floyd sided with Pillow, and the Confederates gave up their hard-won gains and retrenched, handing the initiative to Grant.

"The air was balmy and betokened spring. . . . Before noon of that day many an overcoat was thrown away as a useless burden, which two days later would have prevented suffering and preserved life."

LIEUTENANT HENRY HICKS
2ND ILLINOIS CAVALRY,
on the way to Fort Donelson

Charles Smith was a role model for Ulysses Grant both as Grant's superior at West Point and as his subordinate during the Tennessee Campaign. "His personal courage was unquestioned," Grant wrote, "and he had the confidence of those he commanded as well as those over him."

Leading the way for Grant that afternoon was his former commandant at West Point, Brigadier General Charles F. Smith, who now graciously took orders from a man who had once been a mere cadet under him. "I know a soldier's duty," he told Grant. "I hope you will feel no awkwardness about our new relations." Smith held Grant's left wing, where the Confederates were stretched thin. "All has failed to our right," Grant told him. "You must take Fort Donelson." Smith, renowned for his long mustache, called on his men to charge with bayonets fixed and led them forward on horseback. "He was a grand sight, and inspired every man who looked upon him," wrote one Federal. "The instant that he came in range of the rebel sharpshooters the air around him became sibilant with their bullets." Another soldier who joined in Smith's charge admitted afterward that "I was nearly scared to death, but I saw the old man's white mustache over his shoulder and went on." At considerable sacrifice, his troops drove the enemy from their outer works and held that ground stubbornly against repeated counterattacks.

Smith did not take the fort, but his determined advance helped persuade the Confederates that their position was hopeless. At a council of war that evening, the three generals charged with defending Donelson agreed to surrender their forces. The only dissenting opinion was voiced by Colonel Nathan Bedford Forrest, a wily cavalry commander who would become legendary for his ability to bedevil numerically superior Federal forces. He had detected a gap in Grant's line along the Cumberland River through which he believed Confederates could still escape to Nashville. After the generals rejected that course as too risky, Forrest led 700 men through the gap during the night. John Floyd and Gideon Pillow, for their part, chose to flee by boat rather than face confinement and possible prosecution by the Federals. (Northerners considered Floyd's actions as secretary of war treasonous.) That left Simon Buckner to seek terms from Grant, who informed him bluntly in writing: "No terms except unconditional and immediate surrender can be accepted." When Buckner yielded and news of this great Union victory swept the North, Grant became a national hero. His initials, *U. S.*, came to signify unconditional surrender—and the unyielding determination of Uncle Sam to crush this rebellion and restore the shattered Union.

SHOWDOWN AT SHILOH

THE SURRENDER OF FORT DONELSON WAS A GALLING SETBACK FOR THE CONfederacy in general and for General Johnston in particular. He had lost a sizable portion of his army defending a position he had no confidence in holding. It was an irretrievable blunder, but in the bitter aftermath he demonstrated that Jefferson Davis's faith in him was not entirely misplaced. Already subject to harsh public criticism, he followed a course that was militarily sound but politically unpopular by abandoning Nashville to the fast-advancing Federals and withdrawing his forces from most of Tennessee. The state legislature responded by sending delegates to Richmond to demand the ouster of Johnston, who in their estimation had clearly demonstrated that he was "no general." Davis stood by his man, insisting that if Johnston was not a general, "we had better give up the war, for we have no general."

Johnston's troops hated giving ground, but their morale improved when they realized that this was a tactical withdrawal, meant to lure Grant into a position where he was vulnerable to attack. Grant's confidence and aggressiveness made him highly susceptible to that stratagem. The scorn heaped on Johnston as he withdrew from Tennessee worked to his advantage, for he wanted Grant to believe that his opponents were on the run and would not fight unless he first attacked them. As spring approached, the tide of battle in the West was running in favor of the Union. In early March, Federal forces scored a significant victory at Pea Ridge, Arkansas, loosening the hold of Confederates on that state and effectively ending their hopes of gaining control of Missouri. Later that month, invaders from Texas were foiled in their attempt to seize New Mexico when Federals destroyed their supply train and forced them back to San Antonio. If Grant could follow up his coup at Fort Donelson by crushing the remainder of Johnston's army, Confederate resistance in the West might soon collapse. It was a tantalizing prospect for Grant, who always gave more thought to what he was going to do to his enemies than to what they might do to him.

By April 1, Grant's army had moved southward up the Tennessee River to within 20 miles of the Mississippi border. Johnston's forces were encamped just below that border at Corinth, a vital rail junction west of the Tennessee River. Grant assumed that they were digging in there in anticipation of his attack and that he would have to "root the badger out of his hole." Halleck had forbidden him to challenge the Confederates until he was rein

forced by troops of the Army of the Ohio under Major General Don Carlos Buell, who had occupied Nashville and was delayed by swollen streams in linking up with Grant. The prudent course for Grant while awaiting Buell would have been to encamp on the east bank of the Tennessee, thus placing the river between his army and Johnston's. But he had no fear of being attacked and set up camp on the west bank of the Tennessee at Pittsburg Landing so that his men would be closer to Corinth and ready to advance as soon as Buell's army arrived. "There will be no fight at Pittsburg Landing," he assured one officer. "We will have to go to Corinth, where the rebels are fortified."

Grant's army had been reinforced and now numbered more than 45,000 men, but Johnston had nearly as many troops at Corinth, many of them fresh recruits. He hoped to augment his forces by using cooks and teamsters as soldiers and replacing them with blacks from nearby plantations, but planters refused to part with their slaves. "These people do not seem to be aware how valueless would be their negroes were we beaten," Johnston complained. He entrusted the planning of the attack to Beauregard, who had more battle experience than he did but sometimes lost heart when

Confederates captured at Fort Donelson gather for a group portrait at Camp Douglas, near Chicago. Unlike photographs showing prisoners of war under duress, this picture was evidently taken with the soldiers' cooperation and told of their comradeship in captivity.

> "There will be no fight at Pittsburg Landing, we will have to go to Corinth, where the rebels are fortified."
>
> ULYSSES S. GRANT

> "We shall attack at daylight tomorrow. . . . [By noon] we will water our horses in the Tennessee River."
>
> ALBERT SIDNEY JOHNSTON

faced with adversity. One such crisis of confidence had stricken Beauregard during the battle at Manassas a year earlier, and another overcame him on the evening of April 5 as Confederates moved northward from Corinth and prepared to strike. The men were boisterous, shooting at rabbits and deer as they advanced, and he feared they had lost the advantage of surprise. The Federals would now be "entrenched to the eyes," he warned Johnston, urging him to pull back. Johnston doubted that Grant was thinking defensively and decided to forge ahead. "We shall attack at daylight tomorrow," he told Beauregard. By noon, he promised, "we will water our horses in the Tennessee River."

Sunday, April 6, dawned clear and bright. "It was a most beautiful morning," recalled Corporal Leander Stillwell of the 61st Illinois. "It really seemed like Sunday in the country at home." Federals were polishing their muskets and shining their shoes in anticipation of Sunday morning inspection when they heard cannon booming around Shiloh Church, followed by a "low, sullen, continuous roar. There was no mistaking that sound. That was not a squad of pickets emptying their guns on being relieved of duty; it was the continuous roll of thousands of muskets, and told us that battle was on."

Encamped near Shiloh Church and caught in the Confederate onslaught was the division of General Sherman, who shared Grant's disdain for defensive preparations. "I always acted on the supposition that we were an invading army; that our purpose was to move forward in force," Sherman wrote afterward. "We did not fortify our camps against attack, because we had no orders to do so, and because such a course would have made our raw men timid." Like Grant, who was suspected of being an alcoholic, Sherman had to overcome charges that he was temperamentally unfit for command. He had lost charge of the Army of the Ohio to Buell after suffering what amounted to a nervous breakdown and later credited Grant with rehabilitating him. "He stood by me when I was crazy," Sherman said with dark humor, "and I stood by him when he was drunk." Fortunately for the Federals, Sherman was not crazy at Shiloh and Grant was not drunk. The owner of the house Grant commandeered as his headquarters, across the river in the town of Savannah, attested that the general was "thoroughly sober" when he heard the distant sound of cannon fire while sipping coffee at the breakfast table. "Gentlemen, the ball is in motion," he said to his staff officers, "let's be off." Within 15 minutes, Grant was crossing the Tennessee by steamboat to Pittsburg Landing to organize a defense.

Sherman had little hope of holding his exposed position, but he made the oncoming Confederates pay dearly for the ground they gained. One regiment, the 6th Mississippi, lost 300 of its 425 men in repeated charges before Sherman's troops at last gave way. Other Federal divisions were falling back as well, and some Confederates paused to celebrate in the abandoned camps by claiming trophies or consuming food their foes had been cooking for breakfast—an irresistible temptation for men who had eaten little on the hard march from Corinth. "There was an abundance of prepared food," recalled one soldier from Tennessee, who came upon a woman in camp, "caring for her son. She begged for mercy. I told her we were not out to hurt women or children, only armed men." Dead and wounded Federals littered the ground, another

Federals of the 21st Missouri Infantry typify the motley forces who fought at Shiloh, where most men on both sides were recent recruits and sported a variety of weapons and outfits.

Confederate observed: "They were mangled in every conceivable form. Some were in the last agonies of death. I could not pass a wounded man without saying 'God have mercy on him.' "

By midmorning, the beleaguered Federals had formed a new defensive line along a sunken wagon road fringed by woods that offered them cover as Confederates advanced across open ground to the south. Assailing that line were troops under Major General Braxton Bragg, a headstrong Tennessean who thought his men could break through without artillery support. Not until much of a brigade had been lost in fruitless assaults on that "Hornet's Nest" did Confederates call up big guns to blast the stubborn defenders.

Concerned that the attack was bogging down, Johnston rode forward to get things moving. Along the way, he came upon large numbers of injured men, many of them captured Federals. Johnston left his staff surgeon behind to tend them. "Look after these wounded people, the Yankees among the rest," he said. "They were our enemies a moment ago. They are prisoners now." Around two that afternoon, Johnston rallied troops who had lost the will to fight and spurred them across a peach orchard in full bloom, forcing the Federals back along their left flank near the river, where he hoped to break through and cut Grant off. Moments after mounting that charge, however, Johnston reeled and slumped in his saddle. A bullet had severed an artery in his right

1 PITTSBURG LANDING *The steamboat Tycoon, far right, served as a hospital for Union wounded. Next to her is the Tigress, Grant's headquarters.*

2 SHILOH CHURCH *From this small log meeting house, the Rebels launched what would be the bloodiest battle in U.S. history up to that time.*

5 THE HORNET'S NEST *Thure de Thulstrup's painting depicts one of eleven Confederate assaults ordered by Braxton Bragg on Prentiss's position.*

THE BATTLE OF SHILOH

REELING FROM DEFEATS IN WEST TENNESSEE, GENerals Beauregard and A. S. Johnston launched an offensive to regain the state and keep Union forces from marching on the critical railroad junction at Corinth, Mississippi.

Having concentrated more than 40,000 men at Corinth, including those of Braxton Bragg from the Gulf Coast, Beauregard planned to hit Ulysses S. Grant's army before Don Carlos Buell could arrive at Pittsburg Landing 1 to reinforce him. On the morning of April 6, 1862, Rebels came screaming out of the woods near Shiloh Church 2, surprising the divisions of William T. Sherman and Benjamin M. Prentiss. "My God, we're attacked," cried Sherman as his orderly fell dead at his side from a volley.

For the rest of the brutal day of fighting, the Confederates steadily forced Union forces back toward the landing, nearly two miles from their starting point. Grant organized an artillery line 3 along a ridge to help stem the Rebel advance. A. S. Johnston went personally to the front to rally his troops and was shot dead 4. Holding the center of the Union line was Prentiss 5, who dug in along a country lane that the Union referred to as the Sunken Road and that the Rebels called the Hornet's Nest.

With just 4,500 men Prentiss fended off 18,000 Confederates, who pounded the Hornet's Nest with field guns and infantry for hours until Prentiss finally surrendered near sunset. But his tenacity bought enough time for Grant to reorganize his line and for Buell to arrive with reinforcements. Nathan Bedford Forrest watched Buell's army 6 cross the river during the night and predicted "We'll be whipped like Hell." The morning of April 7 would prove him right. ■

Robert Knox Sneden's map is titled "The Battle of Pittsburg Landing," the Union name for the conflict. The North eventually accepted the name Shiloh.

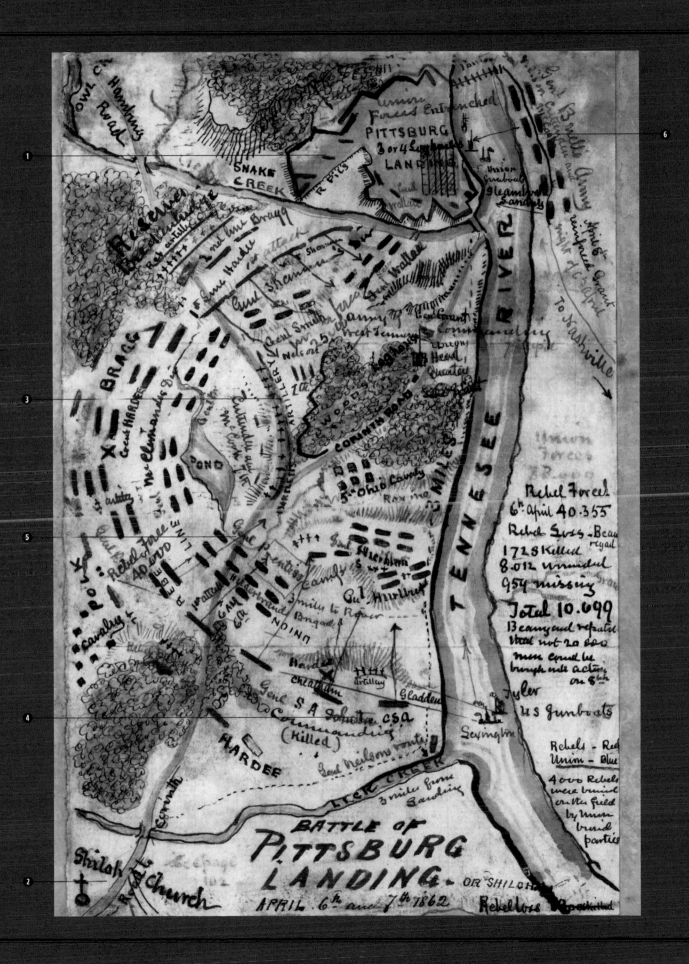

leg. Without a surgeon at hand to apply a tourniquet, he died within minutes.

Beauregard, who had set up headquarters in Shiloh Church, did what he could to sustain the attack after Johnston's death, but time was running out. Beauregard's battle plan had been cumbersome from the start, and when things went awry, his rote response was to send in fresh units where the action was hottest. That meant pounding away at Federal strongpoints like the Hornet's Nest rather than outflanking them. Not until late afternoon did Brigadier General Daniel Ruggles of Bragg's Corps assemble enough firepower—62 cannon in all—to shatter resistance in the Hornet's Nest. It was every man for himself, recalled George McBride of the 15th Michigan, one of several thousand Federals flushed from the nest by that terrific barrage and the Confederate charge that followed: "I was never so frightened before, never ran so fast, was never in such a storm of bullets. Out of that fire I came alive and unharmed, but it was a marvel."

By holding out as long as they did, the defenders of the Hornet's Nest bought time for Grant to form a formidable last line of defense on high ground above Pittsburg Landing. As daylight waned, Bragg tried to crack that line by summoning what remained of his corps for one last push. "Sweep everything forward," he ordered. "Drive the enemy into the river." But as his men struggled through a swampy ravine toward the landing, they came under the com-

---

[EYEWITNESS]

Lieutenant William C. Thompson

6TH MISSISSIPPI INFANTRY, CLEBURNE'S BRIGADE

William Thompson joined the Simpson Fencibles, Company B of the 6th Mississippi, in the summer of 1861.
At Shiloh the 6th went into battle with the brigade of Brigadier General Patrick Cleburne, part of Hardee's Corps.
In a series of desperate assaults against the Federal right on April 6, the regiment lost 48 killed and 247 wounded,
76 percent of the 425 men engaged in battle.

THE HEART-RENDING SCENE at the hospital is one I would like to forget. Piles of dead soldiers were all around, and lying in rows were others who were dying. Doctors and their assistants were moving among the wounded, examining and aiding those who were not beyond help. The screams from the operating table resounded through the woods, for the surgeons were taking off arms and legs of a succession of men carried to them. Teams drawing ambulances were being urged to hasten, hauling the wounded from the field and back to a safer place. Other wagons were collecting and bringing in more wounded. They were being unloaded like so many butchered hogs, and the wagon beds were streaming blood. Once unloaded, the wagons were off to the front again, to collect more unfortunates. Many were dead when unloaded, others died soon afterwards. ∎

"The screams from the operating table resounded through the woods."

This silk flag of the 6th Kentucky Infantry, presented to the unit by the ladies of Huntsville, Alabama, was probably the one carried by the regiment at Shiloh.

bined fire of Grant's artillery and two Federal gunboats on the Tennessee. Bragg withdrew his battered forces only after Beauregard ordered him to, assuring him that their victory was "sufficiently complete."

"My God, was a victory ever sufficiently complete?" responded Bragg, who thought Beauregard was letting Grant off the hook. In truth, any chance the Confederates had of crushing Grant's army had passed earlier in the day when they became embroiled in the punishing fight for the Hornet's Nest. What Beauregard did not know was that much of Buell's army had reached Savannah during the day and would begin crossing to Pittsburg Landing that evening. After barely staving off defeat, Grant could smell victory. "Well, Grant, we've had the devil's own day, haven't we," Sherman said to him. "Yes," Grant replied impassively. "Lick 'em tomorrow, though."

There was little rest for the weary that night as Federal gunboats on the river continued to barrage the Confederates. "At midnight," one Tennessean recalled, "a heavy rain set in, accompanied by peal after peal of thunder, together with the roaring of the cannon and the bursting of shell. The flashes of lightning revealed the ghastly features of the dead. . . . Oh, what a night of horrors that was!" Nathan Forrest's cavalry reported that Federal reinforcements were crossing the river by the thousands, but Forrest's warning never reached the confident Beauregard. "I thought I had General Grant just where I wanted him and could finish him up in the morning," he wrote.

The battle resumed at daybreak on April 7, and this time it was the Confederates who were caught by surprise and forced back. In furious fighting around Shiloh Church, Confederates counterattacked and held the Federals off for a while, but Beauregard's army was exhausted and near collapse. That afternoon, he ordered his forces to withdraw to Corinth. A determined pursuit by Grant might have finished them off, but the Federals too had reached their limit. "I wanted to pursue, but had not the heart," Grant wrote. He could ask no more of troops who had "fought desperately for two days."

Neither side had much to celebrate after this ferocious struggle. Grant could claim victory because he had held his ground and driven Beauregard back to Corinth, which the Confederates would later abandon. But the casualties at Shiloh were appalling and left both armies in shock. As Sherman put it, "The scenes on this field would have cured anyone of war." Each side had lost more than 1,700 men killed and 8,000 wounded, making this by far the bloodiest battle yet fought on American soil. Beauregard's fine reputation in the South was spoiled, and Grant too came under a storm of criticism for being overconfident and letting down his guard. Some in Washington called for his dismissal, but Lincoln offered him a memorable endorsement: "I can't spare this man; he fights." Indeed, Grant emerged from Shiloh with new respect for Confederate powers of resistance and a new understanding of what it would take to defeat these Rebels. They would hold out stubbornly until they no longer had the capacity to wage war, he recognized. To deprive them of that capacity meant bleeding them dry in battle and destroying their economy by ravaging fields and factories and consuming "everything that could be used to support or supply armies." From the carnage at Shiloh came Grant's conviction that complete victory could be achieved only through total war.

"The flashes of lightning revealed the ghastly features of the dead. . . . Oh, what a night of horrors that was!"

Confederate soldier at Shiloh

"As far as the eye can see, the water is rolling, foaming and dashing over the shoals. . . . This is no time for man to war against man."

Soldier's diary,
on rounding Cape Hatteras in heavy seas with Burnside's expedition

THE COASTAL WAR

IN JANUARY 1862, WHILE GRANT WAS LAYING PLANS TO ADVANCE UP THE TENnessee River, 13,000 Federal troops embarked from Annapolis, Maryland, aboard a motley fleet of ferryboats, schooners, barges, and tugs to conduct the largest amphibious assault yet on Confederate territory. Their target was Roanoke Island, nestled between the coast of North Carolina and the Outer Banks. Federals had gained access to the sheltered waters within the Outer Banks in August 1861 by seizing enemy forts guarding Hatteras Inlet. By crossing that inlet and capturing Roanoke Island, they would command both Pamlico and Albemarle Sounds and could range freely along much of the North Carolina coast, attacking ports such as New Bern, the state's second largest town after Wilmington.

If successful, this operation would reinforce the naval blockade imposed by President Lincoln just days after the Civil War began. The coastal war between Confederates seeking to break that blockade and Federals attempting to close harbors and occupy ports intensified in early 1862 as the landing in North Carolina was followed by the first-ever battle between ironclads and a daring naval assault on New Orleans.

Commanding the forces bound for Roanoke Island was Brigadier General Ambrose Burnside, a methodical Rhode Islander who proved well suited for this meticulous operation, in which the army furnished troops and transports while the navy provided gunboats. Burnside had to assemble transports of sufficiently shallow draft to pass through treacherous Hatteras Inlet, where any vessel displacing more than eight feet of water was sure to run aground on shifting sands. He sought recruits from the northeast coast who had been to sea before and could withstand a voyage that would take them past storm-wracked Cape Hatteras in midwinter. Those men knew that ships with shallow drafts built to navigate rivers and bays would be unstable in high seas. Burnside tried to reassure them by shifting his headquarters from a large steamer to the fleet's smallest boat before his unlikely assortment of commercial vessels entered service. "Their weaknesses were known to me," he wrote, "but they were the best that could be procured, and it was necessary that the service should be performed even at the risk of losing life by shipwreck."

After departing Annapolis on January 9, his transports linked up with gunboats and supply ships at Fort Monroe near the mouth of the Chesapeake and entered the Atlantic. Rounding Cape Hatteras in heavy seas, Burnside's puny flagship *Picket* was put to the test. "It seemed for a time as if she would surely be swamped," he related. "We passed a most uncomfortable night. Everything on deck that was not lashed was swept overboard; and the men, furniture, and crockery below decks were thrown about in a most promiscuous manner." Conditions were little better for the men aboard larger vessels, one of whom noted in his diary: "As far as the eye can see, the water is rolling, foaming and dashing over the shoals. . . . This is no time for man to war against man." High winds buffeted the fleet for nearly two weeks, causing some ships to run aground and preventing others from crossing Hatteras Inlet. When conditions improved, Burnside found that the inlet was only six feet deep, too shallow for most of his vessels to cross. Resourceful captains broke through by driving steamers against the sandbar as the tide was running out. The strong current swept sand from under the keels, and the channel was soon deep enough for the entire fleet to enter Pamlico Sound.

This invasion of enemy waters went uncontested. All the Confederates had in the way of a navy here was a so-called mosquito fleet of eight lightly armed gunboats, which had been withdrawn to the northern end of Roanoke Island in anticipation of the Federal assault. The site of the first English colony in North America, Roanoke Island was strategically significant because it commanded the narrow passage between Pamlico Sound and Albemarle Sound, which lay close to Virginia and the Confederate capital. A few thousand troops defended the island, but they were poorly armed and badly outnumbered by Burnside's men, who came ashore in early February. After their ordeal at sea, they were glad to be back on land, and not even pouring rain could dampen their spirits. As one soldier from Massachusetts recalled: "We sat down to the fire, took off our shoes to dry them, wrang the mud out of our pants and stockings, stirred up the fire, talked, laughed, smoked and got smoked until morning."

General Ambrose Burnside, who led the Federal amphibious assault on Roanoke Island portrayed below, had such distinctive facial hair that soldiers made a play on his name and coined the term "sideburns."

On February 8, Burnside's men attacked. Brightly clad Zouaves from New York charged the entrenched Confederates head on, shouting their battle cry—"Zou! Zou! Zou!"—while other units outflanked the defenders and sealed their fate. Nearly 2,500 Rebels were captured, and Yankee gunboats went on to crush the mosquito fleet. This victory, which came shortly before Fort Donelson fell to Grant's troops, cheered Northerners who had had little to celebrate since the war began and caused deep concern in Richmond, where Confederate leaders feared Burnside would cut their supply lines to the south while General McClellan's army descended on them from the north. As it turned out, Burnside's forces did not advance far enough inland to threaten Richmond, but they raised hell on the North Carolina coast, seizing Elizabeth City in mid-February and New Bern a month later. As Confederates abandoned New Bern, they torched supply depots, and the fire spread, fueled by tar and turpentine stored on the docks. Smoke and fumes engulfed the port, and civilians fled in panic. To one officer who witnessed the scene, it was as if the wrath of God had descended. "As I looked upon it," he wrote, "I could think of nothing but Sodom and Gomorrah." Parts of the town escaped the flames, but New Bern remained under Federal control for the remainder of the war.

A DUEL BETWEEN IRONCLADS

NOWHERE WAS THE BLOCKADE MORE GALLING TO CONFEDERATES THAN IN NARrow Hampton Roads, where Federal warships kept opposing vessels bottled up in the James River and prevented Richmond from communicating by sea with the outside world. The necessity of breaking that blockade gave birth to a remarkable invention—an ironclad that proved vastly superior to wooden warships and might have won the battle for Hampton Roads single-handedly had it not met its match in the form of a Federal prototype rushed into service to meet this threat. The Confederate ironclad was widely known as the *Merrimack*, named for the wooden steamship Federals torched when they abandoned Norfolk in 1861. But when Confederates salvaged that hulk, they converted it into a new vessel, the *Virginia*, sheathed in iron plating made at the Tredegar Iron Works in Richmond, the South's leading arsenal. Unlike smaller ironclads produced for the Federals by James Eads in St. Louis, built to navigate rivers and duel with shore batteries, the hulking *Virginia* was designed to smash ships in coastal waters. Measuring 275 feet long, it carried a crew of 330 men and had ten guns and

The hulking Confederate ironclad Virginia, also known as the Merrimack, duels at close range with the smaller Federal ironclad Monitor during their historic encounter in Hampton Roads on March 9, 1862.

Lieutenant S. Dana Greene
U.S.S. *MONITOR*

After about four hours of indecisive action the Monitor's commanding officer, Lieutenant John L. Worden attempted to ram the Virginia's stern hoping to damage her rudder or propeller. As the Monitor closed a shell from the Virginia's stern pivot gun struck the Federal ironclad's pilothouse wounding Worden and temporarily sending the vessel out of control. Greene took command and, uncertain about damage to the Monitor's steering, steered the ship into shallow water.

SOON AFTER NOON A SHELL from the enemy's gun, the muzzle not ten yards distant, struck the forward side of the pilot-house directly in the sight-hole, or slit, and exploded, cracking the second iron log and partly lifting the top, leaving an opening. Worden was standing immediately behind this spot, and received in his face the force of the blow, which partly stunned him, and, filling his eyes with powder, utterly blinded him. The injury was known only to those in the pilot-house and its immediate vicinity. The flood of light rushing through the top of the pilot-house, now partly open, caused Worden, blind as he was, to believe that the pilot-house was seriously injured, if not destroyed; he therefore gave orders to put the helm to starboard and "sheer off." Thus the *Monitor* retired temporarily from the action, in order to ascertain the extent of the injuries she had received. At the same time Worden sent for me, and ... I went forward at once, and found him standing at the foot of the ladder leading to the pilot-house.

He was a ghastly sight, with his eyes closed and the blood apparently rushing from every pore in the upper part of his face. He told me that he was seriously wounded, and directed me to take command. I assisted in leading him to a sofa in his cabin, where he was tenderly cared for by Dr. Logue, and then

"My nerves and muscles twitched as though electric shocks were continually passing through them. . . . I lay down and tried to sleep—I might as well have tried to fly."

I assumed command. Blind and suffering as he was, Worden's fortitude never forsook him; he frequently asked from his bed of pain of the progress of affairs, and when told that the *Minnesota* was saved, he said, "Then I can die happy."

When I reached my station in the pilot-house, I found that the iron log was fractured and the top partly open; but the steering gear was still intact, and the pilot-house was not totally destroyed, as had been feared. In the confusion of the moment resulting from so serious an injury to the commanding officer, the *Monitor* had been moving without direction. Exactly how much time had elapsed from the moment that Worden was wounded until I had reached the pilot-house and completed the examination of the injury at that point, and determined what course to pursue in the damaged condition of the vessel, it is impossible to state; but it could hardly have exceeded twenty minutes at the utmost. During this time the *Merrimac*, which was leaking badly, had started in the direction of the Elizabeth River; and, on taking my station in the pilot-house, and turning the vessel's head in the direction of the *Merrimac*, I saw that she was already in retreat. A few shots were fired at the retiring vessel, and she continued on to Norfolk. . . .

My men and myself were perfectly black with smoke and powder. . . . I had been up so long, and had been under such a state of excitement, that my nervous system was completely run down. . . . My nerves and muscles twitched as though electric shocks were continually passing through them. . . . I lay down and tried to sleep— I might as well have tried to fly. ∎

a protruding iron ram at the bow for puncturing enemy hulls, but its bulk made it awkward and sluggish. "From the start we saw that she was slow, not over five knots," recalled Lieutenant John Taylor Wood; "she steered so badly that, with her great length, it took from thirty to forty minutes to turn."

This big project could not be kept secret, and Federals responded by building an ironclad called the *Monitor*. Work on the *Virginia* was so far along when Swedish-born naval engineer John Ericsson began designing the *Monitor* that nothing of similar dimensions, he noted, "could possibly be completed in time to meet her." The *Monitor* would be a hundred feet shorter than its Confederate rival, with only two guns. But those guns would pivot in a turret, which meant that the craft itself would not have to turn laboriously to take aim. To offset the greater firepower of the *Virginia*, the *Monitor* had an extremely low profile. Only the gun turret amidships and the pilot house, located near the bow, protruded noticeably above water.

Ericsson undertook to build the ironclad in three months and nearly met that target, but his 100-day wonder proved a severe trial for the crew that left New York on March 6 for Hampton Roads. "It was at once evident that the *Monitor* was unfit as a sea-going craft," wrote Lieutenant S. Dana Greene. Waves pounded the pilot house, and water streamed in "with such force as to knock the helmsman completely round from the wheel." Neither the commander in the pilot house nor Lieutenant Greene in the gun turret could see much of their surroundings. It was like being "shut up in a revolving drum," remarked Greene, who sometimes lost his bearings. Both sides were so intent on winning the race to Hampton Roads that they hurried their ironclads into service with their potential unproven and defects unremedied.

The *Virginia*, which had only a short journey to make from Gosport Navy Yard in Norfolk, entered Hampton Roads on March 8 while the *Monitor* was still churning southward in the Atlantic toward the mouth of Chesapeake Bay. Enforcing the blockade in Hampton Roads were five wooden warships. The *Virginia*'s commander, Flag Officer Franklin Buchanan, hoped to destroy them all, beginning with the first two ships he encountered: the 50-gun frigate *Congress* and the 24-gun sloop *Cumberland*. After exchanging shots with both, Buchanan set out to ram the smaller *Cumberland*. The sloop's pilot watched in horror as the ironclad came plowing through the water "like a huge half-submerged crocodile." Its fearsome iron ram pierced the hull of the *Cumberland* and stuck there before breaking off as the sloop went down. The *Virginia* then turned on the *Congress*, which ran aground in shallows off Newport News and fell prey to hot shots that set the frigate ablaze. Many shots fired at the ironclad glanced harmlessly off its sloping sides, rendered slippery with pork fat, but others found openings and did damage, knocking out two of ten guns, killing two men, and wounding Buchanan and 18 others. By day's end, however, the *Virginia* had

Officers inspect the gun turret of the Monitor, dented by shots from the Virginia, after the hot battle between the ironclads. The Monitor's designer, John Ericsson, faulted the Navy Department for ordering powder charges cut in half, which reduced the risk of the Monitor's guns bursting but gave them less punch.

> **"After making preparations for the next day's fight, we slept at our guns, dreaming of other victories in the morning."**
>
> LIEUTENANT JOHN TAYLOR WOOD OF THE CONFEDERATE IRONCLAD *VIRGINIA*

destroyed two warships and was still capable of wreaking havoc. "The armor was hardly damaged," wrote Lieutenant Wood. "After making preparations for the next day's fight, we slept at our guns, dreaming of other victories in the morning."

Those dreams went unfulfilled. By dawn, when the *Virginia* began prowling for fresh victims, the *Monitor* had reached Hampton Roads and was guarding the frigate *Minnesota*, which had run aground. The *Monitor* "appeared but a pigmy compared to the lofty frigate which she guarded," observed Wood. "But in her size was one great element of her success." Indeed, the *Monitor*, likened by one observer to "a tin can on a shingle," presented a much smaller target than the *Virginia* and had a shallower draft, enabling it to run rings around its stronger but clumsier opponent. "Drawing 22 feet of water we were confined to a narrow channel," Wood explained, "while the *Monitor*, with only 12 feet immersion, could take any position, and always have us in range of her guns." It was maneuverability against power, and in the fierce duel that followed neither side had a clear edge. For four hours, the *Monitor* and *Virginia* traded blows, at distances that ranged from a half mile to a few yards. The pounding they took "would have sunk any other vessel," Wood reckoned, but when the smoke cleared both ironclads were still afloat. The *Monitor* pulled back after a shell exploded against the pilot house and blinded its commander, Lieutenant John Worden. The *Virginia* was in no condition to prolong the battle and returned to Gosport Navy Yard for repairs.

Southerners applauded the *Virginia*'s bold foray and claimed victory, but Federals prevailed in the long run by maintaining their grip on Hampton Roads and producing many more ironclads over the course of the war than their opponents did. Confederates could not break the blockade, but they often evaded it, for the U.S. Navy lacked the resources to seal off every Southern port. Blockade-runners carried Southern cotton to Great Britain and other foreign countries, and incoming vessels brought wartime necessities such as medicine and rifles. Meanwhile, the Confederate Ordnance Department stepped up domestic production of arms and ammunition. Clothing and shoes would remain in short supply, but for the remainder of the conflict Southern troops would be as well armed as their opponents.

Confederates also made gains on the high seas by preying on U.S. merchant ships and claiming them and their cargo as prizes of war. In 1862, two ships designed for commerce raiding were produced for the Confed-

Sailors aboard the Wabash, the flagship of Admiral Samuel Du Pont, perform in concert to relieve the tedium of Federal blockade duty, which Du Pont called "the most onerous service in the world."

THE PIRATE RAPHAEL SEMMES

THE MAN CARICATURED BY CARtoonist Thomas Nast as a jaunty pirate had been, for nearly 35 years, a distinguished member of the U.S. Navy as well as a successful attorney. But there was no doubt where Raphael Semmes's loyalties lay when his adopted state of Alabama seceded. Maryland born and a veteran of the Mexican War, he joined the Confederate Navy in April of 1861 and took command of the C.S.S. *Sumter*, a steamer-turned-commerce raider. In June Semmes successfully ran the Federal blockade of New Orleans, launching a career that would see him become the most notorious raider of the war.

"Her lines were easy and graceful," Semmes wrote of the *Sumter*, "and she had a sort of saucy air about her." Saucy might have described Semmes as well, who took to raiding with gusto, quipping that "chasing a sail is very much like pursuing a coy maiden, the very coyness sharpening the pursuit." After six months aboard the *Sumter*, during which time he successfully raided 18 U.S. merchant ships, Semmes took the ship to Gibraltar for a much-needed overhaul. Cornered there by U.S. warships in January of 1862, he escaped to England, where he was promoted to captain and given command of a newly constructed British vessel, christened the *Alabama*.

The *Alabama* was a 220-footlong steam-powered sloop built for speed, and for commerce raiding. It could make 13 knots under sail and steam, and it was armed with eight guns: a large Blakely 110-pounder

> **"The name of your ship has become a household word wherever civilization extends. Shall that name be tarnished by defeat? The thing is impossible!"**
>
> RAPHAEL SEMMES TO HIS CREW,
> *before his Alabama engaged the Kearsarge*

rifled gun, a pivoting 8-inch smoothbore Dahlgren gun, and six 32-pounders mounted broadside. Taking command in August of 1862, Semmes flexed his new ship's muscles against a Yankee whaling fleet in the Azores before grabbing headlines with his sinking of the U.S.S. *Hatteras* off the coast of Texas in January of 1863. The *Hatteras* had been one of the U.S. Navy's most successful blockaders. The *Alabama*, disguised under a British flag, surprised the gunboat and overpowered her in a 40-minute battle.

For the next year and a half, *Alabama* prowled shipping lanes from the Atlantic to the East Indies. Semmes captured more than 60 U.S. merchant ships with a value of more than $6 million, which was enough to make him one of the Union's most wanted. The U.S.S. *Kearsarge*, captained by Lieutenant John A. Winslow, who shared quarters with Semmes during the Mexican War, blockaded the *Alabama* at the port of Cherbourg, France, in June of 1864, finally wrecking the Confederate raider in little more than an hour of fighting. The men of the *Kearsarge* knew the significance of the victory. "Nothing could restrain the enthusiasm of the men," wrote ship's surgeon John M. Browne. "Cheer succeeded cheer...as each projectile took effect."

Semmes was wounded in the battle but was rescued from his sinking ship by a British yacht, which took him to England to recuperate. After the war he was pardoned of treason charges and returned to Mobile. ∎

Captain Raphael Semmes, called Old Beeswax because of his shiny handlebar mustache, relaxes on the Alabama's deck while at anchor off Cape Town.

eracy in Britain in violation of that nation's neutrality laws. Christened the *Florida* and the *Alabama*, they seized scores of merchant ships before the U.S. Navy finally hunted them down. Northerners denounced Captain Raphael Semmes of the *Alabama* as a pirate, but he was acting on orders to inflict on Yankee merchantmen "the greatest injury in the shortest time." For all their notoriety, he and other Confederate raiders had little impact on the Northern economy compared to the toll taken by the blockade, which made imported goods scarce and ever more expensive in the South. Confederate leaders compounded inflation by issuing paper currency unsupported by gold, which went for military purchases from abroad. By 1864, the Confederate dollar had a real purchasing power of less than a nickel, and a pound of coffee cost $50.

The Capture of New Orleans

DAVID GLASGOW FARRAGUT HAD SPENT 50 YEARS IN THE U.S. NAVY PREPARING for this opportunity. Some in Washington doubted his loyalty, for he hailed from Tennessee and made his home in Virginia. But when friends there urged him to side with the Confederacy, he declined, warning them: "You fellows will catch the devil before you get through with this business." Relegated to a desk job by superiors wary of his Southern background, he received a boost from his foster brother, Commander David Dixon Porter, son of a naval hero who had adopted Farragut and taken him to sea as a boy. Porter used his connections in Washington to promote a plan he hoped would make him as famous as his father. He wanted to smash the Confederate forts guarding the mouth of the Mississippi River. He secured command of the gunboats that would bombard the forts, and at his urging Farragut was chosen to lead warships past those strongholds and force the surrender of New Orleans, which would then be occupied by troops. Promoted from captain to flag officer, the 60-year-old Farragut relished this long-awaited chance. As he wrote to his wife: "I have now attained what I have been looking for all my life—a flag—and having attained it, all that is necessary to complete the scene is a victory."

This risky venture, carried out in the spring of 1862, was the boldest attempt yet by Federals to move beyond blockading Confederate ports to taking possession of them. Thus far, most naval operations had been aimed at forts that were unimposing. The two bastions guarding the entrance to the Mississippi River, Fort Jackson and Fort St. Philip, were among the strongest in the Confederacy. Hefty structures of brick and stone bristling with big guns, they stood like sentinels on either side of the river, across which stretched a cordon of heavy iron chains suspended between hulks to snag ships trying to run the gantlet. "Nothing afloat could pass the forts," wrote author George Washington Cable of New Orleans, and many there shared that belief.

Porter hoped that his fleet of 19 schooners, armed with heavy mortars that lobbed 200-pound shells, would force the surrender of the Confederate forts and ease Farragut's passage upriver. But five days of relentless bombardment beginning on April 18 failed to achieve the desired result. Farragut could wait no longer. "Whatever is to be done will have to be done quickly," he declared, "or we shall again be reduced to a blockading squadron." To run the forts, he first had to sever the chain barrier across the river. Lieutenant Charles Cald-

"I have now attained what I have been looking for all my life—a flag— and having attained it, all that is necessary to complete the scene is a victory."

DAVID GLASGOW FARRAGUT
Flag officer of the West Blockade Squadron

A Southerner who stuck with the Union, David Farragut was relieved to learn that the target of his naval expedition in 1862 would be New Orleans and not his hometown of Norfolk, Virginia.

well did that by driving his gunboat *Itaska* at full speed against the chain and riding up over it, snapping it under the weight of his vessel. The path was open, but Farragut would still have to contend with the defiant forts and with a Confederate flotilla that included gunboats, fire rafts—driven against enemy ships to set them ablaze—and two ironclads: the *Manassas*, built for ramming; and the unfinished *Louisiana*, towed into place to serve as a floating battery.

Shortly after midnight on April 24, Farragut set his fleet of 18 ships in motion. "A more desperate, a more magnificent dash was never made," wrote Captain Thomas Craven of the *Brooklyn*, which advanced behind Farragut's flagship *Hartford*. After passing the forts largely unscathed—gunners there had difficulty spotting their targets amid the dense clouds of gun smoke shrouding the river—the *Hartford* was struck by a fire raft. "Don't flinch from that fire, boys," Farragut shouted as crewmen extinguished the blaze. "There's a hotter fire than that for those who don't do their duty!" The *Brooklyn* was rammed head-on by the *Manassas* but stayed afloat, and the hard-hitting ironclad drew Farragut's fury. "Sink that damned thing," he ordered. Pounded mercilessly, the *Manassas* exploded. Confederates later scuttled the immobile and ineffective *Louisiana*. By dawn, Farragut had a clear path up the Mississippi, having lost just one ship.

On April 25, he reached New Orleans. More than 15,000 Federal troops were heading upriver from the Gulf to occupy the city, and the few thousand militiamen defending New Orleans withdrew. Farragut sent two officers, Captain Theodorus Bailey and Lieutenant George Perkins, ashore to deliver an ultimatum to the mayor. Angry civilians crowded around them, shouting threats. "About every third man there had a weapon out," observed George Washington Cable. Yet the officers forged ahead, "unguarded and alone, looking not to right or left, never frowning, never flinching, while the mob screamed in their ears, shook cocked pistols in their faces, cursed and crowded, and gnashed upon them. So through the gates of death those two men walked to the City Hall to demand the town's surrender. It was one of the bravest deeds I ever saw done."

Mayor John Monroe refused to surrender and left it to occupying Federals to haul down Confederate flags over New Orleans and raise the Stars and Stripes. The city was placed under the stringent command of General Benjamin Butler, who became known as Beast Butler for his provocative edicts, including one in which he declared that any female who insulted or showed contempt for a Federal soldier "by word, gesture, or movement" would be "treated as a woman of the town plying her avocation." Butler was not advocating rape, as some residents feared. His order meant that women who offended soldiers would be charged like prostitutes with disorderly conduct. But his grim presence and infuriating pronouncements cast a pall over once-festive New Orleans. "A gloom has settled o'er my spirit," wrote one resident, 16-year-old Clara Solomon, "a gloom envelopes our dearly beloved city." That gloom could be felt as far away as Richmond, where people were bracing for a massive Federal assault that threatened to overwhelm the Confederate capital and crush Southern hopes for independence.

General Benjamin "Beast" Butler, portrayed here as a satanic figure, was also known as "Spoons" for allegedly pilfering silverware from homes in New Orleans, where he commanded Federal occupation forces. Already notorious in the South for harboring escaped slaves as contraband of war, his actions in Louisiana made him despised.

Anne Brantley Heard

RESIDENT OF NEW ORLEANS

*On May 4, 1862, Anne, a recent refugee from her home in New Orleans, wrote a letter to her sister Sara describing
the fall of the city on April 29 to Federal naval forces under Flag Officer David G. Farragut.
The New Orleans resident recounted the chaos she witnessed during the evacuation and destruction of Confederate property
and the flight of city residents in expectation of the arrival of Federal occupiers. In her letter Heard lamented
the failure of Confederate forces to effectively defend the Crescent City.*

I HAD TO LEAVE N.O. IN SUCH a hurry that I hadn't time to answer your last letter or to ship the things I had purchased for you and sister Amelia. As you may suppose, my hegira was affected with difficulty and precipitation.

The Yankees passed the forts on Wednesday night; and all day Thursday and Friday boats and cars were loaded down transporting government stores, munitions, and specie and troops. On Friday I could have gone as many ladies did on the open freight trains. But not a cart, carriage, or dray could I find for love or money to take my trunks, so that I was obliged to remain in town twenty-four hours after the arrival of the fleet in front of our levee.

I have never witnessed such a scene as our streets presented on the day when their imposing fleet of magnificent frigates came steaming up the river calmly and grandly; and what was truly aggravating —most gracefully and confidently. The very heavens were thick with the smoke of our consuming wealth. The streets ran with molasses and turpentine and the river was flaming with burning wrecks and hulks that we had given to the flames to save from the enemy. And even women and children were rushing to and fro in a state of the

"Old and young men wept from mortification and women wrung their hands in agony."

wildest excitement. Rage, fear, humiliation, and grief ruled the hour. Old and young men wept from mortification and women wrung their hands in agony.

The fury of the populace was such that it was difficult to restrain them from committing violence upon the officers who came ashore to demand the city's surrender. As it was, several persons in the crowd who cheered for Lincoln, to give signs of joy upon the landing of the delegation from Commander Farragut, were shot down. Of course

you know the result of the conference between General Lovell and the Yankee officer—and twenty-four hours later between Farragut and the Mayor.

Lovell affected an evacuation by Friday night, and on Saturday the once venerated but now degraded, desecrated and execrable Stars and Stripes was elevated upon Mint and Astrom House under the dictation of their sovereign guns.

Was not Mayor Monroe's letter a brave and dignified surrender? The forts below had not surrendered when I left the city at 10 o'clock on Saturday morning, and still holding out, had prevented the passage of transports up, so that no forces had landed or were expected to land until the transports arrived.

Then I suppose Picayune Butler may be expected to inaugurate Lincoln authority in detail. Major Clinck under General Lovell's order evacuated Ft. Pike simultaneously with the evacuation of the city.

The forts were forcefully bombarded, and made a noble resistance. Our gallant but feeble little navy also fought with desperate valor and did great damage to the enemy's superb and monster fleet. But alas it was totally annihilated, and from few of our lost vessels is there but one left to tell the story. ■

THE CAPTURE OF NEW ORLEANS

ROBERT KNOX SNEDEN'S MAP OF THE DEFENSES BELOW New Orleans details the imposing obstacle course David Farragut had to run in order to capture the South's largest city. On April 23 Farragut brought his fleet just outside the longest range of fire ❶ from the 128 guns of Forts Jackson and St. Philip, the Scylla and Charybdis of the channel. His mortar schooners ❷ had been shelling the forts with 3,000 rounds a day for six days, to little effect. Finally, at 2 a.m. on April 24, Farragut sent three divisions of 17 warships ❸ through the gantlet while his mortar fleet continued to bombard the forts.

Farragut's fleet took heavy fire from the forts, and on the water the Confederates threw everything they had at him. Tugs pulled fire scows and fire barges ❹ down the river. Rebel gunboats like the *Manassas* ❺ tried to ram Union ships and had some success, sinking the *Varuna*. Below Fort St. Philip was the ironclad *Louisiana* ❻, which, though unfinished, still had 16 working guns. And above the forts was a small flotilla ❼ commanded by Flag Officer John K. Mitchell.

All but four of Farragut's fleet got through in the hour-and-a-half assault, which cost the Union 37 men and 147 wounded. The entire Confederate fleet in New Orleans was destroyed, either by the Union or the Rebels themselves. ■

J. Joffray's 1862 painting depicts Farragut's fleet triumphantly running the defenses of New Orleans on April 24. The tremendous shelling in such a contained area created a striking pyrotechnic display. His fleet steamed into the city the next day as "crowds on the levee howled and screamed with rage," according to one onlooker. The Union flag was raised over the city April 29, beginning the martial rule of Benjamin Butler.

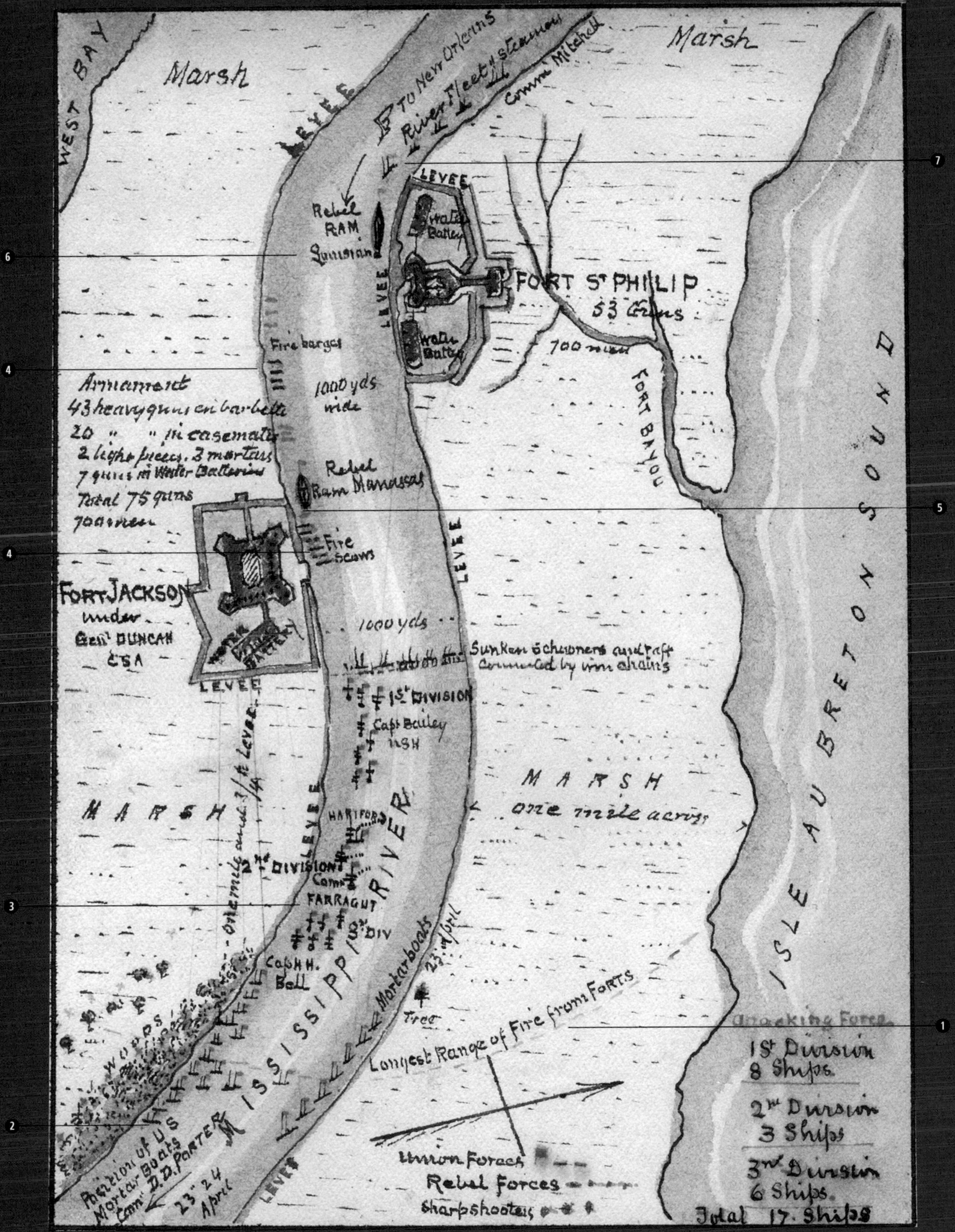

Marsh

WEST BAY

Marsh

To New Orleans

Rebel River Fleet & steamers

Comm Mitchell

Marsh

LEVEE

LEVEE

Rebel RAM Louisiana

7

LEVEE

Water Battery

FORT St PHILIP

53 Guns

6

Fire barges

1000 yds wide

Water Battery

700 men

FORT BAYOU

4

Armament
43 heavy guns en barbette
20 "   " in casemate
2 light pieces. 3 mortars
7 guns in Water Batteries
Total 75 guns
700 men

Rebel Ram Manassas

5

4

Fire scows

FORT JACKSON
under
Gen'l DUNCAN
CSA

Water Battery

LEVEE

1000 yds

Sunken Schooners and raft connected by iron chains

MARSH
one mile across

ISLE AU BRETON SOUND

LEVEE

1st DIVISION

Capt Bailey
USN

HARTFORD

3

2nd DIVISION
Comm.
FARRAGUT
3rd DIV

Cap'n H.H. Bell

One mile and 3/4 to Levee

MARSH

Mortarboats

23rd April

Tree

2

WOODS

Position of US Mortar boats
Comm. D.D. PORTER

23rd 24 April

MISSISSIPPI RIVER

LEVEE

Longest Range of Fire from FORTS

1

Union Forces
Rebel Forces
Sharpshooters

Attacking Force

1st Division
8 Ships

2nd Division
3 Ships

3rd Division
6 Ships

Total 17 Ships

CHRONOLOGY

March 17, 1862 **McClellan's Army of the Potomac begins embarking from Alexandria, Virginia, for Fort Monroe to launch campaign against Richmond.**

April 16 **Battle of Burnt Chimneys (Virginia)**

May 3 **Besieged Confederates withdraw without a battle from Yorktown.**

May 5 **Battle of Williamsburg (Virginia)**

May 23 **Battle of Front Royal (Virginia)**

May 31-June 1 **Battle of Seven Pines, or Fair Oaks, near Richmond**

June 25-July 1 **Seven Days' Battles around Richmond**

June 26 **Battle of Mechanicsville**

June 27 **Battle of Gaines's Mill**

July 1 **Battle of Malvern Hill**

August 3 **Lincoln recalls McClellan's army.**

"If General McClellan did not want to use the army, I would like to borrow it."

ABRAHAM LINCOLN

THE STRUGGLE FOR RICHMOND

GEORGE MCCLELLAN DID NOT SIMPLY COMMAND THE ARMY OF THE Potomac. He possessed it. This was "my army," he said, "as much as any army ever belonged to the man that created it." Since taking charge of Federal forces around Washington after their humiliating defeat at Bull Run in July 1861, the 35-year-old general had raised morale among discouraged veterans and tens of thousands of fresh recruits. He drilled them incessantly and brought them together for grand reviews that filled them with pride and devotion. He promised not to risk their lives prematurely and deplored the way public figures had taken up editor Horace Greeley's cry "Forward to Richmond!" and prodded raw troops into battle at Bull Run. As one of his soldiers wrote: "The rank and file think he is just the man to lead us on to victory when he gets ready and not when Horace Greeley says to go."

Pressure was building for McClellan to move against Confederates in Virginia, however. By February of 1862, President Lincoln figured that this Young Napoleon had had six months to work his huge army of well over 100,000 men into shape and should be strong enough to whip General Joseph Johnston, whose forces remained entrenched at Manassas, site of their victory in July. Lincoln favored a plan in which Federal troops would move south from Washington and threaten Johnston's flank east of Manassas, forcing him to "come out of his entrenchments & meet us in the open field," as one officer put it. But McClellan had other ideas. Based on exaggerated reports from his intelligence chief, Allan Pinkerton, he believed Johnston had as many as 150,000 troops. McClellan planned to circumvent that army by transporting his forces by boat down the Potomac to Chesapeake Bay and landing them at Urbanna, located near the mouth of the Rappahannock River some 50 miles east of Richmond. From there he hoped to advance on the Confederate capital before Johnston could redeploy to save the city. "I will stake my life, my reputation on the result," McClellan declared.

Lincoln worried that this plan would draw too many troops away from Washington and expose the capital to attack. McClellan promised to leave a sufficient force to protect the city, but some there doubted him. Radical Republicans worried that McClellan, a Democrat, was not fully committed to crushing the rebellion. Before the war, Northern Democrats like Stephen Douglas had argued that it was better to appease Southerners than to risk a ruinous conflict for the purpose of abolishing slavery and granting blacks equal rights. Such a revolution was just what radicals like Senator Sumner of Massachusetts hoped to achieve, but moderates like McClellan hoped to win the war without drastic social changes. "I will not fight for the abolitionists," he wrote his wife. He believed that the radicals "had only the negro in view, &

not the Union." They feared he might betray the Union by stopping short of complete victory or by leaving Washington prey to an attack that would shock Northerners and discredit the Republican leadership.

In early March, McClellan recalled, he met with Lincoln to discuss what the president called "a very ugly matter"—accusations that the general meant to strip Washington of defenders and give over "to the enemy the capital and the government." McClellan found it hard to believe that someone of "Lincoln's intelligence could give ear to such abominable nonsense" and took offense when Lincoln used the word "treason" to describe his alleged neglect of the capital's defenses. "Upon this I arose," McClellan related, "and, in a manner perhaps not altogether decorous towards the chief magistrate, desired that he should retract the expression, telling him that I could permit no one to couple the word treason with my name." Lincoln replied that he was merely repeating what others had said, "and that he did not believe a word of it." He had reason to resent the haughty McClellan— who had once had refused to see Lincoln when the President called on him—but did not find his political views offensive. Lincoln himself differed with radicals in his party and was not ready to make the war a crusade against slavery. What troubled him was McClellan's reluctance to risk his beloved army in battle against Confederates so close to Washington. "If General McClellan did not want to use the army," Lincoln once remarked, "I would like to borrow it."

McClellan's critics were not soothed to learn in mid-March that Confederates had abandoned Manassas and withdrawn south of the Rappahannock River, leaving behind so-called Quaker guns, made of wood but painted to look like real cannon. "The fortifications are a humbug," wrote one reporter, "and McClellan has been damnably fooled." In fact, McClellan had received accurate reports on the fake guns, but that did not cause him to lower his inflated estimate of enemy troop strength. With fewer than 50,000 men, Johnston had pulled back, burning bridges as he did so, in order to put the Rappahannock and other rivers in northern Virginia between his army and McClellan's larger force and to be closer to Richmond if it came under attack. In the process, he forced McClellan to alter his plans, for Confederates waiting below the Rappahannock could quickly counter a landing at Urbanna. Instead, he would land with his troops at Fort Monroe, outside Hampton

George McClellan stands beside his wife, Ellen, in whom he confided frequently by letter during his campaigns. "Who would have thought, when we were married," he wrote her as he took charge of the Army of the Potomac, "that I should so soon be called upon to save my country?"

> ## "It seems clear that I shall have the whole force of the enemy on my hands, probably not less than 100,000 men."
>
> GENERAL GEORGE MCCLELLAN

Roads. From there, they would advance overland to Richmond up the Peninsula, bounded by the York and James Rivers and embracing such historic sites as Yorktown and Williamsburg. The Peninsula was defended by no more than 15,000 Confederates. If McClellan moved quickly, he might dispense with that opposition before Johnston's troops arrived in sufficient numbers to impede his advance.

Some questioned whether this was the best approach to Richmond, but it was not the scheme of a commander who was holding anything back in his efforts to win the war. McClellan intended to prove his critics in Washington wrong. "Officially speaking," he wrote as he embarked for the Peninsula, "I feel very glad to get away from that sink of iniquity."

A COLOSSUS IN MOTION

MCCLELLAN WAS A MASTER OF LOGISTICS, OR MOVING AND SUPPLYING TROOPS, and the movement of his massive army to Fort Monroe went swiftly and surely. Between March 17 and early April, some 120,000 men, 15,000 animals, 1,200 wagons and ambulances, and 44 artillery batteries were shipped to the tip of the Peninsula from the Potomac River port of Alexandria, near Washington. One British observer likened the feat to the "stride of a giant." Edmund Ruffin, the old fire-eater who had promoted secession and taken one of the first shots at Fort Sumter, watched from Norfolk through a lens as Federal transports gathered off Fort Monroe. "It was impossible to count the vessels," he wrote. By now, the ironclad *Virginia* had been repaired, and its menacing presence kept Federal ships from threatening Norfolk or venturing up the James River toward Richmond. But the equally formidable *Monitor* was patrolling Hampton Roads for the Union, allowing the U.S. Navy to detach several gunboats from its blockading squadron there and send them up the York River to support McClellan's advance.

McClellan hoped to have more than 150,000 men at hand as he moved up the Peninsula, but Lincoln withheld one of his corps, comprising 38,000 men under General Irvin McDowell, to defend Washington. McClellan fumed at this high-level interference, calling it "the most infamous thing that history has recorded," but his forces still vastly outnumbered their foes on the Peninsula. Commanding the Confederates was Major General John B. Magruder, who had a flair for theatrics and staged impressive demonstrations by his troops to make them appear more numerous than they were. Holding a line that extended across the Peninsula from York-

Men of the 96th Pennsylvania Infantry parade with bayonets gleaming at their camp outside Washington. The 96th was one of more than 150 regiments of the Army of the Potomac that advanced on Richmond under McClellan.

town along the Warwick River, they were stretched thin. Yet McClellan worried that Magruder had been reinforced, and reports from scouts in observation balloons failed to enlighten him.

On April 6, Brigadier General Winfield Scott Hancock, a rising young star from Pennsylvania, led a reconnaissance in force across the Warwick River and found a weak spot in the enemy line where he thought a breakthrough could be achieved. But McClellan put more stock in the deceptive testimony of Confederate prisoners Hancock brought back, who claimed that Magruder now had 40,000 men and would be bolstered by Johnston's entire army in a day or two. "It seems clear that I shall have the whole force of the enemy on my hands," McClellan concluded, "probably not less than 100,000 men." Unaware that few of Johnston's troops had yet reached Yorktown, McClellan settled in for a siege. Lincoln was dismayed. "The present hesitation to move upon an intrenched enemy," he wrote McClellan, "is but the story of Manassas repeated." If Lincoln was so eager to attack, McClellan wrote his wife, "I was much tempted to reply that he had better come & do it himself." Magruder welcomed the reprieve and remarked scathingly: "No one but McClellan could have hesitated to attack."

McClellan still had a chance to confound his critics and score a major victory at Yorktown. Adept at siege warfare, he had heavy guns hauled laboriously into place over muddy roads that were corduroyed, or covered with logs, to bear the weight. His troops were reassured by the firepower he amassed and by the thought that Yorktown was where George Washington and his French allies had laid siege to the British and won the American Revolution. Confederates in the opposing lines found this patriotic setting no less heartening. "The old earthworks and entrenchments of the French were still well preserved," wrote one South Carolinian, "and our thoughts went back and took in with reverence the stirring times of the old days." But as the siege dragged on, men found their surroundings less inspiring. "I wish some of the grumblers at the north that are in such a hurry to have a fight could come down here and try it on," wrote Lieutenant Charles Brewster of 10th Massachusetts Infantry. "We get to sleep at night, jump up three or four times in the night and form line of battle, find it a false alarm and lie down again, get up in the morning and strip off our clothes and go to digging wood ticks out of our flesh." Men broke the monotony by bantering with enemies entrenched nearby. One Yankee, when asked by Rebels what unit he was with, claimed for his tiny state far more regiments than it could ever produce by shouting back: "150th Rhode Island!"

On April 16, McClellan sent a brigade from Vermont against the Confederates at the weak spot identified earlier by Hancock, a place called Burnt Chimneys, to keep them from strengthening their position. The Vermonters gamely forded the Warwick River and drove Confederates from their rifle pits, creating an opening that a more venturesome commander might have exploited by throwing in additional troops. But McClellan had a plan and stuck to

"No one but McClellan could have hesitated to attack."

MAJOR GENERAL JOHN B. MAGRUDER, *commander of Confederates on the Peninsula*

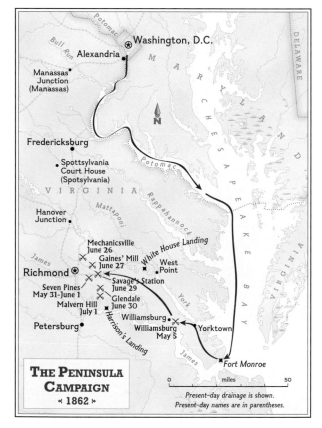

McClellan's army moved by boat from Alexandria to Fort Monroe and then marched up the Peninsula, besieging Confederates at Yorktown and clashing with them at Williamsburg before meeting the defenders of Richmond in several hard battles.

it. Reckoning that his objective had been achieved, he pulled back and proceeded with methodical preparations for a massive bombardment and assault on May 5. By then, he figured to have such superiority in artillery that he hoped to defeat the Confederates, who now had nearly 50,000 men at Yorktown, "with but little loss of life."

On May 3, anticipating McClellan's attack, Johnston withdrew his forces from Yorktown. Once again, as at Manassas in March, McClellan gained ground but let an army heavily outnumbered by his own slip away. Among his men, joy at taking Yorktown gave way to regrets. "We seemed to be celebrating a great victory and forgot our tremendous and useless labor during the siege operations," one sergeant wrote. Another officer spoke for many in the army when he lamented that the Rebels had gotten off without a fight, "as we could have taken them all prisoners and ended the war."

Johnston was intent on falling back to the outskirts of Richmond and making his stand there, but heavy rain slowed his artillery and supply wagons. On

Union artillery officers stand beside huge mortars at Yorktown capable of hitting targets more than two miles away with 220 pound shells. Hauled into place by teams of up to 100 horses, few of these siege guns were fired before Confederates abandoned Yorktown.

May 5, forces sent ahead by McClellan caught up with Johnston's rear guard at Williamsburg. It was the first big test for the Army of the Potomac, and the challenge proved too much for the commander on the spot, Brigadier General Edwin "Bull" Sumner, a crusty old officer with a booming voice who was better at fighting battles than directing them. Unlike his resourceful Confederate opponent, Major General James Longstreet, he failed to bring all his strength to bear, and thousands of Federals within striking distance remained idle. Officers under Sumner pressed the fight, however, among them Brigadier General Philip Kearny, a one-armed former soldier of fortune who boasted that he could "make men follow me to hell," and Winfield Scott Hancock, who nearly outflanked Longstreet north of town before the anxious Sumner recalled him. Hancock's men were withdrawing as ordered when Confederates attacked, taunting them with cries of "Bull Run!" because they looked to be on the run. Spoiling for a fight, the Federals turned on their foes and routed them. "Hancock was superb," declared McClellan, who arrived from Yorktown late in the day. His army took Williamsburg but lost nearly 2,300 men in the process, 600 more than Longstreet's force, which withdrew in good order.

One day after the Battle of Williamsburg, Abraham Lincoln arrived by boat at Fort Monroe to see for himself where matters stood. McClellan's progress was encouraging, but Lincoln was dismayed to find Norfolk still in enemy hands as Confederates withdrew from the Peninsula and left that town exposed. Prodded into action by the president, 78-year-old Major General John Wool led 5,000 troops ashore along the bay east of Norfolk on May 9 and marched on the port. Confederate forces abandoned Norfolk to Wool after demolishing Gosport Navy Yard and blowing up the famed ironclad *Virginia*, which had too deep a draft to retreat with other vessels upriver. Lincoln relished his brief stint as a field commander. "He fairly hugged General Wool," wrote Secretary of the Treasury Salmon P. Chase, who returned with him to Washington after a "brilliant week's campaign." Meanwhile, a newly commissioned Union ironclad, the *Galena*, was leading a squadron of gunboats that included the *Monitor* up the James River to bombard Richmond. On May 15, the squadron was stopped just short of its goal by a battery atop 200-foot-high Drewry's Bluff commanded by Colonel Custis Lee, Robert E. Lee's eldest son. In a scene reminiscent of the artillery duel at Fort Donelson in February, Lee's men, who were safely out of range of the *Monitor*'s guns, battered the heavily armored *Galena* with plunging fire and drove the gunboats back downriver.

By late May, McClellan's forces were drawn up along the Chickahominy River northeast of Richmond. Some units were within ten miles of the city, close enough to hear church bells ringing there. McClellan eagerly awaited McDowell's Corps, which Lincoln had promised him for the assault on the capital. But those plans were upset by Confederates under Major General Stonewall Jackson, who was waging a brilliant campaign in Virginia's Shenandoah Valley that rekindled fears for Washington's safety as the struggle for Richmond neared its climax. Jackson, who never had more than 17,000 men, outmaneuvered much larger Federal forces by driving his "foot cavalry"—

troops who marched up to 35 miles a day—relentlessly across terrain he knew far better than his foes. "Old Jack is a hard master," one of his men complained, but they soon recognized that hard marching brought swift victories and held down casualties, which Jackson could ill afford. As he said one evening before ordering his men back on the road after two hour's rest: "I am obliged to sweat them tonight, that I may save their blood tomorrow." By ousting Federal troops from Front Royal at the northern end of the Shenandoah on May 23, he drew within 70 miles of Washington and prompted Lincoln to send McDowell's Corps to the valley in response, thus denying McClellan reinforcements that would have given him an advantage of more than two to one over his opponents.

As it was, McClellan's army still greatly outnumbered Johnston's. When Johnston learned that McDowell's Corps was not moving toward Richmond, he decided to attack before the situation changed and his foe grew any stronger. McClellan, meanwhile, railed at Lincoln and his Cabinet for being taken in by Jackson's grand diversion, protesting in one letter: "Heaven save a country governed by such counsels!"

CHAOS AT SEVEN PINES

JEFFERSON DAVIS MIGHT HAVE RESTED EASIER IN RICHMOND HAD THE CITY'S FATE been in the hands of another General Johnston—Albert Sidney Johnston of Texas, who died in battle at Shiloh in April. Unlike that fallen hero, Joseph Johnston of Virginia never had the full confidence of his commander-in-chief. Some said the two men had been at odds ever since they quarreled over a

Federal engineers complete a corduroy road in a swampy area near the Chickahominy River by packing dirt over a bed of stones and logs. Many men campaigning in this area came down with so-called Chickahominy fever, which may have been malaria or some other disease endemic to these swamplands.

JACKSON'S VALLEY CAMPAIGN

THE MAN WHO EARNED THE nickname "Stonewall" at Bull Run lived up to his new moniker, and then some, with a campaign of diversion and obstruction in the Shenandoah Valley that quite possibly saved Richmond from falling in the spring of 1862. Using speed and the lay of the land to maximum advantage, General Thomas Jackson foiled the attempts of three Union commands to destroy his small army, whose furious marching earned them a nickname of their own: "Jackson's foot cavalry."

As part of the Federals' Peninsula Campaign, Major General Nathaniel P. Banks was charged with expelling Jackson from the valley, clearing the way for Irvin McDowell and George McClellan to converge on Richmond. Jackson's orders from Joseph E. Johnston were simply to keep Banks busy. But Jackson, emboldened by bad intelligence, led 3,400 men into Kernstown in March against what turned out to be a 9,000-man infantry division commanded by Brigadier General James Shields, and were routed. The cloud of defeat, though, contained a silver lining: Lincoln, feeling threatened by Jackson's persistence, decided to keep Banks in the valley and McDowell's Corps near Fredericksburg, depriving McClellan of more than 30,000 troops.

"If the enemy can succeed so readily in disconcerting all our plans by alarming us first at one point, then at another," said McDowell after his march was halted, "he will paralyze a large force with a very small one." Jackson's strategy was a brilliant study in just that: "Always mystify, mislead and surprise the enemy. Never fight against heavy odds if . . . you can hurl your own force on only a part. A small army may thus destroy a large one."

Jackson embarked on his Valley

> **"It was said by some of the boys who timed us that we once marched three miles in thirty-three minutes."**
>
> ONE OF JACKSON'S INFANTRYMAN

Campaign with 17,000 men, half the enemy's strength. In May Jackson faked a move to Richmond by marching his army across the Blue Ridge, then trained back and won the Battle of McDowell on May 8. Banks's division expected the next attack at Strasburg. Instead, Turner Ashby's cavalry feinted attacks at Strasburg while Jackson marched across Massanutten Mountain into the Luray valley and routed a small Union force at Front Royal on May 23. Suddenly Jackson was ten miles east of Banks's flank with a two-to-one man advantage.

Ashby was one of two men instrumental in helping Jackson outmaneuver the Federals. Known as the Black Knight, he was "light, active, skilful, and we are tormented by him like a bull with a gadfly," wrote one Union soldier. The other was the mapmaker Jedediah Hotchkiss, whose detailed surveying of the valley gave Jackson a tremendous advantage over his opponents in navigating the tricky terrain. The Hotchkiss map Jackson carried was eight and a half feet long.

THE FOOT CAVALRY STRIKES

FROM FRONT ROYAL, JACKSON'S ARMY MARCHED NORTH AND won the Battle of Winchester on May 25, forcing Banks across the Potomac and taking so many supplies off him that the Rebels took to calling him "Commissary Banks." Lincoln ordered McDowell and Frémont, now in command west of the Blue Ridge, to converge on Strasburg, cutting off Jackson's escape route back through the valley. For all practical purposes, the coordinated attack on Richmond was scotched.

Though both Frémont's and McDowell's forces (under Shields's command) were closer to Strasburg,

Stonewall Jackson's cap, a relic of his days at the Virginia Military Institute, was a reflection of his view of life—as he once told his wife, "I like simplicity."

Jackson beat them there along the Valley Pike, slipping through on June 1. The speed with which his men marched through the valley and then back again—646 miles in 48 days all told—is what earned them comparison to cavalrymen. But this glory came at a high price. "He druv us like Hell," said one veteran. An officer said that Jackson considered "all who were weak and weary, who fainted by the wayside, as men wanting in patriotism." Another criticized his "utter disregard for human suffering."

In fact, Jackson was almost without an army for the spring, driving his troops to near mutiny during the winter with an ill-conceived campaign into West Virginia. The same men who would come to call him "Old Jack" during the Valley Campaign had earlier called him "Old Tom Fool." Jackson's famous eccentricities—his aversion to pepper and his habit of sucking lemons on the battlefield—certainly played into this, as well as his religious fervor. "Praying and fighting appeared to be his idea of the 'whole duty of man'," said General Richard Taylor.

After escaping through Strasburg, the chase was on, and

Artist and cartographer David English Henderson painted The Halt of the Stonewall Brigade, depicting Jackson and his staff resting in the Shenandoah Valley. The work vividly shows the rolling and often rugged terrain Jackson's foot cavalry had to traverse during their breakneck marching campaign.

the combined forces of Frémont and Shields, marching parallel on either side of the Shenandoah River, threatened to overwhelm Jackson's army. Ashby once again kept the two commands distracted and separated, picking fights and burning bridges until he was killed June 6 near Harrisonburg in a skirmish with the Pennsylvania Bucktails. Jackson made it to Port Republic, setting up defenses near the only intact bridge, with Frémont and Shields stranded on opposite sides of the river from one another.

A token force under Richard S. Ewell fought with Frémont at the Battle of Cross Keys on June 8, keeping him at bay while Jackson concentrated the rest of his force, almost 8,000 men, against 3,000 of Shields's men at the Battle of Port Republic on June 9. Whipped again, the Union slowly retreated from the valley. Jackson had won five battles against three Union commands totaling 33,000 men, bringing superior numbers to each battle save Cross Keys. In all he diverted 60,000 Union troops from Richmond, and Jackson himself took on an aura of invincibility that would last until his death. ∎

woman as cadets at West Point. But the more immediate problem was that Davis, chronically short of resources, longed for a commander here who could do more with less. Johnston's awareness of the enemy's strength reinforced his penchant for tactical withdrawals, at which he excelled. Davis considered him overcautious and wanted him to attack before McClellan crossed the Chickahominy and "matured his preparations for a siege of Richmond." Instead, Johnston waited until his opponent had pushed two of his five corps south across the river and set out to smash that exposed flank. It was a great opportunity, but his complex plan of attack called for Confederates to advance in several columns on separate paths, far out of sight of one another, before converging on the foe. At odds with Davis, Johnston did not consult him or his military adviser, Robert E. Lee, who might have helped refine the plan.

Johnston's attack got off to a bad start on May 31 when the usually reliable General Longstreet took the wrong road and led an entire division astray. That left much of the fighting to troops under Major General Daniel Harvey Hill of North Carolina, who rode up front, calmly smoking a cigar. "I saw that our men were wavering," he said, "and wanted to give them confidence." Hill's troops bore down on Brigadier General Silas Casey's shaky Federals, who were new to battle and fell back in disarray. "Old Casey was as brave as a lion," one witness wrote, and roared at his men to hold their ground, but to no avail. As Hill's troops pushed through Casey's camp toward a crossroads called Seven Pines, however, they were hit in the flank by the irrepressible Phil Kearny, who reveled in battle and was not too fine about it. When an officer asked him where to deploy, he replied that any place would do: "You'll find lovely fighting all along the line." Among the Confederates facing Kearny was Colonel John B. Gordon of Alabama, who was leading troops into battle when he saw that his younger brother, a captain under him, had fallen wounded. "He was lying with a number of dead companions near him," Gordon recalled. "He had been shot through the lungs and was bleeding profusely. I did not stop; I could not stop, nor would he permit me to stop. There was no time for that—no time for anything except to move on and fire on."

Belatedly, Longstreet got back on track and sent in troops to support Hill's hard-pressed division, including a brigade of Virginians led by Colonel John C. Kemper. But the Federals were ready for them. "Every deadly projectile which could take human life and maim and disfigure was showered upon us," recalled Alexander Hunter of the 17th Virginia Infantry. Things got even hotter for the Confederates when Bull Sumner pushed his corps across a rickety log bridge over the flood-swollen Chickahominy and bolstered Union forces below the river. Late that afternoon, General Johnston brought up reinforcements. An officer with him could not keep from flinching when he heard shells bursting and bullets whizzing by. "Colonel, there is no use dodging," Johnston told him; "when you hear them they have passed." Moments later, Johnston was hit twice, in the shoulder and the chest, and fell from his horse. He regained consciousness long enough to ask an aide to retrieve his sword and pistols. The sword, he explained, "was the one worn by my father in the old Revolutionary War and I would not lose it for ten thousand dollars." Johnston

"You'll find lovely fighting all along the line."

FEDERAL BRIGADIER
GENERAL PHILIP KEARNY,
at Seven Pines

Aeronaut Thaddeus Lowe, who performed reconnaissance for McClellan, ascends in his balloon, Intrepid, while men on the ground hold mooring ropes to keep the craft from drifting away. Such ascents yielded little useful intelligence because much of the Peninsula was forested, shielding Confederates from aerial detection.

survived but had to be replaced as commander—a twist of fate that altered the course of this second American Revolution.

The Battle of Seven Pines continued the next day, June 1, under Johnston's second-in-command, Major General Gustavus Smith. Unnerved by the responsibility, Smith spent an agonizing night before ordering the attack renewed. Longstreet and other officers doubted his resolve and held back forces to cut their losses, which were already appalling. The chaotic battle ended that afternoon with the Confederates having gained nothing for their sacrifice—more than 6,000 casualties, compared to 5,000 for the Federals. On June 2, Davis sacked Smith and entrusted the defense of Richmond to Robert E. Lee, a commander perfectly suited by temperament to challenge McClellan.

LEE TAKES CHARGE

MCCLELLAN WELCOMED THE CHANGE IN COMMAND. "I PREFER LEE TO JOHNston," he wrote, surmising that Lee—whose plans for defending western Virginia had misfired in 1861—was "wanting in moral firmness when pressed by

Men of Battery C, 3rd U.S. Artillery—one of many such Regular Army units bolstering McClellan's forces around Richmond—prepare for battle. On May 31 at Seven Pines, one five-gun U.S. battery fired 343 rounds, subjecting opposing Confederates to "a tremendous fire," an officer reported, "which they were unable to stand."

Private Drury L. Armistead

STAFF, MAJOR GENERAL JOSEPH E. JOHNSTON

*While leading his men in the fighting at Seven Pines, Confederate General Joseph E. Johnston was
severely wounded by shell fragments. One of his couriers, Drury Armistead of the 3rd Virginia Cavalry,
rode to the stricken general's aid. Armistead recalled his success in retrieving Johnson's treasured sword and pistols.
After the battle Johnston presented one of the pistols to Armistead, engraved on one side:
"From General Joseph E. Johnston to D. L. Armistead," and on the reverse, "Seven Pines."*

GENERAL JOHNSTON AND staff rode back about two hundred yards to an elevated position near a small house, which he occupied until he was wounded. The fire of artillery and musketry in our front was then terrific. I being in a few yards of where General Johnston sat on his horse, dismounted and stood with my horse before me. I had an oil cloth strapped on the front of my saddle directly in front of my breast. The minnie balls were flying so very thick I thought I would stoop a little behind my horse, when as I stooped a bullet tore through the oil cloth, just missing the top of my head. It was a powerful close shave. About this time fresh troops going into battle stopped to load their muskets near where I stood, and double-quicked towards the enemy. When the line moved forward after loading, there was an old fellow who had not finished loading, and while thus standing, a shell struck the ground in a few feet of him; but he coolly remarked to himself, "you cannot do that again!" During this time the battle was raging with great fury all along the line.

Most of General Johnston's staff having been sent off on duty except

> ## "The sword was the one worn by my father in the old Revolutionary War."
>
> MAJOR GENERAL JOSEPH E. JOHNSTON

myself and Colonel ____, and the air seeming to be alive with whizzing bullets and bursting shells, Colonel ____ would move his head from side to side, as if trying to dodge them. General Johnston turned toward him and smiling said: "Colonel, there is no use of dodging; when you hear them they have passed." Just after saying this a shell exploded immediately in his front, striking the General from his horse, severely wounded and unconscious. I immediately sprang forward, catching him up in my arms, carried him out of the enemy's fire. Others coming to my assistance we moved him back about a quarter of a mile, and laying him down, hastily sent for a stretcher.

He then regained consciousness, and finding that he had lost his sword and pistols said: "The sword was the one worn by my father in the old Revolutionary War and I would not lose it for ten thousand dollars; will not some one please go back and get it and the

pistols for me?" And several others and myself volunteered. On returning to the battle-field we found our line had been considerably pressed back and the spot where General Johnston fell to be midway between the line of battle, which was blazing in all its fury, with men falling all around like leaves. I dashed through our line to the spot where the General had fallen, snatched up the sword and pistols, jumped upon my horse and was making back to our lines, when I hadn't got more than twenty yards when one of the pistols fell out of my hand. I quickly sprang to the ground, picked it up, when just as I did so a discharge of grape from a battery of artillery planted within a hundred and fifty yards from where I was, tore up the earth all around me; but I leaped upon my horse and reached our lines in safety, where I met one of the men who had volunteered to go back for the sword and pistols. He demanded me to turn them over to him. I said: "No; I will take them to the General myself." He replied, "I am your superior officer, and have the right to order you." I said, "Superior officer or not, you will not get this sword and these pistols unless you are a better man than I am, and I don't think you are." ∎

heavy responsibility & is likely to be timid & irresolute in action." It was McClellan's firmness that would now be tested, however. "I feel sure of success," he wrote his wife after Seven Pines, but success in this arena came at a forbidding price. "I am tired of the sickening sight of the battlefield, with its mangled corpses & poor suffering wounded!" he confided. "Victory has no charms for me when purchased at such cost." Could he bear to see the army he nurtured battered and bloodied relentlessly by an opponent he misread? Beneath Lee's genteel exterior beat the fierce heart of a warrior willing to expose his forces to huge risks and horrific punishment in pursuit of victories that would break the Union's will and end the war.

Men close to Lee such as Colonel Joseph Ives caught glimpses of the fire within that flared up when he was challenged. When one Confederate officer questioned whether Lee had the audacity required "to meet the enemy's superior force," Ives replied emphatically: "His name might be Audacity. He will take more desperate chances, and take them quicker, than any other general in this country, North or South." Lee came to embody the Confederate spirit of resistance, which ran highest when Southerners were under siege. "Richmond must not be given up; it shall not be given up!" he vowed.

Many in that beleaguered city shared his resolve. As McClellan and his troops approached Richmond, women there stitched together 30,000 sandbags for Confederate fortifications in two days. Sick and wounded troops who could have lingered in the city's hospitals hurried back into line to defend the capital. John Beauchamp Jones, a War Department clerk, met with a soldier from South Carolina who looked about 15 and had his hand in a sling. "A ball had entered between the fingers of his left hand and lodged near the wrist, where the flesh was much swollen," Jones noted. But the youngster was smiling and wanted no sympathy. "I'm going to the hospital just to have the ball cut out, and will then return to the battlefield," he declared. "I can fight with my right hand."

McClellan proceeded against Richmond as he had against Yorktown. "I will bring up my heavy guns, shell the city, and carry it by assault," he wrote. His preparations were elaborate and time-consuming, slowed by bad weather and sloppy roads. Meanwhile, Lee had his men dig in to discourage the Federals, who now had four of their five corps south of the Chickahominy, from advancing any closer to the city. Those precautions reinforced McClellan's assumption that his supposedly timid opponent would remain on the defensive. In fact, Lee was preparing to take a huge gamble by leaving a small portion of his army entrenched below the Chickahominy to shield Richmond while the remainder crossed to the north and linked up with Jackson's troops from the Shenandoah Valley to smash McClellan's exposed right flank above the river.

To reconnoiter that flank, Lee sent his dashing young cavalry commander, Brigadier General Jeb Stuart, out with 1,200 troopers on an expedition that became legendary. After crossing the Chickahominy northwest of Richmond on June 12 and gathering intelligence as ordered, Stuart kept going and rode clear around McClellan's army. Along the way, he destroyed supplies, clashed with enemy forces—and bedeviled his accomplished father-

> "I am tired of the sickening sight of the battlefield, with its mangled corpses & poor suffering wounded! Victory has no charms for me when purchased at such cost."
> GENERAL GEORGE MCCLELLAN

> "Richmond must not be given up; it shall not be given up!"
> GENERAL ROBERT E. LEE

"Stuart must be a
great general to foil his
father-in-law."

CONFEDERATE LIEUTENANT
JOHN ESTEN COOKE

*The dashing Confederate cavalry commander
James Ewell Brown (Jeb) Stuart thrilled the
South by riding clear around McClellan's army
on a reconnaissance mission in June. Newspapers were "filled with accounts of the expedition," one of Stuart's aides remarked, "none
accurate, and most of them marvelous."*

in-law, Brigadier General Philip St. George Cooke, a Unionist from Virginia in charge of Federal cavalry. Another member of this divided family, Confederate Lieutenant John Esten Cooke—Philip Cooke's nephew—rode with Jeb Stuart and called it a "splendid affair." Philip Cooke just missed catching up with them as they crossed back over the Chickahominy on a hastily improvised bridge east of Richmond on June 14 and completed their coup. "Stuart must be a great general to foil his father-in-law," concluded a jubilant John Esten Cooke.

Late that month, the struggle for Richmond came to a furious climax with the Seven Days' Battles, which began on June 25 with an attempt by McClellan to advance south of the Chickahominy River and bring his siege guns closer to Richmond. The Federals gained some ground in hard fighting around Oak Grove, but reports that Stonewall Jackson's forces were on their way from the Shenandoah to reinforce Lee stunned McClellan and put him on the defensive. On June 26, Lee attacked Federals dug in north of the Chickahominy near the town of Mechanicsville, trusting that Jackson would hurry his men into line to support that assault. For once, Jackson and his stalwarts—exhausted by months of hard campaigning—rested when the enemy was near and missed the battle. Without them, the Confederates took a terrible beating. It was "a bloody and disastrous repulse," wrote General D. H. Hill, who saw one of his regiments, the 44th Georgia Infantry, lose more than 300 of its 500 men. "We have again whipped the secesh badly," exulted McClellan. "I almost begin to think we are invincible." Yet he made no move against the vulnerable Confederate forces below the Chickahominy, where General Magruder, shielding Richmond with fewer than 25,000 men against three times as many Federals, again staged clever demonstrations to intimidate his opponents.

While McClellan held back, Lee pressed forward, renewing his attack on June 27 against Major General Fitz-John Porter, who had remained above the Chickahominy to guard Federal supply lines with his corps of nearly 30,000 men and made his stand now on high ground near Gaines's Mill. Lee threw everything he had except Magruder's troops against Porter—some 55,000 men in all, including Jackson's force, which rallied after a night's rest and reached the field that afternoon while the battle was raging. Lee challenged the long-awaited hero of the Shenandoah to live up to his reputation. "That fire is very heavy," he remarked, gesturing to the smoke-shrouded plateau where Porter's Federals were repulsing one charge after another. "Do you think your men can stand it?

"They can stand almost anything," Jackson shot back. "They can stand that!" Then he began dispatching orders and sucking on a lemon—a sure sign to his troops that they were in for a hard fight. Many other Civil War battles lasted longer, but few matched the intensity of this firestorm. "We slaughtered them big," one Pennsylvanian recalled, "and they killed a great many of us." Late that day, Brigadier General John Bell Hood, a daring young officer placed recently under Jackson's command, pushed his Texas Brigade up

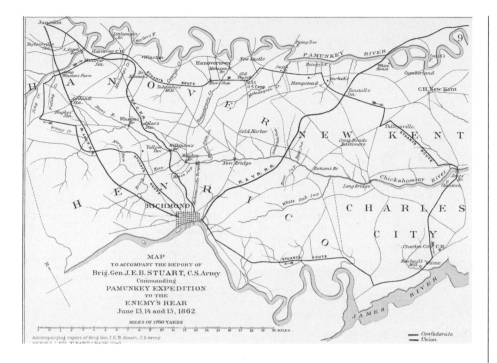

the slope and punctured the enemy line with a thunderous volley that one Federal called "the most withering I ever saw delivered." As attackers poured through the breach, Union batteries to the rear unleashed fearsome canister blasts that cut down dozens of Confederates at a time. "There was dreadful carnage in their ranks," one gunner observed, "but each horrible gap was instantly closed up, and the column pressed forward." Unhinged by Hood's breakthrough, Porter's men fled the field and retreated across the Chickahominy as darkness fell.

Nearly 3,000 Federals were captured and 4,000 killed or wounded at Gaines's Mill in a fateful battle that cost the Confederates almost 9,000 casualties but broke the siege of Richmond. That night, after blaming Secretary of War Edwin Stanton and other high officials in writing for withholding reinforcements and doing their best "to sacrifice this army," McClellan announced what he called a "change of base." He would withdraw to Harrison's Landing on the James River, where he hoped to hold off Lee's forces with the aid of Federal gunboats and supply ships.

Over the next few days, Lee kept up the pressure, hoping to cut off McClellan's retreat and crush his army. But the wary Yankees beat back several Rebel onslaughts, the last coming on July 1 at Malvern Hill, near Harrison's Landing. Lee, audacious to a fault, suffered more than 5,000 casualties there assailing a forbiddingly strong position to no gain. "It was not war," concluded D. H. Hill, "it was murder." Afterward, officers urged McClellan to strike back at Lee—who had lost one fourth of his army in the past week—and try for Richmond. But McClellan would not attack unless his forces were heavily reinforced and abandoned Malvern Hill to hunker down at Harrison's Landing. The combative Phil Kearny was outraged and protested "this order of retreat," which he felt could only be prompted "by cowardice or treason."

Lincoln withheld judgment and visited McClellan by boat at Harrison's

> ## "It was not war— it was murder."
>
> CONFEDERATE GENERAL D. H. HILL, *at Malvern Hill*

Landing to see if it was still possible to renew the offensive. But the general taxed his chief's patience to the limit by asking for 100,000 more troops and warning him by letter not to make the war a crusade against slavery—a radical step Lincoln was now seriously considering as a way of depriving Confederates of slave labor and galvanizing the Northern war effort. After more than a month in limbo, McClellan was recalled, and he and his forces were shipped north. In Richmond there was great relief but little joy, for the carnage of the Seven Days was overwhelming and inescapable. "The whole city is a hospital and the very atmosphere is poisoned & loathsome," wrote one soldier there. Southerners who had defied the Union to preserve their old ways were beginning to suspect that when this bloody revolution was over, life would never be the same.

[EYEWITNESS]

General Robert E. Lee
COMMANDER, ARMY OF NORTHERN VIRGINIA

In the aftermath of the hard-fought Seven Days Campaign, Lee dispatched an official report to Confederate Adjutant General Samuel Cooper. After detailing the battles, Lee admitted his disappointment that McClellan's army had not been destroyed. Nevertheless, he concluded, the outcome of the battles had been extraordinary and he acknowledged his respect for the newly forged Army of Northern Virginia. In his typical fashion, Lee attributed ultimate success, however, to "the Sovereign Ruler of the Universe."

UNDER ORDINARY CIRCUMstances the Federal Army should have been destroyed. Its escape was due to the causes already stated. Prominent among these is the want of correct and timely information. This fact, attributable chiefly to the character of the country, enabled General McClellan skillfully to conceal his retreat and to add much to the obstructions with which nature had beset the way of our pursuing columns; but regret that more was not accomplished gives way to gratitude to the Sovereign Ruler of the Universe for the results achieved. The siege of Richmond was raised, and the object of a campaign, which had been prosecuted after months of preparation at an enormous expenditure of men and money, completely frustrated. More than 10,000 prisoners, including officers of rank, 52 pieces of artillery, and upward of 35,000 stands of small-

"Under ordinary circumstances the Federal Army should have been destroyed."

arms were captured. The stores and supplies of every description which fell into our hands were great in amount and value, but small in comparison to those destroyed by the enemy. His losses in battle exceeded our own, as attested by the thousands of dead and wounded left on every field, while his subsequent inaction shows in what condition the survivors reached the protection to which they fled. . . .

Among the dead will be found many whose names will ever be associated with the great events in which they all bore so honorable a part. For these, as well as for the names of their no less distinguished surviving comrades, who earned for themselves the high honor of special commendation, where all so well discharged their duty, reference must necessarily be made to the accompanying reports. But I cannot forbear expressing my admiration of the noble qualities displayed, with rare exceptions, by officers and men, under circumstances which demanded the exercise of every soldierly virtue. ■

"I think we shall at least change the theater of war from the James to north of the Rappahannock."

GENERAL ROBERT E. LEE

NORTH TO ANTIETAM

ROBERT E. LEE EARNED HIGH PRAISE IN THE SOUTH FOR DEFENDING Richmond, but he was not about to rest on his laurels. Once he felt sure the city was safe, he planned to march his army north and drive Union troops back toward their own capital. "I think we shall at least change the theater of war from the James to north of the Rappahannock," he wrote. Although his immediate goal was to defeat Federal forces in Virginia, larger possibilities loomed on the horizon. An attack on fortified Washington might prove too costly for his army, but Union-controlled Maryland was ripe for invasion. Some Southerners felt it was time they moved beyond defending their own soil and took the fight to the enemy. The idea appealed to Lee, who believed that only bold action would allow the upstart Confederacy to topple the Union goliath. If he did not force the issue, he feared, Northern might would soon crush Southern resistance. Driven by a sense of urgency, he launched a bold campaign in early August that would carry Confederates triumphantly back to Manassas and on into Maryland, culminating in an explosive showdown at Antietam that would be remembered as America's bloodiest day.

If Lee needed any incentive to move aggressively against the Federals to his north, he found it in the provocative edicts of their commander, Major General John Pope. A 40-year-old Kentuckian, Pope had recently ousted Confederates from fortifications along a great bend in the Mississippi River near New Madrid, Missouri. That cleared the way for a Union fleet to seize Memphis in June, leaving Vicksburg as the chief obstacle to Federal control of the Mississippi. The promising Pope was summoned to Washington to command the newly formed Army of Virginia while McClellan's Army of the Potomac was being driven from Richmond. He considered McClellan overcautious and took a swipe at the Young Napoleon in a proclamation issued to his troops. "I have come to you from the West," Pope announced, "where we have always seen the backs of our enemies; from an army whose business it has been to seek the adversary and to beat him when he was found." Men should dismiss from their minds defeatist phrases such as "lines of retreat" and think only of moving forward: "Success and glory are in the advance."

Lee grew angry with his blustering opponent when he learned that Pope had ordered the arrest of all "disloyal male citizens" within his lines. Those who refused to pledge allegiance to the United States, Pope added, would be banished from occupied territory and executed as spies if they returned. Civilians who attacked Federal troops or property would be shot without a trial, he warned, and people harboring such guerrillas would have their homes "razed to the ground." Lee responded by threatening to retaliate against Federal officers if civilians were killed. "I want Pope to be suppressed," he told

Stonewall Jackson. Informed that a nephew of his had enlisted with the Union and was serving in northern Virginia, Lee remarked that he might forgive the young man for "fighting against us if he had not have joined such a miscreant as Pope."

The indignation Lee felt strengthened his resolve to move quickly against Pope's army, which was roughly equal in size to his own and would soon receive additional forces from McClellan as his army withdrew from the Peninsula by boat. Those reinforcements would prove a mixed blessing, for they included a corps commanded by General Fitz-John Porter, who revered McClellan and despised Pope. Lee, meanwhile, was reorganizing his army to ensure that his top commanders were men he could trust. "I plan and work with all my might to bring the troops to the right place at the right time," he wrote. Beyond that, the outcome was in the hands of God—and the battle-tested subordinates to whom Lee delegated great responsibility. He divided his Army of Northern Virginia into two commands, or wings, one led by Stonewall Jackson and the other by James Longstreet, and drew up plans that were flexible enough to allow those gifted and strong-willed generals to exercise their judgment. To try to dictate their every move, he reckoned, "would do more harm than good."

On August 3, Lee received a report confirming his suspicions that Federal forces would soon leave the Peninsula and head up the Chesapeake to reinforce Pope's army. Confident that Richmond was no longer in danger, Lee instructed Jackson to advance on Pope's forces around Culpeper, below the Rappahannock River. Jackson had nearly 25,000 men, including a division led by Major General Ambrose Powell Hill, a hot-tempered Virginian who resented the secretive Jackson for keeping him in the dark. "I do not know whether we march north, south, east, or west," A. P. Hill remarked before they set out. "General Jackson has simply ordered me to have the division ready to march at dawn." Despite the lack of rapport between the two men, Hill's fast-moving light division nicely complemented Jackson's hard-marching "foot cavalry," as veterans of his Shenandoah Valley campaign were known.

On August 9, Jackson's vanguard came up against Federals led by Major General Nathaniel Banks near Cedar Mountain, south of Culpeper. Banks, an inexperienced corps commander under Pope, took a big risk by throwing his 9,000 men against Jackson's much larger command, but he struck at the right time. A. P. Hill, confused by vague marching orders, had not yet reached Cedar Mountain with his troops when the battle erupted. "The heat was excessive, more than flesh and blood could stand," one soldier recalled, but the day grew even hotter when Federals rushed unexpectedly from the woods and slammed into Confederates on Jackson's left, forcing them back in disarray. Jackson was shocked to learn that his trusty Stonewall Brigade had given way and that one of his best officers, Brigadier General Charles Winder, had been killed.

"I have come to you from the West, where we have always seen the backs of our enemies."

MAJOR GENERAL JOHN POPE,
*Federal commander of
the newly formed Army of Virginia*

John Pope, after taking command of Federal forces in northern Virginia in June, issued statements that antagonized both his opponent Robert E. Lee and his fellow commander George McClellan. "The Pope bubble is likely to be suddenly collapsed," wrote McClellan, who predicted that this "paltry young man who wanted to teach me the art of war" would soon be "in full retreat or badly whipped."

Fugitive slaves seek refuge at a Federal camp near the Rappahannock River in Virginia in August. Harbored as "contraband," such fugitives aided the Union war effort in many ways, including building fortifications and alerting commanders to enemy movements.

But he moved quickly to rally his men. "Your general will lead you," he shouted with sword raised. "Follow me!" Jackson was "lit with the inspiration of heroism," one witness wrote. "The men would have followed him into the jaws of death itself; nothing could have stopped them and nothing did."

Jackson's rally and the belated arrival of Hill's division turned the tide. By nightfall the battered Federals were back where they started, having lost almost 2,400 men, some of them victims of sunstroke, which killed soldiers on both sides. Jackson suffered a thousand fewer casualties than Banks, but his failure to communicate clearly with Hill and other subordinates made this fight tougher for his forces than it should have been. Although the battle was inconclusive, the result was hard for Pope to swallow. His stated policy was to move forward relentlessly and attack, but he now had to regroup at Culpeper, and he would soon have to fall back as Lee pressed him harder, demonstrating that bold words were no substitute for a well-conceived offensive.

There was little joy in the Federal camp after the battle. Pope and his senior corps commander, General Irvin McDowell, were sitting together under an apple tree when soldiers carried a dead man by on a litter, followed by troops wielding picks and spades. Observing this grim procession, Pope remarked, "Well, there seems to be devilish little that is attractive about the life of the private soldier." McDowell, unsettled by his own defeat at Bull Run a year earlier and unsure if Pope would fare any better, thought his observation should not be limited to privates. Life was not looking very attractive, McDowell ventured to say, for soldiers of "any grade."

RETURN TO MANASSAS

SHORTLY AFTER THE BATTLE OF CEDAR MOUNTAIN, LEE COMMITTED 30,000 MEN under Longstreet to the campaign and made plans to isolate Pope below the Rappahannock by sending cavalry under Jeb Stuart to destroy a bridge over that river. Before Stuart could accomplish his mission, however, Union troopers raided his camp and captured an officer carrying documents that divulged Lee's plan, prompting Pope to withdraw north of the Rappahannock. Stuart, who lost his distinctive plumed hat in the raid, got even a few days later by raiding Pope's headquarters at Catlett's Station while the general was away and making off with his dress uniform. "You have my hat and plume," Stuart wrote Pope. "I have your best coat." He proposed a "fair exchange," but Pope had larger concerns than retrieving his coat. Of more importance were dispatches Stuart seized at Catlett's Station, confirming that Pope would soon be reinforced by Fitz-John Porter's Corps and other elements of McClellan's army. That news spurred Lee to take one of his biggest gambles ever. Conventional wisdom called for a commander in his position, facing a numerically superior foe, to concentrate his forces. Instead, he divided his army by sending Jackson and his men on a wide sweep to the west and north of Pope's army that would bring them around through Thoroughfare Gap, a pass in the Bull Run Mountains, to Manassas.

As Jackson headed off on August 25, Longstreet remained along the Rappahannock with his forces and demonstrated menacingly, seeking, as he put it, "to impress Pope with the idea that I was attempting to force a passage to his front." The real danger, however, lay not to Pope's front but to his rear, where Jackson would soon appear. As the Federals fell back to deal with that threat, Lee would move with Longstreet's command to Manassas on the same path taken by Jackson and throw his entire army against Pope while he was distracted and off balance.

Pope could not imagine that Lee would do something so daring and unorthodox. When he learned that Jackson had raided a Federal supply depot near Manassas on the night of August 26, he thought it was merely a foray and assumed that Jackson would soon head west to join the rest of Lee's army, which Pope believed was destined for the Shenandoah Valley. Pope had two corps under McDowell and Major General Franz Sigel stationed near Thoroughfare Gap, where they could have blocked Longstreet's command and prevented Lee from reuniting his army, but he summoned them now to Manassas to help nab Jackson's raiders. "If you will march promptly and rapidly at the earliest dawn of day," Pope instructed McDowell late on August 27, "we shall bag the whole crowd."

Jackson played his part to perfection. After announcing his presence by raiding the Manassas supply depot—where he allowed his hungry men to gorge on food but destroyed hundreds of barrels of liquor, explaining that he feared

"**The men would have followed him into the jaws of death itself; nothing could have stopped them and nothing did.**"

Confederate officer with Stonewall Jackson at Cedar Mountain

the effects of "that whiskey more than I do Pope's army"—sent his three divisions off on separate paths to Stony Ridge, a strong position behind the embankment of an unfinished railroad. From there, Jackson could either launch attacks or fight defensively. Pope had little idea of his strength or intentions until late in the day on August 28 when Jackson saw Federals marching down the nearby Warrenton Turnpike and decided to strike. It was his task now to preoccupy Pope until Lee and Longstreet moved in to deliver the knockout blow.

"Bring out your men, gentlemen!" Jackson instructed his officers, whose troops were waiting eagerly in the woods along Stony Ridge. "From the woods arose a hoarse roar like that from cages of wild beasts at the scent of blood," wrote Captain William Blackford. "Then all advanced in as perfect order as if they had been on parade, their bayonets sparkling in the light of the setting sun and their red battle flags dancing gayly in the breeze."

Crossing Brawner's Farm, Jackson's troops bore down on Federals led by Brigadier General John Gibbon, a West Pointer from North Carolina who had three brothers in Confederate ranks. Gibbon had outfitted his Midwestern recruits in black hats worn by regular U.S. troops and hoped that pride and polish would make up for their lack of experience. One member of his Black Hat Brigade, Philip Cheek of the 6th Wisconsin Infantry, recalled a comrade complaining as they marched down the turnpike that soon "this damn war will be over and we will never get into a battle!" Moments later, a shell fired by Jackson's gunners flew over their heads, and they were battling for their lives. As Confederates came on, Cheek recalled, they raised the shrill Rebel yell. "There is nothing like it this side of the infernal region," he remarked, "and the peculiar corkscrew sensation that it sends down your backbone under these circumstances can never be told."

Gibbon's men stood up to the challenge, and the fighting along the turnpike raged into the evening. One Confederate officer, Brigadier General William B. Taliaferro, marveled afterward at how the two sides faced each other at close quarters for hours, exchanging one murderous volley after another: "Out in the sunlight, in the dying daylight, and under the stars they stood, and although they could not advance, they would not retire. There was some discipline in this but there was much more of true valor." Taliaferro himself was badly wounded, and Gibbon lost more than 900 of his 2,100 men before the contest ended inconclusively that night.

While the Second Battle of Bull Run (Manassas) was unfolding around Brawner's Farm that afternoon, Lee and Longstreet were approaching Thoroughfare Gap off to the west. Confederates were well into the gap when, as one soldier recalled, "the bullets began to sing through our ranks and some men fell. We had no idea of danger until then." That fire came from Federals sent to hold the pass by McDowell, who took that precaution despite orders from Pope to move his entire corps to Manassas. Although McDowell had good reason to depart from those instructions, he failed to inform his superior, and Pope remained ignorant of the gathering threat to his west. By nightfall, Longstreet's men had ousted the opposing Federals and were filing through the gap.

"From the woods arose a hoarse roar like that from cages of wild beasts at the scent of blood."

CONFEDERATE CAPTAIN
WILLIAM BLACKFORD,
at Manassas

Lee and Longstreet reached Manassas with their forces before noon on August 29 to find Jackson under fierce pressure. "Hadn't we better move our line forward?" suggested Lee, hoping that an attack by Longstreet south of the turnpike would help relieve Jackson to the north. "I think not," replied Longstreet, who wanted to know what his troops were up against before he sent them groping through the woods into battle. Pope did not share Longstreet's caution—or Lee's capacity to trust in his subordinates. Although he had little idea what awaited his forces south of the turnpike, he ordered Porter's Corps there "to push into action at once," hoping to outflank Jackson. Porter did not receive the order until late afternoon and suspected that the Confederates to his front—the bulk of Longstreet's command—were too strong to be dislodged before nightfall. No admirer of Pope, he disregarded his instructions and sat tight.

The stalemate south of the turnpike left Jackson's men facing relentless attacks along the unfinished railroad to the north. Around 5 p.m., General Philip Kearny—whose troops had fought hard around Richmond before moving to reinforce Pope—entered the fray, hurling his division against Jackson's left flank with strong words. "Fall in here, you sons of bitches," he urged his men, "and I'll make major generals of every one of you!" Holding Jackson's left was A. P. Hill, whose men were near exhaustion and running short of ammunition. "General, your men have done nobly," Jackson replied when Hill informed him of their plight. "If you are attacked again you will beat the enemy back." Only nightfall could relieve the pressure on the Confederates,

Federal troops view wreckage along the tracks after Stonewall Jackson's troops struck the Federal supply depot at Manassas Junction on the night of August 26, looting the contents of boxcars and wagons before burning them.

Men of the all-German 41st New York Infantry, pictured here, served under German-born General Franz Sigel at the Second Battle of Bull Run, where they were caught in the devastating attack by James Longstreet's Confederates on August 30.

and it seemed the sun would never set. "No one knows how long sixty seconds are, nor how much time can be crowded into an hour," wrote Jackson's aide, Lieutenant Henry Kyd Douglas, "unless he has been under the fire of a desperate battle, holding on, as it were by his teeth, hour after hour, minute after minute, waiting for a turning or praying that the great red sun, blazing and motionless overhead, would go down." At last, darkness descended, and Jackson's line held.

By the morning of August 30, Pope had ample notice that Confederate reinforcements had arrived in force. But he believed their objective was simply to rescue Jackson's beleaguered troops. Determined not to let them escape, Pope made a fatal error by moving Porter's Corps and other units below the turnpike to the north to join in a climactic assault on Jackson, who had been bolstered with artillery and held the attackers off. That left only about 8,000 Federals south of the turnpike, facing 25,000 men under Longstreet, who was ready to strike. That afternoon, Lee closed the trap on the befuddled Pope, launching Longstreet's command against his opponent's pitifully exposed flank. The Confederate onslaught was overwhelming, but Federals caught in the storm did not yield without a fight. Andrew Coats of the 5th New York Infantry, a Zouave regiment, saw scores of his comrades mowed down. "War has been designated as Hell," he wrote, "and I can assure you that where the regiment stood that day was the very vortex of Hell. Not only were men wounded, or killed, but they were riddled." Zouaves fought desperately to save their regimental colors—a cherished symbol of the ties that bound men together as a unit through such terrible ordeals. Both of the regiment's color-bearers and seven of eight color guards were killed, but the survivors clung to their banner and retreated with it. One witness later saw their colonel sitting "immobile on his horse, looking back at the battle as if paralyzed, while his handful of men, blackened with dust and smoke, stood under the colors silent as statues."

By evening, Pope's forces were in full retreat, streaming back over Henry House Hill and across the Stone Bridge spanning Bull Run in a scene eerily reminiscent of the first battle here. This time, the Federals fell back in good order, putting up enough of a fight as they withdrew to save face and preserve their army. But soldiers with a sense of history felt they were reliving a nightmare. "It's another Bull Run!" a furious Phil Kearny said that evening to John Gibbon, who tried to soothe him: "I hope not quite as bad as that, General." Kearny found little solace in the fact that troops under Major General Jesse Reno and other commanders were still gamely resisting the Confederate advance. "Reno is keeping up the fight," he told Gibbon. "He is not stampeded. I am not stampeded. You are not stampeded. That is about all, sir—my God, that's about all." Kearny, who had suffered under McClellan and Pope this summer, could not bear to see his brave men beaten for lack of inspired leadership of the sort Lee demonstrated. The Union would find its champions eventually, but Kearny would not be part of that resurgence. On September 1, while holding off Confederates at Chantilly with Pope's rear guard, he died in action.

Second Bull Run was one of the war's longest and costliest battles. Some 25,000 men—16,000 Federals and 9,000 Confederates—were reported dead, wounded, or missing, with the difference between the two sides largely attributable to the thousands of Federals captured. Surgeons, nurses, and burial parties were overwhelmed by the carnage. At one field infirmary, the wounded lay on the ground "as thick as a drove of hogs in a lot," wrote Confederate surgeon Spencer Welch. "They were groaning and crying out with pain, and those shot in the bowels were crying for water." Welch and another surgeon were forced to amputate a soldier's arm without chloroform: "I held the artery and Dr. Hout cut it off by candle light." It was hard to imagine anything surpassing the bloodshed here. But many soldiers on both sides who survived this harrowing ordeal would soon engage in an even fiercer battle in neighboring Maryland.

THE ROAD TO ANTIETAM

DESPITE LEE'S STUNNING VICTORY, THE CONFEDERACY WAS NO CLOSER TO WINNING the war now than it had been when the year began. If Lee remained at Manassas, his hungry troops would find little to eat in an area where Pope's Federals had foraged exhaustively, and he would face the same dilemma Joseph Johnston had confronted in March—how to cope with a much larger

"It's another Bull Run!"
UNION GENERAL PHILIP KEARNY

Federal army around Washington that could either challenge his forces head on or circumvent them and renew pressure on Richmond. His army was reduced to less than 45,000 men, no match for the forces of Pope and McClellan, who together had more than 100,000 troops around Washington. Realistically, Lee had two choices. He could secure his army by withdrawing southward below the Rappahannock or westward into the Shenandoah Valley. Or he could advance into western Maryland, where his men could obtain food and might receive aid from Confederate sympathizers. Union troops were sure to pursue him, but some would have to be left behind to guard Washington, and Lee had a better chance of outmaneuvering and defeating a numerically superior foe amid the hills and valleys of western Maryland than around Washington.

Lee's decision to invade Maryland ran counter to the defensive strategy favored by Jefferson Davis, and Lee tactfully dissuaded the president from joining him in the field by stressing the hazards of the journey. "I cannot but feel great uneasiness should you undertake to reach me," he wrote. Lee admitted that his army was not well supplied for an invasion. "The men are poorly provided with clothes," he informed Davis, "and in thousands of instances are destitute of shoes. Still we cannot afford to be idle, and though weaker than our opponents in men and military equipments, must endeavor to harass, if we cannot destroy them." On September 4, he led his army to the Potomac near Leesburg, Virginia, where the river was shallow enough to be forded, and crossed over to Maryland. Having recently injured his hands in a fall, Lee had to ride in an ambulance, but his men happily removed their trousers and waded across, singing "Maryland, My Maryland."

In Washington, President Lincoln responded to news of Pope's defeat with grim determination. "We must whip these people now," he declared, and he could see that Pope was not up to that task. Over the strenuous objections of Secretary of War Stanton and other Cabinet members, he named George McClellan commander of all forces around Washington. "We must use the tools we have," he explained, and no one was better than McClellan at rousing demoralized troops and preparing them for battle. As Lincoln put it, "If he can't fight himself, he excels in making others ready to fight." He had much to prove after failing to take Richmond, and Lincoln hoped he would be more aggressive now, if only to silence his many critics. "McClellan is working like a beaver," Lincoln noted approvingly. "He seems to be aroused to doing something." By September 7, McClellan had an army of nearly 85,000 men marching in pursuit of Lee. "I certainly hope that after this campaign," wrote one of his soldiers, Wilbur Fisk of Vermont, "we can write of something beside disaster, slaughter, defeat, and skedaddle."

Lee, in a proclamation addressed to Marylanders, portrayed his campaign as an effort to liberate them from Federal occupation. "The people of the

"I have never seen a mass of such filthy, strong-smelling men; the scratching they kept up gave warrant of vermin in abundance."

Resident of Frederick, Maryland, after Confederates passed through the town

In a sketch by artist Alfred Waud, who witnessed the scene, Federal scouts put up token resistance as Lee's Confederates in the distance cross the Potomac from Virginia into Maryland on September 4. Although the crossing otherwise went unopposed, Lee's men were not at liberty to bathe in the river. "We needed a good washing of our bodies," one of them wrote, "but wading in the water did us no good in that direction."

Federal scouts and guides such as these men with the Army of the Potomac kept McClellan informed on Confederate movements in Maryland, but he continued to believe that Lee's army was more than twice its actual strength.

South," he declared, "have long wished to aid you in throwing off this foreign yoke, to enable you again to enjoy the inalienable rights of freemen, and restore independence and sovereignty to your state." But most people in western Maryland—a region of small farming communities with few slaves—were loyal to the Union and hostile to these Confederates invaders. Some jeered as Lee's men passed, and others watched in sullen silence, surprised at how ragged and desperate they looked. "I have never seen a mass of such filthy, strong-smelling men," remarked one observer after Confederates passed through the town of Frederick; "the scratching they kept up gave warrant of vermin in abundance." Another witness felt humiliated that "this horde of ragamuffins could set our grand army of the Union at defiance." A number of Lee's men were in such poor shape that they were no longer willing or able to keep up with the march and headed home. Lee's losses through straggling largely offset the reinforcements he received from Richmond and left him with only about half as many troops as McClellan commanded.

Never one to bow to adversity, Lee again divided his outnumbered forces, as he had before Second Manassas. On September 10, he sent the bulk of his troops off with Stonewall Jackson to seize two Federal strongholds in west-

ern Virginia, Martinsburg and Harpers Ferry. Martinsburg was lightly defended, but Harpers Ferry with its garrison of more than 10,000 Federals would hold out until Confederates seized the heights around town and hauled up big guns. Lee needed those two towns to secure supply lines from the Shenandoah Valley, which would allow him to prolong his offensive and perhaps even invade Pennsylvania. But his divided forces would be in jeopardy if McClellan attacked before they reunited as planned at Boonsboro, Maryland. The danger was even greater than Lee realized, for on September 13 Federals strolling through a recently abandoned Confederate campground outside Frederick found a copy of Lee's orders wrapped around some cigars. The discovery gave a huge boost to McClellan, who had been advancing slowly and warily, taken in by misleading reports that Lee had as many as 120,000 troops. Now he had a chance to smash Lee's divided forces if he moved quickly. "I have all the plans of the rebels," he wired Lincoln, "and will catch them in their own trap if my men are equal to the emergency. . . . Will send you trophies."

On September 14, McClellan's troops pushed westward from Frederick and clashed with Confederates holding gaps on South Mountain through which roads passed to Boonsboro and Harpers Ferry. Lee, who was anxiously awaiting the return of his forces from Harpers Ferry and suspected that his plans had been intercepted, brought up troops from Boonsboro to delay McClellan at South Mountain. Confederates managed to hold out there until evening, when they were ousted in sharp fighting. McClellan's forces missed a chance that night to press ahead to Harpers Ferry before Confederates seized the town and linked up with Lee. On September 15, Lee fell back to Sharpsburg, Maryland, near the Potomac, and learned to his great relief that Jackson had taken Harpers Ferry and would soon join him. Surveying the Sharpsburg area, Lee chose a strong defensive position near the town on high ground west of Antietam Creek. "We will make our stand on those hills," he declared as McClellan's forces approached.

By September 16, Lee had most of his army reassembled there. One notable exception was A. P. Hill's light division, which remained in Harpers Ferry to secure that town and would set out for Sharpsburg the next morning. McClellan had been poised east of Antietam Creek, within striking distance of Lee, for 24 hours, but he did not position his troops for battle until late on the 16th, when he pushed two of his six corps across the creek north of Sharpsburg. His attack would be launched there at dawn against Lee's left flank, while other forces crossed the creek to the south to join the battle. McClellan's delay would prove costly, but he would never have a better opportunity to fulfill the hopes of his commander in chief. "God bless you, and all with you," Lincoln wired him. "Destroy the rebel army, if possible."

> "I have all the plans of the rebels, and will catch them in their own trap if my men are equal to the emergency. . . . Will send you trophies."
>
> GENERAL GEORGE MCCLELLAN TO PRESIDENT LINCOLN

After capturing war-ravaged Harpers Ferry (opposite), Confederates there rushed to join the remainder of Lee's army at Sharpsburg, Maryland, where the Lutheran church on Main Street (above) was damaged in the fierce battle that erupted nearby at Antietam Creek on September 17. The building served afterward as a hospital.

Clara Barton

UNION NURSE

In 1862 Barton organized a private relief agency to assist the sick and wounded of the Army of the Potomac. She established field hospitals at Cedar Mountain and Second Manassas and, at Antietam, she pushed her wagons past stalled Federal supply trains to arrive at a barn near the Cornfield at about noon. Under fire, Barton set about recovering and treating the wounded.

A MAN LYING UPON THE GROUND asked for drink—I stooped to give it, and having raised him with my right hand, was holding the cup to his lips with my left, when I felt a sudden twitch of the loose sleeve of my dress the poor fellow sprang from my hands and fell back quivering, in the agonies of death—A ball had passed between my body—and the right arm which supported him—cutting through the sleeve, and passing through his chest from shoulder to shoulder.

There was no more to be done for him and I left him to his rest—I have never mended that hole in my sleeve—I wonder if a soldier ever does mend a bullet hole in his coat?

The patient endurance of those men was most astonishing as many as could be were carried into the barn, as a slight protection against random shot—just outside the door lay a man wounded in the face—the ball having entered the lower maxillary on the left side, and lodged among the bones of the right cheek—his imploring look drew me to him—when placing his fingers upon the sharp protrubrance, he said Lady will you tell me what this is that burns so I replied that it must be the ball which had been too far spent to cut its way entirely through—

It is terribly painful he said won't you take it out? I said I would go to the tables for a surgeon "No! No!"

"Oh! God—what a costly war—This man could laugh at pain face death without a tremor, and yet weep like a child over the loss of his comrades and his captain."

he said, catching my dress—"they cannot come to me, I must wait my turn for this is a little wound." You can get the ball, there is a knife in my pocket—please take the ball out for me.

This was a new call—I had never severed the nerves and fibers of human flesh—and I said I could not hurt him so much—he looked up, with as nearly a smile as such a mangled face could assume saying—

"You cannot hurt me dear lady—I can endure any pain that your hands can create—please do it,—t'will relieve me so much."

I could not withstand his entreaty—and opening the best blade of my pocket knife—prepared for the operation—Just at his head lay a stalwart orderly sergeant from Illinois ... who had a bullet directly through the fleshy part of both thighs—he had been watching the scene with great interest and when he saw me commence to raise the poor fellow's head, ... with a desperate effort he succeeded in raising himself to a sitting posture—exclaiming as he did so, "I will help do that"—and shoving himself along upon the ground he took the wounded head in his hands and held it while I extracted the ball and washed and bandaged the face. . . .

Returning in half an hour I found him weeping ... I thought his effort had been too great for his strength—and expressed my fears—"Oh! No! No! Madam," he replied—"It is not for myself I am very well—but—pointing to another just brought in, he said, "This is my comrade and he tells me that our regiment is all cut to pieces—that my captain was the last officer left—and he is dead."

Oh! God—what a costly war—This man could laugh at pain face death without a tremor, and yet weep like a child over the loss of his comrades and his captain. ∎

THE BLOODIEST DAY

FOR BRIGADIER GENERAL ALPHEUS WILLIAMS, WHOSE FEDERALS GROPED THEIR way into position west of Antietam Creek around 2 a.m. on September 17, that night was unforgettable: "so dark, so obscure, so mysterious, so uncertain." Men knew that a great battle was coming, and many felt as he did that it might well determine the "fate of our country." It was a sobering thought for a commander: "So much responsibility, so much intense, future anxiety!"

The struggle began at first light, when Major General Joseph Hooker, aptly known as "Fighting Joe," threw his corps against Stonewall Jackson's forces on Lee's left. Emerging from the woods north of town, Hooker's men entered a cornfield that became the scene of almost-unimaginable slaughter over the next few hours. Lurking in the trees west of that field and behind a wooden fence to the south were Confederate infantry and artillery, whose blasts cut down oncoming Federals like so many cornstalks. Major Rufus Dawes of the 6th Wisconsin Infantry, advancing with General John Gibbon's Black Hat Brigade, ordered his men to lie flat, but there was no shelter for them in this storm. "The bullets began to clip through the corn, and spin through the soft furrows," Dawes recalled. "Shells burst around us, the fragments tearing up the ground, and canister whistled through the corn above us." Pressing ahead, his men stood and exchanged thunderous volleys with Confederates behind the fence. Men on both sides "were knocked out of the ranks by dozens," Dawes related, but the surviving Federals kept going: "We jumped over the fence, and pushed on, loading, firing, and shouting as we advanced. There was, on the part of the men, great hysterical excitement, eagerness to go forward, and a reckless disregard of life, of everything but victory."

Like so many other brave charges by both sides at Antietam, this one was ultimately repulsed. Fearing a breakthrough, Jackson sent in reserves led by the hard-driving General John Bell Hood, whose men forced the enemy back and advanced into the Cornfield, where they in turn were exposed to murderous fire. Hood's 1st Texas Infantry lost 186 of 226 men in the bloodbath, the steepest casualty rate for any regiment during the war. Overall, Hood lost nearly 1,400 of his 2,300 men in less than an hour. "Where is your division?" an officer asked him afterward. "Dead on the field," he replied. Hooker, for his part, saw 2,600 of his 9,000 men killed or wounded in and around the Cornfield. "The slain lay in rows precisely as they had stood in their ranks a few minutes before," he wrote. "It was never my fortune to witness a more bloody, dismal battlefield."

Both Federal corps commanders opposing Jackson this morning fell victim to enemy fire. Hooker was shot in the foot and was carried from the field, and Major General Joseph Mansfield was mortally wounded in the chest. Replacing Mansfield as corps commander was Alpheus Williams, whose forces renewed the battle around the Cornfield and drove Confederates back toward

> **"The slain lay in rows precisely as they had stood in their ranks a few minutes before."**
>
> UNION GENERAL JOSEPH HOOKER, *at Antietam*

Confederates wounded at Antietam lie under tents at a makeshift Federal field hospital at Keedysville, Maryland, near Sharpsburg. Other injured Confederates were retrieved by their own side and carried in wagons across the Potomac to Shepherdstown, Virginia, where as one resident put it: "They filled every building and overflowed into the country."

the Dunker Church—situated on the Hagerstown Turnpike a mile north of Sharpsburg—before Jackson shored up his line and stemmed the Federal tide. "The roar of the infantry was beyond anything conceivable to the uninitiated," Williams wrote. "If all the stone and brick houses of Broadway should tumble at once the roar and rattle could hardly be greater, and amidst this, hundreds of pieces of artillery, right and left, were thundering, as a sort of bass to the infernal music." Another soldier described the explosive fighting around the Cornfield as "a great tumbling together of all heaven and earth." By nine in the morning, some 8,000 men had been killed or wounded there, and the Battle of Antietam had barely begun.

McClellan, who still grossly overestimated Confederate strength and feared a counterattack, was slow to commit more troops to this struggle. Not until 10 a.m. did General Ambrose Burnside receive orders to launch his corps of 11,000 men against Lee's right wing south of Sharpsburg. That crucial advance was then stalled for nearly three hours by a single brigade of some 550 Georgians, who held the west bank of Antietam Creek and beat back repeated Federal efforts to cross what became known as the Burnside Bridge. Commanding the Georgians was Brigadier General Robert Toombs, who had stepped down as Confederate Secretary of State to prove himself in a great battle. "I will retire if I live through it," he promised his wife. Toombs survived the test, but many in his brigade did not. "So many men were shot down," wrote Lieutenant Theodore Fogle of the 2nd Georgia Infantry, "that the officers filled their places and loaded and fired their guns."

By holding off Burnside's advance until afternoon, Toombs's Brigade bought precious time for Lee, who shifted troops from his right to cope with an attack launched near the Dunker Church at midmorning by General Edwin "Bull" Sumner. True to his nickname, Sumner charged impulsively into the fray, paying little heed to advice offered by Alpheus Williams, who knew the ground here and the dangers that awaited Sumner's Corps. With one of his three divisions held in reserve and another trailing far behind, Sumner led 5,400 men into the woods west of the Hagerstown Turnpike. His plan was to outflank the enemy, but instead he exposed his own flank to attack by Confederates advancing from the south. "By God, we must get out of this!" Sumner shouted when he realized the fix he was in. "Back boys, for God's sake, move back!" His men would have to fight their way out, for Confederates were working around their flank to their rear. Among those caught in that envelopment was Captain Oliver Wendell Holmes, Jr., of the 20th Massachusetts Infantry, a future Supreme Court justice. Holmes saw one of his men, an Irish immigrant, firing to the rear and hit him with the flat of his sword, thinking he had taken leave of his senses. Then the truth dawned on him. "The enemy is behind us!" a soldier shouted, and Holmes ordered the rest of his company to face about and follow the example of that alert Irishman. Moments later, Holmes took a bullet through the neck and joined a grim roster of more than 2,000 casualties suffered by Sumner in his ill-considered advance.

Throughout the battle, both sides showed a remarkable capacity to rebound from bloody setbacks, and so it was with the Federals after this debacle. Troops of Alpheus Williams's Corps rallied in defense of Sumner's retreating

"By God, we must get out of this! . . . Back boys, for God's sake, move back!"

UNION GENERAL EDWIN "BULL" SUMNER

Colonel John B. Gordon

6TH ALABAMA INFANTRY, RODES'S BRIGADE

At Antietam Gordon's 6th Alabama occupied part of the fire-swept sunken farm road that came to be called the Bloody Lane. Severely injured, the 30-year-old former lawyer and coalmine operator would return to action in March 1863 and end the war with the rank of major general. After the war Gordon served in the United States Senate and as governor of Georgia.

THE FIRST VOLLEY FROM THE Union lines in my front sent a ball through the brain of the chivalric Colonel Tew, of North Carolina, to whom I was talking, and another ball through the calf of my right leg. On the right and the left my men were falling under the death-dealing crossfire like trees in a hurricane. . . . Both sides stood in the open at short range and without the semblance of breastworks, and the firing was doing a deadly work. Higher up in the same leg I was again shot; but still no bone was broken. I was able to walk along the line and give encouragement to my resolute riflemen, who were firing with the coolness and steadiness of peace soldiers in target practice. When later in the day the third ball pierced my left arm, tearing asunder the tendons and mangling the flesh, they caught sight of the blood running down my fingers, and these devoted and big-hearted men, . . . pleaded with me to leave them and go to the rear, pledging me that they would stay there and fight to the last. I could not consent to leave them in such a crisis. . . .

A fourth ball ripped through my shoulder, leaving its base and a wad of clothing in its track. I could still stand and walk, although the shocks

> **"On the right and the left my men were falling under the death-dealing crossfire like trees in a hurricane."**

and loss of blood had left but little of my normal strength. . . . I thought I saw some wavering in my line, near the extreme right, and Private Vickers, of Alabama, volunteered to carry any orders I might wish to send. I directed him to go quickly and remind the men of the pledge to General Lee, and to say to them that I was still on the field and intended to stay there. He bounded away like an Olympic racer; but he had gone

less than fifty yards when he fell, instantly killed by a ball through his head. I then attempted to go myself, although I was bloody and faint, and my legs did not bear me steadily. I had gone but a short distance when I was shot down by a fifth ball, which struck me squarely in the face, and passed out, barely missing the jugular vein. I fell forward and lay unconscious with my face in my cap; and it would seem that I might have been smothered by the blood running into my cap from this last wound but for the act of some Yankee, who, as if to save my life, had at a previous hour during the battle, shot a hole through the cap, which let the blood out. ∎

Confederate dead nearly fill the Bloody Lane in this photograph by Alexander Gardner. Gardner noted that the body leaning against the bank at lower right was that of a Rebel colonel— probably Colonel Tew of the 2d North Carolina.

2 DUNKER CHURCH *At the center of the morning's horrific violence was the whitewashed church of the pacifist Dunker sect.*

3 SUMNER'S CHARGE *Bull Sumner's 2nd Corps was surprised on three sides in a counterattack near the West Woods and all but wiped out.*

4 BURNSIDE BRIDGE *The view from the Confederate side of Antietam's southernmost bridge, where Rebels picked off Burnside's men trying to cross.*

THE BATTLE OF ANTIETAM

McCLELLAN'S PLAN AT SHARPSBURG WAS TO HAVE three corps deliver a massive assault on Lee's left flank while Ambrose Burnside's 9th Corps crossed Antietam Creek to the south to antagonize Lee's right. Poor coordination, though, allowed Lee to parry an army of 87,000 with just 45,000 men.

Joseph Hooker launched the battle at dawn on September 17, marching his 1st Corps down the Hagerstown Turnpike and clashing with Stonewall Jackson's Corps in the West Woods and the Cornfield of the Miller farm [1]. Hooker's report would state that "every stalk of corn . . . was cut as closely as could have been done with a knife, and the [Confederates] slain lay in rows precisely as they had stood. "

Joseph Mansfield's 12th Corps attacked near the Dunker Church [2], suffering heavy losses, including both Mansfield, who was killed, and Hooker, who was wounded. Finally, a division of Bull Sumner's 2nd Corps, led by Major General John Sedgwick, launched a third wave of attack [3] and were assaulted from three sides, suffering 2,200 casualties in half an hour. Burnside's failure to cross the creek [4] in the morning had allowed Lee to reinforce his left.

Sumner's remaining divisions fell back to the Sunken Road [5], known after as the Bloody Lane because of the carnage — 5,500 casualties in four hours. A Northern war correspondent who arrived as the Rebels were falling back described a "ghastly spectacle" where "Confederates had gone down as the grass falls before the scythe." McClellan declined to send his fresh reserves into the battered Confederate center, and later in the day A.P. Hill's division [6] arrived from Harpers Ferry to save Lee's right flank. A truce was called the next day in light of more than 23,000 total casualties. ■

The farmland around Sharpsburg, Maryland, became such a violent theater that "the whole landscape," according to a Union soldier, "for an instant turned slightly red."

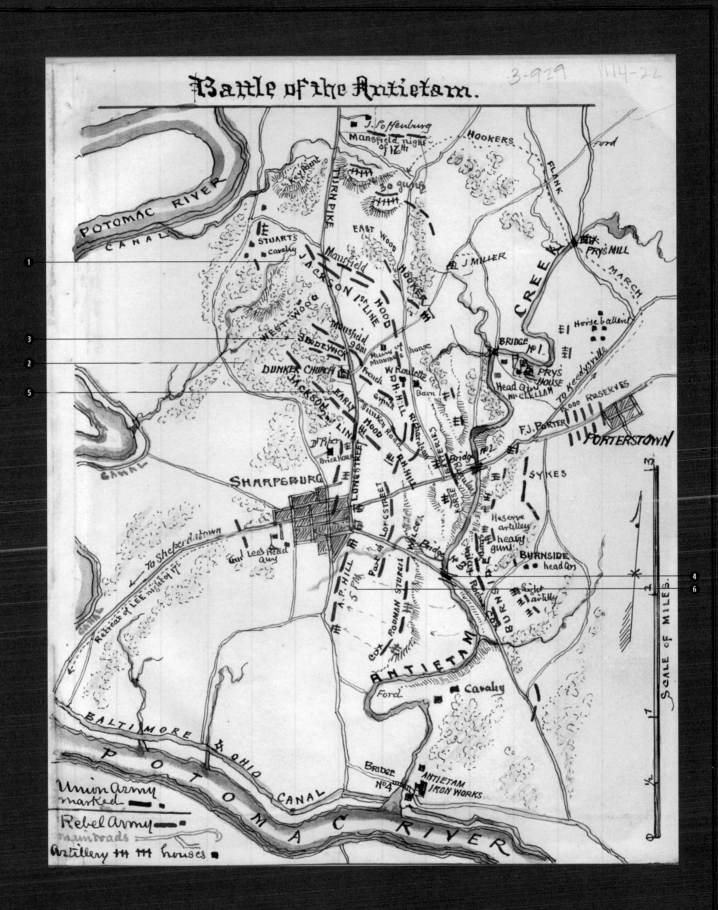

Battle of the Antietam.

forces and drove the pursuing Confederates back, inflicting heavy casualties on them. Meanwhile, the two divisions Sumner had left behind before blundering into the woods entered battle against Confederates holding the Sunken Road, a dirt path intersecting the Hagerstown Turnpike south of the Dunker Church. Among the Confederates entrenched in that worn-down road were troops of the 6th Alabama Infantry under Colonel John Gordon, who urged his men to hold their fire as the Federals came on. "Soon they were so close that we might have seen the eagles on their buttons," he recalled; "but my brave and eager boys still waited for the order." When he finally gave that order and his men let loose, he added, "the effect was appalling. The entire front line, with few exceptions, went down in the consuming blast."

One Federal wave after another crashed against this Confederate barricade before New Yorkers led by Colonel Francis Barlow seized a knoll overlooking the Sunken Road and began shooting down into the trench. Colonel Gordon sustained multiple wounds and fell unconscious, and his flustered successor misinterpreted an order he received and called for retreat. "Sixth Alabama, about face; forward march!" he shouted, setting off a stampede as Confederates fled the Sunken Road, leaving behind so many dead they formed a solid line that "one might have walked upon," a Union soldier observed. "They lay just as they had been killed apparently, amid the blood which was soaking the earth."

By mid-afternoon, Lee had exhausted his reserves and could only pray that A. P. Hill's men would arrive soon from Harpers Ferry. Federals had finally secured the Burnside Bridge and were driving Confederates on Lee's right back toward Sharpsburg, threatening to sever his line of retreat to Virginia. Two of six Union corps had yet to enter the battle, but McClellan was swayed by warnings from the discouraged Sumner and held them back. "Most of us think that this battle is only half fought and half won," one Federal officer complained to a reporter at headquarters. "There is still time to finish it. But McClellan will do no more." Around four that afternoon, Hill reached Sharpsburg after an eight-hour march and threw his troops at once against Burnside's Federals. It was a close fight and a critical one, but McClellan did not see fit to commit any of his 20,000 well-rested reserves against Hill's weary forces. As evening approached, Burnside's men gave way and fell back across the bridge they had car-

Lincoln and McClellan face each other in camp near Antietam in early October. Dismayed that the general had not yet moved in pursuit of Lee two weeks after the battle, Lincoln complained that the army had become "McClellan's bodyguard."

Federals prepare a mass grave at Antietam in this photograph by Alexander Gardner. One man told of searching in vain for his son's grave here: "Oh how dreadful was that place to me, where my dear boy had been buried like a beast of the field!"

ried at such cost. Confederates were glad to see the sun set on a day that was nearly disastrous for them. As Longstreet wrote afterward: "Ten thousand fresh troops could have come in and taken Lee's army and everything in it."

A MISSED OPPORTUNITY

THE ULTIMATE TRAGEDY OF THIS BLOODIEST DAY—WHICH LEFT MORE THAN 10,000 Confederates and 12,000 Federals dead, wounded, or missing—was that it did not end the Civil War and its dreadful carnage. For that, some Unionists blamed McClellan, who made no effort to renew the battle on September 18 or prevent Lee from withdrawing with his forces to Virginia. As Colonel Thomas Welsh of Burnside's Corps wrote bitterly: "The whole Rebel Army could have been captured or destroyed easily before it could have crossed the Potomac—but indeed it seems to me that McClellan let them escape purposely." Yet McClellan was just one of many Civil War commanders who let their vulnerable opponents slip away after a devastating battle that left both sides shocked and exhausted. And not even his fiercest critics could deny him credit for forging the army that fought with such determination at Antietam and forced the Confederate invaders to retreat. What held McClellan back and prevented him from taking great risks in pursuit of a great victory was not just his innate caution but his failure to recognize that this war was now a fight to the finish, a relentless struggle for America's future that would not end until his resilient foes were mercilessly pursued and utterly defeated. Until that happened, there would be more bloody days, more battlefields littered with bloated corpses, more young men cut down in droves and buried in mass graves.

"Perhaps you don't know how we bury the dead," wrote Roland Bowen of the 15th Massachusetts Infantry to the father of his friend and company mate Henry Ainsworth, who fell at Antietam and was placed in a common grave before Bowen could retrieve his body for private burial. The trench in which Ainsworth lay, Bowen explained, was 25 feet long, six feet wide, and a mere three feet deep. Forty bodies were placed in it in two tiers, separated by a layer of straw. The only marker at the grave was a board inscribed, "15th Mass. buried here." It took more than one trench to hold the dead from this ill-fated regiment, which suffered a staggering 334 casualties at Antietam. So vast were the losses on this single day that a single life seemingly counted for little. "Henry is the 3rd corpse from the upper end on the top tier next to the woods," Bowen informed his friend's bereft father. "Mr. Ainsworth, this is not the way we bury folks at home. I am sorry, but I was too late to have it different."

"Henry is the 3rd corpse from the upper end on the top tier next to the woods."

ROLAND BOWEN
15TH MASSACHUSETTS INFANTRY,
to the father of his friend

A plaque at the base of a tree at Antietam marks the grave of John Marshall of the 28th Pennsylvania Infantry. Some soldiers who died in battle here were buried individually by comrades for the benefit of family members, who might then transfer the remains to graveyards back home.

> **"If I could save the Union without freeing *any* slave I would do it, and if I could save it by freeing all the slaves I would do it, and if I could save it by freeing some and leaving others alone I would also do that."**
>
> ABRAHAM LINCOLN

EMANCIPATION AND ENDURANCE

IT WAS NOT THE GREAT VICTORY LINCOLN HOPED FOR, BUT IT WOULD DO. For months, as Federal forces suffered one setback after another, he had put off this proclamation, awaiting a triumph that would lend force to his words. Now as Confederates withdrew after the Battle of Antietam, Lincoln felt confident enough to proceed. "I wish it was a better time," he told his Cabinet on September 22. "The action of the army against the rebels has not been quite what I should have best liked. But they have been driven out of Maryland." He had made a vow and was ready to honor it: If God blessed the Union with victory, Lincoln would "crown the result by the declaration of freedom to the slaves."

He admitted there might be others better qualified for the role of Great Emancipator. Among his Cabinet were Republican stalwarts such as William Seward and Salmon Chase who had taken stronger stands against slavery before the war than he did. Indeed, Lincoln owed his nomination in 1860 partly to the fact that he was not viewed as an abolitionist or an advocate of racial equality. Although he believed that the promise of equal rights in the Declaration of Independence applied to blacks as well as whites, he feared that the differences between the two races might be too great to overcome and favored sending freed slaves to other countries to form their own colonies. Free blacks denounced Lincoln for advocating racial segregation through colonization and showing "contempt for Negroes," as the former slave and abolitionist Frederick Douglass put it. "This is our country as much as it is yours," an African-American in Philadelphia wrote Lincoln, "and we will not leave it."

What earned Lincoln the respect of these critics, ultimately, was his capacity to heed opposing arguments and evolve in his thinking. "I shall adopt new views so fast as they shall appear to be true views," he wrote. Few in his position would have granted a hearing to a black leader who publicly scolded him, but Lincoln would meet more than once with Frederick Douglass before the war was over. "He treated me as a man," wrote Douglass; "he did not let me feel for a moment that there was any difference in the color of our skins!" Through such encounters, Lincoln moved toward accepting African-Americans as an integral part of the Union and its war effort. The Emancipation Proclamation he issued on September 22 was a big step in that direction, but he still had far to go. As he wrote shortly before taking that step: "If I could save the Union without freeing any slave I would do it, and if I could save it by freeing all the slaves I would do it, and if I could save it by freeing some and leaving others alone I would also do that."

In his proclamation, Lincoln emancipated some and left others alone by declaring slaves free only in states that remained in rebellion as of January 1, 1863. The proclamation did not apply to slaves states outside the Confeder-

acy such as Missouri and Kentucky. Nor did it apply to occupied areas of the Confederacy. Skeptics pointed out that the proclamation did not actually free any slaves, since it applied only to areas where Union forces as yet had no authority. But the consequences of declaring slaves free in those large parts of the South beyond Federal control were enormous. As Lincoln stated in the proclamation's key passage, all slaves in areas that were still in rebellion against the United States as of New Year's Day "shall be then, thenceforward, and forever free; and the executive government of the United States, including the military and naval authority thereof, will recognize and maintain the freedom of such persons." This was an invitation for slaves to leave their masters and seek refuge in areas under Federal control, thus depriving Confederates of slave labor vital to their economy and war effort. And by declaring those slaves "forever free," Lincoln was ruling out a negotiated settlement of the war, unless Confederate leaders gave in and accepted an end to slavery as the price of peace. He exempted slaveholders in loyal states and occupied areas from the proclamation because his war powers as president applied only to enemies, but a government that eliminated slavery by force of arms in rebellious states would not long tolerate slavery anywhere else in the nation.

For all its exceptions and qualifications, the Emancipation Proclamation was a revolutionary document that redefined the Civil War and aroused passions on both sides. One Southern newspaper denounced this "fiendish proclamation" as an attempt to incite "servile insurrection in the Southern States and thus consign our women and children to indiscriminate butchery." Opinion in the North was divided, with many Democrats faulting Lincoln and his "Abolition-Republican party" for favoring blacks over whites. As the Harrisburg Patriot & Union editorialized: "The simple question to be decided is, whether the white man shall maintain his status of superiority, or be sunk to

Former slaves cultivate their own crops on Hilton Head Island in South Carolina, taken by Federal forces in late 1861. Lincoln's Emancipation Proclamation encouraged slaves in Confederate territory to seek freedom in these occupied areas. Some freedmen proclaimed their loyalty to the Union by wearing cast-off Federal uniforms, as shown here, or by enlisting as soldiers and fighting to destroy slavery and the Confederacy.

the level of the negro. Equality of races is demanded by the Abolitionists; they claim that socially, civilly and politically the black man should be the equal of the white. The Democrats deny and oppose this." Most Republicans, for their part, backed emancipation and felt it ennobled their cause. "Slavery is the great enemy to the constitution and the Union," proclaimed the *Rutland Herald*. "Down with slavery, now and forever!" Some called for blacks to be enlisted by the Union as soldiers, a proposal soon to be enacted.

A War of Wills

SOUTHERNERS WERE ENCOURAGED BY THE INCREASINGLY BITTER POLITICAL debate in the North over emancipation and race. The setback at Antietam dampened Southern hopes of prevailing on the battlefield, but Confederates did not have to conquer the North to preserve their independence. They could achieve that goal by avoiding defeat and remaining united in opposition while Unionists quarreled and lost heart. A war that many people once thought would be a sprint to victory had become an endurance race, and willpower would have as much to do with the outcome as firepower. Confederates had their own quarrels that grew sharper as the war dragged on, many of them concerning how much power the central government should exercise over the states. The Confederacy was born in rebellion against Washington, and some of those resentments were transferred to Richmond when President Davis and the Confederate Congress tried to further the war effort by asserting powers such as taxation and conscription.

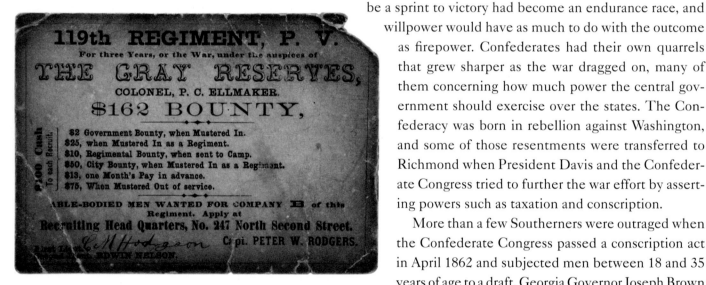

A recruiting card for the 119th Pennsylvania Infantry offers volunteers a bounty that cannot be collected in full until they complete their service, thus discouraging bounty jumpers from claiming their reward and running off. One infamous bounty jumper enlisted and deserted 32 times before he was court-martialed and sent to prison.

More than a few Southerners were outraged when the Confederate Congress passed a conscription act in April 1862 and subjected men between 18 and 35 years of age to a draft. Georgia Governor Joseph Brown considered this a violation of states' rights and declared defiantly: "I cannot permit the enrollment of conscripts under the act of Congress." Others regarded conscription as an assault on individual rights and denounced provisions allowing men who were drafted to hire substitutes to serve in their place—something only the wealthy could afford to do—and exempting from service planters and overseers responsible for more than 20 slaves. This inequitable draft increased anti-Confederate sentiment in areas such as the hill country of North Carolina, where few people had slaves or the means to purchase substitutes. As one woman there wrote bluntly, "The common people is drove off to fight for the big mans negro." The ultimate rebels in the South were poor whites in remote areas who felt that Confederate authorities had no more right than Federal officials did to draft them, tax them, impress their livestock for military use, or otherwise make their hard lives even harder.

Northern officials encountered similar resistance when states there began drafting men in the summer of 1862. Those efforts failed to meet the rising demand for troops, and Congress in 1863 would institute a nationwide draft of men between the ages of 20 and 45 and set quotas for each congressional district. Some wealthy districts filled their draft quotas by offering hefty bounties to lure volunteers from poor districts—among them unscrupulous bounty jumpers, who enlisted, deserted, and enlisted again for profit. Here as in the South, draftees were allowed to purchase substitutes, fueling resentments in poor neighborhoods where men were paid to enlist, or forced to fight, while the wealthy avoided service. Hostility to conscription—and to a war waged to free blacks from slavery—was greatest among Irish immigrants and other poor whites in urban areas. The *New York News* spoke for them when it denounced conscription as the "tool of Emperors, who cannot trust the patriotism of their subjects," and argued that instead of drafting "white men to serve the blacks," the government should pursue "Negotiation, Compromise, and Peace."

Despite such misgivings, many men of little means enlisted freely on both sides simply because they felt it was their duty. Among the Federal casualties at Antietam were 540 men of the Irish Brigade, made up largely of immigrants living in New York City who volunteered for service and hoped to return as a unit to Ireland one day to free their homeland from British rule. The majority of people in the North and the South were willing to make the sacrifices required of them so long as they believed victory was within reach. In late 1862, as the mounting costs of war weighed heavily on Unionists and Confederates alike, the opposing armies struggled for a breakthrough that would boost confidence at home and make the price of continuing the struggle even harder for their opponents to bear.

BATTLING FOR KENTUCKY

"OUR PROSPECTS HERE, MY DEAR SIR, ARE NOT WHAT I EXPECTED," WROTE GENeral Braxton Bragg to Jefferson Davis on September 25 as Bragg's troops moved toward a showdown with Federals in Kentucky. Like Lee in Maryland, Bragg had entered Kentucky hoping to win support from the populace. His troops received a warm welcome as they crossed over from Tennessee, wrote Sam Watkins of the 1st Tennessee Infantry: "The bands played 'Dixie' and 'Bonnie Blue Flag,' the citizens cheered, and the ladies waved handkerchiefs and threw us bouquets." But fewer Kentuckians joined Confederate ranks than fought for the Union. Many simply wanted to remain peacefully at home on their farms. "Their hearts are evidently with us," wrote Major General Edmund Kirby Smith, who joined in the Confederate campaign, "but their blue-grass and fat cattle are against us."

For Bragg, the contest for Kentucky was a chance to show skeptics that he was qualified to lead the Army of the Mississippi, which had fought at Shiloh under two commanders with larger reputations than his own: Albert Sidney Johnston and P. G. T. Beauregard. After Johnston died at Shiloh and Beauregard was removed by Davis for abandoning Corinth, Mississippi, to the enemy, Bragg took charge of an army he regarded as little better than a mob and cracked down on the troops. "He loved to crush the spirit of his men," wrote Sam Watkins. "The more of a hangdog look they had about them the better was General Bragg pleased." Yet this seemingly aggressive commander was surprisingly reluctant to commit himself. The invasion of Kentucky was General Smith's idea, and Bragg was slow to assert his seniority and take charge of

> **"The common people is drove off to fight for the big mans negro."**
> *North Carolina woman denouncing the Confederate draft*

the campaign. When Kentuckians hesitated to volunteer, he occupied the state capital, Frankfort, and installed a Confederate governor there so he could legally conscript troops. That scheme was sure to antagonize independent-minded Kentuckians of all persuasions, but it was cut short. On October 4, just hours after the new governor was sworn in, Bragg abandoned the capital to approaching Federals to assemble his scattered forces for battle.

Like Bragg, the Federal commander pursuing Confederates in Kentucky, General Don Carlos Buell, had much to prove. He had barely reached Shiloh with his army in time to help Grant avert disaster there, and his pace since then had been far too slow to satisfy his superiors, who nearly removed him from command in September. Buell was not to blame for delays caused by Confederate cavalry under Brigadier General Nathan Bedford Forrest and Colonel John Hunt Morgan, whose men burned bridges, severed telegraph lines, and otherwise disrupted enemy movements and communications. But some Federals faulted Buell for not being tough enough on civilians who helped those raiders and mounted their own attacks. Buell disapproved of reprisals taken by subordinates such as Colonel John Beatty, who responded forcefully when guerrillas in one town ambushed a train carrying his troops. Hereafter, he warned the populace, "every time a train was fired upon we should hang a man." Beatty then set fire to the town. Buell had another officer, Colonel John Turchin, court-martialed and dismissed for reprisals against civilians, but Lincoln reinstated and promoted Turchin, sending a clear signal that he favored strong measures against Confederates in and out of uniform.

If Buell did not shape up, Lincoln had his eye on possible successors, including Buell's second-in-command, George Thomas, and Major General William Rosecrans, who had driven Confederate forces from Iuka, Mississippi, on September 19 and then had beaten back a furious attack at nearby Corinth two weeks later. Under pressure from Washington, Buell moved with newfound urgency and caught up with Bragg's forces at Perryville, Kentucky, south of Frankfort, on October 8. Bragg had not brought all his troops together there and had only about 16,000 men at hand. He thought he was facing a small portion of Buell's army, when in fact 60,000 Federal troops awaited his Confederates west of town. "Do not scatter your forces," he was warned by Major General William Hardee, his most experienced corps commander. "Strike with your whole strength." But Bragg pressed ahead at Perryville and defied the odds.

Leading the Confederate attack were Tennesseans under Major General Benjamin Cheatham, who shouted "Give 'em hell, boys!" His men proceeded to do just that, driving the Federals on Buell's left back for more than a mile. Buell learned of the attack belatedly at his headquarters to the rear and failed to exploit his numerical superiority. An entire Federal corps remained inactive that day on his right, facing only a small force of Confederate cavalry. Fortunately for Buell, he had a young prodigy up front who needed no prompting, 31-year-old Brigadier General Philip Sheridan. Sensing that Bragg had thrown most of his forces against Buell's left, Sheridan advanced against the weak side of the Rebel line and drove Confederates there back into the streets of Perryville, negating Bragg's earlier gains. The battle ended as a draw,

"This war is ours. We must fight it out ourselves."

JEFFERSON DAVIS

with both sides suffering around 4,000 casualties in sharp fighting between two armies that were growing accustomed to war and learning to play by its deadly rules. "There was no cringing, no dodging," wrote one participant. "The men stood right straight up on the open field, loaded and fired, charged and fell back as deliberately as if on drill." That night, Bragg recognized what he was up against—Buell's entire army—and withdrew his outnumbered forces before dawn.

Both commanders at Perryville were barraged by criticism afterward. When Buell let Confederates retreat unhindered from Kentucky into Tennessee, President Lincoln removed him in favor of Rosecrans. Bragg, for his part, was denounced by his officers and was even faulted by his own wife for losing Kentucky to Buell. "I had hoped he could have been overtaken & driven out," she wrote Bragg sternly. Jefferson Davis, who knew what it was like to face detractors on all sides, gave Bragg a sympathetic hearing and decided to stick with him, but these were bitter days for the president. Hopes of expanding the Confederacy to include Kentucky and other border states were fading. And another dream harbored by Davis since the war began— that Great Britain might recognize and aid the Confederacy—was now dead. The British would not back the South after its recent setbacks, and having

Dead men and horses litter the field at Corinth, Mississippi, after Confederates attacked Battery Robinett (background) on October 4 and were driven back. The body of Colonel William Rogers of the 2nd Texas Infantry, who led the attack, lies to the left of the tree stump at center. "The men fell like grass," wrote one Confederate at Corinth, where entrenched Federals led by General William Rosecrans scythed down wave after wave of attackers, inflicting nearly 5,000 casualties on forces under General Earl Van Dorn.

abolished slavery within their own realm, they would not oppose Lincoln and emancipation. "This war is ours," Davis told the Confederate Congress bluntly. "We must fight it out ourselves."

SLAUGHTER AT FREDERICKSBURG

THE GLOOM WAS NEARLY AS THICK IN WASHINGTON AS IN RICHMOND. IN FALL elections, Democrats critical of the Emancipation Proclamation and Lincoln's handling of the war won races for governor in New York and New Jersey and gained 32 seats in the House of Representatives, substantially reducing the Republican margin there. Some of the victors were so-called Peace Democrats, branded Copperheads by their opponents, who accused them of poisoning the war effort by urging compromise with the South. Lincoln acknowledged privately that "the ill-success of the war" was deepening divisions within the Union and felt he could no longer tolerate generals who were slow to pursue enemy forces. In early November, after learning that McClellan had failed to prevent Lee's troops in the Shenandoah Valley from crossing the Blue Ridge and placing themselves between Federal forces and Richmond, he gave up on the general. "I said I would remove him if he let Lee's army get away from him, and I must do so," Lincoln told his trusted advisor, Francis P. Blair, Sr. "He has got the slows, Mr. Blair."

McClellan should not have been surprised when Lincoln's order reached him at his headquarters near Warrenton, Virginia, on November 7. It was no secret that he opposed both the Emancipation Proclamation and a recent decree by Lincoln suspending the writ of habeas corpus throughout the Union, thus allowing military authorities to jail suspected subversives without a hearing. In a letter to a prominent New York Democrat, McClellan criticized Lincoln for "inaugurating servile war, emancipating the slaves, & at one stroke of the pen changing our free institutions into a despotism—for such I regard as the natural effect of the last proclamation suspending the habeas corpus throughout the land." Lincoln did not want to make McClellan a martyr in the eyes of his fellow Democrats and removed him for military reasons, but he was under growing political pressure in Washington to oust this troublesome commander. "They have made a great mistake," McClellan wrote afterward. "Alas for my poor country!" What most shocked him was the choice of Ambrose Burnside to succeed him—a general he considered "not fit to command more than a regiment." Burnside had done well as leader of the expedition to coastal North Carolina early in the year, but his corps had faltered at Antietam. He did not seek command of the army and accepted only when told the honor would otherwise go to Joseph Hooker, whom he resented.

Once in charge, Burnside moved quickly to circumvent Lee's army at Culpeper by shifting forces southeastward from Warrenton to Falmouth, across from Fredericksburg. If his troops could cross the Rappahannock River there

> "If you make the attack as contemplated, it will be the greatest slaughter of the war; there isn't infantry enough in our whole army to carry those heights."
>
> FEDERAL COLONEL RUSH HAWKINS, AT FREDERICKSBURG

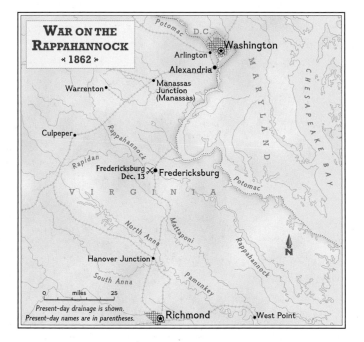

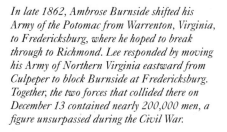

In late 1862, Ambrose Burnside shifted his Army of the Potomac from Warrenton, Virginia, to Fredericksburg, where he hoped to break through to Richmond. Lee responded by moving his Army of Northern Virginia eastward from Culpeper to block Burnside at Fredericksburg. Together, the two forces that collided there on December 13 contained nearly 200,000 men, a figure unsurpassed during the Civil War.

before Lee awoke to the threat and moved to intercept them, they would be barely 50 miles from Richmond, with little to prevent them from advancing on the capital. By November 18, much of the Army of Potomac had reached Falmouth, moving so quickly that officers accustomed to McClellan's glacial advances were left rubbing "their eyes in mute astonishment," a reporter noted. Lee was unsure of Burnside's whereabouts and Federicksburg was lightly defended, but heavy rains swelled the Rappahannock, making it difficult to ford, and pontoons Federal engineers needed to bridge the river did not arrive from Washington for more than a week. By the time Burnside's forces were ready to cross in early December, Lee's army had occupied the high ground around Fredericksburg in anticipation of an attack. "On the Confederate side all was ready," recalled Lieutenant William Owen of Lee's artillery, "and the shock was awaited with stubborn resolution."

Having lost the advantage of surprise, Burnside now lost the confidence of his officers. "If you make the attack as contemplated, it will be the greatest slaughter of the war," warned Colonel Rush Hawkins, a brigade commander under Burnside; "there isn't infantry enough in our whole army to carry those heights." So strong was Lee's position that he would have been hard to defeat even with half as many troops as his opponent, but he had been substantially reinforced since Antietam and now had some 75,000 men to contend with Burnside's army of more than 115,000. Burnside felt he had no choice but to forge ahead, given Lincoln's expectations. "I know where Lee's forces are, and I expect to surprise him," he declared. Few offensives during the war were more thoroughly anticipated than this one, however, or launched with greater foreboding by officers and men.

On December 12, Federals crossed the Rappahannock on pontoon bridges and prepared to attack Lee's army the following day. James Longstreet's Confederates held Marye's Heights, just west of Fredericksburg, and Stonewall Jackson's forces held Prospect Hill, overlooking the river south of town. Burnside hoped that his left wing, consisting of two corps under the overall command of Major General William Franklin, could outflank Jackson's forces, but as Franklin's men advanced on the morning of the 13th they were pinned down by murderous artillery fire. Unable to find a way around Jackson, Major General George Meade instead challenged him head on by sending his division of Pennsylvanians up the wooded slope. "They went in beautifully," Meade reported, and achieved the first and only Federal breakthrough of the battle before Jackson's reserves drove them back. Franklin, who had no faith in Burnside's plan, concluded that further exertions were useless and withheld the bulk of his forces, leaving nearly 20,000 troops uncommitted on the Federal left while attacks proceeded against Longstreet's virtually impregnable position on Marye's Heights.

Lee was with Longstreet as Federals by the thousands marched bravely into battle and was stirred by the spectacle. "It is well that war is so terrible—we should grow too fond of it," he remarked. Many Confederates looking down from the heights shared Lee's sense of awe as their opponents advanced into the maelstrom in near perfect order. "How beautifully they came on!" recalled Lieutenant Owen. "Their bright bayonets glistening in the sunlight made the

FRENCH MARY

Among the thousands of Union casualties at Fredericksburg, one woman stands out. Mary Tepe (above), known to soldiers as "French Mary," was struck in the heel by a musket ball as she comforted men of the 114th Pennsylvania Infantry, a Zouave regiment she followed as a vivandière, or female sutler. Not all sutlers—who peddled goods to troops at sometimes-inflated prices—were as beloved as Mary. One war correspondent called them "a wretched class of swindlers," but Mary did more than sell pies, tinned meats, tobacco, and other fare to troops in need. She also washed and mended their clothing. And during battles she carried a small keg to the front lines at considerable risk and offered troops who were cold, weary, or wounded sips of whiskey, which was considered a healthy stimulant in those days.

Little is known of Mary's life before the Battle of Fredericksburg. She reportedly emigrated from France to Philadelphia, where she married a tailor named Bernardo Tepe and followed him as a vivandière when he enlisted with the Union and went to fight in Virginia. Grateful Zouaves credited her with braving enemy fire in 13 battles. For her courage at Fredericksburg, she was decorated by her corps. ■

Private William Kepler

4TH OHIO INFANTRY, KIMBALL'S BRIGADE

*Dubbed the "Gibraltar Brigade" for its service at Antietam, Nathan Kimball's brigade led the Federal assault
on Marye's Heights. The 4th's commander, Colonel John S. Mason, led his own regiment along with the 8th Ohio and
1st Delaware in advance of the brigade as skirmishers. As they deployed below the heights, the brigade came under murderous
artillery and rifle fire and was unable to reach its objective. The regiment fell back, losing 5 killed and 65 wounded.
William Kepler survived and in 1886 he authored a history of his regiment's service.*

COLONEL MASON, COMMANDing the skirmishers, near noon gave the order to advance. Colonel Godman now commands: "Attention! Shoulder arms. Forward—file right—March!" Our regiment, now numbering nineteen officers and ninety-eight enlisted men, moves in the advance, rapidly out Princess Ann street, to the rear of the town, crosses the canal bridge and we are just in the very act of climbing up an embankment two to three feet high, and can plainly see the rebels upon redoubts on Marye Heights move rapidly to and fro, while Godman riding coolly at our head, gives the order: "Deploy as skirmishers! By the left flank!" when there is a puff of smoke on the Heights and two men fall; immediately several more cannon belch forth fire and smoke and sixteen more fall; ... The wounded are immediately laid in back of the embankment or helped to the house a few rods to our right and soon cared for by Surgeon Morrison. ...

We continue on the run up the slope over the rise of ground, down the further slope, under a continued storm of missiles, which does now but little damage to our thin line; we cross a ravine, with its mud and fence, then up the Marye Heights slope, a triple line of rebel skirmishers rapidly vanishing behind a stone wall from which

> **"The sight is horrible and heart-rending; hundreds of the bleeding and mangled are dragging themselves from the dead and dying, are trampled upon by the thousands, many of whom in the excitement hardly knew whither they were going save to the certain slaughter."**

there now comes volley after volley from some half a dozen lines of rebels; again one after another of our boys fall; human nature cannot endure facing such a storm of bullets and not reply; we have reached the crest of the slope and open a vigorous fire.

We hug the ground for some time, hoping reinforcements would soon come to help us drive the enemy from the stone wall; General Kimball's other four regiments now come over the hill behind us on the run, closing the gaps that are made in their ranks by the storm of missiles; they reach us, drop down by our side, and open fire. ...

Nearly an hour has passed by since the ordeal began, when the Second Brigade of our division forms at the canal and comes charging midst a terrific hurling of shot and shell; crosses the ravine, comes up the slope, drops down at the crest and joins the general fusilade against the stone wall. In like manner at intervals of less than half an hour comes brigade after brigade, doing just the same things, rush over the plain for one-third of a mile, over dead, wounded and dying, closing up the gaps, while the showers of lead and iron leave the field more difficult to cross because of the increased number of mangled remains that must not be trampled into the earth. ...

Thousands of men come over the slope and get down at the crest with us before the Heights and there remain, while on the hill and slope behind and among us the sight is horrible and heartrending; hundreds of the bleeding and mangled are dragging themselves from the dead and dying, are trampled upon by the thousands, many of whom in the excitement hardly knew whither they were going save to the certain slaughter. Wounded men fall upon wounded; the dead upon the mangled; the baptism of fire adds more wounds and brings even death to helpless ones; as we look back the field seems covered with mortals in agony; some motionless, others are dragging themselves toward the rear; ... on the front line there is no safety. ■

line look like a huge serpent of blue and steel. . . . We could see our shells bursting in their ranks, making great gaps; but on they came, as though they would go straight through and over us. Now we gave them the canister, and that staggered them." Federals who withstood that barrage came up against Confederate infantry in a sunken road behind a stone wall. "A series of braver, more desperate charges than those hurled against the troops in the sunken road was never known," wrote Longstreet in tribute to his foes, "and the piles and cross-piles of dead marked a field such as I never saw before or since."

Observing the carnage from Fredericksburg, General Hooker concluded that "it would be a useless waste of life to attack with the force at my disposal." Only at Burnside's insistence did Hooker agree to commit his troops that afternoon and sacrifice "as many men as my orders required." Nightfall brought an end to the slaughter but no end to the suffering as a bitter chill descended and many of the wounded died of exposure. "We are slaughtered like sheep, and no result but defeat," wrote Captain William Nagle of the Irish Brigade, which advanced boldly under its emerald banner and paid dearly, with one regiment losing all 16 of its officers. "It can hardly be in human nature for men to show more valor, or generals to manifest less judgment," a reporter on the scene concluded. Burnside—who suffered over 12,500 casualties at Fredericksburg, or 7,000 more than Lee—was devastated and had to be dissuaded from personally leading another attack the next morning that could have been suicidal for him.

Back in Washington, Lincoln felt the loss as keenly as Burnside did. Never in this year of trials had he come closer to the brink of utter hopelessness. "If there is a worse place than Hell, I am in it," he remarked. But he did not lose faith in his cause or his capacity to further it. As Senator William Fessenden of Maine remarked at year's end, nothing could shake Lincoln's conviction that "he was specially chosen by the Almighty for this crisis, and well chosen."

> ## "It is well that war is so terrible—we should grow too fond of it."
>
> GENERAL ROBERT E. LEE

Confederate infantry massed behind this stone wall at Fredericksburg beat back repeated assaults by opposing Federals, who suffered further punishment from artillery on Marye's Heights. "All that day we watched the fruitless charges, with their fearful slaughter, until we were sick at heart," wrote Alexander Hunter of the 17th Virginia Infantry, who saw an entire line of Federals swept away as they approached the stone wall. "I forgot they were enemies," he added, "and only remembered that they were men."

THE SOLDIER'S LIFE

BETWEEN BATTLES, SOLDIERS OF both the North and South had hardships aplenty to deal with, not the least of which was sheer boredom. Camp life was a never-ending series of chores and drills, with a little time in between to play games and indulge vices. As the war dragged on, the soldier's life became more dismal, and desertion significantly affected both sides.

"Fancy the comforts of such a life as this!" wrote Private Randolph Shotwell of the 8th Virginia Infantry. "Roused at dawn [for] the company-roll; then . . . rub the skin off of your knuckles, trying to start a fire . . . and devote the next hour to trying to boil a dingy tin-cup of so-called coffee." Shotwell was a prep-school boy writing about his first winter away from home. Later in the war he would remember his winter quarters fondly: "Even the discomforts of Centerville would be recalled as positive luxuries."

Armies generally marched and fought when it was warm and holed up over the winter. An assortment of tents, cabins, and log-and-canvas structures took the place of home. Tepee-shaped Sibley tents could hold up to 18 men and were equipped with a stove. Camp food was deplorable (regimental cooks were called dog robbers), and traveling vendors called sutlers offered alternatives such as cakes and sardines, but at inflated prices.

Adequate food was even more of a challenge for soldiers on campaign, who had to subsist on field rations carried in their haversack, usually salted pork, hardtack, and coffee. The incursions of Northern armies and damage to transportation systems sometimes made rations scarce in the South. A Rebel claimed to have once seen fellow soldiers "reduced to the extremity of picking grains of corn out of the horses' dung, washing it, and parching it for food." Tenting became a luxury for armies on the move as well. The dog or pup tent was improvised, which allowed a pair of soldiers to combine two five-foot squares of canvas, carried on their backs, with a stick or their musket as a ridge-pole. More often than not, tent flies, ponchos, and blankets served as shelter.

When encamped, "we drill, and sometimes we stop to eat a little," wrote one Pennsylvania soldier. Universally practiced and just as universally hated, drilling was supposed to instill a sense of soldierly discipline into amateur ranks. When not drilling, soldiers were kept busy with chores like caring for horses and equipment, building roads, and digging latrines. Between supper at 6:30 and lights out at 9:00, men not on picket duty had only time to kill, and gambling and drinking often did the trick. According to one Texan, men "who never threw a card before the war began [would] lose the last Confederate dollar they had." Alcohol supposedly was restricted to senior officers, but whiskey was prevalent, and as with gambling, men who never knew the vice before the war succumbed out of boredom or shell shock.

Sports were encouraged as alternatives to cards and drink. One of the most popular, especially on the Union side, was the relatively new game of baseball. Though the homemade balls were softer and the rules slightly different, the game played was the same one played when the National League was established in 1876. ■

> ### "If you could look into our tents, you would not wonder that consolation is sought for in whiskey."
> CONNECTICUT OFFICER

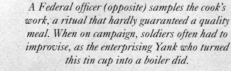

A Federal officer *(opposite) samples the cook's work, a ritual that hardly guaranteed a quality meal. When on campaign, soldiers often had to improvise, as the enterprising Yank who turned this tin cup into a boiler did.*

The most ubiquitous item in either the Rebel or Yankee ration bag was a square flour-and-water biscuit called hardtack. Often bug-infested after storage, hardtack was "unsuitable for anything that claims to be human," according to a Vermont private. Foraging (right), though illegal, was often necessary, and few were better at it than Private Billy Crump, shown here with spoils for Colonel Rutherford B. Hayes's 23rd Ohio. Crump once netted 50 chickens, 2 turkeys, a goose, 20 dozen eggs, and 30 pounds of butter on a single expedition.

Pipes, such as this meerschaum model belonging to Private Stephen H. Leonard of the 3rd Massachusetts Volunteer Cavalry, were among the most treasured luxuries, as evidenced by the photo of General Fitz-John Porter's staff bivouacked during the 1862 Peninsula Campaign. "Most of the soldiers with whom I was thrown . . . smoked tobacco as a constant habit," one Alabama infantryman recalled. "In those days I esteemed such indulgence next to a necessity, and an inexpressible delight."

The wife of a soldier in the 31st Pennsylvania poses next to her husband and children before doing the wash at Camp Pendleton in northern Virginia. The Army allowed each regiment to have four laundresses in camp, but the men were on their own during campaigns.

A Federal soldier mends his uniform while others pass the time writing letters. Soldiers in the field found themselves doing all sorts of unaccustomed chores, and referred to their sewing kits, such as the one shown here, owned by confederate soldier H. C. S. Green, as "housewives." Below, Federals fighting in the Wilderness campaign take advantage of a break to swim in Virginia's North Anna River. Hygiene was a casualty of most campaigns, and men looked forward to the luxury of a bath or a shave.

Though discouraged by some commanders, card playing was probably the most popular form of recreation in both Northern and Southern regiments. Union playing cards such as these, with patriotic motifs in place of the usual suits, were found in many knapsacks. The Federal blockade eventually forced Confederates to make their own playing cards.

Two Federal soldiers square off for a bare-knuckle boxing match near their camp in Petersburg, Virginia, in April 1865.

Though church services and the Bible were common, clergymen often struggled to keep their flock's morale from sagging. Father Thomas Mooney of New York City (above) helped motivate his state's Irish 69th before Bull Run by christening a cannon, an unorthodox ploy that earned him a rebuke from his bishop.

CHAPTER 3

1863

VICTORY OR DEATH

EARLY ON THE MORNING OF DECEMBER 31, 1862, NEAR MURFREES-boro, Tennessee, a great, gray horde of Confederates rushed from the woods west of Stones River and launched a desperate battle that would continue into the new year. Soldiers on both sides who had seen combat and knew how murderous it could be fought with grim resolve, as if aware that something larger than their own life was at stake. One Confederate officer wrote that his troops "leapt forward like men bent on conquering—or dying in the attempt." Many Federals fell back under the shock of that onslaught, but others held their ground. One Union officer proud-ly noted that his men were "determined to stop the sweeping tide or die." Like their equally determined foes, they were obey-ing an ancient imperative, echoed on battlefields down through the ages: "Victory or Death!"

The Battle of Stones River was a fitting start to the momentous year of 1863. It was not just the fate of soldiers or armies that hung in the balance now but the fate of the rival nations for which they fought. The struggle at Murfreesboro in January was followed by crucial confrontations at Vicksburg, Chancellorsville, Gettysburg, and Chattanooga. None of these battles decided the war, but col-lectively they tipped the scales. By year's end, the Union would be much closer to victory, and heroic measures would be required to prolong the life of the Confederacy. As Jefferson Davis said, "We are now in the darkest hour of our political existence." ∎

Federals of the Army of the Potomac wait solemnly for orders to advance before the Battle of Chancellorsville in May 1863. Robert E. Lee, commanding the opposing Confederates, told General Lafayette McLaws on the eve of the battle, "It must be victory or death, for defeat would be ruinous."

Taking Vicksburg

IT WAS NOT A HAPPY NEW YEAR FOR WILLIAM SHERMAN. A FEW DAYS EARLIer, on December 29, 1862, his Federals had suffered a bloody repulse at Chickasaw Bluffs, near Vicksburg. He now had to abandon plans to capture that fortified town, situated on high ground overlooking the Mississippi. "I assume all the responsibility and attach fault to no one," he wrote in his official report on January 3, "and am generally satisfied with the high spirit manifested by all." He summed up the situation more bluntly in a letter to his wife: "Well we have been to Vicksburg, and it was too much for us, and we have backed out."

Sherman hated to admit defeat, but he was not the first Federal commander who had tried and failed to take Vicksburg. David Farragut, after capturing New Orleans, had twice led fleets up the Mississippi in 1862 and bombarded the town, but the damage he did was slight compared to the harm done to his own ships by Vicksburg's batteries and the Confederate ironclad *Arkansas*. When Farragut gave up the fight in late July and returned to New Orleans, the best he could say for his efforts was that they "showed the enemy that we were prompt and always ready to be upon them with a sharp stick."

It would take more than a sharp stick to force the surrender of Vicksburg. One of the few things on which Abraham Lincoln and Jefferson Davis agreed

> "Well we have been to Vicksburg, and it was too much for us, and we have backed out."
>
> MAJOR GENERAL WILLIAM T. SHERMAN, *after the Battle of Chickasaw Bluffs*

Ulysses Grant relied heavily on William Sherman (right), who expressed doubts about Grant's plan to take Vicksburg in 1863 but later judged it "one of the greatest campaigns in history."

was the strategic significance of this hub, which linked the core of the Confederacy to the Confederate Southwest by river and rail. Through Vicksburg from Louisiana, Arkansas, and Texas came shipments vital to Southerners and their war effort, including beef, grain, and weapons of European manufacture imported through Mexico to avoid the Federal blockade. As Davis put it, Vicksburg was the "nailhead that held the South's two halves together." And as long as Confederate batteries remained atop the bluffs and dominated the river below, Vicksburg would also serve to divide the Union by preventing Federals from moving freely between occupied Memphis and New Orleans and keeping Midwestern farmers from transporting their produce by barge to the Gulf of Mexico for shipment to the East Coast. Some freight moved across the Union by rail, but rates were steep and space limited as railroads strained to meet military demands. Lincoln had conducted cargo downriver to New Orleans on a flatboat as a young man, and he now placed a premium on controlling the Mississippi. "The war can never be brought to a close until that key is in our pocket," he said of Vicksburg; "I am acquainted with that region and know what I am talking about, and, valuable as New Orleans will be to us, Vicksburg will be more so."

Urged on by their superiors in Washington, Sherman and his boss, Ulysses Grant, spared no effort to take Vicksburg. For Grant, it was an opportunity to show those who blamed him for letting down his guard at Shiloh that he was equal to any challenge. After the Battle of Shiloh, Grant had endured what amounted to a public scolding when his department chief, Henry Halleck, came down from St. Louis to supervise the Army of the Tennessee. At one point, Grant considered calling it quits, but Sherman dissuaded him. "You could not be quiet at home for a week when armies are on the move," Sherman told him, predicting he would soon be back in favor. Within a month, Halleck restored Grant to independent command, and Lincoln then cleared the way for him to become head of operations along the Mississippi by summoning Halleck to Washington to serve as general in chief of Federal forces.

Grant hoped to show that Lincoln's trust in him was well placed by capturing Vicksburg quickly, but his first campaign to that end in late 1862 went badly awry. His plan was to advance southward with 40,000 men from Tennessee along the railroad to Jackson, the capital of Mississippi, where he would then turn west toward Vicksburg, 40 miles away. He anticipated that Confederates would concentrate against him before he reached Vicksburg, leaving that town vulnerable to an assault from the north by Sherman, who would come down from Memphis with more than 30,000 troops. But Grant was unable to protect his railroad supply lines from punishing cavalry raids by Nathan Bedford Forrest, who had driven Federals to distraction in Tennessee earlier in the year and now did the same here. Forrest was a "law unto himself," one of Grant's aides remarked, "and was constantly doing the unexpected at all times and places." His men destroyed 50 miles of track, severed

A cotton planter from Mississippi with no formal military training, Nathan Bedford Forrest had a genius for mounting cavalry raids that confused and intimidated Union forces. As he said to his men on one occasion, "Shoot up everything blue and keep up the scare."

telegraph lines, and otherwise bedeviled Grant's army. Meanwhile, a separate cavalry force under Major General Earl Van Dorn, a fiery Mississippian born to raise hell, torched Grant's supply base at Holly Springs on December 20. The raids "cut me off from all communication with the North," Grant wrote. "I determined, therefore, to abandon my campaign."

Sherman, out of touch with Grant, went ahead with his part of the deal, bringing troops down the Mississippi from Memphis by boat and turning up the Yazoo River just north of Vicksburg to a landing near Chickasaw Bluffs, where Confederate artillery and infantry awaited his men in force and barred their way into town. Sherman had little chance of taking Vicksburg on his own but put his foes to the test on December 29 by sending troops across a bog to the base of the bluffs, where they were pinned down under withering fire for hours before retreating. In this woefully one-sided battle, the Confederates suffered fewer than 200 casualties and inflicted nearly ten times as many losses on Sherman's force. Afterward, a journalist reported, wounded Federals lay in the bog "under a soaking rain, uncared for, and many who had fallen on their faces and were unable to turn themselves smothered in the mud." Persistent rain and heavy fog prevented Sherman from renewing the attack the next day, and he gave up.

A short time later, he met with Admiral David Dixon Porter, whose gunboat fleet supported his offensive. "General Sherman came on board my flagship, drenched to the skin," Porter recalled. "He looked as if he had been grappling with the mud and got the worst of it." After a long silence, he burst out: "I have lost seventeen hundred men, and those infernal reporters will publish all over the country their ridiculous stories about Sherman being whipped, etc."

"Only seventeen hundred men!" Porter exclaimed. "That is nothing;

> **"I have lost seventeen hundred men, and those infernal reporters will publish all over the country their ridiculous stories about Sherman being whipped, etc."**
>
> GENERAL WILLIAM SHERMAN
>
> **"Only seventeen hundred men! That is nothing; simply an episode in the war. You'll lose seventeen thousand before the war is over."**
>
> REAR ADMIRAL DAVID DIXON PORTER

The Warren County Courthouse, completed in 1860, dominates the skyline of Vicksburg, built on a steep bluff overlooking the Mississippi that Confederates reinforced with batteries, making the town a forbidding obstacle for Federals approaching by river.

simply an episode in the war. You'll lose seventeen thousand before the war is over." Then he offered Sherman a drink along with a few words of encouragement: "We'll have Vicksburg yet before we die."

Passengers and freight arriving here at Vicksburg by steamboat from Louisiana and other states along the Mississippi River could continue by rail to such destinations as Jackson, Mississippi, and Mobile, Alabama.

STRUGGLE AT STONES RIVER

WHILE SHERMAN DEALT WITH HIS DEFEAT AT CHICKASAW BLUFFS, ANOTHER FEDeral commander, William Rosecrans, faced a far greater crisis in a desperate battle that erupted not far from Nashville, Tennessee, on the last day of 1862 and concluded on January 2. Events in Tennessee had considerable impact on Grant's Vicksburg campaign. So long as Rosecrans maintained a firm grip on Nashville and kept opposing forces led by Braxton Bragg on the defensive, Grant could concentrate all his resources on seizing Vicksburg. Bragg, for his part, had already been asked to divert 7,500 men—nearly one-fifth of his army—to Mississippi to strengthen Vicksburg against Grant. Bragg did so at the insistence of Jefferson Davis, who was under pressure from his fellow Mississippians to hold Vicksburg at all costs. This further strained Davis's relationship with Joseph Johnston, who, after recovering from wounds suffered at Seven Pines outside Richmond, took overall command of Confederate forces between the Appalachians and the Mississippi. Johnston thought it was better to commit troops against Federals in the field than to concentrate forces at Vicksburg. If reinforcements had to be sent there, he argued, they should come from Arkansas, not from Bragg's hard-pressed army in the crucial state of Tennessee. Bragg could not make the sacrifice Davis demanded of him, Johnston warned, "without exposing himself to inevitable defeat."

Davis realized that his decision placed Bragg in something of a predicament. After visiting him in mid-December at his encampment near Murfreesboro, some 30 miles southeast of Nashville, he left Bragg the option to withdraw if pressed. "Fight if you can," Davis advised, "and fall back beyond the Tennessee." That meant possibly retreating all the way to Chattanooga, on the Georgia border. Davis's vague instructions did not help Bragg clarify his thinking as Rosecrans advanced against him from Nashville at Lincoln's urging. Bragg was a mercurial figure, who could be cocky and combative one day and unsure of himself the next. He needed support from his seasoned corps commanders, William Hardee and Leonidas Polk, but he no longer had their trust.

Here as at the Battle of Perryville in Kentucky a few months earlier, Bragg faced an army significantly larger than his own but chose not to remain on the defensive. He could have dug in outside Murfreesboro, along the east bank of Stones River, as Rosecrans descended with his troops from Nashville to the northwest. Instead, he shifted most of his forces west of the river on December 30 in preparation for an attack. That was the "Yankee side," as Sam Watkins of the 1st Tennessee put it, and he and others considered this "bad generalship." But Bragg's bold move gave him the opportunity to outflank his opponents and cut them off. Around midnight, a vigilant Federal officer, Brigadier General Joshua Sill, spotted large numbers of Confederates moving into position for that flank attack and informed Phil Sheridan, his division commander. Sheridan then warned his corps commander, Major General Alexander McCook, but McCook was slow to alert other officers under him and they were slow to respond. Only Sheridan's men were fully prepared for the avalanche that was about to hit.

At dawn on December 31, Confederates of Hardee's Corps attacked west of the river and overwhelmed their startled opponents, turning the Federal right and threatening Rosecrans's army with annihilation. To some who had fought at Shiloh, where Federals were surprised in their encampments, the onslaught here seemed eerily similar. "The coffee pots and frying pans were on the fires steaming as we went through their camp," recalled one Confederate. "Many were still in their 'pup' tent asleep and were killed while lying there," another wrote. As the surviving Federals retreated, he added, it was "every fellow for himself and the devil take the hindmost." Units to the rear

General Braxton Bragg, who led Confederate forces at Stones River, was a stubborn man who did not welcome criticism. "When he has formed his opinion," one colleague remarked, "no advice of all his officers put together can shake him."

were caught in the rout, and soldiers threw down their guns and ran. "If there was anything more disgraceful at Bull Run than the scenes I witnessed, I have not seen it described," wrote one Union soldier at Stones River. "All around us, and often breaking through us, was a yelling mob; officers weeping or swearing; soldiers demoralized and shivering."

Here as at Shiloh, however, the Federals narrowly averted disaster, thanks largely to the efforts of Sheridan, whose men were braced for the shock and gave ground grudgingly near the center of the Federal line while the right wing caved in. They had to fall back because they were running out of ammunition and in danger of being cut off, but their fighting retreat—which claimed the life of General Sill, who had alerted Sheridan to the threat—wore down the opposing Confederates and gave Rosecrans time to respond. He had been planning to launch his own attack that morning, but Bragg had beaten him to the punch. "This battle must be won," he insisted when he learned at headquarters of the collapse on his right. He then hurried to the front to repair the damage. "Wherever the battle raged most fiercely," recalled Surgeon Eben Swift, "General Rosecrans bore his charmed life," exposing himself to the same risks his men faced and urging them on. At one point, a cannonball passed within a few feet of him and decapitated his close friend and chief of staff, Lieutenant Colonel Julius Garesché. Rosecrans's coat was spattered with blood, and those who saw him afterward feared he had been wounded. "No," he told them. "That is the blood of poor Garesché."

By midday, Rosecrans had stemmed the rout on his right. Bragg then abandoned his flanking movement and attacked the enemy salient, or the protruding portion of the Federal line, which bent like a fish hook around a cedar grove called the Round Forest, known to those who fought there as Hell's Half Acre. A Confederate breakthrough in that critical sector, situated near the west bank of the river astride a turnpike and railroad to Nashville, could have been fatal for Rosecrans. But he was alert to the danger and sent all available artillery—50 cannon in all—to support his infantry there. The brunt of the fighting was borne by a brigade led by Colonel William Hazen, who had battled Comanches on the Plains before the war and was used to being in tight spots. When his Federals began to run short of ammunition, he ordered them to "fix bayonets and hold your ground." An all-out assault might have overwhelmed them, but Bragg and Leonidas Polk repeated the same mistake made at the Hornet's Nest at Shiloh by sending in units piecemeal against a forbidding Federal strongpoint. As evening approached, Confederates made one last push to capture Hell's Half Acre, but the big guns there were too much for them. "In the fading light," recalled Spencer Talley of the 28th Tennessee Infantry, "the sheets of fire from the enemy's cannon looked hideous and dazzling."

Bragg shrugged off this setback at day's end and thought he was on the brink of victory. "The enemy has yielded his strong position and is falling

> **"All around us, and often breaking through us, was a yelling mob; officers weeping or swearing; soldiers demoralized and shivering."**
>
> *Union soldier at Stones River*

After fighting at Stones River, men of the 18th Ohio Infantry commemorated the battle on their regimental flag. Such flags were carried into action by a color guard of up to eight soldiers and defended to the death.

"My poor Orphans! My poor Orphan Brigade! They have cut it to pieces!"

CONFEDERATE MAJOR GENERAL JOHN C. BRECKINRIDGE

back," he wired Richmond that night. "God has granted us a happy New Year." He fully expected his opponents to pull out the next day, but he misjudged them. "This army does not retreat," insisted General George Thomas when Rosecrans asked his corps commanders if they should withdraw to Nashville. By sticking to their guns, the Federals placed Bragg in a quandary. He had entered battle with 7,000 fewer troops than Rosecrans and had suffered similar losses. Now Bragg feared that his opponent, who had tens of thousands of troops elsewhere in Tennessee, would call up reinforcements. He would have to defeat Rosecrans soon or withdraw. After deliberating for more than a day, Bragg decided to renew the battle by attacking Federals who had crossed to the east side of the river above Murfreesboro and occupied a ridge that commanded the field there. Capturing that high ground was sure to be costly for Bragg's men, and if they succeeded they would be prominent targets for Federal batteries on the west bank.

Among the forces assigned that grim task were men of the so-called Orphan Brigade, Confederates from Kentucky who were homeless now that their state was under Federal control. Their division commander, Major General John C. Breckinridge of Kentucky, a former vice president who ran against Lincoln in 1860 as candidate of the Southern Democrats, vehemently protested Bragg's order. "This attack is made against my judgment," he told a subordinate before launching the assault late on the afternoon of January 2. "Of course we all must try to do our duty and fight the best we can." His men did just that, charging up the ridge and driving their foes across the river, only to come under a blistering barrage from Federal artillery on the west bank. It was as if they had "opened the door of Hell," one witness wrote, "and the devil himself was there to greet them." Among those mortally wounded in the desperate attack was the commander of the Orphan Brigade, Brigadier General Roger Hanson, who had denounced Bragg's order as "murderous" before setting out. As the battered remnants of his brigade were forced back by the resurgent Federals at dusk, Breckinridge could not hold back tears. "My poor Orphans!" he exclaimed. "My poor Orphan Brigade! They have cut it to pieces!"

After this futile sacrifice, Bragg had little choice but to retreat. Nearly 19,000 men had been killed or wounded at Stones River, with casualties roughly equal on both sides, but the losses weighed much heavier on Bragg, who was left with only about 25,000 soldiers fit for duty. As his

In a sketch by Alfred Mathews, a military topographer who witnessed the battle, Federals wade across Stones River late on January 2 and repulse Confederates of Breckinridge's division.

hungry, ragged troops fell back toward Chattanooga, their disdain for Bragg reached legendary proportions, inspiring a tale that says much about this embattled general and his beleaguered men. As the story goes, Bragg was riding with his staff officers when he came upon a stray Texan on the road who failed to recognize him and looked suspiciously like a straggler.

"Don't you belong to Bragg's army?" asked the general.

"Bragg's army!" the Texan replied in disbelief. "Why, he's got no army! One half of it he shot in Kentucky, and the other half has been whipped to death at Murfreesboro!"

GRANT'S WINTER OF DISCONTENT

GRANT WAS FREE NOW TO CONCENTRATE ON VICKSBURG, BUT HE FELT MORE LIKE a prisoner, hemmed in by foul weather. The swampy terrain around Vicksburg could be hard to negotiate in any season, but the heavy rains and floods that occurred this winter all but ruled out a ground campaign by Grant before spring. While laying plans for that offensive, Grant kept troops busy on laborious engineering projects designed to circumvent obstacles that prevented Federal ships from freely navigating the Mississippi or landing troops up the Yazoo River where they could approach Vicksburg from the east, the town's more vulnerable side. Grant called these projects "experiments," but they proved little except to show that men who battled the elements here were bound to lose.

The first such undertaking involved digging a mile-long canal just west

> **"While we worked on that canal almost one half the men was sick and could not work. . . . They were dying every day like mice and no wonder."**
>
> *Union sergeant under General Sherman*

Troops of Sherman's Corps labor on a canal designed to allow boats to circumvent a horseshoe bend in the Mississippi at Vicksburg and bypass artillery there. Sherman concluded that the project was a "pure waste of human effort."

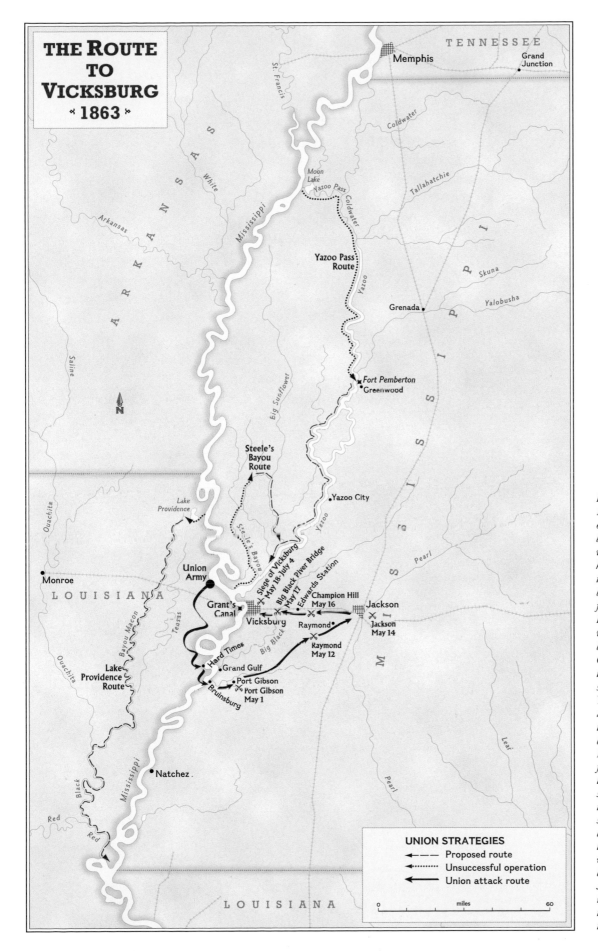

THE ROUTE TO VICKSBURG ✦ 1863 ✦

TENNESSEE

Memphis

Grand Junction

St. Francis

Coldwater

Moon Lake

Yazoo Pass

Coldwater

Tallahatchie

Yazoo Pass Route

Skuna

Yalobusha

Grenada

Yazoo

Mississippi

White

Arkansas

A R K A N S A S

Saline

Fort Pemberton
Greenwood

Big Sunflower

Steele's Bayou Route

Lake Providence

Yazoo City

Big Black

Steele's Bayou

Yazoo

Union Army

Grant's Canal

Siege of Vicksburg
May 18–July 4

Big Black River Bridge
May 17

Edwards Station

Champion Hill
May 16

Jackson

Jackson
May 14

Pearl

Vicksburg

Raymond

Hard Times

Grand Gulf

Raymond
May 12

Monroe

Bayou Macon

Ouachita

LOUISIANA

Lake Providence Route

Port Gibson

Port Gibson
May 1

Bruinsburg

M I S S I S S I P P I

Leaf

Natchez

Mississippi

Black

Red

Red

Pearl

N

LOUISIANA

UNION STRATEGIES
➡ - - - Proposed route
➡ •••••• Unsuccessful operation
➡ ——— Union attack route

0   miles   60

In the early months of 1863, Grant made laborious efforts to skirt Vicksburg's defenses, including work on the canal at the horseshoe bend, just west of town, and a much longer bypass extending westward from the Mississippi to Lake Providence and southward along creeks and bayous to the Red River. Grant's forces also explored two routes east of the Mississippi—one employing Yazoo Pass and the other Steele's Bayou—in an effort to circumvent Confederate batteries on the lower Yazoo River and attack Vicksburg from the northeast. When those efforts failed, Grant settled on a daring offensive that would carry his forces southward along the west bank of the Mississippi to the vicinity of Grand Gulf, where they would cross by boat and advance inland to Jackson, Mississippi, thus isolating Vicksburg before they turned and seized the town from the east.

of Vicksburg across a peninsula in neighboring Louisiana formed by a horseshoe bend in the Mississippi River. Engineers reckoned that this canal would allow vessels to move up and down the river without passing under Vicksburg's big guns, but Confederates responded by placing a menacing battery across from the canal's southern end, and the task proved too much for Sherman's men in any case. "Our canal here don't amount to much," he wrote. Floodwaters and shellfire from a monstrous Confederate cannon called Whistling Dick disrupted the troops as they toiled in the muck, forcing them to seek shelter, and diseases such as dysentery and typhoid fever took a steep toll. "While we worked on that canal almost one half the men was sick and could not work," a sergeant wrote. "They were dying every day like mice and no wonder."

An even more ambitious project involved clearing a navigable passage from the Mississippi River some 40 miles above Vicksburg to Lake Providence, a mile inland on the Louisiana side, and from there southward along bayous to the lower Red River, which enters the Mississippi well below Vicksburg. Opening a channel to Lake Providence was manageable, but the route beyond proceeded through a dense cypress swamp that could take months or years to clear even with the best tools available.

Grant let the work proceed for a while, reasoning that "employment was better than idleness for the men," before calling a halt to the project in March. Meanwhile, his troops were exploring another route east of the Mississippi that they hoped would bring them around to Vicksburg's back door. That scheme involved reopening Yazoo Pass, well north of Vicksburg, thus enabling steamers to reach the upper Yazoo River and land forces northeast of Vicksburg without coming under fire from batteries downriver at Haynes's Bluff and nearby Chickasaw Bluffs, where Sherman's men had come to grief in December. Yazoo Pass had long been employed by boatmen until it was sealed off with a levee to prevent floods. By destroying that levee, Federals hoped to reach Vicksburg by the path of least resistance.

Although Grant sometimes made use of this liquor cabinet, his drinking binges were infrequent and did not affect his performance as a commander. President Lincoln once asked what brand of whisky he favored, "for if it made fighting generals like Grant, I should like to get some of it for distribution."

When engineers blew the levee in February, water from the flood-swollen Mississippi entered the pass in a raging torrent, clearing the way for steamers carrying 4,500 Federal troops. Sergeant Samuel Byers of the 5th Iowa Infantry was among those pioneers. "We would have not been more excited at being told to start over Niagara Falls," he recalled. His transport, carrying 500 men, was whirled round "like a toy skiff in a wash tub," he added. "We all held our breath as the steamer was hurled among floating logs and against overhanging trees." Their wild ride ended a short time later when they entered Moon Lake, where they found the rest of their fleet intact. "It was luck, not management, that half the little army was not drowned," Byers asserted. After this rousing start, he added, the expedition slowed to a crawl: "Now for days and days our little fleet coursed its way toward Vicksburg among the plantations, swamps, woods, bayous, cane-brakes, creeks, and rivers of that inland sea." In mid-March, they came up against an obstacle they had not anticipated—a hastily constructed Confederate fort. Dubbed Fort Pemberton, after Major General John Pemberton, commander of Vicksburg's defenses, it was held by 1,500 men, who had blocked the channel with sunken ships. When the Federals tried to break through, they came under galling cannon fire and retreated ignominiously, heading back through Yazoo Pass.

For Byers and others on board, this was a memorable adventure—"we private soldiers had great fun," he wrote—but for Grant it was another setback in a season of disappointments. Admiral Porter would conduct one more experiment: an attempt to evade the batteries on the lower Yazoo by seeking a passage through Steele's Bayou, north of Vicksburg. But Grant had lost faith in such diversions, and higher authorities were beginning to lose faith in him. Some in Washington were calling for a new commander to reenergize what looked to be a stalled campaign. "I think Grant has hardly a friend left, except myself," remarked Lincoln. It was enough to drive a man to drink, and Grant sometimes yielded to that temptation as the pressures on him mounted. His chief of staff, John Rawlins, the son of an alcoholic, kept a close watch over him and threatened to quit if he failed to remain sober. "No officer or civilian ever saw any open drinking at General Grant's headquarters," one journalist who traveled with him attested. "This was wholly and solely the result of Rawlins's uncompromising attitude, and Grant's acquiescence in what he knew to be for his own good."

Rawlins served as Grant's conscience in other ways as well. Earlier in the winter, he had strongly protested when Grant tried to discourage illicit purchases of Southern cotton by Northern merchants, some of whom were Jewish, by banning all Jews from his sprawling department. Among those evicted by Grant's order were staunch Unionists such as Cesar Kaskel of Paducah, Kentucky, who led a delegation to the White House and persuaded Lincoln to overturn the order. Because it "prescribed an entire class, some of whom are fighting in our ranks," Halleck informed Grant, "the President deemed it necessary to revoke it."

Lincoln did not object to severe measures taken by Grant and other Federal commanders against Confederate sympathizers in occupied territory. One order Grant issued would have evicted from their homes all those who had a brother, son, or father serving in Confederate ranks. That edict was not enforced, but Grant's men routinely took food and other property from Southerners without compensation. One conscientious Union soldier, Daniel Allen of Illinois, watched in dismay as troops raided a cotton plantation near Chickasaw Bluffs and seized "everything they could carry," leaving the place in flames. On another occasion, he saw Union troops destroying the homes of slaves. "Alas," he wrote, "how long am I doomed to witness such scenes?"

Grant was not vindictive by nature and did what he could to see that Confederate prisoners were well treated. His harsh occupation policies stemmed

> **"I think Grant has hardly a friend left, except myself."**
> ABRAHAM LINCOLN

On the night of June 16, Admiral Porter's gunboat fleet runs past Vicksburg, exchanging shots with Confederate batteries on the bluff. The spectacular gun battle, heard up to 60 miles away, did little damage, and Porter's fleet slipped downriver largely unscathed to facilitate the crossing of Grant's army below Grand Gulf at month's end.

"It was the grandest spectacle of my life. . . . Our batteries were in full play, blazing away at the line of gunboats making their way past them and giving them shot for shot."

Confederate General Dabney Maury, *on Vicksburg*

from his conviction that Southerners would not give up the fight until they were thoroughly drained and defeated, economically and militarily. The harder he bore down, he reckoned, the sooner the slaughter would end. As spring approached in 1863, he devised a daring plan to break the deadlock at Vicksburg and capture that prize faster than any of his critics and even many of his admirers thought possible. He was convinced by his experiments that there was no point in trying to reach Vicksburg's eastern flank from the north. Instead, he would move his men south along the west bank of the Mississippi while Porter's gunboats ran Vicksburg's batteries at night. Then his army would cross to the east bank with Porter's help and sweep up and around Vicksburg like a snake encircling its prey. He was taking a huge risk, for Confederates had other strongholds on the Mississippi below Vicksburg at Port Hudson, Louisiana, and Grand Gulf, Mississippi, where Grant hoped to ferry his army across. And once he moved inland he would be cut off from his base of supplies. No one thought more highly of Grant than Sherman, but in April, on the eve of this offensive, Sherman strongly urged him to abandon the campaign. Grant thanked him for his "friendly advice" but told him it was time to press ahead: "You will be ready to move at ten o'clock tomorrow morning."

CLOSING THE TRAP

IT WAS A FESTIVE EVENING IN VICKSBURG. MANY CONFEDERATE OFFICERS THERE were attending a ball, but Major General Dabney Maury was asleep at home with his wife on the night of April 16 when they were roused by thunderous cannon fire over the Mississippi. Maury called for his slave Jem to saddle his horse. Jem "seemed to be always awake," Maury related, "no matter at what hour he might be called, and he could 'catch a horse' quicker than any one I ever saw. By the time I was booted and spurred, the horse was ready at the door, and I mounted and galloped off toward the sound of the firing." Maury reached the bluffs overlooking the river just in time to see Porter's fleet rounding the bend on its way downriver. "It was the grandest spectacle of my life," he wrote. "Our batteries were in full play, blazing away at the line of gunboats making their way past them and giving shot for shot." A few shells lobbed by the Federals landed in town and disrupted the ball, and "the gallant young officers dashed away to their posts, leaving the ladies to their own devices." Fearing this might be the start of a wholesale bombardment, Maury sent a message to his wife to leave town, but she had a baby to care for and stayed put. This was not an assault on Vicksburg, it turned out, but the prelude to something worse—a siege that would leave the inhabitants no way out.

As Porter's fleet slipped downriver, losing one steamer to Vicksburg's batteries, Grant's troops were making their way slowly southward through marshlands west of the river. "It was terrible marching at the best," noted Porter, who had to convey most of the supplies by boat and made a second run past Vicksburg on April 22. A week later, his gunboats bombarded Grand Gulf, 25 miles below Vicksburg, in preparation for the crossing there. Confederate batteries fired back with a vengeance and did so much damage to the fleet that Grant changed his plans, sending his troops farther south along the west bank until they were safely out of range of the big guns. They were tired of marching through the muck but responded readily when Grant appeared on horseback and urged them along.

If Confederate forces had converged on Grant and contested his crossing, they could have wrecked his campaign, but General Pemberton was distracted by artful diversions carried out separately by Sherman and Colonel Benjamin Grierson, a former music teacher who wanted nothing to do with horses when

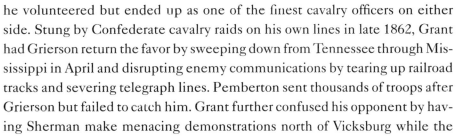

The ambitious David Dixon Porter did not like playing second fiddle to anyone, but by helping Farragut take New Orleans and Grant take Vicksburg, he won the fame he had long sought.

he volunteered but ended up as one of the finest cavalry officers on either side. Stung by Confederate cavalry raids on his own lines in late 1862, Grant had Grierson return the favor by sweeping down from Tennessee through Mississippi in April and disrupting enemy communications by tearing up railroad tracks and severing telegraph lines. Pemberton sent thousands of troops after Grierson but failed to catch him. Grant further confused his opponent by having Sherman make menacing demonstrations north of Vicksburg while the bulk of the army prepared to cross to the south. Brigadier General Carter Stevenson fell for Sherman's ruse and sent an alarming message to Pemberton shortly after he dispatched forces to Grand Gulf to oppose Grant's crossing, "The demonstrations at Grand Gulf must be only a feint," Stevenson wrote. "Here is the real attack. . . . Send me reinforcements." Pemberton promptly recalled the troops he had sent south, and Grant brought his forces across the Mississippi unopposed at month's end. At last, he wrote, "I was on dry ground on the same side of the river with the enemy." And Pemberton still did not know what he was up to.

Before closing in on Vicksburg, Grant had to reckon with Confederate forces in the vicinity. He began by beating back a stiff challenge from Brigadier General John Bowen, a Confederate from Missouri who had been a neighbor of Grant's in St. Louis before the war. Bowen led some 6,000 men from Grand Gulf and gave the Federals a hard fight at nearby Port Gibson on May 1 before retreating to Vicksburg. Grant then set out for Jackson, hoping to seize the capital and its vital railroad junction before Joseph Johnston arrived from Tennessee with reinforcements. Johnston urged Pemberton to abandon his static defense of Vicksburg and challenge Grant in the field, but Pemberton felt compelled by his instructions from Jefferson Davis to guard Vicksburg closely. Grant exploited this rift by thrusting his army between Pemberton and the approaching Johnston. After defeating Confederates at Raymond on May 12, Federals barged into Jackson on the 14th, forcing the outnumbered Johnston to fall back to the north. In two weeks since crossing the river, Grant had isolated Vicksburg at a cost of some 1,500 Federal casualties—a small price by the punishing standards of this war. The

Benjamin Grierson wreaked havoc behind Confederate lines by leading cavalrymen from La Grange, Tennessee, down through Mississippi to a Federal camp on the outskirts of Baton Rouge, Louisiana (above).

campaign took its toll on the countryside, however, as Federals lived off the land and destroyed nearly everything of strategic value to the enemy, including large parts of Jackson. "Foundries, machine shops, warehouses, factories, arsenals and public stores were fired as fast as flames could be kindled," one journalist there reported.

Belatedly, Pemberton heeded Johnston's urgings and took action, leaving around 10,000 troops within Vicksburg's defenses and venturing out with 23,000 men. On May 16, they collided with Grant's forces at Champion's Hill, midway between Vicksburg and Jackson. Pemberton held the high ground, and Sherman's Corps had not yet arrived from Jackson, but Grant had 32,000 men at hand and hoped to crush his opponent and take Vicksburg in a rush. As Federals approached Pemberton's forces on the ridge and came under fire, Samuel Byers of the 5th Iowa saw Grant "leaning complacently against his favorite steed, smoking—as seemed habitual with him—the stump of a cigar. His was the only horse near the line, and must, naturally, have attracted some of the enemy's fire." Byers feared for his commander: "What if Grant should be killed and we be defeated here—in such a place and at such a time? I am sure everyone who recognized him wished him away; but there he stood— clear, calm, and immovable."

Grant's plan was for troops under Major General James McPherson, an avid young West Pointer, to attack from the north, while another corps led by Major General John McClernand, a political appointee, advanced from the east and caught Pemberton in a pincer. McClernand was a former Illinois Congressman, as was Major General John Logan, a division commander in McPherson's Corps. McClernand had risen higher by exploiting his ties to President Lincoln, but Logan was superior in ability and loomed larger in this battle. After gaining ground early on, McPherson's Federals were stunned by a counterattack mounted by John Bowen, who had distinguished himself at Port Gibson.

Grant threw in reinforcements, including Byers's 5th Iowa, to regain the initiative. As they advanced, Byers recalled, they passed retreating Federals, holding up "their bleeding and mangled hands to show us that they had not been cowards." Some of them were laughing—a common reaction under the stress of battle—and yelled at the reinforcements: "Wade in and give them hell." Logan, meanwhile, stepped up pressure on the Confederates by launching his troops against Bowen's flank with words that were "forcible, inspiring, and savored a little of brimstone," as a listener put it. When one regiment took heavy casualties and began to retreat, Logan whipped it back into line. "General, the rebels are awful thick up there," an officer objected, to which Logan replied vehemently: "Damn it, that's the place to kill them—where they are thick!"

Ultimately, Bowen's hard-fighting Confederates gave way. Grant nearly trapped Pemberton's forces, but McClernand unaccountably failed to advance, and most of the Rebels got away, retreating across the Big Black River toward Vicksburg that evening. "Had McClernand come up with reasonable promptness," Grant wrote, "I do not see how Pemberton could have escaped with any organized force." As it was, Grant's victory at Champion's

> **"General, the rebels are awful thick up there."**
>
> *Union officer to Major General John Logan at Champion's Hill*

> **"Damn it, that's the place to kill them— where they are thick!"**
>
> *General Logan's reply*

> ### "This is a death struggle, and will be terrible."
> GENERAL SHERMAN, *outside Vicksburg*

Hill—which cost the Confederates almost 4,000 casualties and the Federals nearly 2,500—all but sealed Vicksburg's fate. "Until this moment I never thought your expedition a success," Sherman told him frankly after the battle. "I could never see the end clearly until now."

A SLOW DEATH

MARYANN LOUGHBOROUGH EMERGED FROM CHURCH ON SUNDAY MORNING, MAY 17, to find Vicksburg bracing for the worst amid unconfirmed rumors of Pemberton's defeat. "Sullen and expectant seemed the men," she wrote, "tearful and hopeful the women." Those hopes were soon crushed as retreating Confederates began streaming into town, "worn and dusty with the long march." She heard bystanders scolding the soldiers and crying "Shame on you!" But she did not join in. As the wife of a Confederate officer, she took pity on Vicksburg's downcast defenders: "I could not but feel sorry for the poor worn fellows, who did seem indeed heartily ashamed of themselves."

Soon all of Pemberton's surviving forces, some 30,000 troops in all, were back within the fortifications of Vicksburg—trapped there with several thousand civilians. With Grant's army hemming them in by land and Porter's fleet blocking the Mississippi, they could not obtain food, supplies, or reinforcements. Grant hoped to avoid a prolonged siege and tried twice that week to v . On May 19, Sherman's men led the way and were stopped cold by the Confederates, who had strengthened their barricades considerably in recent weeks. "This is a death struggle, and will be terrible," Sherman wrote his wife afterward.

As if to confirm that grim prophesy, Grant launched a larger and deadlier assault on May 22, preceded by a massive artillery barrage. As men of the 20th Ohio Infantry prepared to charge the forbidding Confederate works, they entrusted their rings, pictures, and other keepsakes to the cooks, who would not see action. "This watch I want you to send to my father if I never return," said one man. "I am going to Vicksburg, and if I do not get back just send these little trifles home, will you?" asked another.

Confederates gave their foes credit for advancing bravely into a murderous firestorm. "As they rushed up the slope to our works they invariably fell backwards, as the death shot greeted them" one Mississippian wrote. "And yet the survivors never wavered. Some of them fell within a few yards of our works. . . . They came into the very jaws of death and died." Thomas Higgins, color-bearer of the 99th Illinois Infantry, amazed Confederates by advancing alone toward their works with flag in hand after those around

Refugees like this family, with their earthly possessions piled in a wagon, fled Grant's advancing army and took refuge in Vicksburg, swelling the town's population during the siege that began in May.

him had been shot down. "Come on, you brave Yank, come on!" they yelled, dropping their guns and raising their hats. "He did come, and was taken by the hand and pulled over the breastworks," wrote one soldier, "and when it was discovered that he was not even scratched, a hundred Texans wrung his hands and congratulated him upon his miraculous escape from death."

Few in his position were so fortunate. On this, the worst day of the campaign, 500 Federals died and more than 2,500 were wounded to no gain. "We'll have to dig our way in," Grant concluded. That meant extending trenches ever closer to the Confederate works and tightening his grip on the defenders until

---

[EYEWITNESS]

Alice Shirley
RESIDENT OF WEXFORD LODGE

Born in Vicksburg to a family of Northern stock, Alice and her brothers kept their Union sympathies to themselves when their state seceded. Federal troops later besieged their home, Wexford Lodge, which fell within the front lines. With their home riddled with shot and shell, the family was forced to seek refuge in a cave in a nearby ravine. They soon moved into an abandoned slave cabin behind Federal lines.

THE CONFEDERATES, knowing that they must soon retreat behind their fortifications at Vicksburg, began their preparations by destroying what they could outside, and burned all the houses in the vicinity; but my mother's persistent refusal to go out of hers, and her determination to prevent its destruction, delayed its being set on fire until the Federals made their appearance on the hills to the east of us. The poor fellow who was appointed to do the work, while holding the ball of blazing cotton to the corner of the house, was struck by a bullet of the pursuing vanguard, and crept away under the shelter of some planks, where he died alone. His body was found the next day and was buried under the corner of the house.

My mother and the old home were greeted with a shower of bullets and shell from the advancing army. One shot passed her as she stood in an open doorway. A piece of shell struck the top of a chimney and tore it away, and passing into an upper room, shattered a bedstead.

"War, terrible war, had come to our very hearthstone."

She thought rapidly; the thing to be done was to hang out a flag of truce, and quickly she secured a sheet to a broom handle, and sending it by our carriage driver to the upper front porch where it might be seen from a distance, it was soon waving a truce to the bullets.

Now all was confusion and excitement. The great hosts advanced rapidly, and the house, the grounds, the road, and the woods behind were soon alive with Union soldiers, and that same afternoon the fighting began. Bullets came thick and fast, shells hissed and screamed through the air, cannon roared, the dead and dying were brought into the old home. War, terrible war, had come to our very hearthstone, and here my mother and brother remained for three days. The two house servants stayed by them. Household treasures were soon destroyed under the ruthless hand of the soldier. Daguerreotypes prized so highly by the family, letters, valuable papers, etc., etc., quickly disappeared. A dinner set of beautiful china which had been packed away in a box for safe keeping, was taken out, piece by piece, and smashed.... Choice books were carried off, furniture was destroyed, but through the kindness of some officers our trunks and the best of our furniture were saved; among these were the piano and melodeon. ■

they cracked. "The Boa Constrictor is drawing his coils around us with all his strength," wrote Major Raleigh Camp of the 40th Georgia Infantry as Grant methodically laid siege to Vicksburg. "He has found that he cannot kill his victims at one stroke with his fangs, so he has concluded to crush us out by the squeezing process." Confederates at the barricades were constantly being sniped at or bombarded, and more than a few of the shells lobbed at them landed in town, prompting civilians to take shelter in caves dug out of the soft clay soil. Some of those caves collapsed, burying people. About 50 civilians were wounded or killed during the siege, and the hot, sleepless nights in the shelters were an ordeal for all. "I shall never forget my extreme fear during the night," wrote Maryann Loughborough, "and my utter hopelessness of ever seeing the morning light." The sounds of shells plummeting and exploding left her "cowering in a corner, holding my child to my heart."

[EYEWITNESS]

Lucy McCrae
RESIDENT OF VICKSBURG

The daughter of a well-to-do Vicksburg merchant, Lucy McCrae took shelter with her family and some 200 other refugees from the Federal bombardment in one of the city's supposedly bombproof caves. In her diary the young teenager recorded the horrifying experience of being buried alive when a shell collapsed a portion of the roof.

ONE NIGHT MOTHER FIXED our beds for us, putting my brothers on a plank at one side, and putting me near Mary Ann; but, spoiled and humored child that I was, I decided not to stay near Mary Ann. . . . The Rev. Dr. Lord of the Episcopal Church was suffering with a sore foot and leg, which was all bandaged and propped on a chair for comfort. He said, "Come here, Lucy, and lie down on this plank." Dr. Lord was almost helpless, but he assisted me to arrange my bed, my head being just at his feet. The mortars were sending over their shells hot and heavy; they seemed to have range of the hill, due, it was said, to some fires that a few soldiers had made on a hill beyond us. Everyone in the cave seemed to be dreadfully alarmed and excited, when suddenly a shell came down on the top of the hill, buried itself about

"As soon as the men could get to me they pulled me from under the mass of earth. The blood was gushing from my nose, eyes, ears, and mouth."

A resident of besieged Vicksburg prays for deliverance from Federal shell fire in one of the many bombproof shelters excavated into the city's hillsides and bluffs.

six feet in the earth, and exploded. This caused a large mass of earth to slide from the side of the archway in a solid piece, catching me under it. Dr. Lord, whose leg was caught and held by it, gave the alarm that a child was buried. Mother reached me first, and a Mrs. Stites, who was partially paralyzed, with the assistance that Dr. Lord, who was in agony, could give, succeeded in getting my head out first. The people had become frightened, rushing into the street screaming, and thinking that the cave was falling in. Just as they reached the street over came another shell bursting just above them, and they rushed into the cave again. Then came my release. Mother had cried in distressing tones for help, so as soon as the men could get to me they pulled me from under the mass of earth. The blood was gushing from my nose, eyes, ears, and mouth. ∎

The only hope for those trapped in Vicksburg was that Joseph Johnston would come to their relief. By late June, he had amassed some 30,000 troops around Jackson and regained control of the state capital. But Grant too had been heavily reinforced in recent weeks and now had nearly 80,000 men, enough for him to maintain a stranglehold on Vicksburg while he detached a large force under Sherman that discouraged Johnston from advancing on Vicksburg until it was too late and later drove him from Jackson. Meanwhile, a separate Federal army led by Major General Nathaniel Banks was besieging Port Hudson, roughly midway between Vicksburg and New Orleans. The Confederate garrison there had been substantially reduced in May when more than 5,000 troops left to defend Vicksburg. Now the South risked losing both strongholds, leaving the Union in control of the Mississippi. Much blame was heaped on Pemberton and Johnston for the looming disaster, but both were appointed by Jefferson Davis, who bore ultimate responsibility. By insisting that Vicksburg—which Pemberton deemed "the most important point in the Confederacy"—be held at all hazards, Davis raised the stakes substantially, but he did not have strong enough cards in hand or sufficient assets in reserve to make good on his gamble.

On July 3, General Bowen crossed the lines at Vicksburg under a flag of truce and proposed an armistice. Pemberton's troops were exhausted, hungry, and in poor health. Bowen himself was suffering from dysentery and would not live long. Grant at first insisted on unconditional surrender but then offered Pemberton's men parole, meaning that they would be exchanged for Federal captives if they pledged not to take up arms again. After midnight, Pemberton accepted Grant's terms and surrendered Vicksburg and its garrison. There was no boasting or blustering afterward from Grant or his men. As the beaten Confederates laid down their arms and marched off, Grant noted with satisfaction, "Not a cheer went up, not a remark was made that would give pain." To the contrary, Federals offered their foes food, water, and condolences. "Many a ration was divided," recalled Samuel Byers, "many a canteen filled, and many were the mutual, sympathizing wishes that the cruel war might soon be over."

The full magnitude of Grant's victory became clear several days later, when Confederates at Port Hudson learned of Vicksburg's fate and surrendered, thus ending the struggle for the Mississippi. "The Father of Waters again goes unvexed to the sea," remarked a grateful President Lincoln. July 4, 1863, was soon recognized as the most significant day of the war and one of the most fateful days in American history. As Federals were taking possession of Vicksburg that morning, Robert E. Lee was counting his losses at Gettysburg and bringing to a close an offensive as momentous as Grant's campaign. When the results on both those fronts hit home, Southerners were devastated. As Confederate Ordnance Chief Josiah Gorgas wrote in his diary: "Yesterday we rode on the pinnacle of success—today absolute ruin seems to be our portion."

> "Yesterday we rode on the pinnacle of success—today absolute ruin seems to be our portion."
> CONFEDERATE ORDNANCE CHIEF JOSIAH GORGAS

> "The Father of Waters again goes unvexed to the sea."
> ABRAHAM LINCOLN

Two scenes leading to the fall of Vicksburg adorn the cover of Harper's Weekly. At top, on July 3, Confederate General John Bowen and Colonel L. M. Montgomery are led blindfolded to the tent of Brigadier General Stephen Burbridge, who sent them along to Grant for preliminary talks. At bottom, later that same day, Grant and Major General John Pemberton, the commander of Vicksburg's defenses, work out the details of the Confederate surrender, which took effect on July 4.

In the bottom right corner of his map, Robert Knox Sneden neatly sums up the capture of Vicksburg: "General Grant completely divested the city in June 1863 and it surrendered 4th July. The enemy losing in the entire campaign 40,000 prisoners and 300 guns." The 8th Wisconsin Infantry (left) went into every battle with their eagle, Old Abe, which became one of the most famous regimental mascots of the war. The Eagle Brigade was part of Sherman's May 22 assault on the city, which ended in heavy Union casualties. Old Abe survived several wounds before being mustered out in 1864.

THE SIEGE OF VICKSBURG

ULYSSES S. GRANT'S SECOND CAMPAIGN AGAINST VICKS-burg was a plan so ambitious that his most trusted subordinates opposed it. Few Rebels feared for the safety of their "Gibraltar of the West" until the evening of May 17, when John Pemberton's retreating army, having failed to stop Grant in the open, came home "hollow-eyed, ragged, bloody," according to one observer. It was "humanity in the last throes of endurance."

The Confederates dug in behind a formidable line of redoubts to the east of Vicksburg ❶. Grant ordered William Sherman to launch an attack on May 19 that was repulsed with heavy casualties ❷. A subsequent attack on May 22 cost the Union another 3,000 men as Sherman, James McPherson, and John McClernand met fierce resistance along the Graveyard Road, the Baldwin Ferry Road, and at the Railroad Redoubt ❸. Grant then proceeded to lay siege to the city. Of the failed assaults, he wrote, "they would not have worked so patiently in the trenches if they had not been allowed to try [to attack]."

Sherman's first sally had forced the Rebels to evacuate Haines's Bluff ❹, allowing Union boats to dock on the Yazoo River and supply Grant. Meanwhile, the Confederates were trapped between Grant's army on one side and David Porter's gunboats on the other, forcing them to hope for relief from Joseph Johnston that never came.

Throughout June, the Union continued to dig approaches toward Confederate lines and tried to penetrate their defenses by mining their earthworks. On June 25, engineers of McPherson's Corps tunneled beneath the 3rd Louisiana Redan and detonated 2,200 pounds of black powder ❺. They set off another blast July 1, but in both cases discovered that the Confederates had simply withdrawn to a new line of defense.

But by the end of June, Rebel soldiers and civilians were reduced to eating horses, rats, and dogs. Most became sick with dysentery, malaria, scurvy, and diarrhea, and Pemberton surrendered the city on July 4 ❻. ■

3 RAILROAD REDOUBT *The 22nd Iowa charges the Confederate breastworks of the Railroad Redoubt in the second failed frontal assault on the city.*

5 LOUISIANA REDAN *The 45th Illinois charges into a 50-foot-wide crater blasted out of Confederate earthworks by a Federal mine.*

6 SURRENDER *The Stars and Stripes is raised over the Warren County courthouse July 4, just before food is distributed to starved residents.*

"That winter was probably the most dreary and miserable we had. . . . There were thousands on duty in the perpetual snow and mud, without shoes, often no blanket, hardly any overcoats, and many without coats, nothing often but a ragged homespun shirt."

CAPTAIN ALEXANDER HASKELL
ARMY OF NORTHERN VIRGINIA,
recalling the winter of 1863

THE ROAD TO GETTYSBURG

FOR THE TWO WAR-WEARY ARMIES FACING EACH OTHER IN VIRGINIA, IT was a lull between storms. After their explosive encounter at Fredericksburg in December, they had settled into winter camps on either side of the Rappahannock River. Men welcomed the respite, but inactivity could be as hard on troops as marching and fighting. The imminent threat of death in battle faded, only to be replaced by the perils of disease, malnutrition, and exposure. "That winter was probably the most dreary and miserable we had," recalled Captain Alexander Haskell of Lee's Army of Northern Virginia. "The suffering from cold, hunger, and nakedness was intense and widespread. There were thousands on duty in the perpetual snow and mud, without shoes, often no blanket, hardly any overcoats, and many without coats, nothing often but a ragged homespun shirt." Shortages of food and clothing grew worse for Confederates as Federals occupied their territory, tightened the blockade, and took control of the Mississippi. Families sent aid to soldiers in camp, Haskell noted, "but much of this was lost by defective transportation, and for the poor fellows from across the Mississippi nothing could come."

Lee himself lived frugally that winter, as Haskell discovered when he visited the general's headquarters in early 1863. "He chanced to come out just as I was taking my leave," Haskell wrote, "and as it was the hour for dinner he politely insisted on my sharing the meal." If the young captain expected a feast, he was mistaken. As they entered the tent, he related, "there was before us a crude board table with camp stools around it; on it a beautiful glass dish of 'Virginia Pickles' sent by some hospitable Virginia lady; the balance of the dinner was a plate of corn bread, or 'pones,' and a very small piece of boiled bacon." After saying grace, Lee explained to his guests that his Irish servant Mike had "harder work than we have in Quarters, and must be fed." He then cut a thick slice for Mike, Haskell noted, laid it aside, and offered each of his guests and himself a portion that was "but a fraction of Mike's."

This was typical of Lee, whose consideration for men of all ranks helped earn him the lasting devotion of his troops in circumstances that would have demoralized other armies. Soldiers called him "Marse Robert" and felt he had their best interests at heart even during the hardest campaigns. "The boys never cheer him," wrote Corporal Edmund Patterson, "but pull off their hats and worship." For all his personal charms, Lee could not have commanded such loyalty without success in battle. Much as he did as a host by stretching that "very small piece of boiled bacon" as far as possible, he made the most of limited resources as a commander by repeatedly defeating armies larger and better equipped than his own. He could not hope to perform such feats much longer, however, if his army grew much weaker. Losses to desertion

and disease were mounting, and his men were so malnourished he was not sure how much more he could ask of them. "I fear they will be unable to endure the hardships of the approaching campaign," he wrote in late March. "Symptoms of scurvy are appearing among them, and, to supply the place of vegetables, each regiment is directed to send a daily detail to gather sassafras buds, wild onions, garlic, lamb's quarter, and poke sprouts."

For now, the poor condition of his troops and the numerical superiority of the Federals across the river forced him to remain on the defensive. But if his opponents happened to squander their advantage and leave him an opening, he would attack with everything he had. He could not afford to play a waiting game. One more winter of hardship and stalemate such as this and his army might be driven back toward Richmond and ultimate defeat. However, if the year ended with Federals in retreat and the Union demoralized, Northern voters might reject Abraham Lincoln in 1864 in favor of a Democrat willing to end the war on terms favorable to the South. If his army prevailed, Lee wrote to his wife, "there will be a great change in public opinion at the North. The Republicans will be destroyed."

LINCOLN CHANGES HORSES

THINGS LOOKED EVEN WORSE FOR THE FEDERALS CAMPED NORTH OF THE RAPpahannock as the year began than for the Confederates to their south. The disaster at Fredericksburg haunted the Army of the Potomac and left its commander, Ambrose Burnside, in disrepute. When he reviewed one of his corps in mid-January, he was "coldly received by the men," an officer observed.

Federal troops of the Army of the Potomac wade through a bog in January 1863 during their so-called mud march, an abortive effort by General Ambrose Burnside to renew his offensive against Lee's forces in Virginia. Several days of rain slowed the army to a crawl and forced Burnside to cancel the operation, ruining any chance he had to regain the confidence of his men. "Burnside rode along yesterday and was followed by hooting and yells," an officer wrote on January 23, shortly before Lincoln removed him as commander.

Asked to give three cheers for their commander, they could not manage even one. Subordinates were plotting to have Burnside removed, and soldiers were upset with unsanitary living conditions and shortages of food and other supplies that failed to reach camp because of mismanagement and corruption. Officers at headquarters were dining on "canvasback ducks and champagne," one lieutenant observed, while privates were so poorly fed that diarrhea and scurvy were "almost universal." All this contributed to an epidemic of desertions. Men were running off in "squads of fifteen or twenty at a time," one soldier wrote, "and they are very rarely brought back." In late January, the army's tally of deserters reached an appalling 25,000.

By then, it was clear to Lincoln that Burnside must go. With some reluctance, he entrusted the troubled Army of the Potomac to the outspoken Joseph Hooker, who had openly criticized both Burnside and his commander in chief, remarking to a reporter that nothing would go right in Washington "until we had a dictator, and the sooner the better." Hooker disliked his nickname, "Fighting Joe," because it made him sound hot-headed, but Lincoln did not mind having a fighter in charge of the army, so long as he showed some sense. Instead of applying the whip to urge his commander forward, as he had done with McClellan, he tightened the reins a bit to keep the high-spirited Hooker from attacking recklessly. In a thoughtful letter, Lincoln scolded and encouraged him in equal measure. "Only those generals who gain successes, can set up dictators," he told him. "What I now ask of you is military success, and I will risk the dictatorship." Lincoln urged Hooker to be prudent without losing his combativeness: "Beware of rashness, but with energy, and sleepless vigilance, go forward, and give us victories."

Hooker treasured the letter and said appreciatively of Lincoln, "He talks to me like a father." Far from rushing into battle, he recognized that his troops were in no condition to fight and set about improving their living conditions and raising morale. He overhauled the army's supply system and issued the troops fresh vegetables and soft bread in place of their despised hardtack. "His 'soft bread' order reaches us in a tender spot," wrote one of his grateful men. Hooker also cleaned up filthy camps and hospitals, slashed the desertion rate by tightening security and granting men more generous furloughs, set up an intelligence bureau that gave him a far more accurate view of enemy strength than McClellan ever had, and created a separate cavalry corps to rival that of Jeb Stuart on the Confederate side.

Hooker's cavalrymen were goaded into action in late winter when Brigadier General Fitzhugh Lee, Robert E. Lee's nephew, raided their camp and left a provocative note for Brigadier General William Averell, a former classmate of his at West Point. "I wish you would put up your sword, leave my state, and go home," Lee wrote. "If you won't go home, return my visit, and bring

"When Old Jo fights he will win a splendid victory or suffer a terrible defeat."

Federal officer on Joseph Hooker

Major General Joseph Hooker, who replaced Burnside, had a self-assurance that bordered on arrogance. When he came to Washington from California to offer his services to the Union Army shortly after the First Battle of Bull Run, he told President Lincoln bluntly: "I am a damned sight better than any general you had on that field."

A well-fed chaplain stands with hands behind his back among Pennsylvania troops camped north of Fredericksburg in early 1863. Hooker improved conditions after he took charge of the army, and tidy encampments such as this one, with clean streets and snugly built log huts, became commonplace.

me a sack of coffee." Coffee was scarce in the wartime South, where most people made do with chicory and other substitutes. Urged on by Hooker, Averell took up the challenge, crossing the Rappahannock at Kelly's Ford with 3,000 men on March 17 and clashing sharply with Lee's troopers. Cavalry battles like this one, which cost the Confederates more than 130 casualties and the Federals nearly 80, were considered mere skirmishes by infantrymen. "Whoever saw a dead cavalryman?" they asked mockingly. Among the dead in this clash, however, was one of the South's most admired young officers, Major John Pelham, a dashing 24-year-old from Alabama who happened to be visiting a young woman in the neighborhood when the battle broke out and could not resist joining in. Afterward, Averell left a sack of coffee for Lee with a message attached: "Dear Fitz: Here's your coffee. Here's your visit. How do you like it?"

The clash at Kelly's Ford signaled that the winter's respite was ending and that hostilities would soon resume in earnest. "We are ready for a fight & the men have never been so well," wrote a sergeant from Massachusetts. But doubts lingered among troops who had seen their hopes dashed repeatedly and regiments shot to pieces. "Our culinary condition has been much improved," observed a lieutenant from Indiana, adding, "like a herd of poor oxen they are fattening us for the slaughter." Hooker was grooming his men for a purpose, and no one doubted what that was. "We are to have hard marching and hard fighting," one captain from Wisconsin concluded, and the stakes were sure to be high, "for when Old Jo fights he will win a splendid victory or suffer a terrible defeat."

CONVERGING ON CHANCELLORSVILLE

HOOKER WAS DETERMINED TO AVOID ANOTHER BATTLE OF FREDERICKSBURG, where Federals crashed head-on into an impenetrable Confederate wall. His intention was to outflank Lee, forcing him to abandon his fortifications at Fredericksburg and retreat toward Richmond or risk battle in the open field with an army much larger than his own. Hooker had a good idea of the strength of Lee's army, left with only around 60,000 men after two divisions under General Longstreet went off to counter an expected enemy thrust in southeastern Virginia, near Fort Monroe. With more than 130,000 Federal troops at hand, Hooker felt sure of victory. "My plans are perfect," he said, "and when I start to carry them out, may God have mercy on General Lee, for I will have none."

This sort of talk made his commander in chief nervous. "It seems to me that he is overconfident," Lincoln said of Hooker, whose campaign got off to a bad start. In mid-April, he sent 10,000 cavalrymen under Brigadier General George Stoneman off on a wide sweep around Lee's western flank to cut his lines of supply and communication with Richmond. That alone, Hooker believed, would force his opponent to retreat or face defeat, but it was not to be. Stoneman was slow to get moving and had few of his troopers across the Rappahannock before heavy rains swelled the river and made it impassable. While waiting for the weather to improve, Hooker overhauled his plans. Stoneman would go ahead with his foray when the river subsided, but at the same time Hooker would launch a massive flanking movement by his infantry, sending four corps totaling more than 70,000 men upstream, where they would cross at fords and converge on Chancellorsville, a crossroads 10 miles west of Fredericksburg. To disguise his intentions, Hooker would leave some men in camp as reserves and send two corps downstream to cross the Rappahannock below Fredericksburg and divert Lee's attention from the huge threat gathering to his west. It was a bold and imaginative scheme, one that Colonel E. Porter Alexander, an artillery officer under Lee, considered "the best strategy conceived in any of the campaigns ever set on foot against us."

Hooker maintained strict secrecy, and troops involved in the flanking march launched on April 27 knew only that they were leaving camp, presumably for good. "Gather up everything you want!" the call went out. "We're not coming back!" Men stuffed their knapsacks with overcoats, blankets, skillets, and other goods. "Some of the boys looked like moving vans on legs," recalled William Southerton of the 75th Ohio Infantry. Predictably, many of those belongings were soon discarded as overloaded men found they could not keep up the pace. With or without their possessions, troops were glad to be on the move. Men of Southerton's regiment were singing the "Battle Hymn of the Republic" when Hooker and his staff rode by. "Our boys threw their caps high into the air, shouted hurrahs to the general," he related. "Hooker's bright blue eyes sparkled with pride and confidence."

Hooker had reason to be proud, for his plans were unfolding beautifully.

"It seems to me that he is overconfident."

ABRAHAM LINCOLN,
on General Hooker

Lieutenant Colonel Rufus R. Dawes

6TH WISCONSIN INFANTRY, MEREDITH'S BRIGADE

In 1861 Rufus Dawes helped raise a company of the 6th Wisconsin. Appointed captain, he served with his regiment at Second Manassas, South Mountain, Antietam, and Fredericksburg. On the night of April 28, 1863, Dawes, now a lieutenant colonel, joined his men in crossing the Rappahannock River to secure the way for John Reynolds's Corps south of Fredericksburg.

WE LEFT CAMP AT NOON OF the 28th, camped same night near the river four miles below Fredericksburg. About 11 . . . started again for the river hoping to surprise the Rebels by a "coup de main" by rushing two regiments over in boats, storming & carrying the rifle pits, thus clearing the way for a pontoon bridge. For this perilous duty the 6th & 24th Michigan were selected. An honor most high. We moved along so slowly in the fog & rain and so much noise was made by the donkeys of the pontoon train that we had little hope of surprising. Sure enough when, near daylight we got the pontoons about half launched in the river. Crack, smash, whiz, ping, came the musketry volleys of long lines of Grey Backs in the pits. . . .

The 24th Michigan and the 14th Brooklyn Zouaves were brought rapidly into line on our right and left and for ten minutes we kept up a tremendous musketry fire. But it was demonstrated that we could gain nothing that way. The rebels were on higher ground & in rifle pits, and it was destruction to lay under their fire. So we moved back in good order, out of range. . . .

At nine o'clock, Gen. Reynolds [sent] down that the 6th and 24th must cross and carry the pits. . . . Troops were moved down along

> **"I stood up in the bow of the boat, . . . swinging my sword in one hand and cheering on the oarsmen, holding my pistol in the other to shoot them if they wavered or flinched."**

the edge of the river and batteries planted on the hills to fire back at the Rebels as hard as they could. . . . After these dispositions had been made, we moved down over the open field in line of battle. . . . The rebels opened fire on us, and our men along the river, and the batteries returned their fire. We moved down in line until within two hundred yards of the boats, then . . . double quicked and into

the boats the men plunged. . . . The storm of bullets was perfectly awful. "Heave her off." . . . "Show the army why the old Sixth was chosen to lead them." . . . I stood up in the bow of the boat, . . . swinging my sword in one hand and cheering on the oarsmen, holding my pistol in the other to shoot them if they wavered or flinched. Across the river, we tumbled into the mud or water waist deep, waded ashore, crawled & scrambled up the bank. . . . Crack—crack, for two minutes and the Rebels were running like sheep over the field or throwing down their arms as prisoners. I took the flag swung it as a signal of our victory, and such a shout of triumph as went up from the thousand anxious spectators on the north bank of the river. ∎

Crowded into pontoon boats, men from Reynolds's Corps prepare to cross the Rappahannock in this sketch by artist Alfred Waud.

Three brothers from Georgia—Daniel, John, and Pleasant Chitwood—strike a menacing pose after enlisting in a militia company called the Bartow County Yankee Killers, which became part of the 23rd Georgia Infantry and served under Lee in Virginia. Pleasant Chitwood died at a hospital in Richmond in 1862, and Daniel and John were captured at Chancellorsville.

"I retired from his presence with the belief that my commanding general was a whipped man."

Major General Darius Couch,
on meeting with Hooker at Chancellorsville

By April 30, he had all four corps involved in the flanking movement safely across the river and approaching Chancellorsville. Lee was now aware of that gathering threat, but most of his army remained around Fredericksburg, preoccupied with Federals who had crossed the Rappahannock there to divert attention from the main thrust upstream. Stonewall Jackson proposed driving those Yankees back into the river, but Lee suspected they were a diversion and gambled on that hunch by stripping his defenses at Fredericksburg to the bone and sending most of his forces to Chancellorsville with Jackson. Lee once remarked that he feared the Federals would keep changing commanders until they found one he did not understand. Thus far Hooker had eluded his understanding, but Lee was beginning to take his measure. Hooker assumed that placing the bulk of his forces on Lee's flank at Chancellorsville would leave his opponent at a loss. "From that moment all will be ours," Hooker had assured his officers. Yet Lee was conceding nothing and acting as if this was his opportunity, his moment.

The Union troops around Chancellorsville found themselves in a forlorn area called the Wilderness, consisting of swamps and scrubby woodlands with tangled undergrowth. Troops moving along roads here came upon occasional clearings, but the dense foliage disguised enemy movements. "We are across the river and have out-maneuvered the enemy," wrote corps commander George Meade on the night of April 30, "but are not yet out of the woods." Hooker had little idea of the terrain here before he crossed the Rappahannock and set up headquarters that evening at the Chancellor House, near the crossroads. "I was not prepared to find it an almost impenetrable thicket," he remarked afterward. "It was impossible to maneuver."

Hooker expected Confederates to remain on the defensive as his troops moved out toward Fredericksburg on the morning of May 1. Around midday, however, Jackson's troops collided with Federals led by Major General George Sykes as his corps was about to emerge from the Wilderness east of Chancellorsville. Hooker ordered Major General Darius Couch to support Sykes, and Couch hurried forward with a division from his corps, led by the accomplished Winfield Scott Hancock. But Hooker then had second thoughts as he received reports on Jackson's strength. To continue the advance, he concluded, would be "hazarding too much," and he ordered his forces to return to Chancellorsville and take up defensive positions. Couch was bitterly disappointed. "In no event should we give up our ground," he declared, and Hancock and Sykes agreed. They appealed to Hooker, but he was adamant. "Nothing was to be done but carry out the command," Couch wrote. That evening at headquarters, Hooker tried to soothe Couch, assuring him: "I have got Lee just where I want him; he must fight me on my own ground." But to find Hooker hunkering down for "a defensive battle in that nest of thickets was too much," Couch recollected, "and I retired from his presence with the belief that my commanding general was a whipped man."

Hooker was not whipped yet, but he had surrendered the initiative to his opponents and would never recover it. He would not be fighting on his "own ground," for Confederates knew far more about this tangled Wilderness than he did. That very night, Jackson learned from his topographical engineer, Major Jedediah Hotchkiss, of a circuitous route on back roads that would allow his troops to swing around to the south of Chancellorsville and attack Hooker from the west while he was expecting a blow from the east. Conferring with Lee, Jackson proposed taking some 30,000 men on that flanking march, leaving Lee with fewer than 15,000 troops east of the crossroads to contain 72,000 Federals. Lee concluded from the day's events that Fighting Joe had lost his punch and readily approved Jackson's proposal. Unlike Hooker, Lee was not afraid of hazarding too much.

Lost in the Wilderness

JACKSON'S MARCH ON MAY 2 DID NOT GO UNDETECTED. Hooker warned Major General Oliver Howard that his exposed corps west of Chancellorsville was at risk of being attacked, but Howard did little to prepare. Most Federal commanders informed of Jackson's movement believed it signaled a Confederate retreat. One of the few officers to take the threat seriously was Colonel Robert Reily of the 75th Ohio. "Some of us will not see another sunrise," he told his men. When Jackson launched his attack late that afternoon, Reily's Ohioans bravely held their ground "until both flanks were overlapped by the enemy, which was bearing down upon them like an avalanche," reported a captain in the regiment. Reily died in the onslaught, and 150 of his men were killed or wounded. Gathering momentum, Jackson's troops rolled eastward toward Chancellorsville along the Orange Turnpike, driving everything before

Lee, holding a map prepared by topographical engineer Jedediah Hotchkiss, confers with Stonewall Jackson on the night of May 1, shortly before Jackson launched his pivotal flanking march at Chancellorsville.

them—rabbits, deer, and terrified Federals, many of whom did not stop running until they reached the crossroads. "It seemed to me that the whole army had gone to pieces in a panic," recalled Sergeant Luther Mesnard of the 55th Ohio, who was caught up in the rout with the rest of Howard's Corps. "I look back to this as the darkest day in my experience."

That evening, Jackson rode forward with staff officers to the front, hoping to revive the attack, which was faltering with the fading light. As they were returning in the dark, Confederate pickets mistook them for enemies and opened fire, severely wounding Jackson and killing others in his party. Later that night, a surgeon amputated his left arm. "God be praised that he is yet alive," Lee remarked when he learned of Jackson's condition. "He has lost his left arm, but I have lost my right."

Command of Jackson's Corps fell first to A. P. Hill and then when Hill too was wounded, to Jeb Stuart, who resumed the attack early on May 3. Hooker found himself hemmed in, with the smaller Confederate force to the east under Lee's direct command serving as the anvil while Stuart's men to the west hammered the Federals bunched up around Chancellorsville. Confederate gunners led by Colonel Alexander seized the high ground at Hazel Grove, a hilltop farm near the crossroads, and shelled the Chancellor House as Hooker stood on the porch, shattering a pillar and knocking him unconscious for several minutes. Dazed by the blow, he

"He has lost his left arm, but I have lost my right."

GENERAL LEE,
after learning of Jackson's injury

This last portrait of Stonewall Jackson was taken just days before he was wounded by friendly fire on the night of May 2 in the wooded area at right, west of Chancellorsville. His wife, Mary Anna, visiting him at camp in late April with their daughter, urged him to have the picture taken and remarked afterward, "I never saw him look so handsome and noble."

Mary Anna Morrison Jackson

WIFE OF LIEUTENANT GENERAL THOMAS J. JACKSON

After receiving the news that her husband had been wounded, Mary Anna Jackson, accompanied by her brother, Lieutenant Joseph G. Morrison, traveled from Richmond to Guinea Station, a plantation stop on the R.F.&P Railroad. Arriving on May 7, Mary Anna rushed to a nearby overseer's house at Fairfield Plantation that had been provided for use as shelter for the stricken general. There she remained with her husband until he died, three days later.

FROM THE TIME I REACHED HIM he was too ill to notice or talk much, and he lay most of the time in a semiconscious state; but when aroused, he recognized those about him and consciousness would return. Soon after I entered his room he was impressed by the woeful anxiety and sadness betrayed in my face, and said: "My darling, you must cheer up, and not wear a long face. I love cheerfulness and brightness in a sickroom." . . . Thinking it would cheer him more than anything else to see the baby in whom he so delighted, I proposed several times to bring her to his bedside, but he always said, "Not yet; wait till I feel better." He was invariably patient, never uttering a murmur or complaint. Sometimes, in slight delirium, he talked, and his mind was then generally upon his military duties— caring for his soldiers, and giving such directions as these: "Tell Major Hawkes to send forward provisions to the men;" "Order A. P. Hill to prepare for action"; "Pass the infantry to the front," etc. . . .

Early on Sunday morning, the 10th of May, I was called out of the sick-room by Dr. Morrison, who told me that the doctors, having done everything that human skill could devise to stay the hand of death, had lost all hope, and that my precious, brave, noble husband could not live! Indeed, life was fast ebbing away, and they felt they

"Let us cross over the river and rest under the shade of the trees."

must prepare me for the inevitable event, which was now a question of only a few short hours. As soon as I could arise from this stunning blow, I told Dr. Morrison that my husband must be informed of his condition. I well knew that death to him was but the opening of the gates of pearl into the ineffable glories of heaven; but I had heard him say that, although he was willing and ready to die at any moment that God might call him, still he would prefer to have a few hours' preparation before entering into the presence of his Maker and Redeemer. . . .

I therefore felt it to be my duty to gratify his desire. He now appeared to be fast sinking into unconsciousness, but he heard my voice and understood me better than others, and God gave me the strength and composure to hold a last sacred interview with him, in which I tried to impress upon him his situation, and learn his dying wishes. When I told him the doctors thought he would soon be in heaven, he did not seem to comprehend it, and showed no surprise or concern. But upon repeating it, and asking him if he was willing for God to do with him according to His own will, he looked at me calmly and intelligently, and said, "Yes, I prefer it, I prefer it." I then told him that before that day was over he would be with the blessed Saviour in His glory. With perfect distinctness and intelligence, he said, "I will be an infinite gainer to be translated." . . .

Mrs. Hoge now came in, bearing little Julia in her arms. . . . As soon as they entered the door he looked up, his countenance brightened with delight, and he never smiled more sweetly as he exclaimed, "Little darling! sweet one!" . . . He now sank rapidly into unconsciousness, murmuring disconnected words occasionally, but all at once he spoke out very cheerfully and distinctly the beautiful sentence which has become immortal as his last: "Let us cross over the river and rest under the shade of the trees." ∎

THE BATTLE OF CHANCELLORSVILLE

WHILE GRANT WAS MARSHALLING HIS ARMY against Vicksburg in the West, new Union commander Joseph Hooker launched a plan to destroy Lee in Virginia. At the Battle of Chancellorsville Lee once again showed his ability to parry a large force with a smaller one, while the noted gambler, Hooker, failed to live up to his Fighting Joe nickname.

Hooker divided his army of 120,000 into three parts. A force of 40,000 feigned an attack on Fredericksburg [1]. The rest crossed the Rappahannock far upstream to maneuver around Lee, by the evening of April 30, 70,000 Union infantry were at the Chancellorsville mansion [2], ready to attack Lee from behind.

"Hooker could play the best game of poker I ever saw," wrote a former colleague, "until it came to the point where he should go a thousand better." Lee called Hooker's bluff, leaving just 10,000 men at Fredericksburg and bringing the bulk of his army to Chancellorsville. After being told by Jeb Stuart that Hooker's right flank was exposed, he sent Stonewall Jackson's Corps on a 12-mile march around the Federals [3].

Jackson's 30,000 men managed to sneak through the Wilderness along a local charcoal road, and on May 2, came bursting from the woods to stun Hooker's Corps [4]. Disorganized fighting continued into the night, with Stonewall Jackson being shot by his own men. The next day Union troops at Fredericksburg under John Sedgwick took Marye's Heights [5] and began marching for Chancellorsville. But Lee, thanks to Hooker's timidity, was able to redirect part of his army and stop Sedgwick's advance at Salem Church [6]. Despite an advantage of 75,000 men to 25,000, Hooker withdrew his forces back across the river. ■

Robert Knox Sneden's map, drawn west to east top to bottom, shows the shifting battle lines between April 29 and May 5 as the Union first closed around Lee's army and then retreated.

2 CHANCELLORSVILLE MANSION *The large house owned by the Chancellor family became Hooker's headquarters, until Confederate artillery set it afire.*

5 MARYE'S HEIGHTS *Confederates lie dead in the same Sunken Road they had defended in the Battle of Fredericksburg a few months earlier.*

6 SALEM CHURCH *Union forces bivouac on the west bank of the Rappahannock shortly before their bloody engagement around Salem Church.*

temporarily relinquished command to General Couch—but only on condition that he withdraw from Chancellorsville toward the Rappahannock. Federals abandoned the burning Chancellor House to their enemies, who could smell victory now and saluted Lee joyously when he appeared there on horseback around noon. In the words of his aide, Major Charles Marshall, the men hailed their triumphant chief with "one long, unbroken cheer, in which the feeble cry of those who lay helpless on the earth blended with the strong voices of those who still fought." As he watched Lee riding amid that adoring throng, Marshall thought that "it must have been from such a scene that men in ancient times rose to the dignity of gods."

Hooker's about-face negated determined efforts by Federals of Major General John Sedgwick's Corps to break through at Fredericksburg on May 3 and link up with the rest of the army near Chancellorsville, as ordered. Fixing their bayonets, Sedgwick's men carried Marye's Heights in a rush, avenging the dreadful Union losses in December, but it was only a symbolic victory. With Chancellorsville in hand, Lee was able to spare enough forces to repulse Sedgwick that afternoon at Salem Church, several miles west of Fredericksburg. Over the next few days, the Army of the Potomac drew on bitter experience and executed a fighting retreat across the Rappahannock. "Fearful blunders were made and many lives were thrown away," concluded Edward Taylor of the 4th Michigan Infantry, who felt like many others in the army that Hooker had yielded prematurely and failed to live up to his bold words: "How different the result from his anticipations! Instead of the enemy retreating we retreated!"

Lee had little time to savor his stunning triumph at Chancellorsville. He had inflicted more than 17,000 casualties on his foes but suffered nearly 13,000, a proportionally larger loss for his forces than for the Federals. If his army remained in a defensive posture and continued to endure such blows, it would eventually break. While he still had the strength, he would try instead to break the will of his opponents and bring them to terms by taking the offensive and advancing northward. But he would have to do so without his right arm, Stonewall Jackson, who developed pneumonia after undergoing surgery and was told by his wife on Sunday, May 10, that doctors could do no more for him. "Very good," replied Jackson, a deeply religious man who believed that all events were ordained by God and considered it a blessing to leave the world on a Sunday. "Let us cross over the river and rest under the shade of the trees," he said just before he died. It was a heavy loss for Lee, who was soon to cross into enemy territory and would face an even greater ordeal there.

INVADING PENNSYLVANIA

THE BATTLE OF GETTYSBURG MIGHT NEVER HAVE OCCURRED IF CONFEDERATE Secretary of War James Seddon had won his point. Seddon was a Virginian, but after Chancellorsville he proposed detaching Major General George Pickett's division of Virginians from Lee's army and sending it to relieve Vicksburg, which was under mounting pressure from Grant. Lee strongly objected, arguing that the division might arrive too late to save Vicksburg and warning that unless he retained all his forces and received reinforcements, he might

"I concur entirely in your views of the importance of aggressive movements."

JAMES SEDDON
CONFEDERATE SECRETARY OF WAR,
to General Lee

have to fall back to defenses around Richmond. Such was Lee's prestige that even President Davis, a Mississippian determined to hold Vicksburg, sided with him in this matter. Meeting with Lee in Richmond in mid-May, Davis, Seddon, and other Confederate leaders approved his plans for an offensive northward into Pennsylvania. "I concur entirely in your views of the importance of aggressive movements," Seddon assured Lee. By advancing northward, it was hoped, he would relieve pressure on Richmond, allow his hungry troops to forage in enemy territory, and demoralize Unionists, undermining Lincoln's war effort. Lee expected a battle with pursuing Federals and saw this as a "fair opportunity to strike a blow," but neither he nor anyone else anticipated the titanic struggle that loomed at Gettysburg.

While Lee won support at high levels and gathered reinforcements, Joseph Hooker lost prestige and saw his army diminished by the losses at Chancellorsville and the departure of troops whose enlistments had expired. Lincoln, appalled by the recent defeat and alarmed by harsh criticism of Hooker by his subordinates, stuck with him only because other candidates were reluc-

Dead horses surround a wrecked caisson of the Washington Artillery of New Orleans, which withdrew with other Confederate forces from Marye's Heights, overlooking Fredericksburg, when Federals under General Sedgwick broke through there on May 3. A day later, the photographer who took this picture—Andrew J. Russell, an officer assigned to document the work of the U.S. Military Railroads—came under fire with his commander, Brigadier General Herman Haupt (standing at left), when Confederates reclaimed Fredericksburg.

tant to accept the position. Having tried McClellan "a number of times," Lincoln told a journalist, "he saw no reason why he should not try General Hooker twice." That was hardly a ringing endorsement, and General in Chief Halleck, long at odds with Hooker, made things worse for him by offering him few reinforcements. When Lee's 75,000 men moved northward in June, Hooker pursued with around 93,000 men, a significantly smaller army than he had at Chancellorsville.

There was still plenty of fight left in the Army of the Potomac. One captain likened the men to bulldogs: "You can whip them time and again, but the next fight they go into, they are in good spirits, and as full of pluck as ever. . . . Some day or other we shall have our turn." In early June, Hooker ordered his new cavalry commander, Major General Alfred Pleasonton, to "disperse and destroy" Lee's cavalry, now back under the command of Jeb Stuart, as the Confederates moved westward from Fredericksburg to around Culpeper—the first step in a journey that would carry them across the Blue Ridge into the Shenandoah Valley and northward into Pennsylvania.

Before dawn on June 9, some 8,000 Union troopers supported by 3,000 infantrymen gathered along the north bank of the Rappahannock and prepared to cross over and attack Stuart's 10,000-man corps camped around Brandy Station, a stop on the Orange & Alexandria Railroad near Culpeper. The Confederates were surprised and might have been overwhelmed had Pleasonton's two-pronged offensive unfolded as planned. One wing led by Brigadier General John Buford, a keen officer with a knack for being in the right place at the right time, crossed at Beverly Ford promptly at 5 a.m. and bore down on Stuart's troopers from the north. But Federals who were supposed to cross simultaneously at Kelly's Ford a few miles downstream and swing around to the south lost their way in the dark and did not enter battle until mid-morning. That allowed Stuart's troopers to deal with Buford first before the second wave hit their flank. Even so, it was a close fight and a furious one—the largest cavalry battle fought during the war. "Such charging and yelling was never before witnessed and heard on this continent," wrote Major Walter Taylor, Lee's adjutant. Opposing ranks of troopers met head on with "an indescribable clashing and slashing," a Federal cavalryman recalled.

Federal troopers withdrew across the Rappahannock that evening after suffering more than 850 casualties, nearly 350 more than the Confederates. Stuart's Corps had not been destroyed or dispersed, and it would serve now as Lee's rear guard, preventing the enemy from following in pursuit as Confederates crossed the Blue Ridge into the Shenandoah Valley. Leading the way was Jackson's old corps, now under the command of Major General Richard Ewell, who had lost a leg in the Second Battle of Bull Run. Succeeding Jackson was a tall order, but the troops admired "Old Bald Head," as Ewell was known, and rewarded him with victory in mid-June by seizing Winchester—a hotly contested town at the northern end of the valley that changed hands many times during the war—and taking more than 3,000 prisoners. That cleared the way for Ewell and Lee's two other corps commanders, James Longstreet and A. P. Hill, to cross the Potomac into Maryland. "Here we are, ladies," one Confederate said to women there who eyed them

"You can whip them time and again, but the next fight they go into, they are in good spirits, and as full of pluck as ever. . . . Some day or other we shall have our turn."

Federal officer, describing the Army of the Potomac

Slashing with sabers, opposing cavalrymen battle for possession of a regimental flag at Brandy Station on June 9. A Union trooper who fought here wrote that "those who resisted were sabered or shot till they reeled from their saddles, the victor rushing madly on to engage another foe."

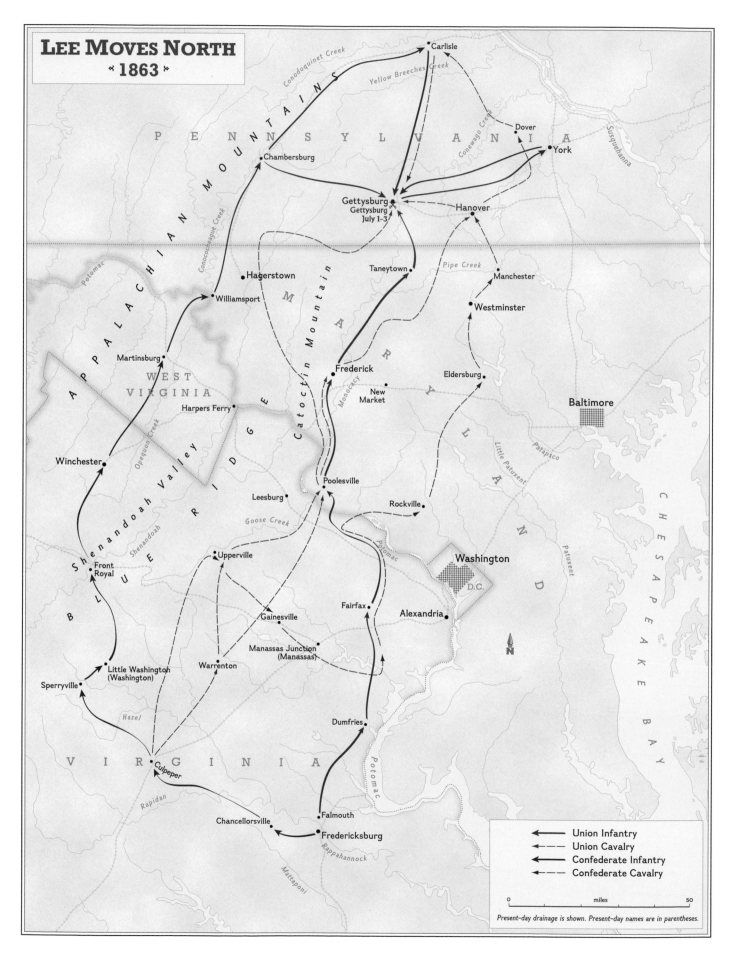

LEE MOVES NORTH
✦ 1863 ✦

PENNSYLVANIA

Carlisle

Dover

York

Conodoquinet Creek

Yellow Breeches Creek

Conewago Creek

Susquehanna

APPALACHIAN MOUNTAINS

Chambersburg

Gettysburg
Gettysburg
July 1–3

Hanover

Taneytown

Pipe Creek

Manchester

Hagerstown

Catoctin Mountain

Williamsport

Westminster

Potomac

Martinsburg

MARYLAND

WEST
VIRGINIA

Frederick

Eldersburg

Monocacy

New
Market

Baltimore

Harpers Ferry

Opequon Creek

Poolesville

Little Patuxent

Patapsco

Winchester

Leesburg

Rockville

Goose Creek

BLUE RIDGE

Shenandoah Valley

Shenandoah

Front
Royal

Upperville

Washington

D.C.

Patuxent

Fairfax

Gainesville

Alexandria

Sperryville

Little Washington
(Washington)

Warrenton

Manassas Junction
(Manassas)

N

CHESAPEAKE BAY

Hazel

Dumfries

VIRGINIA

Culpeper

Potomac

Rapidan

Chancellorsville

Falmouth

Fredericksburg

Rappahannock

Mattaponi

	Union Infantry
	Union Cavalry
	Confederate Infantry
	Confederate Cavalry

0   miles   50

Present-day drainage is shown. Present-day names are in parentheses.

disapprovingly, "as rough and ragged as ever but back again to bother you."

They would not be in Maryland for long. By the last week of June, they had entered Pennsylvania and were raising havoc. Much like Federal troops in the South, they ransacked farms and stores, largely ignoring Lee's directive that civilians were to be compensated for goods taken from them. Some invading Confederates seized not only property but people—blacks who had fled slavery in the South or were suspected of being fugitives. Philip Schaff of Chambersburg, Pennsylvania, saw "negroes captured and carried back into slavery (even such as I know to have been born and raised on free soil), and many other outrages committed." Hooker's slow response to this alarming invasion prompted Lincoln to remove him in favor of George Meade, who, unlike Hooker, had strong support from the generals serving under him. Meade had no choice but to accept the honor, for it came as an order. "Well, I've been tried and condemned without a hearing," he remarked, "and I suppose I shall have to go to execution."

Meade was quick to pursue Lee's forces. "I am going straight at them," he wrote his wife, "and will settle this thing one way or the other." Leading the pursuit was John Buford's cavalry division. On June 30, Buford's men entered the town of Gettysburg, Pennsylvania, a hub where many roads met and two great armies would soon collide. With the exception of Jeb Stuart, who was off raiding enemy supply lines, all elements of Lee's army were within a day's march of Gettysburg. Closest was the corps of A. P. Hill, who learned that night of the Federal presence in Gettysburg from an officer who had gone there seeking shoes for Lee's ill-clothed men. Hill informed Lee that he would advance the next morning from Cashtown to Gettysburg, eight miles to the east, to "discover what was in my front." He then gave Major General Henry Heth permission to lead that advance "and get those shoes." But this was about much more than shoes. It was about finding the enemy and seizing control of a strategic crossroads. Buford sensed what was coming. When an officer in Gettysburg commented that he doubted the Rebels would cause much trouble the following day, Buford replied sharply: "They will attack you in the morning and they will come booming—skirmishers three deep. You will have to fight like the devil until supports arrive."

COLLISION AT THE CROSSROADS

HETH'S MEN WERE NOT EXPECTING MUCH OF A FIGHT WHEN THEY SET OUT FOR Gettysburg along the Chambersburg Pike at first light on July 1. The Yankees sighted there the day before were probably just militia, they figured, and would be quickly swept aside. As one artillerist recalled: "We moved forward leisurely smoking and chatting as we rode along, not dreaming of the proximity of the enemy." Awaiting Heth's 7,500 men on ridges west of town were Buford's 3,000 Federal troopers, who would fight dismounted, like infantry. "I had

"**Here we are, ladies, as rough and ragged as ever but back again to bother you.**"

Confederate soldier to Maryland women

Confederates remove their trousers before fording a stream on their way to Pennsylvania. As shown at left, Lee's path (red) took his army west of the Blue Ridge in Virginia while the pursuing Army of the Potomac followed a parallel path (blue) to the east. Lee's three corps traveled separately and raided various towns in Pennsylvania before reuniting at Gettysburg to confront the oncoming Federals.

gained positive information of the enemy's position and movements," Buford wrote, "and my arrangements were made for entertaining him." The first of his men to greet the enemy that morning was Lieutenant Marcellus Jones of the 8th Illinois Cavalry, who took aim at a distant Confederate officer on horseback and fired the opening shot of the most destructive battle ever fought on American soil. Jones missed his target, but over the next three days more than 43,000 men would become casualties here.

Neither commander sought this showdown at Gettysburg. Only two of Meade's eight infantry corps were within striking distance of Gettysburg on the morning of July 1. Meade expected battle near Taneytown, Maryland, 14 miles to the south, where he was preparing defenses. Lee had instructed his officers to avoid a "general engagement" until his three infantry corps, operating separately, reunited near Gettysburg. Lee was with Longstreet's Corps, which began the day at Chambersburg, 25 miles to the west, and would not do battle today. Ewell's Corps was closer, about a half day's march north of Gettysburg, and would join Heth's division and other elements of A. P. Hill's Corps that afternoon in fighting that spread like wildfire. Although Lee's subordinates exceeded his orders in sparking this conflagration, their actions were in keeping with the aggressive spirit of their commander and the army he forged. The Yanks they collided with were equally combative and determined to stand up to these Johnnies, as they referred to the Rebels. "They came forward with a rush," recalled Lieutenant Colonel Rufus Dawes of the 6th Wisconsin, a veteran of Antietam and other hard battles with Lee's army, "and how our men did yell, 'Come on, Johnny, come on.'"

Dawes and his men were part of the hard-fighting Iron Brigade—originally known as the Black Hat Brigade—thrown into action around mid-morning by their corps commander, Major General John Reynolds, who found Buford's

Major General Henry Heth (top), who led Confederates on July 1 to Gettysburg (above), expected to find only militia guarding the town and was surprised to encounter Federal troops in force. "I did not know that any of your people were north of the Potomac," he told a Union officer afterward.

troopers under heavy pressure from Heth's Confederates. "The enemy is advancing in strong force," he wrote Meade back at Taneytown. "I will fight him inch by inch." When the Iron Brigade moved in to support Buford's men, the Confederates recognized who they were up against. "Here are those damned black-hat fellows again!" one man exclaimed. "This is no militia." It came as a shock for Heth. "I struck the Iron Brigade and had a desperate fight," he wrote. He lost over 20 percent of his forces in this struggle, which proved even costlier for the Iron Brigade, with one regiment, the 24th Michigan Infantry, losing nearly 400 of its 500 men. Heth was shot in the head but survived with a cracked skull when the bullet struck the lining of his hat, which had been stuffed with paper to make it fit. General Reynolds was riding close behind the Iron Brigade when he was hit in the neck and fell dead. "I have seen many men killed in action," wrote his orderly, "but never saw a ball do its work so instantly as did the ball which struck General Reynolds."

After a lull around midday, the fighting resumed in earnest as Confederates of Ewell's Corps arrived from the north and Federals of Oliver Howard's Corps poured in from the south. Lee could hear the distant sounds of battle as he approached with Longstreet's Corps from the west and rode ahead to assess the situation. His first instinct when he reached Gettysburg was to rein in his overzealous officers. "I do not wish to bring on a general engagement today," he emphasized. "Longstreet is not up." But the battle was now raging beyond control, and Lee had little choice but to add fuel to the fire and try for victory. One of Ewell's divisions, commanded by 34-year-old Major General Robert Rodes, was being chewed up as Rodes launched ill-coordinated attacks along an unfinished railroad north of the Chambersburg Pike. But another division, led by Major General Jubal Early—a grizzled old warrior who bore down hard on his men and even harder on his enemies—had yet to enter battle and was approaching the exposed flank of Howard's Corps from the northeast. The combined impact of Early's assault and renewed pressure by A. P. Hill's troops along the Chambersburg Pike west of Gettysburg proved too much for the Federals, and they caved in. Thousands were captured as Lee's men overran Gettysburg. As one Union officer put it: "Defeat and retreat were everywhere."

As Federals fell back through Gettysburg, General Winfield Scott Hancock rode in from the south with orders to take charge and stand fast until Meade arrived with more forces that night. As one officer put it, Hancock's "imperious and defiant bearing heartened us all." He swiftly asserted authority over General Howard—who was senior to him in rank and at first objected to taking orders from him—and rallied the troops on high ground south of Gettysburg. "I think this is strongest position by nature upon which to fight a battle that I ever saw," he said to Howard as they stood on Cemetery Hill. As yet, their troops held only that hill and nearby Culp's Hill, but their defensive line would eventually extend southward for three miles along Cemetery Ridge to a peak called Little Round Top. Lee was not about to concede the high ground to his foes without a fight and ordered Ewell to

"They came forward with a rush, and how our men did yell, 'Come on, Johnny, come on.'"
LIEUTENANT COLONEL RUFUS DAWES
6TH WISCONSIN INFANTRY IRON BRIGADE

"Here are those damned black-hat fellows again! This is no militia."
Confederate soldier, confronting the Iron Brigade

This hat was worn by Sergeant Philander Wright, wounded at Gettysburg while serving with the 2nd Wisconsin Infantry. His regiment was part of the Iron Brigade, also known as the Black Hat Brigade for the tall felt hats the men wore, adopted from the Regular Army.

Private Andrew Park

42ND MISSISSIPPI INFANTRY, DAVIS'S BRIGADE

On the morning of July 1, Andrew Park splashed across Willoughby Run as part of Major General Henry Heth's attack against units of Darius N. Couch's Federal Corps below Seminary Ridge. Park and his fellow Mississippians collided with Federal troops under Brigadier General Lysander Cutler near an unfinished railroad cut, and during the fierce action, Park witnessed the capture of the regimental colors of the 56th Pennsylvania Infantry.

AFTER FORMING HIS COMMAND, Col. Hugh R. Miller walked down the line, and stated that if there was a man there who could not stand the smell of gunpowder he had better step out, for we were going into a fight. To my astonishment one poor fellow went to him and said: "Colonel, I just cannot go into a fight today, for if I do I will get wounded or killed." The Colonel, with an oath, ordered him back into line. Just at this moment General Davis and staff rode up and gave the command to move forward, and to let nothing stop us. . . .

I should have stated in the beginning that we were thrown into a fine field of wheat as I ever saw. We had not gone more than three or four hundred yards in this field until we met the enemy's skirmishers. We drove them in, and they fell back over their main line. This drew us up to within fifty or sixty yards of that line, where they were lying down in the wheat. They rose up and resting on one knee fired the first volley. But they shot too high, and but few of our men were hurt. We received orders to fire and charge. This broke their line, and they retreated down the railroad cut . . . Our troops on the left were ordered to fire right oblique; and those on the right to fire left oblique. In this manner we poured

> **"I could have walked a half or three quarters of a mile on the dead soldiers of the enemy and not have put my feet on the ground."**

This flag of the 6th Wisconsin Infantry was carried during the fighting on July 1st at Gettysburg.

volley after volley into them as they ran down this railroad cut. I think there never was such slaughter as we made. . . . The enemy now brought up more troops when we were about a half mile from the town. They were very strong now, while our forces consisted of only Heth's division; so we received orders to fall back and wait for reinforcements. We fell back about three hundred yards. We had been

fighting about two hours and our loss was quite heavy. . . .

When we arrived on the ground where we first began the fight in the morning we could see no Yankees. But about three hundred yards farther to our right we [saw] standing two flags; one of which was the flag of Pennsylvania and the other the National flag. There seemed to be no one about them; and Col. Miller called to his men and asked if he had a man in his regiment that could or would bring those flags to him. In an instant Willie Clarke, a fourteen year old lad, said: "I can," and started after them. At about the same time five others started, two them being from my regiment (42nd) and three from the Second regiment.

Willie Clarke outran the rest, having had a little the start of them, and got there first, and threw his arms around the flag-staff. But, low and behold! the flags were not alone, for six Yankees were there, and a hand to hand fight began. Two men from the 42nd were wounded and two from the 2nd killed and the other wounded. Five of the Yankees were killed, and the sixth took the flags and started off with them. But Willie Clarke shot him before he got fifty yards and brought [the flags] to Colonel Miller without receiving a scratch. ■

seize the heights "if practicable." The late Stonewall Jackson might well have found it practicable to attack, but Ewell felt his corps had done enough that day and held back. "Everybody was in fine spirits," recalled Colonel William Allan of Ewell's staff. "After all, we had gained a great victory." The next morning, they would awake to find Meade and his army commanding the field.

"THE GREAT BATTLE OF THE WAR"

THROUGH THE NIGHT, UNION TROOPS HURRIED TOWARD GETTYSBURG, RESTING only briefly before continuing on. General John Gibbon, former commander of the Iron Brigade, roused the men of his division at three in the morning, had them marching at four, and brought them into line on Cemetery Ridge with the rest of Hancock's Corps before six. If any of them doubted that a deadly confrontation was brewing, he spelled things out for them. As Isaac Taylor of the 1st Minnesota Infantry noted in his diary: "Order from Gen. Gibbon read to us in which he says this is to be the great battle of the war & that any soldier leaving the ranks without leave will be instantly put to death."

Lee was up well before dawn on July 2, laying plans for an attack that he hoped would shatter Meade's army before it fully assembled. Meade's largest corps, consisting of 14,000 men under General John Sedgwick, would not reach Gettysburg until late afternoon. Time was of the essence, but Lee found it uncommonly difficult to prod his forces into battle. He had always relied mightily on his corps commanders, but today with so much hanging in the balance

Little Round Top (foreground) was fiercely contested on July 2 as Federals struggled to maintain possession of the hill, which anchored their left wing at the southern end of the battlefield. If Confederates seized the bare crest and placed artillery there, wrote Brigadier General John Geary, whose Federals occupied Little Round Top on the night of July 1, they would have "an opportunity of enfilading our entire left wing and center with a fire which could not fail to dislodge us."

"Order from Gen. Gibbon read to us in which he says this is to be the great battle of the war & that any soldier leaving the ranks without leave will be instantly put to death."

ISAAC TAYLOR
1ST MINNESOTA INFANTRY,
GETTYSBURG, JULY 2

he felt hampered by his top lieutenants. Jeb Stuart's long absence and Richard Ewell's failure to seize the heights had placed him in a bind. No less disturbing was the resistance he faced from his "old warhorse," James Longstreet, who urged Lee to avoid an attack at Gettysburg, where the terrain favored the Federals, and seek ground of his choosing where he could wage a defensive battle. Lee saw no point in trying to outmaneuver Meade without Stuart's cavalry to screen his movements. "The enemy is here," he insisted, "and if we do not whip him, he will whip us."

At Lee's urging, Longstreet gathered his corps for battle. But he seemed listless and resentful that afternoon as his men moved southward into position for an attack on Meade's vulnerable left flank, held by Major General Daniel Sickles. A political appointee from New York who had murdered his wife's lover and won acquittal by pleading temporary insanity, Sickles was careless about heeding orders. Instructed to hold a line that culminated at Little Round Top—whose bare crest commanded the surrounding countryside— he left that strategic hill unguarded and advanced his corps nearly a mile west of its assigned position to occupy a peach orchard on what looked to him to be more defensible ground. That impulsive move confused both sides. Officers under Longstreet whose line of attack was now blocked by Sickles's Corps asked him for new instructions, but he was in no mood to alter Lee's plan. "We must obey the orders," he insisted. Meanwhile, Meade had ridden to the Peach Orchard to reprimand Sickles, who promised to withdraw to his assigned position. "I wish to God you could," Meade replied as Confederate artillery opened up, "but the enemy won't let you!"

Confusion deepened into chaos when fighting erupted around four. Lee's plan called for units to attack en echelon from south to north with a trip-hammer effect that would place mounting pressure on the Federals. But nothing went quite as planned that day.

Major General George Meade, who replaced Hooker as commander of the Army of the Potomac shortly before the Battle of Gettysburg, brought unity and resolve to the army's disgruntled officer corps. As Brigadier General John Gibbon wrote after learning of Meade's appointment, "I now feel my confidence restored and believe we shall whip these fellows."

Leading the way on Lee's far right was General John Bell Hood, a seasoned commander whose men had been in the thick of the fighting at Antietam and other battles. When Longstreet refused to modify Lee's plan, Hood did so on his own authority and sent troops against Sickles's left and around his flank toward Little Round Top. Hood's left arm was shattered by a shell fragment soon after the attack began and he was carried from the field, leaving his forces in a jumble as they negotiated fiendishly difficult terrain in unbearably hot weather. Some of them entered the Devil's Den, where granite boulders made it impossible for them to maintain formation as they came up against Federals on Sickles's flank and grappled with them. It was "more like Indian fighting than anything I experienced during the war," recalled one Confederate "Each side wanted the protection of those rocks," wrote another, who surprised six Federals crouching behind a massive boulder and told them to drop their guns. "Young man, where is your troops?" one of his prisoners asked. "I told them I was it," he related, "and showed them to the rear."

While much of Hood's division struggled with the enemy around the Devil's Den, several regiments succeeded in outflanking Sickles's Corps and made their way up Little Round Top. Shortly before they began their ascent, Colonel Strong Vincent took it upon himself to defend that hill and led his Federal brigade to the crest. "This is the left of the Union line," Vincent told Colonel Joshua Chamberlain, whose 20th Maine Infantry occupied the very end of that line. "You are to hold this ground at all costs." Chamberlain and his men withstood several assaults by men of the 15th Alabama before fixing bayonets and counterattacking. "The whole line flung itself down the slope through the fire and smoke upon the enemy," recalled Captain Ellis Spear. That brave charge ended the Confederate threat here, but the right flank of Vincent's Brigade was giving way under pressure from men of the 4th and 5th Texas Infantry, who threatened to seize a Union battery that had just been placed atop the hill. Into the breach rushed Federals led by Brigadier General Stephen Weed, who won the fight by hurrying his men to the summit after Colonel Vincent was mortally wounded but lost his own life in the process when a bullet severed his spine. An aide tried to offer him hope, but he knew better. "I'm as dead a man as Julius Caesar," he said.

With their position now secure, Union gunners atop Little Round Top blasted away at Confederates below. The surviving Texans fell back down the slope and found what shelter they could in a rocky area at the base of the hill known as the Slaughter Pen. Major Jefferson Rogers of the 5th Texas urged them to "stand fast," but as Sergeant Valerius Giles noted, few of them were standing: "The balance of us had settled down behind rocks, logs, and trees." Just then, a courier from Brigadier General Evander Law, filling in for the injured Hood, arrived with a message for Rogers. "General Law presents his compliments," he announced, "and says hold this place at all hazards." Rogers glared at the courier and shot back: "Compliments, hell! Who wants any compliments in such a damned place as this? Go back and ask General Law if he expects me to hold the world in check with the Fifth Texas Regiment." As more and more officers on both sides were killed or wounded, battle plans broke down, yet men kept fighting and dying. "Night began settling around us, but the carnage wore on," Giles recalled. "There seemed to be a viciousness in the very air we breathed."

By 7 p.m., the fighting had spread northward to Cemetery Hill and Culp's Hill, where General Ewell belatedly launched attacks on Federals who were now firmly entrenched. Between those two hills and Little Round Top to the south, meanwhile, Meade's forces faced one furious attack after another. Hardest hit were the exposed men of Sickles's Corps in the Peach Orchard and the nearby Wheat Field, which came to resemble the Cornfield at Antietam as bodies piled up amid the stalks. Before entering that killing ground, troops of the Irish Brigade received absolution from their chaplain, who warned them there would be no Christian burial for "the soldier who turns his back upon the foe." They went in faithfully and gained ground, but the struggle for the Wheat Field was soon overshadowed by a blistering assault launched across the Peach Orchard by Mississippians under Brigadier General William Barksdale. Advancing toward a farm where General Sickles was

"Night began settling around us, but the carnage wore on. There seemed to be a viciousness in the very air we breathed."

CONFEDERATE SERGEANT VALERIUS GILES, *in the Slaughter Pen*

A Confederate soldier lies dead in the Devil's Den. Evidence suggests that the photographer, Timothy O'Sullivan, had the body moved about 40 yards and placed in the sharpshooter's nest for dramatic effect.

"I found them foaming at the mouth as if mad."

Confederate soldier attempting to comfort the wounded

---

headquartered, they "sped swiftly across the field and literally charged the goal," one Confederate recalled. As Sickles fell back with his troops, he was severely wounded in the leg, and General Hancock took charge of what remained of his corps. Hancock then launched a counterattack in which Barksdale fell mortally wounded. "Tell my wife I am shot, but we fought like hell," he told a surgeon before dying.

Meade, meanwhile, remained at his headquarters near Cemetery Ridge and funneled reinforcements to Hancock, who made good use of them. No sooner had he repulsed Barksdale's charge than he faced another stiff challenge from Brigadier General Cadmus Wilcox, who advanced toward a gap in the Federal line on Cemetery Ridge and threatened to break through. To buy time until help arrived, Hancock sent the 262 men of the 1st Minnesota—who had been told that morning to prepare for the "great battle of the war"—against Wilcox's entire brigade. "Every man realized in an instant what that order meant," wrote Lieutenant William Lochren, "death or wounds to us all, the sacrifice of the regiment to gain a few minutes' time and save the position." With bayonets fixed, they charged down the slope and held the Confederates off until reinforcements arrived. Only 47 of the Minnesotans, fewer than 20 percent, escaped death or injury.

That desperate encounter summed up this great battle, in which Confederates advanced more than once to the brink of victory only to be beaten back. The last such charge occurred after dark when the Louisiana Tiger Brigade clawed its way up Cemetery Hill and captured a Federal battery before being repulsed. Finally, around ten, the din of battle ceased, leaving only the dreadful cries of the wounded—a chilling chorus that some who survived this struggle found harder to bear and harder to forget than the sight of mute, mangled corpses. The howls of men writhing in agony were "so distressing," one Confederate recalled, "that I approached several with the purpose of calming them if possible. I found them foaming at the mouth as if mad."

The Final Sacrifice

AT DAWN ON JULY 3, LEE MET WITH LONGSTREET TO SPUR HIS RELUCTANT warhorse back into battle. Lee's plan was for Longstreet to strike the center of the Union line on Cemetery Ridge while Ewell kept up pressure on the Federal right by attacking Culp's Hill. A. P. Hill's Corps would remain in reserve, ready to exploit a breakthrough on Cemetery Ridge and seal

The bodies of Union dead, stripped of their shoes by scavengers, lie near the Peach Orchard, where Confederates shattered Sickles's exposed corps on July 2. One survivor, Robert Carter of Massachusetts, described the struggle here as "a perfect hell on earth . . . not to be surpassed, nor ever to be forgotten in a man's lifetime."

James Longstreet (top) admired Major General George Pickett (bottom) for his "magnetic presence" and was reluctant to send him against the heart of the Union line on July 3. "I don't want to make this attack," Longstreet told Colonel E. Porter Alexander, Lee's artillery commander. "I would not make it even now, but that General Lee has ordered and expects it."

the victory. Longstreet, who had been reluctant to attack Meade's flank the day before, was even more strongly opposed to this frontal assault, which would require his men to advance in full view of Union artillery and infantry and would, he feared, prove as disastrous as the bloody Federal attacks at Fredericksburg. His corps would be bolstered today by the 6,000 men of George Pickett's division, newly arrived from Chambersburg, where they had been serving as the army's rear guard in the absence of Jeb Stuart, who had finally returned from his untimely foray. Aside from Pickett's division, however, Longstreet had only about 9,000 men fit to fight. "It is my opinion," he told Lee, "that no fifteen thousand men ever arrayed for battle can take that position." Lee replaced some of Longstreet's battle-weary brigades with units from Hill's Corps but insisted that the attack go forward with a force amounting to about 13,000 men. "Never was I so depressed as on that day," Longstreet recalled. "I felt that my men were to be sacrificed, and that I should have to order them to make a hopeless charge."

While Lee overrode strong objections from his trusted subordinate, Meade and his corps commanders were in full agreement. Meeting at his headquarters the night before, they had voted unanimously to hold their ground. As Major General John Newton said at that council, two days of fighting "had ended in consolidating us into a position immensely strong." Meade and his officers agreed to remain on the defensive but left open the possibility of launching limited attacks to correct their lines where Confederates had made inroads. When Major General John Slocum learned that Rebels had seized trenches at the base of Culp's Hill overnight, he decided a correction was in order. "Drive them out at daylight," he commanded, but it would not be that easy. Instead of retreating when they came under artillery fire, the Confederates attacked, surging up the hillside over the bodies of men killed the day before toward Federals who unleashed withering volleys from behind log breastworks. "It appeared to me as if the whole of my company was being swept away," recalled David Howard, whose Confederate 1st Maryland Battalion was torn apart by Unionists from the same part of that state. Afterward, recalled Colonel James Wallace on the Federal side, "we sorrowfully gathered up many of our old friends & acquaintances & had them carefully & tenderly cared for." Ewell prolonged the costly assaults, hoping to hold out until Longstreet's attack began, as Lee directed. But by noon, Ewell's forces were spent. The steep price his men paid this morning on Culp's Hill would not prevent an even greater sacrifice that afternoon on Cemetery Ridge.

Lee could only pray that a massive artillery bombardment would shatter Federal defenses on the ridge and allow his risky frontal assault to succeed in the absence of diversionary attacks. Around midday, Colonel E. Porter Alexander amassed more than 160 big guns and unleashed a cannonade of unprecedented ferocity. "The whole air above and around us was filled with bursting and screaming projectiles," recalled John Gibbon. His corps commander, Hancock, cheered frightened troops by riding along the lines without flinching as the bombardment continued. When an aide urged him not to risk his life, he replied memorably: "There are times when a corps commander's life does not count." Hancock wanted Federal gunners to respond in full force, but the

army's artillery chief, Brigadier General Henry Hunt, had his batteries fire sparingly to conserve ammunition. Then around 2:30, Hunt ordered his gunners to cease fire, hoping to give the impression that the Confederates had won the artillery duel when in fact most of their shots had flown high of the mark and done little damage. His gambit worked. Alexander, who was running short of ammunition now in any case, called for the attack.

"General, shall I advance?" Pickett asked Longstreet, who could not bring himself to speak and simply bowed his head. "My brave Virginians are to attack in front," Pickett wrote his fiancée moments before entering battle. "Oh, may God in mercy help me as He never helped before!" This was known to posterity as Pickett's Charge, but he was one of three division commanders involved in the attack, the others being Brigadier General J. Johnston Pettigrew and Major General Isaac Trimble. Pickett advanced on the right and Pettigrew and Trimble on the left, with their forces converging on Cemetery Ridge at a spot called the Angle, where the Federal line jutted forward slightly. Observers on both sides marveled at the skill and tenacity with which the Confederates maintained formation as their ranks compressed and men fell by the hundreds to enemy shellfire. "Through our field-glasses we could distinctly see the gaps torn in their ranks, and the ground dotted with dark spots—their dead and wounded," wrote Major General Carl Schurz of Howard's Corps. "But the brave rebels promptly filled the gaps from behind or by closing up on their colors, and unshaken and unhesitatingly they continued their onward march." As they approached the Angle, they came under staggering fire from troops in front and on their flanks and fell in heaps. The

Pickett's Charge reaches a furious climax as Federals beat back surging Confederates (right) at the Angle in this painting by Peter Frederick Rothermel of Pennsylvania, who drew on eyewitness accounts. As one Union soldier described the fighting: "Foot to foot, body to body and man to man they struggled, pushed and strived and killed."

"My brave Virginians are to attack in front. Oh, may God in mercy help me as He never helped before!"

GENERAL GEORGE PICKETT, *before entering battle*

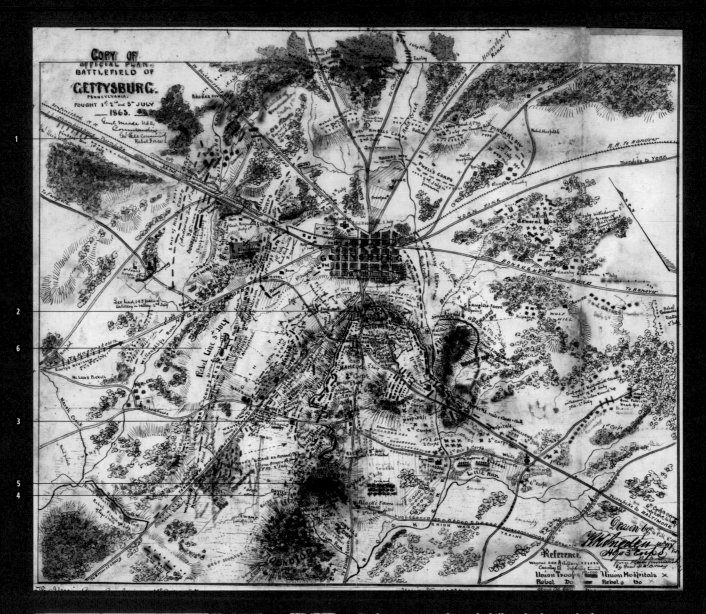

Dark green areas indicate the hills and ridges south of town along which the Union established its "fishhook" defensive line during the battle's final two days. The only civilian known to have fought at Gettysburg was John Burns (left), a 72-year-old veteran of the War of 1812 who grabbed his flintlock musket and offered his services to the 150th Pennsylvania Volunteers when the fighting began near his home on Chambersburg Street. Burns fought with the Iron Brigade near the McPherson Farm, where he was wounded. He became a national hero, photographed here by Mathew Brady while he was recuperating, immortalized in verse by Bret Harte, and sought out by Lincoln when he came to deliver the Gettysburg Address.

THE BATTLE OF GETTYSBURG

LEE'S VICTORY AT CHANCELLORSVILLE GAVE HIM the courage to mount his second invasion of the North, after the failure at Antietam the previous September. But in a reversal of form, Confederate leadership was shaky and their attack uncoordinated, while Union commanders showed initiative in turning defeat into victory.

The battle began almost inadvertently on July 1 before the main armies were present. General John Buford's small Union cavalry division encountered A. P. Hill's Confederates marching toward Gettysburg along the Chambersburg Pike [1], on a quest for shoes. Richard Ewell's 2nd Corps joined the attack in the afternoon, driving the Federals back through the town and up Cemetery Hill [2]. Lee ordered Ewell to take the hill "if practicable"; Ewell held back, but a Rebel victory seemed imminent by the day's end.

At the start of day two, the Union line of defense curved from Culp's Hill down the length of Cemetery Ridge [3]. James Longstreet's Corps was to roll up the Union left while Jubal Early and others "demonstrated" against Culp's and Cemetery Hills to prevent Meade from shifting his defenses. Brutal fighting took place that afternoon from the Peach Orchard to the Devil's Den [4], but the Union line held, thanks to one of the most fabled episodes of the war. Out of ammunition, the 20th Maine Volunteer Infantry led a bayonet charge down Little Round Top [5] to keep the Rebels off this crucial high ground. The Union also held Cemetery Hill, thanks to their efficiently organized defense, and by day's end Lee's ambitious plan was almost completely thwarted.

Around 3 p.m. on day three, Longstreet reluctantly ordered "Pickett's Charge," from Seminary Ridge across an open plain to Cemetery Ridge [6]. Union fire wiped out half the attackers. Jeb Stuart's cavalry, tied up three miles to the east, never arrived to help, and the battle ended with more than 51,000 total casualties. ■

2 **CEMETERY HILL** *The gatehouse to Evergreen Cemetery was riddled with bullets as Federal troops retreated to the hills south of town.*

4 **DEVIL'S DEN** *A Confederate soldier lies dead among the maze of boulders where some of the most intense fighting occurred.*

6 **SEMINARY RIDGE** *Three of the more than 5,000 Rebels captured during the battle await transport to a Federal prison camp.*

survivors bunched together in a churning mass. Most were repulsed before they reached the Federal line, but a small group of perhaps one or two hundred men rallied around Brigadier General Lewis Armistead of Pickett's division, who waved his hat atop his sword and shouted: "Come on, boys, we must give them the cold steel! Who will follow me?" Surging over a stone wall, they achieved a momentary breakthrough before Federals assailed them from all sides and annihilated them.

That brave leap by Armistead and his followers would be remembered as the Confederate high-water mark. But Lee had come closer to victory a day earlier, and he paid a steep price for renewing the attack on July 3. As his beaten troops retreated from the Angle, what had been an agonizingly close-fought battle at Gettysburg ended as a clear-cut defeat for Lee, who made no attempt to deny that fact or shift blame. "All this has been my fault," he told General Cadmus Wilcox. "It is I that have lost this fight, and you must help me out of it in the best way you can." His aura of invincibility was gone, and his army would never again mount a major offensive. More than half of the 13,000 men who took part in Pickett's Charge were killed, wounded, or captured, bringing Lee's total losses over three days to more than 23,000 men, or nearly one third of his forces. Meade had suffered over 20,000 casualties, and both he

[EYEWITNESS]

Abraham Lincoln
PRESIDENT OF THE UNITED STATES

FOUR SCORE AND SEVEN YEARS ago our fathers brought forth on this continent a new nation, conceived in Liberty, and dedicated to the proposition that all men are created equal.

Now we are engaged in a great civil war, testing whether that nation, or any nation so conceived and so dedicated, can long endure. We are met on a great battle field of that war. We have come to dedicate a portion of that field, as a final resting place for those who here gave their lives that that nation might live. It is altogether fitting and proper that we should do this.

But, in a larger sense, we can not dedicate—we can not consecrate—we can not hallow—this ground. The brave men, living and dead, who struggled here, have

"Four score and seven years ago . . ."

consecrated it, far above our poor power to add or detract. The world will little note, nor long remember what we say here, but it can never forget what they did here. It is for us the living, rather, to be dedicated here to the unfinished work which they who fought here have thus far so nobly advanced. It is rather for us to be here dedicated to the great task remaining before us—that from these honored dead we take increased devotion to that cause for which they gave the last full measure of devotion—that we here highly resolve that these dead shall not have died in vain—that this nation, under God, shall have a new birth of freedom—and that government of the people, by the people, for the people, shall not perish from the earth. ■

and his men were so exhausted that they did little to stop the battered Confederates from retreating to Virginia. "We had them within our grasp," Lincoln complained. "We had only to stretch forth our hands and they were ours. And nothing I could say or do could make the army move."

Lincoln understood how much had been gained at Gettysburg, however. Together with the fall of Vicksburg on July 4, Lee's defeat and retreat, which began that same day, transformed this conflict. Southerners could no longer hope to win the war outright through bold strokes. But Northerners could still lose the war if they lacked the will to see it through, which meant overcoming at terrible cost the continuing resistance of Lee and other Confederate commanders. Lincoln would have to persuade Unionists to pay the fearful price exacted at Gettysburg many times over before victory would be assured. And if he failed to do that and lost at the polls, his successor might concede to Confederates in peace talks. On November 19, 1863, Lincoln attended the dedication of the Gettysburg National Cemetery and argued eloquently for redeeming the sacrifices made there by carrying this fight through to a triumphant finish. As he said in conclusion, it remained to the living to ensure "that these dead shall not have died in vain—that this nation, under God, shall have a new birth of freedom—and that government of the people, by the people, for the people, shall not perish from the earth."

President Lincoln sits bareheaded at center before delivering his Gettysburg Address at the dedication of the Gettysburg National Cemetery on November 19, 1863. A reporter on the scene evoked the historic speech: "The President rises slowly, draws from his pocket a paper, and, when commotion subsides, in a sharp, unmusical treble voice, reads the brief and pithy remarks."

CHRONOLOGY

April 2, 1863 **Richmond Bread Riot**

July 13-16 **New York City Draft Riots**

August 21 **Confederate raider William Quantrill leads deadly attack on town of Lawrence, Kansas.**

August 25 **Federal Brigadier General Thomas Ewing, Jr., retaliates by ordering inhabitants to evacuate four Missouri counties bordering on Kansas.**

"They offer to buy up white men for three hundred dollars each, about one third of what a good negro is worth."

Opponent of the Union draft

War on the Home Front

When Colonel Robert Nugent of the Irish Brigade was wounded at Fredericksburg and sent home to New York City to recuperate, he thought he was leaving the war behind. As he said of that battle: "It was a living hell from which escape seemed scarcely possible." He was fortunate enough to survive the ordeal and recover from his wound, but he soon found himself under attack on the home front when he was placed in charge of drafting men in New York for armed service. That draft drew fierce opposition from many of Nugent's fellow Irish immigrants, who considered him a traitor for enforcing a conscription act that allowed wealthy men to purchase an exemption or a substitute for $300—about as much as the average worker made in an entire year—while poor Irishmen and others of little means were forced into the army. "Colonel Nugent, the recent idol of the Irish," reported the *New York Evening Post*, was now being "cursed beyond measure." His experience was shared in one form or another by many people around the country—North, South, and West—who found that turmoil and strife were no longer confined to the battlefield and that their society as a whole was in a state of war.

On Saturday, July 11, the first draftees were selected by lottery in New York City, and their names appeared in newspapers the following day. At the same time, casualty lists from the Battle of Gettysburg were being posted around town, reminding those who had been drafted, or might soon be, that serving the Union could cost them life or limb. Compounding their resentments were fears that if they were inducted, black laborers might take their jobs at lower wages. Many felt they were being reduced to military servitude to win freedom for blacks, who would then compete with them economically. As one opponent of the draft put it, "they offer to buy up white men for three hundred dollars each, about one third of what a good negro is worth." Throughout the city, people gathered on street corners and in taverns and cursed the draft. One man swore he would rather "blow his own brains out than shoulder the musket in defence of an abolition administration."

Colonel Nugent expected trouble when the draft resumed on Monday morning, July 13, but there was not much he could do about it. To defend the city's draft offices against attack, he could call on no more than 70 men of the Invalid Corps, made up of disabled veterans unfit for combat. The New York police force had only about 1,600 patrolmen, and most of the city's militia units had been sent to Pennsylvania in June to help repel Lee's invasion and had not yet returned. Acting on a tip, Nugent dispatched many of his men to a draft office at Third Avenue and 46th Street that morning. By the time they arrived there, a mob had routed policemen at the site and set the building afire. They first tried to disperse the crowd by firing blanks, then fired real bullets, injur-

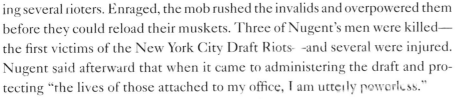

ing several rioters. Enraged, the mob rushed the invalids and overpowered them before they could reload their muskets. Three of Nugent's men were killed—the first victims of the New York City Draft Riots—and several were injured. Nugent said afterward that when it came to administering the draft and protecting "the lives of those attached to my office, I am utterly powerless."

He was not the only official who felt helpless as the violence spread. Police Chief John Kennedy was on his way to the embattled draft office on 46th Street when rioters recognized him, knocked him to the ground, and began kicking and pummeling him. A politician who knew the chief intervened and had him placed in a wagon and carried to safety, but many in the mob thought he was dead and began celebrating. As one journalist reported: "A sort of war-dance was improvised on the spot and cudgels and curses and heels flew in an ungovernable 'shindig.' " Like raiders behind enemy lines, rioters cut communications by pulling down telegraph wires, tearing up tracks, and halting traffic. A mob of several thousand people surrounded an armory on Second Avenue and 21st Street and broke in, seizing weapons and clashing with police before setting the building ablaze. On lower Broadway, police wielding billy clubs got the better of a crowd armed with various weapons by charging down side streets and hitting them in the flank. "For a few minutes," one witness wrote, "nothing was heard but the heavy thud of clubs falling on human skulls, thick and fast as hail stones upon a window pane."

RIOT OR REVOLUTION?

FEW MEN IN NEW YORK WERE MORE THOROUGHLY DESPISED BY THOSE WHO TOOK to the streets on July 13 than Horace Greeley, a fervent Unionist who popularized the slogan, "Forward to Richmond!" That afternoon, an angry crowd

At top, a civilian wearing a blindfold drafts men in New York City for military duty in 1863 by drawing names from a lottery wheel similar to the one shown above. Men could avoid the draft by volunteering for service and receiving a bounty of $300 from Washington; by purchasing a commutation for $300, which exempted them temporarily but left them liable to future drafts; or by purchasing a substitute, which could cost much more than $300 but exempted them permanently.

gathered outside the offices of his newspaper, the *New York Tribune*. As the mob grew larger and louder and threatened to hang Greeley, an editor said to him: "This is not a riot, but a revolution." Fortunately for Greeley and other prominent supporters of the war, the insurgents were not well organized enough to mount a full-fledged rebellion against those in authority. Some rioters were interested only in looting. Others lacked the nerve to make good on their threats and contented themselves with cursing Greeley and others who looked to them like "$300 men," or those wealthy enough to buy their way out of the draft. One such man of means, George Templeton Strong—a Republican lawyer and diarist who strongly favored the war but purchased a substitute rather than risk his life in battle—called the rioters "Celtic devils" and felt threatened by them. "I could not walk four blocks eastward from this house this minute without peril," Strong wrote in his diary as the violence continued. "The outbreak is spreading by concerted action in many quarters."

Rioters hang and burn a black man in Greenwich Village during the mob violence that erupted in New York on July 13 in reaction to the draft. This was one of at least a dozen lynchings committed in the city by rioters who saw the war as benefiting blacks at the expense of whites.

The rioters launched their most venomous assaults not against wealthy whites but against poor blacks. One of the ugliest attacks occurred late Monday afternoon when a mob surrounded the Colored Orphans Asylum on Fifth Avenue and set it afire with the children inside. The orphans escaped harm with the help of firemen and an anonymous bystander described only as an "Irishman," who defied the angry mob. "If there's a man among you with a heart within him," he shouted, "come and help these poor children." The mob then "laid hold of him, and appeared ready to tear him to pieces," recalled Anna Shotwell, the asylum's director. Amid the furor, the children got safely away, she added, "leaving this generous-spirited man in the hands of the ruffians." He was one of many Irish immigrants, some of them policemen and firemen, who stood up to the mob and shielded people from harm at great risk. Few blacks threatened by rioters were as fortunate as the orphans at the asylum. Many were stoned and beaten, and several were lynched. A reporter saw a black man hanged by assailants who then set fire to his clothes, "burning him almost to a cinder." A British visitor asked a bystander what blacks had done to whites to provoke such attacks. "Oh, sir, they hate them here," the man replied; "they are the innocent cause of all these troubles."

The worst of the violence occurred on the night of July 13, but rioting continued for several days afterward. "There will be much trouble today," George Strong predicted in his diary on July 15. "Rabbledom is not yet dethroned any more than its ally and instigator, Rebeldom." He and others suspected that enemy agents were behind the uprising, but there was little to indicate that rioters were in league with the Confederacy other than the fact that some of them denounced Lincoln and cheered for Jefferson Davis.

By Friday, July 17, several thousands troops had reached New York and were patrolling the streets, and order was largely restored. The turbulent draft riots, which left more than 400 people dead or injured, shocked Unionists in general and Republicans in particular. Violent protests against the draft on a smaller scale in Boston and other northeastern cities confirmed that opposition to Lincoln's war policies was widespread. In the Midwest, resistance took a different form as thousands there joined a secret society of Confederate sympathizers called the Knights of the Golden Circle. A grand jury in Indiana reported that there were 15,000 members in that state alone, committed to opposing Federal efforts to raise troops and collect taxes. Democrats charged Republican officials with exaggerating the threat posed by the Knights to frighten the public and justify harsh measures against those who openly protested the war. One editor in New Jersey was hauled into court and fined for denouncing the draft in no uncertain terms. "Those who wish to be butchered will please step forward," he wrote. "All others will please stay at home and defy Old Abe and his minions to drag them from their families."

> **"Those who wish to be butchered will please step forward. All others will please stay at home and defy Old Abe and his minions to drag them from their families."**
>
> *An anti-war newspaper editor from New Jersey*

REBELS AGAINST THE CAUSE

NO NORTHERNER DID MORE TO DEMORALIZE THE SOUTH AND PROMOTE DISSENsion there than Ulysses Grant. His triumph at Vicksburg led many Confederates in that area to conclude that their cause was lost. Among those deflated

The Colored Orphans Asylum is burned and sacked by a New York City mob protesting the military draft. Although the children were inside when the fire was started, they escaped unharmed with the help of firemen and a courageous bystander.

> **"I shall come home, leave or license when I have a mind to. My family are nearer and dearer to me than any Confederacy could be."**
>
> *Soldier from Louisiana*

SUBSTITUTE NOTICES.

WANTED—A SUBSTITUTE for a conscript, to serve during the war. Any good man over the age of 35 years, not a resident of Virginia, or a foreigner, may hear of a good situation by calling at Mr. GEORGE BAGBY'S office, Shockoe Slip, to-day, between the hours of 9 and 11 A. M. [jy 9—1t*] A COUNTRYMAN.

WANTED—Two SUBSTITUTES—one for artillery, the other for infantry or cavalry service. Also, to sell, a trained, thoroughbred cavalry HORSE. Apply to DR. BROOCKS, Corner Main and 12th streets, or to T. T. BROOCKS,
jy 9—3t* Petersburg, Va.

WANTED—Immediately, a SUBSTITUTE. A man over 35 years old, or under 18, can get a good price by making immediate application to Room No. 50, Monument Hotel, or by addressing "J. W.," through Richmond P. O. jy 9—1t*

WANTED—A SUBSTITUTE, to go into the 24th North Carolina State troops, for which a liberal price will be paid. Apply to me at Dispatch office this evening at 4 o'clock P. M.
jy 9—1t* R. R. MOORE.

WANTED—A SUBSTITUTE, to go in a first-rate Georgia company of infantry, under the heroic Jackson. A gentleman whose health is impaired, will give a fair price for a substitute. Apply immediately at ROOM, No. 13, Post-Office Department, third story, between the hours of 10 and 3 o'clock. jy 9—6t*

WANTED—Two SUBSTITUTES for the war. A good bonus will be given. None need apply except those exempt from Conscript. Apply to-day at GEORGE I. HERRING'S,
jy 9—1t* Grocery store, No. 56 Main st.

Notices published in the Richmond Dispatch seek substitutes for men attempting to avoid the draft under Confederate law, which stated that "persons not liable for duty may be received as substitutes for those who are." At first, only those men between 18 and 35 were liable for duty, so draftees purchased substitutes under 18 or over 35. Seeking more troops and hoping to counter charges that this was "a rich man's war but a poor man's fight," the Confederate Congress eventually made men between 17 and 50 liable for duty, repealed the substitute clause, and canceled the exemptions of those who had purchased substitutes, subjecting them once more to the draft.

Rebels were the 30,000 troops he paroled after they surrendered at Vicksburg. "I knew many of them were tired of the war," he wrote, and he reckoned that few of them would make good soldiers if they ever returned to service. They were not supposed to take up arms again until an equal number of Federals were paroled, but Confederate authorities did not have that many to exchange and ordered their own parolees to report for duty without freeing any Federals in return. This angered Union officials—who suspended prisoner exchanges—and antagonized the parolees, who felt they had done their duty and should not be called back. "The men are under the impression that they cannot be held to serve under their parole and are encouraged in it by many people in the country," reported Brigadier General Carter Stevenson. Some of them reported for duty under duress, but as Grant foresaw they proved to be more of a liability than an asset for the army. Others deserted and defied Confederate authorities. "The country is full of paroled prisoners, swearing they will not take up arms again," Grant wrote in late July. "Thousands have crossed the Mississippi and gone west."

Here as in the North, opposition to the draft ran deep. But the strongest challenge to the Confederate government came not from draft resisters but from deserters. Some soldiers ran off because they dreaded combat or were Unionists at heart, but many fought hard for a year or two before deserting because they considered their cause hopeless or felt they had a higher obligation to family members back home. "I shall come home, leave or license when I have a mind to," one soldier from Louisiana wrote. "My family are nearer and dearer to me than any Confederacy could be." More and more Confederates left camp and headed home to help family members as the war dragged on and civilians fell prey to pillaging by their own troops as well as Federals. One man in Alabama complained that Confederates there seized "all my beef cattle and every one of my hogs, not only without my consent, but even without my knowledge, leaving me utterly destitute of meat for my family." Bands of deserters became a law unto themselves in remote areas, defending their own rights and the rights of their kin against Yankees and Confederates alike. One resident of southwestern Virginia noted that deserters there showed no respect for officials: "When halted and asked for their furloughs or their authority to be absent from their commands, they just pat their guns defiantly and say, 'This is my furlough.' "

There were no great explosions of dissent in the South to rival the New York City Draft Riots, but there were numerous run-ins between defiant bands of deserters, sometimes allied with draft resisters, and authorities out to get them. In western North Carolina in early 1863, a band of renegades, many of them deserters from the 64th North Carolina Infantry, raided the town of Marshall and looted the home of Colonel Lawrence Allen while he was away, frightening his wife and children. Allen struck back with a vengeance, leading troops of the regiment against the raiders, who eluded capture until several of their relatives were tortured and revealed their whereabouts. Fifteen men were seized and put before a firing squad without a hearing. "Fire or you will take their place," an officer told soldiers who hesitated to shoot the prisoners. Among those killed was a 13-year-old boy, who begged in vain for mercy.

A larger and more determined band of renegades took hold of Jones County, Mississippi, in the summer of 1863 under the leadership of two deserters: Newton Knight, a Union sympathizer; and Jaspar Collins, who rebelled against fighting a war to defend slavery while planters with 20 or more Negroes were exempt from the draft. With help from poor farmers who shared their disdain for the "slaveocracy"—the Confederacy's slaveholding elite—Knight and his followers held out for nearly a year, raiding plantations, shooting tax collectors, and skirmishing with Confederate troops. It took 200 cavalrymen and a battalion of sharpshooters to bring them to bay. One captured renegade was offered clemency if he agreed to fight for the South. "Hell, no," he replied, and went to the gallows instead.

Unlike Democrats in the North at odds with Lincoln's policies, Southerners disenchanted with the Confederate war effort did not have a political party to represent them. In congressional elections held in the fall of 1863, however, many Confederate representatives who supported Jefferson Davis were challenged by candidates who opposed him. In Galveston, Texas, a Congressman who had voted in favor of the 20-Negro exemption went down to defeat. "A furor was kindled against him on the matter," one observer wrote. "The soldiers and poorer people were carried almost to a man for the upset victor." Davis retained a narrow margin of support in Congress, but in Alabama his opponents won several seats and claimed the governorship. Some blamed the outcome there on a shadowy organization called the Peace Society—the Confederate equivalent of the Knights of the Golden Circle—but the underlying factors that caused voters to rebel were hostility to conscription and festering resentments among soldiers. One official in Alabama noted that "paroled prisoners of the Vicksburg army . . . contributed largely by their votes to the result of the election."

Southern women expressed dissent in various ways, including aiding deserters and draft resisters and taking to the streets in protest. Angered by food shortages and rampant inflation, women joined in so-called bread riots in several Southern cities in 1863. One such disturbance occurred on April 2 in Richmond, where bakeries and other stores were looted. A bystander who saw protesters gathering there asked a young woman if there was a celebration going on. "There is," she replied; "we celebrate our right to live. We are starving. As soon as enough of us get together we are going to the bakeries and each of us will take a loaf of bread. That is little enough for the government to give us after it has taken all our men." Jefferson Davis helped restore order by climbing atop a wagon and addressing the defiant crowd. "You say you are hungry and have no money," he said as he emptied his pockets. "Here is all I have. It is not much, but take it." That was his way of showing that times were hard for everyone in the Confederacy, from the president on down, and the women

> "We are starving. As soon as enough of us get together we are going to the bakeries and each of us will take a loaf of bread. That is little enough for the government to give us after it has taken all our men."
>
> *Woman in Richmond bread riot*

A ringleader stands defiantly with revolver in hand as women raid a bakery during a bread riot that occurred in Richmond on April 2 in response to the soaring cost of food. By 1863, prices in the South had increased eightfold since the beginning of the war and wages had not kept pace, leaving many civilians poor, hungry, and resentful.

Freed slaves embrace their infants at a plantation on St. Helena Island, South Carolina, which was occupied by Federal troops. Many slaves fled to such occupied areas to gain freedom, opportunity, and education, which one fugitive called "the next best thing to liberty."

heeded his order to disperse. But Davis and his advisers worsened inflation by printing too much money and taking in too little revenue. The government did not impose an income tax until 1863, too late to keep the soaring price of food and other necessities in check. "I fear that the poor suffer very much," wrote Judith McGuire of Richmond. "Meal was selling today at $16 per bushel. It has been bought up by speculators. Oh that these hard-hearted creatures could be made to suffer! Strange that men with human hearts can, in these dreadful times, thus grind the poor."

Some Southerners were so opposed to Confederate rule that they welcomed Federal occupation forces. Yankee troops were regarded as liberators by many people in eastern Tennessee, where one Unionist, editor William Brownlow of Knoxville, pledged to "fight the secession leaders till Hell freezes over, and then fight them on the ice." Other Southerners came to terms with Federal authorities for practical reasons, taking an oath of allegiance to the Union to avoid having their property confiscated. Most people in the South deeply resented Federal occupation, however, and some fled their homes rather than live under Yankee domination. Many planters migrated to Texas to avoid losing their slaves to advancing Federals. By one estimate, as many as 150,000 slaves moved to Texas with their masters from occupied Mississippi and Louisiana. Some slaves remained willingly with their owners, but others were coerced. One planter in Arkansas warned his slaves that if Yankees ever got close enough to liberate them, he would line them up "and free you with my shotgun!" Despite such threats, slaves grew bolder and more defiant as word of the Emancipation Proclamation spread. One woman in Texas who took charge of a plantation in 1863, after her husband went off to war, complained that her slaves would not work and refused orders: "Some of them are getting so high on anticipation of their glorious freedom by the Yankees I suppose, that they resist a whipping."

The largest active corps of resisters in the South were the hundreds of thousands of slaves who left their masters and sought freedom under Federal authority. Charitable organizations such as the New England Freedmen's Aid Society sent teachers to educate freed slaves "who had seen the magic of a scrap of writing," as one instructor put it, "and were eager to share such power." Some former slaves worked for Federal officers on military projects or for Northern civilians who acquired abandoned or confiscated plantations. Others toiled for Southerners loyal to the Union. Their employers deducted from their wages the cost of food, clothing, and other items provided to them, meaning that many received little or no cash for their labor and remained in what amounted to servitude. Some enterprising blacks leased land from Federal officials, however, and did well enough to hire other blacks as laborers. "They do full work themselves," one observer wrote, "and being of the same race with those they hire, they succeed in getting good and steady work out of them." The Sea Islands of South Carolina were among the best-administered occupied territories and became a proving ground for postwar efforts to help former slaves become self-sufficient. One of the first black regiments to serve the Union was recruited there. Together with black troops raised in other occupied areas and throughout the North, they helped fulfill the words of Frederick Douglass: "Once let the black man get upon his person the brass letters, U.S.; let him get an eagle on his button, and a musket on his shoulder and bullets in his pocket, and there is no power on earth which can deny that he has earned the right to citizenship in the United States."

TERROR ON THE FRONTIER

THERE WERE MEN WHO KILLED TO END SLAVERY AND MEN WHO KILLED TO DEFEND it. And then there were men like William Quantrill who liked to kill and plunder and used the furor over slavery as an excuse. Raised in Ohio, young Quantrill went west before the war and lived for a while in Lawrence, Kansas, a hotbed

"Once let the black man get upon his person the brass letters, U.S.; let him get an eagle on his button, and a musket on his shoulder and bullets in his pocket, and there is no power on earth which can deny that he has earned the right to citizenship in the United States."

FREDERICK DOUGLASS

Sergeant James Baldwin of Company G, 56th U.S. Colored Infantry, sits proudly for a portrait with the American flag as his backdrop. Union General James Blunt wrote that the black recruits under his command made "better soldiers in every respect than any troops I ever had."

THE GLORY REGIMENT

THE 54TH MASSACHUSETTS WAS just one of 166 regiments of U.S. Colored Troops that contributed nearly 200,000 soldiers to the Union cause. But the first black regiment recruited in the North achieved a lasting fame like none of the others, due in large part to their valor in a failed attack on Fort Wagner, South Carolina. Today they are known commonly as "the Glory regiment," after the 1989 film that helped immortalize them.

Banned by law from armed service at the start of the war, blacks were finally able to enlist thanks to the militia act of 1862 and the Emancipation Proclamation of

> **"Who would be free themselves must strike the blow. . . . This is your golden opportunity."**
>
> FREDERICK DOUGLASS TO BLACK SOLDIERS

1863. Abolitionists and segregationists alike knew the potential consequences: "The iron gate of our prison stands half open," wrote Frederick Douglass in "Men of Color to Arms!," published in the *National Anti-Slavery Standard*. "One gallant rush from the North will fling it wide open, while four million of our brothers and sisters shall march out into liberty."

One of the first official black regiments was the 1st South Carolina Volunteers, who were led by a noted abolitionist, Colonel Thomas Wentworth Higginson of Massachusetts. Encouraged by their successful organization, the Bay State's governor, John Andrew, raised the North's

This somewhat fanciful 1890 lithograph by Kurz and Allison dramatizes the storming of Fort Wagner by the 54th Massachusetts. Colonel Shaw, saber raised, is depicted front and center, either just before or just as he takes a bullet through the heart from one of the Rebel defenders.

first black regiment, the 54th Massachusetts, and hand-picked Colonel Robert Gould Shaw to lead them.

Shaw was the son of prominent abolitionists, later elegized by philosopher William James as a "blue-eyed child of fortune" who rode among the "champions of a better day for man." But Shaw initially resisted Governor Andrew's call to raise and lead an all-black regiment, until he saw the enthusiasm of the volunteers, who came not just from the Bay State, but New York and Pennsylvania as well.

Once the 54th Massachusetts was up and running, Shaw struggled to get supplies for his troops, and he encouraged them to boycott their pay after the government reneged on a promise to pay black soldiers the same as whites. The boycott was eventually successful, but such problems were chronic among the black regiments, who were segregated, paid less, required to purchase their own clothes, not allowed to become officers, and generally used only in garrison and labor battalions.

THE BATTLE OF FORT WAGNER

A LITTLE MORE THAN TWO YEARS after the Rebels captured Fort Sumter, another watershed battle took place in the mouth of Charleston Harbor. On Morris Island, a formidable Confederate earthwork known as Fort Wagner was garrisoned by around 1,800 Rebels. A 30-foot wall stretched east to west from the ocean to a salt marsh, and the approach to the fort was a narrow strip of beach just 60 yards wide. Union forces landed on Morris Island in the summer of 1863 aiming to take the fort, but their first attack failed.

Since taking command of the 54th Massachusetts,

Sergeant William Carney exemplified his regiment's bravery at Fort Wagner by saving the American flag despite being wounded repeatedly. He became the first black soldier to be awarded a Medal of Honor. "Boys, I only did my duty," he said. "The old flag never touched the ground!"

Colonel Shaw had struggled to get them into battle, where he insisted they would prove themselves "true men, worthy of fighting among Whites." For a second attempt on Fort Wagner, Shaw lobbied Major General Quincy Gillmore to let his men see some real action. Gillmore agreed to let the all-black regiment spearhead the second attack, a decision that would irrevocably alter the Northern perception of black soldiers.

On July 18, the 54th Massachusetts led five other brigades, for a total of 5,000 men, across the narrow beach approach in a frontal assault on Fort Wagner. The men suffered heavy casualties rushing the well-defended fort, but managed to reach the parapets in intense fighting. After another hour of brutal hand-to-hand combat, the Federals were forced to withdraw, having suffered around 1,600 casualties to the Rebels' 200. Almost every officer was killed, and no regiment suffered more losses than the 54th Massachusetts, which lost around 40 percent of its regiment, including Colonel Shaw, who was shot dead through the heart just after rallying his men with the words, "Come on 54th!"

When Shaw's father tried to bring his son's body home for burial, the Confederate command reportedly told him, "We have buried him with his Niggers." It was intended as an insult, but it became a rallying cry in the North, and the much-publicized valor of the 54th Massachusetts encouraged further enlistment and mobilization of black troops. According to the *New York Tribune*, the battle "made Fort Wagner such a name to the colored race as Bunker Hill had been for ninety years to the white Yankees." ■

"I hope soon to have troops enough on the Missouri side not only to prevent raids into Kansas but also to drive out or exterminate every band of guerrillas now haunting that region. I will keep a thousand men in the saddle daily in pursuit of them and will redden with their blood every road and bridle path of the border."

FEDERAL BRIGADIER GENERAL
THOMAS EWING

"I'm in for burning Lawrence and killing all the men in the damned town."

One of William Quantrill's Confederate raiders

of abolitionism, where he joined antislavery ruffians called Jayhawkers in raids on proslavery settlements on either side of the Kansas-Missouri border. He cared nothing for the abolitionist cause and would steal slaves and livestock from one owner and sell them to another. True antislavery men in Lawrence like Sheriff Sam Walker saw through him. "He did not deceive me one bit," Walker recalled. "He was a monster of the worst kind." In late 1860, after betraying several abolitionists to a Missouri planter who shot them when they tried to free his slaves, Quantrill fled Lawrence and went over to the other side. Settling in Missouri among proslavery Border Ruffians, he enlisted with the Confederates when war broke out as a captain of partisans, or guerrillas. Among his followers were men as ruthless as he was, including Frank and Jesse James, William "Cole" Younger, and William "Bloody Bill" Anderson. In August 1863, Quantrill set his sights on Lawrence, Kansas. He had a score to settle with abolitionists and Unionists there who had spurned him and sent him packing, and many of his followers felt the same way he did. As one of them said: "I'm in for burning Lawrence and killing all the men in the damned town."

Quantrill's raid on Lawrence was symptomatic of a war that was degenerating in the West into bushwhacking—savage, irregular combat that offered civilians no quarter. Some who rode with Quantrill had fought in conventional battles such as Wilson's Creek, but since that victory, Confederate fortunes had declined in the region. By mid-1863, Missouri and northern Arkansas were largely under Federal control, and Rebels there were reduced to raiding and pillaging. Putting a stop to that bushwhacking was the task of Brigadier General Thomas Ewing, who shared the uncompromising attitude of his brother-in-law, William Sherman, and set out to crush Confederate resistance. "I hope soon to have troops enough on the Missouri side not only to prevent raids into Kansas," he wrote, "but also to drive out or exterminate every band of guerrillas now haunting that region. I will keep a thousand men in the saddle daily in pursuit of them and will redden with their blood every road and bridle path of the border." Ewing infuriated Quantrill's men by rounding up women suspected of aiding the guerrillas and confining them in a dilapidated building in Kansas City that collapsed on August 14. Among those crushed to death in the rubble were a sister of Bill Anderson and a cousin of Cole Younger, both of whom backed Quantrill's proposed raid as a way of defying the hated Ewing and making Unionists pay. "Let's go to Lawrence," Quantrill urged. "We can get more revenge, and more money there than anywhere else in the state."

For Quantrill, who had been struggling to hold his band together as men like Younger and Anderson attracted followers of their own, the raid was an opportunity to reassert his authority. Attacking Lawrence, a town of 3,000 or so inhabitants more than 30 miles west of the Missouri border, was a daunting task, but Quantrill assembled nearly 450 men on horseback and crossed into Kansas on August 19. A Union cavalry officer, Captain Joshua Pike, recognized them as Confederates but let them pass, fearing that his 100 or so cavalrymen would be overwhelmed. Not until Captain Charles Coleman arrived that evening with 80 troopers and took charge of Pike's men did the Federals launch a pursuit, and by then Quantrill had too big a lead. At dawn on August 21, he and his raiders approached Lawrence, which had received no warning of the

WILLIAM QUANTRILL

JESSE JAMES

BLOODY BILL ANDERSON

COLE AND JIM YOUNGER

Confederate bushwhacker William Quantrill attracted followers who shared his penchant for murder and mayhem. He did not have Jesse James with him when he launched his attack on the Unionist stronghold of Lawrence, Kansas, but other notorious members of Quantrill's gang, including Bloody Bill Anderson and Cole Younger, figured prominently in that bloody assault.

Quantrill's raiders bring death and destruction to Lawrence on the morning of August 21, killing prominent Unionists and abolitionists who were slated for execution and other men and boys who were targeted indiscriminately.

"A tempest of fire and death swept through the adjacent streets."

Eyewitness to the carnage in Lawrence, Kansas

impending attack. Quantrill had four Colt revolvers at his belt, and those riding with him were similarly armed. "Kill every man big enough to carry a gun," he told them.

Their first victim in Lawrence was Reverend Samuel Snyder, an abolitionist who had recruited black troops for the 2nd Kansas Colored Regiment. He was milking a cow in his yard outside town when he was gunned down. Twenty black soldiers who had recently enlisted under Snyder were camped in Lawrence, and 22 young white volunteers enrolled in another regiment were sleeping in tents a few blocks away. Those volunteers were boys, playing soldier until they were old enough to fight, but that did not earn them a reprieve. The raiders riddled their tents with bullets, chased down those who fled, and ignored their pleas for mercy. "No quarter for you Federal sons of bitches," one gunman shouted. Only five of the boys escaped death, but the black recruits were more fortunate. Hearing shooting and screaming close by, they got away before they came under attack.

In a large town like this with many avenues of escape, the raiders could not possibly kill all the men, so they concentrated on prominent figures like Mayor George Washington Collamore, whose name was on a death list Quantrill drew up before the attack. Collamore hid from his attackers but died when they burned down his house. The top name on Quantrill's list was Senator James H. Lane, who had led destructive raids by Kansas militiamen against Confederate havens in Missouri. As assailants approached his front door, Lane exited through a rear window in his nightshirt and ran off through a cornfield. To his dying day, Quantrill regretted losing this chance to seize Lane and said of him intently: "I would have burned him at the stake."

Many men staying at the Eldridge House might have died after Quantrill's men surrounded that large hotel had it not been for the efforts of Captain Alexander Banks, a provost marshal in charge of military police in Kansas. Banks appealed to Quantrill as an officer—one who held the rank of captain and claimed to be a colonel—by offering to surrender the hotel if its occupants were treated as prisoners of war. Quantrill agreed, and the guests were spared, forcing the raiders to seek other targets nearby. "A tempest of fire and death swept through the adjacent streets," one witness wrote. After four hours of mayhem, a lookout saw Coleman's Federals approaching in the distance and Quantrill and his raiders made their escape, leaving Lawrence in flames. Two-thirds of the residents lost their homes to fire, and 185 men and boys lost their lives. Reverend Richard Cordley, who survived despite the marauders' threats to "kill all the damned preachers," saw corpses everywhere, "on the sidewalks, in the streets, amid the weeds of the gardens, and in the few remaining homes." Another survivor, John Speer, wandered amid the rubble for days in search of his 17-year-old son Robert. "Help me find my boy," he asked passersby. "They have killed one, and the other I cannot find." Robert had spent the night at the office of a newspaper he worked for, the *Lawrence Republican*, which was torched and incinerated. No remains were found there, but his mother refused to give up hope, setting a place for him each day at the dinner table to which he never returned.

The shocking attack on Lawrence drove General Ewing to retaliate on August 25 by ordering the inhabitants of four counties in Missouri bordering Kansas to leave their homes. He hoped by depopulating that area to deprive bushwhackers of refuge and support. But Quantrill and others continued to kill and plunder—some of them until the end of the war and beyond—while thousands of civilians who bore no blame for their depredations paid the price. As Missourians packed up and moved out, Jayhawkers seeking to avenge the killings at Lawrence crossed over from Kansas, robbed the refugees, and torched their abandoned homes and fields, transforming this once-lovely country into a wasteland that came to be known as the Burnt District.

It was here along the Kansas-Missouri border that the seeds of the Civil War had been planted by abolitionists like John Brown and their proslavery foes. Those seeds bore such bitter fruit that people wondered whether any good would come of this fearful conflict. In the "Battle Hymn of the Republic," based on the abolitionist anthem "John Brown's Body," composer Julia Ward Howe imagined God cleansing the nation of its sins with "his terrible swift sword." As the war expanded and intensified, leaving few homes untouched, the promise of that hymn—that death and destruction would bring renewal and redemption—was for many Americans their last great hope.

"I would have burned him at the stake."

WILLIAM QUANTRILL, *lamenting the lost opportunity to seize Senator James Lane*

Senator James Lane, who survived the attack on Lawrence by fleeing his home, helped provoke Quantrill's raid by leading an assault by Jayhawkers in September 1861 on Osceola, Missouri, where they shot suspected Confederate sympathizers, burned homes, robbed banks, stole livestock, and freed slaves.

> "If we can hold Chattanooga and eastern Tennessee, I think the rebellion must dwindle and die."
>
> ABRAHAM LINCOLN

BREAKTHROUGH AT CHATTANOOGA

FRIDAY, AUGUST 21, WAS DESIGNATED BY JEFFERSON DAVIS AS A DAY OF prayer and fasting. In Chattanooga, Tennessee, where soldiers and civilians were anxiously awaiting an advance by Federal troops to their north, many people dutifully attended services to seek God's help while others went about their business. Around 9 a.m., as prayer meetings were getting under way, Chattanooga was jarred by cannonfire from a Union battery on the north bank of the Tennessee River. "The Yanks made their appearance very suddenly on the opposite side of the river and commenced shelling the town," wrote Colonel Newton Davis of the 24th Alabama Infantry. "You never saw such skidadling in all your life." Shopkeepers and fruit vendors ran for their lives, but the panic was not limited to people in the streets. A Union soldier across the river saw frightened worshippers pouring out of a church in Chattanooga "like bees from a hive." One minister was "in the act of prayer when a shell came hissing near the church," related Confederate General Daniel Harvey Hill. "He went on calmly with his petition to the Great Being 'who rules in the armies of heaven and among the inhabitants of earth,' but at its close, the preacher, opening his eyes, noticed a perceptible diminution of his congregation."

This was the beginning of a fierce struggle for control of Chattanooga, a major rail hub that served as the gateway from Tennessee to Georgia. Hav-

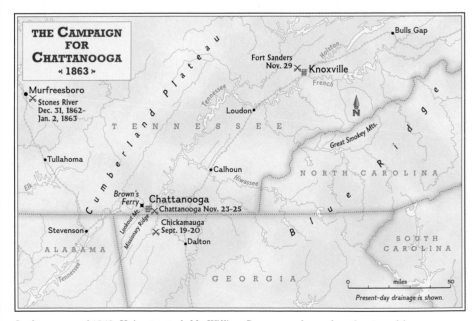

In the summer of 1863, Union troops led by William Rosecrans advanced southeastward from Murfreesboro, repulsing Confederates under Braxton Bragg at Tullahoma and forcing them to abandon Chattanooga in September. After pursuing Bragg's forces across the border into Georgia, Rosecrans was defeated at Chickamauga. Ulysses Grant then took charge and prepared for a showdown with Bragg at Chattanooga while Federals under Ambrose Burnside held out at Knoxville.

ing recently seized control of the Mississippi River, Federals now hoped to drive another wedge through the South by completing the conquest of Tennessee and advancing from Chattanooga into Georgia, thus isolating Virginia and the Carolinas. "If we can hold Chattanooga and eastern Tennessee," Lincoln declared, "I think the rebellion must dwindle and die."

Jefferson Davis, for his part, was just as intent on defending Chattanooga and preventing further Federal advances that might prove fatal to his cause. The recent Confederate defeats at Vicksburg and Gettysburg enabled him to shift troops withdrawn from those areas to Chattanooga, where Braxton Bragg's Army of the Tennessee was desperate for reinforcements. Since retreating from Murfreesboro after the Battle of Stones River in January, he had been thoroughly outmanned and outmaneuvered by his Federal opponent, William Rosecrans, commander of the Army of the Cumberland. Now as Chattanooga came under the gun, Bragg faced the hard choice of holding out there under siege—which might mean losing his army—or abandoning the town and enhancing his dismal reputation for yielding ground. If Bragg stood at the very gates of Heaven and had a chance to join the angels, Southerners jibed, he would fall back and regroup. Disliked by his troops and scorned by his top officers, Bragg was isolated and apprehensive and felt trapped in Chattanooga, set amid steep ridges that concealed enemy movements. "It is said to be easy to defend a mountainous country," he told D. H. Hill, "but mountains hide your foe from you, while they are full of gaps through which he can pounce on you at any time."

The bombardment on August 21 was part of a well-orchestrated effort by Rosecrans to convince Bragg that Chattanooga was under imminent threat of attack from the north while Federal forces crossed the Tennessee River west of town and outflanked the Confederates. Not until month's end did Bragg learn of that flanking movement, and he did not know whether it was a diversion or the enemy's main thrust. He soon found his position in Chattanooga untenable and abandoned the town on September 7, retreating southward below the Georgia border. "Chattanooga is ours without a struggle and East Tennessee is free," Rosecrans wired Washington. The fall of Chattanooga came less than a week after Union troops of the Army of the Ohio led by General Ambrose Burnside—back in command after his disastrous defeat at Fredericksburg—seized Knoxville, Tennessee, where many people opposed secession and greeted the Federals with open arms. As one of Burnside's men recalled: "Old gray-haired men would come out and seize the General's hand, bidding him Godspeed, and men would flock in at every halt to be armed and join us."

To Rosecrans in Chattanooga, the future looked deceptively bright. He

After seizing Chattanooga, William Rosecrans was lionized in his home state of Ohio, where a sheet-music publisher dedicated this song to him. His troops called him "Old Rosy" and admired him for remaining up front during battles and braving enemy fire.

> **"It is said to be easy to defend a mountainous country,
> but mountains hide your foe from you,
> while they are full of gaps through which
> he can pounce on you at any time."**
>
> GENERAL BRAXTON BRAGG AT CHATTANOOGA

had Bragg on the run and hoped to finish him off. But to do so meant abandoning the cautious path he had followed since taking charge of the Army of the Cumberland in late 1862. He had always been slow to advance—too slow for President Lincoln and General in Chief Halleck, who bombarded him with telegrams urging action. His near-defeat at Stones River left him determined not to move forward until he felt sure his forces were ready, and his capture of Chattanooga seemingly vindicated that painstaking approach. Now, however, he ignored the advice of his most accomplished corps commander, General George Thomas, who urged him to consolidate his position at Chattanooga before advancing southward against Bragg. Instead, the overconfident Rosecrans sent his three corps after the Confederates on separate paths.

Meanwhile, Bragg was gathering strength and preparing to strike back. He had already been bolstered by troops withdrawn from Knoxville and was expecting 12,000 men from Lee's Army of Northern Virginia under Lieutenant General James Longstreet, one of the South's most respected commanders. Longstreet's troops were battle-weary after the grueling Gettysburg campaign and were forced to make a roundabout rail journey of nearly 1,000 miles after Federals severed the direct route from Richmond

At right, a climber perches atop Lookout Mountain, overlooking the Tennessee River near Chattanooga. Most of the troops who campaigned here and at Chickamauga were from west of the Appalachians, and some were from west of the Mississippi, including the men of the 8th Kansas Infantry above, who fought for the Union with the Army of the Cumberland.

to Chattanooga. Diarist Mary Chesnut saw them as they passed through South Carolina in the night. "God bless the gallant fellows," she wrote. "Not one man intoxicated—not one rude word did I hear. It was a strange sight—miles, apparently, of platform cars—soldiers rolled in their blankets, lying in rows, heads and all covered, fast asleep. In their gray blankets, packed in regular order, they looked like swathed mummies. . . . A feeling of awful depression laid hold of me. All these fine fellows going to kill or be killed."

Even before Longstreet's Corps arrived, Bragg felt confident enough to take the offensive. Beginning on September 9, he tried to prod his corps commanders into attacking the oncoming Federals while they were divided and vulnerable. His officers were slow to respond and let the opportunity pass, in part because they distrusted their commander, who in D. H. Hill's words had a way of finding "a scapegoat for every failure and disaster." By September 18, Rosecrans had recognized the threat to his army and reunited his forces below Chattanooga along the west bank of a creek called Chickamauga—a Cherokee name meaning River of Blood. His army was still at considerable risk, for with the arrival of Longstreet's Corps, Bragg would have 66,000 men, or several thousand more than his opponent. This was a dangerous place for Rosecrans to do battle and risk all he had gained over the past year. The Confederates to his east seized control of fords and bridges over the Chickamauga on the 18th and began crossing in force that evening. Rosecrans would find it hard to maintain a defensive line west of the river amid dense woodlands interspersed with clearings. As Lieutenant Albion Tourgée of the 105th Ohio Infantry observed: "It was the worst possible region in which to maneuver an army, being without landmarks or regular slopes, and so thickly wooded that it was impossible to preserve any alignment. . . . The commander of a regiment rarely saw both flanks of his command at once. Even companies became broken in the thickets, and taking different directions were lost to each other. Confusion reigned even before the battle began." Such was the setting for two days of unsurpassed fury along the aptly named River of Blood.

CARNAGE AT CHICKAMAUGA

ROSECRANS AND BRAGG HAD SPENT SO MUCH TIME TRYING TO OUTWIT EACH OTHER that they had begun to think alike. Bragg's plan was to sweep around the Federal left flank, or the north end of the line, and cut Rosecrans off from Chattanooga. Rosecrans anticipated that move and shifted George Thomas's Corps to the left on the night of the 18th so that his own line extended farther north than Bragg's. Early on September 19, Thomas received a misleading report that a single Confederate brigade had crossed the Chickamauga on Bragg's right and sent forces to deal with those exposed Rebels. The advancing Federals soon realized what they were up against when they clashed first with cavalrymen led by General Nathan Bedford Forrest, covering Bragg's right flank, and then with several brigades of infantry. Forrest's men were caught by surprise and hard-pressed. Jay Minnich of the 6th Georgia Cavalry recalled that he and his comrades were resting in the woods west of the Chickamauga that morning, convinced that "there was not a Yankee within cannon range—when we were suddenly brought up standing by two volleys deliv-

"It was the worst possible region in which to maneuver an army, being without landmarks or regular slopes, and so thickly wooded that it was impossible to preserve any alignment. . . . Confusion reigned even before the battle began."

LIEUTENANT ALBION TOURGÉE
105TH OHIO INFANTRY,
at Chickamauga

The placid fields and forests around Lee and Gordon's Mills, on Chickamauga Creek, became a killing ground in September when forces led by Bragg and Rosecrans collided here in one of the bloodiest battles of the war.

ered in rapid succession and with such precision as is attained only by practiced and seasoned troops." The cavalrymen could not see their assailants, "so completely were they concealed by the underbrush in our front," but took heavy casualties before reinforcements arrived. "Hold on, boys," Forrest urged his beleaguered troopers, "the infantry is coming."

As Confederate troops of Major General William Walker's Corps entered the fray, the tide turned and the Federals called for help. Thomas sent in more men, and the fighting escalated. Bragg, who began the day "bright and confident," as one officer put it, was dismayed to learn that Thomas's Corps stood in the way of his flanking movement but clung stubbornly to the hope of breaking through there, committing one division after another as the day wore on. As D. H. Hill commented afterward, he was swinging away impulsively at his foe like an "amateur boxer," rather than delivering "the crushing blows of the trained pugilist." Late that morning, Bragg hurled General Benjamin Cheatham's division of Polk's Corps against Thomas's Federals. Many of Cheatham's men were Tennesseans, eager to reclaim Chattanooga, and they fought hard. "We held our position for two hours and ten minutes in the midst of a deadly and galling fire," recalled Sam Watkins of the 1st Tennessee Infantry, commanded by Colonel Hume Field, who stood fast while regiments to his left and right were giving way under fierce pressure. Not until General Forrest rode up and warned him did he realize how desperate his situation was. "Colonel Field, look out," Forrest shouted over the din of battle, "you are almost surrounded; you had better fall back." When the order came to retreat, Watkins related, he and other survivors "ran through a solid line of blue coats. . . . They were upon the right of us, they were upon the left of us, they were in front of us, they were in the rear of us. It was a perfect hornets' nest. The balls whistled around our ears like the escape valves of ten thousand engines. The woods seemed to be blazing; everywhere, at every jump, would rise a lurking foe."

As Cheatham's troops pulled back, Bragg threw in the division of Major General Alexander Stewart. A West Point graduate and professor of mathematics who opposed secession but sided with the Confederacy out of loyalty to Tennessee, Stewart had a mind of his own and was not content with Bragg's vague written orders, which instructed him to "move to the point where the firing had commenced." He confronted Bragg at his headquarters and demanded clarification. The fighting in the woods west of the Chickamauga was so fierce and chaotic that Bragg could scarcely keep up with events there, and all he could do was tell Stewart to be "governed by circumstances." Relying on his own judgment, Stewart moved toward the center of the line, far from where the firing had commenced, and smashed through there in heavy fighting. As Stewart's men surged across the La Fayette Road, they neared Rosecrans's headquarters at the house of a widow named Eliza Glenn. Rosecrans had moved there with his staff a few hours earlier to get closer to the action. Now he was too close for comfort. The fighting was "so terrible and so near us," wrote his aide, Colonel John Sanderson, "that orders were given to mount with a view of falling back to a less dangerous place."

Rosecrans was not about to surrender this ground without a fight and summoned reinforcements. Stewart's Confederates were badly mauled and could not sustain their breakthrough. One of his brigades lost more than 600 men in the attack. Meanwhile, a new threat was emerging that startled Rosecrans. Although he knew that Longstreet's men were on their way to reinforce Bragg, he dismissed reports of their arrival as Confederate fabrications meant to demoralize his troops. In fact, the first of Longstreet's men—a division commanded by General John Bell Hood—had reached the battlefield the day before. Hood's right arm had been shattered at Gettysburg and rendered useless, but he was as keen to do battle as ever. Around 4 p.m., he sent his vaunted Texas Brigade charging across the La Fayette Road near where Stewart broke through. As they advanced, they passed some of Stewart's exhausted men, who were laying low, and shouted out to them: "Rise up, Tennesseans, and see the Texans go in!"

They did not go far. Awaiting them behind breastworks on the far side of the road was the Lightning Brigade of Colonel John Wilder, a resourceful officer from Indiana who had equipped his men with Spencer repeating rifles, which could fire seven shots in far less time than it took men with muskets to load and fire once. Staggered by the fusillade, the Confederates sought shelter in a ditch bordering the road, but it offered them little protection. Within

"They fell in heaps, and I had it in my heart to order the firing to cease, to end the awful sight."

FEDERAL COLONEL JOHN WILDER
LIGHTNING BRIGADE

Private John Munson holds a Spencer repeating rifle—the weapon that made his Lightning Brigade, a mounted infantry unit commanded by Colonel John Wilder, devastatingly effective against Confederates at Chickamauga. "With our Spencer rifles, we felt ourselves to be well-nigh invincible," recalled one soldier in the brigade, which fought dismounted.

two minutes, recalled a sergeant in Wilder's brigade, not a man remained "upon his feet in our front." The ditch was "literally full of dead and wounded," another Federal wrote. Wilder found it hard to stomach the slaughter. "They fell in heaps," he recollected, "and I had it in my heart to order the firing to cease, to end the awful sight."

Nearby, around a farmhouse owned by the Viniard family, other brigades sent in by Hood fared better and came close to shattering the Federal line. Bragg had a division in reserve commanded by Major General Patrick Cleburne, an Irish immigrant who had served in the British Army before settling in Arkansas and was earning a reputation as the Stonewall Jackson of the West. If Cleburne had reinforced Hood's thrust, Rosecrans might have been overwhelmed. But Bragg remained preoccupied with the struggle in the woods to his right, where Thomas had spoiled his plan to outflank Rosecrans. Ordered to attack there, Cleburne's men had to march for several miles from left to right and were not in position to attack until it was nearly dark. Their onslaught stunned Thomas's Federals, who thought fighting was done for the day and were preparing to pull back to a fortified line along the La Fayette Road. As the Confederates advanced, one of them recalled: "The somber woods were lit up by the flashing guns and the night seemed to

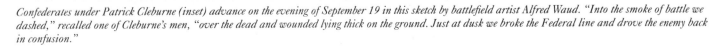

Confederates under Patrick Cleburne (inset) advance on the evening of September 19 in this sketch by battlefield artist Alfred Waud. "Into the smoke of battle we dashed," recalled one of Cleburne's men, "over the dead and wounded lying thick on the ground. Just at dusk we broke the Federal line and drove the enemy back in confusion."

quake and tremble." Cleburne's men were fighting blind. "Accurate shooting was impossible," he wrote. "Each party aimed at the flashes of the other's guns, and few of the shots from either side took effect." In the deepening gloom, Confederate Brigadier General Preston Smith mistook a Yankee for a Rebel straggler and swung at him with the flat of his sword, at which point the startled soldier shot him dead. After driving the Federals back to the La Fayette Road, which was just where Thomas wanted them, Cleburne's men could do no more.

It was a bitter evening for the thousands of wounded men and for those who heard their cries. "The ground upon which we lay had been well fought

Private William J. Oliphant

6TH TEXAS INFANTRY, DESHLER'S BRIGADE

William Oliphant joined the 6th Texas Infantry at Victoria, Texas, in 1861. The regiment served in the Corinth Campaign and was captured at Arkansas Post in January 1863. After their exchange, the survivors were consolidated with the 10th Texas Infantry and a regiment of dismounted cavalry. The new regiment fought at Chickamauga, and of the 667 soldiers who went into action, 20 were killed, 95 were wounded, and 28 went missing. Oliphant was among the injured, suffering wounds in his right arm, left hand, and jaw.

"Bowing our heads and grasping our guns firmly we plunged into this vortex of hell."

LATE IN THE AFTERNOON a mounted officer galloped up to General Deshler, hurriedly spoke a few words and dashed away. The bugle immediately sounded attention and then came the sharp commands "right face, forward, double quick march." Away we went dashing through the Chickamauga River waist deep, and double quicked to the front.

On arriving at the edge of the battle we were quickly thrown into line and ordered to charge. The Texas yell was raised and into the smoke of battle we dashed passing through lines of Confederates who had been driven back by the enemy, and over the dead and wounded lying thick on the ground. Just at dusk we broke the Federal line and drove the enemy back in confusion.

After reforming our lines and resting a short time, we were again ordered forward, the enemy giving way as we advanced. It was now quite dark but just ahead of us was a brilliant light. A field was burning and we were ordered to charge through it. A battery had been stationed in the field and it was still there. It had been captured and recaptured and, then abandoned. The firing of the guns had set fire to the high sedge grass of the field. The fence was on fire and the tall dead trees in the field were blazing high in the air. Dead and wounded men were lying there in great danger of being consumed and the federals occupying the opposite side of the field were pouring a deadly shower of shot and shell through the smoke and flames. Bowing our heads and grasping our guns firmly we plunged into this vortex of hell. On emerging from the fire and smoke, yelling like demons, we dashed at the federals and soon had them flying. It was a fearful place. The heartrending appeals of the wounded, some of whom were scorching, the hissing bullets and screeching shells, made it an experience never to be forgotten. ∎

over during the day," recalled Lieutenant Wilson Vance of the 21st Ohio Infantry, "and as things became quiet we heard the moans and groans of the wounded, which told us that between us and the enemy were lying human beings, torn and mangled, and in agony." One victim whose "speech plainly proclaimed him a Confederate" raised such pitiful cries for help that men of Vance's regiment went out to retrieve him. "I'll never forget ye for this, Yanks," he told them. "You've done me a good turn." The struggle was far from over, and some men who came through the first day unscathed reckoned that their time had come. "I knew the next day would bring us into one of the bloodiest battles the world had ever witnessed," wrote Sergeant Major John Green of the Confederate 9th Kentucky Infantry. "I could not shake off the conviction that I would meet my death in the next day's battle. I offered up a prayer that the Lord would guide me and strengthen me and that when death came it would find me gallantly doing my duty."

Elsewhere on the battlefield that evening, a Union man traded barbs with a Confederate of the Texas Brigade who had been captured. "How does Longstreet like the western Yankees?" the Federal asked. "You'll get enough of Longstreet before tomorrow night!" the Texan replied.

RETREAT TO CHATTANOOGA

ON THE NIGHT OF SEPTEMBER 19, AFTER NARROWLY AVERTING DEFEAT, AN ANXious William Rosecrans summoned his commanders to a war council. "It struck me that much depression prevailed," wrote General Phil Sheridan. "We were in a bad strait unquestionably." One officer who did not appear nervous or depressed was George Thomas, who dozed during the meeting and had one simple refrain when Rosecrans roused him and asked his advice: "Strengthen the left." This was sound advice, for a Confederate breakthrough on the left, where Thomas had been sorely tested, would cut the army off from Chattanooga. But any redeployment of forces by Rosecrans to the left would have to be managed with the utmost care to avoid leaving weak points or gaps elsewhere for Bragg to exploit. Some men close to Rosecrans worried that the strains of battle were beginning to tell on him. Even in the best of times, he was high-strung, obsessing over details and seldom getting to bed before three in the morning. In the past few days, as battle loomed, he had scarcely slept at all. On the morning of September 20, he left his headquarters at the Widow Glenn House "without having a mouthful to eat or drink," noted his aide, Colonel Sanderson. A reporter who knew him well, William Bickham, found him morose and apprehensive. "Rosecrans is usually brisk, nervous, powerful of presence," Bickham wrote, "and to see him silent or absorbed in what looked like gloomy contemplation, filled me with indefinable dread."

Rosecrans had a hot temper and a sharp tongue, but he seldom berated an officer without softening the blow with a kind word or gesture in parting. Today, however, he was no mood to humor those who did not do precisely as he wished. He blasted Major General James Negley, who was ill, for starting his men to the left to bolster Thomas before another division arrived to relieve Negley's on the right. And he came down even harder on Brigadier General Thomas Wood when he did not move up promptly from his position in reserve

"As things became quiet we heard the moans and groans of the wounded, which told us that between us and the enemy were lying human beings, torn and mangled, and in agony."

LIEUTENANT WILSON VANCE
21ST OHIO INFANTRY

"I'll never forgit ye for this, Yanks. You've done me a good turn."

Wounded Rebel thanking Yankee soldiers who saved him

to take Negley's place, citing contrary instructions from his corps commander. "You have disobeyed my specific orders!" Rosecrans thundered. "By your damnable negligence you are endangering the safety of the entire army, and, by God, I will not tolerate it!" This tongue-lashing, delivered to the proud and prickly Wood in the presence of his staff, would have dire consequences for Rosecrans and his army.

The mood was little better among Confederate officers that morning. Overnight, Bragg had reorganized his army into two wings, with Lieutenant General Leonidas Polk commanding on the right and James Longstreet, who arrived around midnight with the remainder of his forces, taking charge on the left. This hasty overhaul created confusion and ill will. D. H. Hill did not learn until shortly before dawn that he was being placed under Polk—who was superior to Hill neither in rank nor ability—and that his corps was supposed to launch the attack on Polk's right at daybreak. Hill's troops were not in position to advance until around 9:30, by which time part of Negley's division had arrived on the Federal left to bolster Thomas.

Among the first of Hill's men to enter battle this morning were Kentuckians of General John Breckinridge's division, who had seen brutal fighting at Stones River. Once again, they found themselves in desperate straits. The attack proceeded en echelon, from right to left, and when the Kentuckians went in the Confederates to their left had not yet come up. As a result, wrote Sergeant Major Green of the 9th Kentucky, "the enemy to our left poured their fire into us as did those directly in our front. . . . our men were falling fast." Green's premonition of death was nearly fulfilled when he was struck in the groin by grape shot—small iron balls fired from cannon—and knocked to the ground. "I thought my entire leg was torn off," he related, "but I looked down & saw my leg was not gone. I felt with my hands & found no blood, but there was a grape shot in my pocket." A pocket book he kept there had deflected the shot, and he escaped serious injury: "I found I could limp along & soon caught up with the regiment which was now within thirty yards of the enemy's breast works giving and taking death blows which could last but a few minutes without utter annihilation."

One Confederate division after another entered the fray over the next hour and crashed against Union breastworks along the La Fayette Road. For some Federals, the pressure was unbearable. Lieutenant Vance of the 21st Ohio, part of Negley's division, found one of his most reliable men, an older soldier in his forties, lying face down behind a tree, sick with fear and claiming to be wounded in the forehead. "The man was unhurt, he was there to fight, and it was my business to see that he did fight," recalled Vance, who struck the soldier repeatedly with the flat of his sword until he returned to the line. A short time later, Vance found him shot dead through the forehead: "As I knelt by the body and searched his pockets for the little trinkets that should be sent to his family, and found there the pictures of the wife and the chubby children, and the locks of hair and soiled and worn letters from home, I felt like a murderer."

As the Confederate attack intensified, the pressure was even greater on higher officers, who knew that a single misstep could mean defeat and

"As I knelt by the body and searched his pockets for the little trinkets that should be sent to his family, and found there the pictures of the wife and the chubby children, and the locks of hair and soiled and worn letters from home, I felt like a murderer."

LIEUTENANT WILSON VANCE
21ST OHIO,
on the death of a soldier he had forced back into line

disgrace. Rosecrans, mistakenly informed that there was a gap in his line to the left of General Wood's division, hastily ordered Wood to close up with the division of Major General John Reynolds "as fast as possible." Wood should have questioned the order and sought clarification, for he knew there was no gap to his left and that complying might create one as he moved behind the division immediately to his left to reach Reynolds. But he was stung by the rebuke he had received earlier for defying "specific orders" from Rosecrans and chose to obey this mystifying command promptly. Wood's decision alarmed his subordinate, Colonel George Buell, whose brigade was coming under fire. "Tell the general that my skirmishers are actively engaged, and I cannot safely make the move," he told a messenger. But Wood was adamant. Orders were orders. As his entire division shifted left, a quarter-mile-wide gap opened in the Union line.

This dreadful gaffe could not have come at a worse time or place for the Federals. The gap lay opposite the Confederate left wing, commanded by Longstreet, who had spent the morning planning a massive assault. Longstreet had put the agonies of Gettysburg behind him and regained his old confidence. Unlike Bragg, who feared disaster and warily committed one division at a time, he felt sure of success and prepared to throw everything he had at the enemy. John Bell Hood, dismayed by the defeatism pervading Bragg's army, wrote that Longstreet was "the first general I had met since my arrival who talked of victory." Around 11:30 a.m., just as the gap opened, Longstreet's command swept forward like a tidal wave, pouring through the breach and swamping the Union right. "The woods in our front seemed alive," wrote an aide to Major General Alexander McCook, whose corps was shattered by Longstreet's charge. "On they came like an angry flood." Assistant Secretary of War Charles Dana was with Rosecrans when the devastating breakthrough occurred. "I had not slept much for two nights," wrote Dana, who was dozing on the grass near the Widow Glenn House when he was jarred awake "by the most infernal noise I ever heard. Never in any battle I had witnessed was there such a discharge of cannon and musketry. I sat up on the grass, and the first thing I saw was General Rosecrans crossing himself—he was a very devout Catholic. 'Hello!' I said to myself, 'if the general is crossing himself, we are in a desperate situation.' "

After trying in vain to stem the rout on his right, Rosecrans fell back with his troops in full retreat through McFarland's Gap toward Chattanooga. His one hope now was that Thomas could hold out long enough on the left to prevent Bragg from pursuing and destroying the army before it reached Chattanooga and organized a defense there. Rosecrans wanted to join Thomas, but his chief of staff, Brigadier General James A. Garfield—destined to become president—persuaded Rosecrans to oversee the defense of Chattanooga while Garfield acted as his liaison with Thomas. Rosecrans reached Chattanooga around four that afternoon, so exhausted that he had to be lifted from his horse.

> **"I sat up on the grass, and the first thing I saw was General Rosecrans crossing himself—he was a very devout Catholic. 'Hello!' I said to myself, 'if the general is crossing himself, we are in a desperate situation.' "**
>
> FEDERAL ASSISTANT SECRETARY OF WAR CHARLES DANA, *at Chickamauga on September 20*

George Thomas, known as "Pap" to his troops, averted disaster for the Federals at Chickamauga on September 20 by holding out with his corps on Horseshoe Ridge as much of the army fell back to Chattanooga. "This hill must be held at all hazards!" he shouted, and as one soldier attested, "his words acted like magic."

Federals of Gordon Granger's reserve corps move in at far right to support Thomas's hard-pressed troops on Horseshoe Ridge. Lieutenant Ambrose Bierce, a Union officer at Chickamauga who later won fame as an author, recalled the stirring sight of General Granger and his reserves "moving soldier-like toward the sound of heavy firing. . . . A few moments later Granger was put in on the right and the fighting was terrific!"

"He had the appearance of one broken in spirit," an officer there wrote.

As the Federal right caved in, George Thomas pulled his troops back from the La Fayette Road and formed a new defensive line on high ground atop Horseshoe Ridge. To retreat now would "ruin the army," he told Garfield that afternoon. "This position must be held until night." Having held off Polk's command earlier in the day, his troops now withstood furious attacks by Longstreet's men. At one point, he dispatched an aide with orders for a brigade commander. "Where will I find you, General, when I return?" asked the aide, who assumed that retreat was imminent. "Here!" Thomas shot back. His men were taking heavy casualties and running short of ammunition but were bolstered by the timely arrival of reserves led by Major General Gordon Granger, who acted on his own authority. "I am going to Thomas, orders or no orders!" Granger declared. Come evening, Thomas was still there on Horseshoe Ridge, overseeing an orderly withdrawal that saved the Army of the Cumberland. This unshakable loyalist from Virginia would be known ever after as the "Rock of Chickamauga."

As the Federals fell back to Chattanooga, Bragg could at last claim victory, but it brought him little credit. Some felt he should have pursued the retreating army and finished it off. That was more easily said than done after a battle as punishing as this was for the Confederates. Bragg had lost over 18,000 men, compared to around 16,000 for Rosecrans, which included nearly 5,000 Federals captured or missing. Few of Bragg's men were captured, but he lost 17,000 men killed or wounded—50 percent more than Rosecrans suffered and more than Lee lost in three days at Gettysburg. Bragg's subordinates feared

he had won the battle but lost the campaign with his costly and ill-coordinated attacks "I am convinced that nothing but the hand of God can save us or help us as long as we have our present commander," Longstreet wrote Secretary of War Seddon on September 26. "Can't you send us General Lee?"

GRANT TAKES CHARGE

DEFEAT WAS OFTEN MORE INSTRUCTIVE THAN VICTORY. THE CONFEDERATE TRIumph at Chickamauga encouraged Jefferson Davis to overlook Bragg's shortcomings and reject an appeal by a dozen generals serving under him that he be replaced. Lincoln, on the other hand, recognized that Rosecrans, for all his earlier achievements, had come undone at Chickamauga, a debacle that left him "confused and stunned like a duck hit on the head," in Lincoln's words. Unlike Davis, who could not send Robert E. Lee west without endangering Richmond, Lincoln had the luxury of calling in his favorite general to meet the crisis at Chattanooga. Since capturing Vicksburg in July, Ulysses Grant had been largely idle. On October 16, he was placed in charge of all Union forces between the Appalachians and the Mississippi and summoned to Chattanooga. Serving under him would be Ambrose Burnside and his Army of the Ohio; William Sherman, Grant's successor as commander of the Army of the Tennessee; and George Thomas, chosen by Grant to take charge of the Army of the Cumberland in place of Rosecrans. On his way to Chattanooga by rail, Grant crossed paths with the departing Rosecrans. "He was very cheerful, and seemed as though a great weight had been lifted off his mind," Grant wrote. "He came into my car and we held a brief interview in which he described

DRUMMER BOY OF CHICKAMAUGA

Many youths under 18 enlisted as soldiers during the Civil War by claiming to be a few years older than they were, but Johnny Clem (above) entered the ranks before he was 10. There was no minimum age for musicians, and he joined the 22nd Michigan Infantry as a drummer, campaigning with the regiment in Tennessee and seeing battle at Shiloh, Perryville, and Stones River. He was a "bright, cheery child," his sister recalled, and "soon made his way into the affections of officers and soldiers." Johnny became the Union's darling when the press touted his exploits at Chickamauga. By one account, he used a sawed-off musket cut down to size for him to shoot a Confederate officer who came at him shouting: "Surrender, you little Yankee devil!" For his valor, he was awarded sergeant's stripes and a silver medal. After the war, he remained in the army for a half century. When he retired at 65 as a major general, he was the last man active in the armed forces who had served in the Civil War. Yet Clem was still a youngster compared to the oldest soldier known to have taken part in that conflict—Curtis King, who enlisted in the 37th Iowa Infantry in 1862 at the age of 80. ■

After Chickamauga—a costly Confederate triumph that men of the 1st Arkansas proudly commemorated on their battle flag (below)—Federals hunkered down in Chattanooga and set up camp there (opposite), tearing down houses to obtain firewood. Bragg had Union forces hemmed in here but chose not to attack, enabling Grant to repair Federal supply lines, bring in reinforcements, and seize the initiative.

"We will hold the town until we starve."

MAJOR GENERAL GEORGE THOMAS, *with Federals at Chattanooga*

very clearly the situation at Chattanooga, and made excellent suggestions as to what should be done. My wonder was that he had not carried them out."

Grant had to make the last part of his journey on horseback because Bragg's Confederates had occupied ridges overlooking Chattanooga and severed Federal supply lines by river and rail. "We will hold the town until we starve," Thomas had pledged, and it looked as if it might come to that. Soldiers were so hungry that the occasional arrival of a wagon train carrying hardtack—which the troops usually spurned if they had anything else to eat—was cause for celebration. Many houses in town had been torn down to fuel campfires. Civilians who had not fled Chattanooga lived in flimsy shacks that one reporter compared unfavorably to "the worst tenements in New York City." Grant was pleased to find that Thomas and his chief engineer, Brigadier General William F. Smith, had a plan to reopen the supply lines and gave them the go-ahead. On the night of October 27, they sent forces down the Tennessee River at night in pontoon boats to drive Confederates from Brown's Ferry, west of Chattanooga, and link up with Federals advancing eastward on the railroad from Memphis, which also connected with Nashville. By month's end, supplies were once again pouring into Chattanooga. "The men were soon reclothed and also well fed," Grant wrote, and "an abundance of ammunition was brought up." He no longer had to worry about holding out against Bragg and could concentrate on defeating him. Now that Grant was in charge, one officer in Chattanooga wrote, "we began to see things move."

Jarred by the defeat at Chickamauga, Grant's superiors in Washington sent him abundant reinforcements, including several divisions under Sherman and 20,000 men from the Army of the Potomac led by General Joseph Hooker,

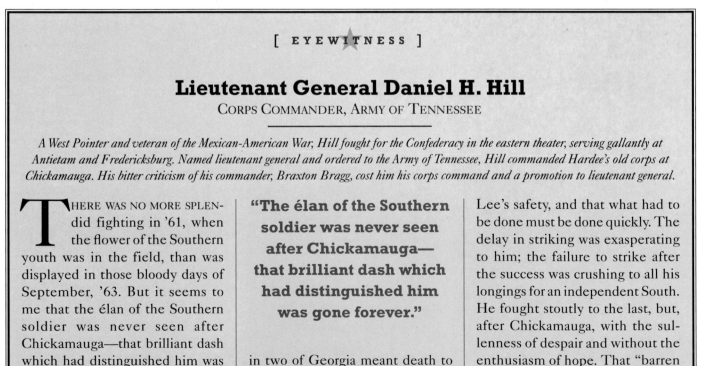

[EYEWITNESS]

Lieutenant General Daniel H. Hill

CORPS COMMANDER, ARMY OF TENNESSEE

A West Pointer and veteran of the Mexican-American War, Hill fought for the Confederacy in the eastern theater, serving gallantly at Antietam and Fredericksburg. Named lieutenant general and ordered to the Army of Tennessee, Hill commanded Hardee's old corps at Chickamauga. His bitter criticism of his commander, Braxton Bragg, cost him his corps command and a promotion to lieutenant general.

THERE WAS NO MORE SPLENdid fighting in '61, when the flower of the Southern youth was in the field, than was displayed in those bloody days of September, '63. But it seems to me that the élan of the Southern soldier was never seen after Chickamauga—that brilliant dash which had distinguished him was gone forever. He was too intelligent not to know that the cutting

"The élan of the Southern soldier was never seen after Chickamauga—that brilliant dash which had distinguished him was gone forever."

in two of Georgia meant death to all his hopes. He knew that Longstreet's absence was imperiling

Lee's safety, and that what had to be done must be done quickly. The delay in striking was exasperating to him; the failure to strike after the success was crushing to all his longings for an independent South. He fought stoutly to the last, but, after Chickamauga, with the sullenness of despair and without the enthusiasm of hope. That "barren victory" sealed the fate of the Southern Confederacy. ■

Grant had a hard journey to Chattanooga, complicated by injuries he received when thrown by a horse, but when he arrived there, he got right down to business. As the men delivered their grim appraisal of the military situation, Grant listened—"immovable as a rock and silent as a sphinx," one officer recalled.

who was seeking vindication after his crushing defeat at Chancellorsville. Bragg, meanwhile, diminished his forces at Chattanooga by sending Longstreet to attack Burnside's Federals at Knoxville. Jefferson Davis, who suggested this diversion, reckoned that Longstreet would take Knoxville unless Grant sent substantial reinforcements there, in which case Chattanooga would be left vulnerable. But the Confederate attempt to reclaim Knoxville failed on both counts. Although urged by Halleck and Lincoln to aid Burnside at Knoxville, Grant decided to keep his forces at Chattanooga and exploit his numerical superiority by defeating Bragg while Longstreet was otherwise occupied. All he could do until that attack unfolded and Bragg was driven out was to "encourage Burnside to hold on." Like Hooker, Burnside was hungry for redemption and assured Grant he was "ready to meet any force the enemy might send against us." After delaying Longstreet's troops on the outskirts of Knoxville, Burnside withdrew to a formidable stronghold called Fort Sanders and repulsed a doomed attack there in late November that cost Longstreet over 800 casualties while the fortified Federals lost only about a dozen men. As one soldier under Burnside exulted, it was "Fredericksburg reversed."

Meanwhile, Grant was proceeding with the formidable task of ousting Bragg's forces from high ground overlooking Chattanooga. Bragg's line extended from Lookout Mountain, a 2,100-foot-high bluff south of town, to Missionary Ridge, which rose 300 feet above the valley floor east of Chattanooga. Hooker's troops were assigned to menace Bragg's left at Lookout Mountain while Sherman's men attacked the Confederate right flank at the northern end of Missionary Ridge near the Tennessee River. Southward on Missionary Ridge lay the heart of Bragg's defenses, and Grant hoped that Thomas's Army of the Cumberland, drained and dejected after Chickamauga, could preoccupy the Confederates there while Sherman outflanked them. Thomas hoped for more than that. He had restored order and morale to his battered army and believed it could win the battle for Chattanooga, if called upon. Thomas had a score to settle with Braxton Bragg. Recently, he had courteously passed along a letter to a Confederate officer from a relative living in Federal-occupied territory by forwarding the letter to Bragg, an acquaintance of his before the war, with a note attached. The note and accompanying letter came back with a curt message: "Respectfully returned to General Thomas. General Bragg declines to have any intercourse with a man who has betrayed his state." A short time later, Sherman asked Thomas if he had heard from Bragg. "Damn him," Thomas responded, "I'll be even with him yet."

STORMING THE HEIGHTS

THIS WAS GRANT'S SHOW, BUT THOMAS AND HIS TROOPS WERE FIRST ON THE STAGE and would perform the last act as well. At midday on November 23, several divisions of the Army of the Cumberland, supported by some of Hooker's troops, advanced eastward from Chattanooga toward Confederate positions in front of Missionary Ridge. Unlike Chickamauga, where commanders could see little of what was unfolding, this was an open arena—the first such theater Grant had ever witnessed where the whole field lay "within one view." His script called for Thomas's men to demonstrate against the enemy to determine if Bragg meant to stand and fight here or was about to pull out, as some reports indicated. "It was an inspiring sight," wrote Lieutenant Colonel Joseph Fullerton, who watched the demonstration unfold with Grant and others on his staff. "Flags were flying; the quick, earnest steps of thousands beat equal time. The sharp commands of hundreds of company officers, the sound of the drums, the ringing note of the bugles, companies wheeling and countermarching . . . all looked like preparations for a peaceful pageant, rather than for the bloody work of death."

Even the Confederates seemed dazzled by the spectacle, which looked at first to be a parade staged to impress them with Union might. But when Federals revealed their intentions and charged toward a fortified mound called Orchard Knob, not far Missionary Ridge, they came under fire "from the enemy's advanced rifle pits," Fullerton observed, and soon the hills were resounding with "a tremendous roll of musketry and roar of artillery." It was clear now that Bragg planned to fight for Chattanooga and the demonstration could have ended there, but the enthusiastic Federals went on to drive the Rebels from their trenches, forcing them back to the base of Missionary Ridge. "You have gave gained too much to withdraw," Thomas instructed General Thomas Wood, who had contributed to defeat at Chickamauga by obeying Rosecrans's fatal order unquestioningly but won credit now for exercising initiative. "Hold your position and I will support you," Thomas assured him.

Ambrose Burnside's triumphant entry into Knoxville was celebrated in Harper's Weekly (inset) as a sign of strong Unionist sentiment in the South. While many in Knoxville welcomed the Federals, others in Tennessee loathed the invaders and mourned when Longstreet's campaign to reclaim the town ended disastrously at Fort Sanders, shown above. Confederate troops found themselves entangled in a web of telegraph wire strung among tree stumps and fallen trees.

Captain John Wilson

8TH KENTUCKY (U.S.) INFANTRY, WHITAKER'S BRIGADE

*On November 24, Federal forces under Major General John W. Geary ascended the steep, heavily timbered slopes of
Lookout Mountain and drove back the Rebel defenders, but the action ended when thick fog blanketed the mountainside.
During the night the Confederates withdrew and before dawn on November 25, Captain Wilson led a detachment
of the 8th Kentucky to the summit, where they unfurled the 8th's national flag.*

WE WERE PLACED IN ONE of the columns on the extreme right that marched around the palisades of Lookout Mountain on the 24th of November. We marched around to the nose or point of the mountain and lay that night above the Craven House. Just before daylight on the 25th, Gen. Whitaker came to our regiment and said: "Col. Barnes, have you an officer that will volunteer to carry your flag and place it on the top of the mountain?"

I said, "General, I will go."

Turning to the regiment, he said: "How many of you will go with Capt. Wilson? I could order you up there, but will not, for it is a hazardous undertaking; but for the flag that gets there first it will be an honor."

Five men went with me. I handed my sword to my color-sergeant to bring up, and I took the flag and started, accompanied by Sergeant James Wood, Company H; Private William Witt, Company A; Sergeant Harris H. Davis, Company E; Sergeant Joseph Wagers, Company B; and Private Joseph Bradley, Company I.

Those who have seen the awe-inspiring precipice at the top of the great mountain can realize what a serious undertaking was before us, not to mention our lack of knowledge concerning the Confeder-

> **"Fortune favored us, and before sun-up I, in front, reached the summit and planted the flag on top of Lookout Mountain."**

ates, who the day before had held Hooker at bay. Dim daylight was dawning. We crept cautiously upward, clutching at rocks and bushes, supporting each other, using sticks and poles and such other aids as we could gather. At every step we expected to be greeted with deadly missiles of some sort from the enemy. But fortune favored us, and before sun-up I, in front, reached the summit and planted the flag on top of Lookout Mountain. It was the highest flag that was planted during the war: Soon other detachments came up and congratulated me and my party, and we were the lions of the day in the Union Army. ∎

General Joseph Hooker sits atop Lookout Mountain in a photograph commemorating the Union victory of the "battle above the clouds."

Later, Thomas rode to the crest of Orchard Knob to congratulate Wood and other officers for exceeding orders and gaining ground.

Grant was heartened by the performance of Thomas's men. "The troops moved under fire with all the precision of veterans on parade," he wrote. He would need all the help he could get, for his show of force on the 23rd prompted Bragg to recall Patrick Cleburne, whom he had just sent to support Longstreet at Knoxville in the mistaken belief that Sherman was on his way there to bolster Burnside. Cleburne's formidable division moved into line at the northern end of Missionary Ridge along with other forces shifted from Bragg's left flank on Lookout Mountain to bolster his right. These moves spelled trouble for Sherman, who would face stiff resistance, but created opportunities for Hooker at Lookout Mountain and for Thomas at the center of the line.

Hooker's orders for November 24 were to make a convincing demonstration against Bragg's left while Sherman attempted to outflank the Confederates on their right. But like Thomas the day before, Hooker had no intention of holding his men back if the opportunity arose to strike a blow at the enemy. Grant left Hooker the option of seizing the heights "if your demonstration develops its practicality," and that was all the license he needed. He was "ordered to take Lookout Mountain," Hooker told a subordinate, stretching the truth somewhat. "Have your command in readiness to move at the earliest dawn of day." The news came as a shock to his troops. "Before night I expect we shall have to climb the side of yonder mountain," Colonel Thomas Champion of the 96th Illinois Infantry told his startled men. "I expect every man to do his duty; I shall try to do mine." Soldiers of the 149th New York Infantry reacted with disbelief when told they were to scale that peak and drive the Rebels from their roost. "Does the general expect us to fly?" they asked. "The men had not breakfasted," one New Yorker recalled. "This announcement took away their appetites."

For all their misgivings, Hooker's men rose to the challenge. Fog shrouded the mountain, disguising their movements from the Confederates, who had just received a new commander, Brigadier General Carter Stevenson, the night before and were in some confusion as Bragg shifted officers and forces from one flank to the other. "Our advance was unopposed and seemingly unnoticed," recalled one of Hooker's men who ascended Lookout that morning. The silence was "almost painful," he added. "Every moment we expected to hear it broken by sharp shots from the rocks overhead." Around midday, they reached a plateau midway up the mountain and clashed sharply with Confederates around the Cravens House, where Stevenson had his headquarters. While fighting continued there, other forces dispatched by Hooker were advancing around the base of Lookout Mountain along the Tennessee River. "In all probability the enemy will evacuate tonight," Hooker predicted. "His line of retreat is seriously threatened by my troops." At Bragg's insistence, Stevenson withdrew overnight. Federals down in the valley looked up at daybreak on November 25 to see a huge American flag unfurled at the summit. Among the proud spectators was Major James Connolly of the Army of the Cumberland. "Lookout was ours," he exulted, "never again to be used as a perch by rebel vultures."

"Before night I expect we shall have to climb the side of yonder mountain."

COLONEL THOMAS CHAMPION
96TH ILLINOIS INFANTRY,
at Lookout Mountain

"Does the general expect us to fly?"

Union soldiers after being ordered to take Lookout Mountain

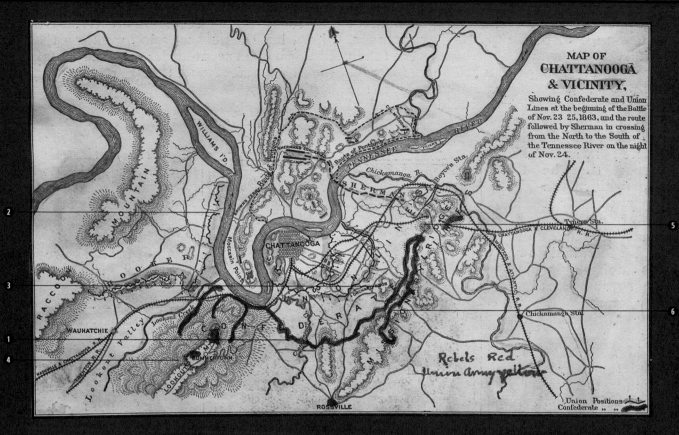

MAP OF
**CHATTANOOGA
& VICINITY,**

Showing Confederate and Union Lines at the beginning of the Battle of Nov. 23 25, 1863, and the route followed by Sherman in crossing from the North to the South of the Tennessee River on the night of Nov. 24.

The seemingly indomitable Confederate lines are shown in red stretching from Lookout Mountain along Missionary Ridge, from which the Rebels laid siege to Chattanooga below. Cartographer Robert Knox Sneden notes in his caption that this is a copy of the official map kept at the U.S. War Department in Washington. (left) One of the heroes of the Army of the Cumberland's impassioned charge up Missionary Ridge was Arthur MacArthur, Jr., a lieutenant in the 24th Wisconsin and the father of future General Douglas MacArthur. MacArthur grabbed the regimental flag, shouting "On, Wisconsin," and planted the colors in front of Bragg's abandoned headquarters.

THE BATTLE OF CHATTANOOGA

THE BATTLE OF CHATTANOOGA PROVED PIVOTAL AT the end of 1863, as Grant's victory over Braxton Bragg opened the "gateway to the Deep South" and made the Atlanta campaign of 1864 possible.

A Union victory in East Tennessee seemed improbable, just two months removed from their worst defeat in the western theater, at Chickamauga. Rosecrans's Army of the Cumberland had retreated 12 miles northeast to Chattanooga, pursued by Bragg's Army of Tennessee, who surrounded the town from positions along Lookout Mountain and Missionary Ridge ❶ and cut off Union supply lines.

Grant, though, now in command of the western armies, replaced Rosecrans with Major General George H. Thomas and devised a new supply route known as the Cracker Line, a shortcut across two spans of the Tennessee River made possible by the capture of Brown's Ferry ❷. No longer faced with starvation, the Union went on the offensive once Sherman's four divisions arrived in mid-November.

On November 23, Thomas moved his men halfway toward Missionary Ridge by capturing a line from Orchard Knob to Bushy Knob ❸. The next day the Union launched a two-pronged attack by Sherman and Hooker against the Rebel flanks. Hooker's men charged up and around Lookout Mountain ❹, capturing the high ground and forcing Bragg to withdraw after the "battle above the clouds." Sherman crossed the Tennessee, but on the morning of November 25 his attack was rebuffed at Tunnel Hill ❺ by Patrick Cleburne's division.

Later that day came one of the most legendary actions of the war. With both Sherman and Hooker stalled, Thomas's men charged up Missionary Ridge ❻ without orders, despite punishing enemy fire. Helped by the fact that Bragg had poorly positioned his artillery, the Army of the Cumberland overwhelmed Bragg's troops, who fled in panic. ■

❹ LOOKOUT MOUNTAIN *Union soldiers ascend above the clouds to plant the highest flag of the war after driving Bragg off the mountain.*

❺ TUNNEL HILL *Sherman's men were stopped cold here by three Texas regiments counterattacking from the crests around the mouth of the tunnel.*

❻ MISSIONARY RIDGE *Sketch artist Alfred Waud captured some of the fierce fighting that took place on the climactic day of the battle.*

Corporal William Montgomery, a color guard for the 76th Ohio Infantry, lost his arm but held on to this bullet-riddled flag in a sharp clash with Bragg's retreating Confederates at Ringgold, Georgia, on November 27. Grant called off his pursuit the next day, satisfied with having ousted Bragg, whose resignation took effect on November 30.

The stage was set for Thomas's troops to finish what they had begun two days earlier. Grant could see now that Sherman was not going to break through on Bragg's right, where Patrick Cleburne was standing fast. "It was a stinging disappointment," recalled an officer who spoke with Sherman that afternoon. "He gave vent to his feelings in language of astonishing vivacity." To break the deadlock, Grant ordered Thomas to advance late in the day against the heart of Bragg's defenses. Once again his objective was limited—to seize Confederate rifle pits at the base of Missionary Ridge—and once again his troops would surpass that goal. "We were crazy to charge," recalled one of his soldiers. As they overran the rifle pits, they came under heavy fire from Confederates entrenched midway up the slope and went after them instinctively. "Boys, I don't want you to stop until we reach the top of that hill," shouted Brigadier General William Carlin, who saw no point in restraining this spontaneous and irresistible advance. "Each soldier moved as his courage and endurance dictated," recalled another officer. Confederates in their path had orders to fire and then withdraw to the crest of Missionary Ridge, a misguided tactic that encouraged the advancing Federals and alarmed Bragg's men up above. "Those defending the heights became more and more desperate as our men approached the top," wrote L. G. Bennett of the 36th Illinois Infantry. "They shouted 'Chickamauga!' as if the word itself were a weapon. . . . They seized huge stones and threw them, but nothing could stop the force of the desperate charge and one after another the regimental flags were borne over the parapet and the ridge was ours."

Grant watched in amazement down below as his troops took control of the battle and surged to victory. "Who ordered those men up the ridge?" he asked Thomas, who disclaimed responsibility but relished the results. "Once those fellows get started," said General Gordon Granger, commander of Thomas's reserve corps, "all hell can't stop them." With their impulsive charge, they shattered Bragg's line and forced him to retreat into Georgia. This was Bragg's last stand—he would soon resign his command—and even soldiers who disdained him could not help feeling sorry for him. "Poor fellow, he looked so hacked and whipped and mortified and chagrined at defeat," recalled Sam Watkins. The battle cost Bragg over 6,500 casualties—many of them prisoners captured on Missionary Ridge—compared to losses of under 6,000 for the Federals, a relatively light toll for a triumph of this magnitude. With their breakthrough at Chattanooga, they secured Tennessee and cleared the way for Sherman's devastating drive through Georgia in the year to come.

Back east, 1863 ended much as it began, with the lines drawn midway between Washington and Richmond and the outcome still very much in doubt. But out west, this was a year of momentous gains for the Union. Many soldiers engaged in these western campaigns still felt that they were involved in "a side show of the big show," as Sam Watkins put it. But the fate of the Union now depended largely on three men from the Midwest—Lincoln, Grant, and Sherman—and hundreds of thousands of troops from their region who were gradually dismantling the Confederacy west of the Appalachians while Jefferson Davis and those faithful to his cause were left to hope and pray for deliverance.

THE CAVALRYMAN'S FLAIR

"The rascals are brave, fine riders, bold to rashness and dangerous in every sense."

WILLIAM T. SHERMAN, *on the Confederate cavalry*

N O REGIMENTS FOUGHT THE WAR WITH MORE BRIO than those of the cavalry. Embodied by the flamboyant Jeb Stuart or the rakish George Custer, the cavalryman considered himself the heir to a knightly tradition—dashing, gallant, and fearless. His plumed hat, jangling spurs, and swaggering style provoked envy among the foot soldiers. "Whoever saw a dead cavalryman?" scoffed one. But these flashy warriors were fierce and often reckless in their pursuit of victory and glory, and brilliant leadership, especially in the South, helped make the cavalry perhaps the most important branch of the service by the end of the war.

The cavalry's primary advantage was an ability to move swiftly over long distances. As such, its traditional functions were to reconnoiter, screen the army's movements from enemy scouts, guard against surprise attacks by patrolling the flanks, raid enemy supply lines, and chase down defeated and fleeing infantry. But over the course of the war the American cavalryman expertly blended two European models—the classical light cavalry and the heavily armed dragoon—into a force that could use mounts to scout with agility or ride full-force into battle. A British admirer wrote that "the Americans struck the true balance between shock and dismounted tactics," and became "the model of the efficient cavalryman."

In the South, mounted soldiers served another, less official purpose—as a shadow force of guerrillas, led by the likes of John Singleton Mosby, whose elusive raids earned him the nickname "Gray Ghost." Mosby was a scourge to Union forces in northern Virginia, striking

With his golden hair and audacious attitude, George Armstrong Custer (opposite) embodied the swashbuckler. He graduated at the bottom of his West Point class but became the youngest Union general of the war, described by his men as "the idol, as well as the ideal" and "the foremost cavalry officer of his time." A lawyer turned outlaw, John Singleton Mosby (left) used the Confederacy's Partisan Ranger Act to organize his guerrilla cavalry group.

MOSBY'S JACKET

CAVALRY BADGE

outposts and supply trains with small squads of men, and once capturing a Northern general in his bed ten miles from Washington, D.C.

Mosby's depredations were but one example of the success enjoyed by the Confederate cavalry early in the war. Outgunned and outmanned by the Union in most respects, the Rebels were decidedly superior on horseback. Their leaders had grown up on horses, the scions of Virginia gentry, and their mounted regiments were more efficiently organized as a separate division rather than dispersed throughout their armies, as they were on the Union side.

THE MAKING OF A KNIGHT-ERRANT

THE NORTH EVENTUALLY CAUGHT ON TO THE IMPORTANCE of a well-trained, well-organized cavalry. But producing able cavalrymen was easier said than done. Fighting on horseback required mastering skills that would have disabused the infantryman of his notion that horse soldiers had it made. War brought on fast learning, but even so, it took at least a year to train a man to be a competent cavalryman.

"Some of the boys had never ridden anything since they galloped on a hobby horse," lamented a New York officer, who watched as new recruits inadvertently gouged their horses with their spurs or failed to secure their saddles. Even more challenging for the young cavalryman was learning to care for his mount, a demanding piece of equipment. Each trooper was his own groom, veterinarian, and liveryman, and inexperience cost the lives of thousands of horses due to exhaustion and starvation.

It didn't take long for the cavalryman to appreciate that failure to keep his horse in fighting shape meant he was at best useless and at worst, a significant liability. "One of the first lessons taught the inexperienced trooper," wrote a Federal officer, "was to take better care of his horse than he did himself." Newly recruited cavalry soldiers quickly "became most scrupulous in smoothing out wrinkles in saddle blankets, in dismounting to walk steep hills, [and] in giving frequent rests to their jaded animals."

Properly equipping a cavalryman was no simple matter either. It was three times as expensive to arm and equip a cavalryman versus an infantryman, mainly

Riding in formation was one of the many new skills needed by the cavalry recruit. At right, the headquarters flag of the Army of the Potomac's Cavalry Corps carries the crossed sabers that served as the branch of service badge for all Union cavalrymen. The gold silk flag at left was made by the ladies' aid society of the London Bridge Baptist Church of Princess Anne County for the Princess Anne Cavalry, 14th Virginia Cavalry Battalion, which seized Virginia's Gosport Naval Yard at the start of the war.

because breech-loading carbines, the light rifles preferred by horse soldiers, were so much more expensive than muskets, as was their ammunition. Southerners had to provide their own mounts, a fact that helped give the Union a decided advantage as the war progressed.

THE CAVALRY IN BATTLE

THE SOUTH'S AFFINITY FOR MOUNTED ARMS PRO-duced naturally gifted cavalry leaders who had great success early in the war. In the West, Nathan Bedford Forrest continually menaced Union armies by raiding garrisons, cutting supply lines and communications, burning bridges, and destroying railroads. A self-made man, Forrest had raised and equipped his own cavalry battalion, and despite having no previous military experience, became legendary for his daring maneuvers and his innovative combination of mounted and dismounted tactics that were perfect for the thick woods of western Tennessee and northern Mississippi. The "Wizard of the Saddle" was instrumental in thwarting Grant's first assault on Vicksburg, stranding the Union commander in enemy territory without a supply line, and Sherman himself declared, "There will never be peace in Tennessee till Forrest is dead."

In the East, the bane of the Yankees was the charismatic Jeb Stuart, who became the most famous horseman of the war in large part because of his daring feats of reconnaissance. Called the "eyes of the army" by Lee, Stuart twice literally rode circles around McClellan's huge army in 1862, earning a permanent place in Southern lore. Stuart also played a critical role in winning the Battle of Chancellorsville in 1863, both through his reconnaissance and by taking command of Stonewall Jackson's Corps when the general was shot down.

Forrest and Stuart helped convince the Yankees that there was some wisdom to Napoleon's belief that "an army weak in cavalry rarely achieves great success." A reversal in Union fortunes came most unexpectedly from Benjamin Grierson, an

SLOUCH HAT

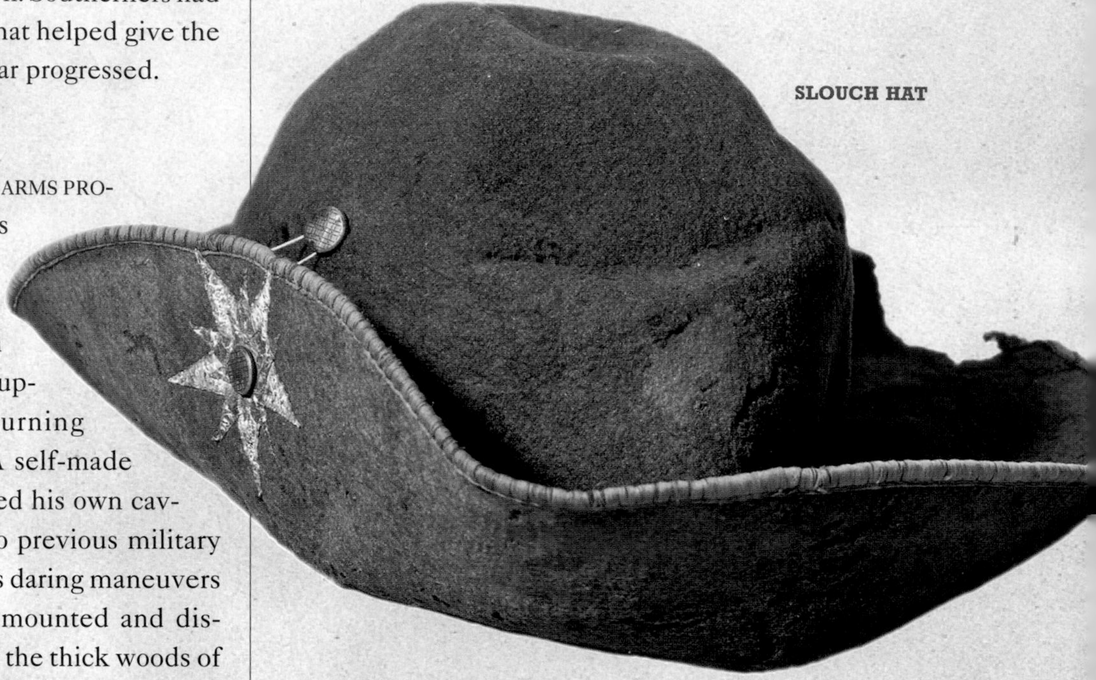

Typical of the cavalryman's flair was to take the infantryman's felt slouch cap and wear it with one side of the brim cocked up. The owner of this model, James Wilson Poague of the 1st Virginia Cavalry, further embellished it with a fixed gold star.

GAUNTLET

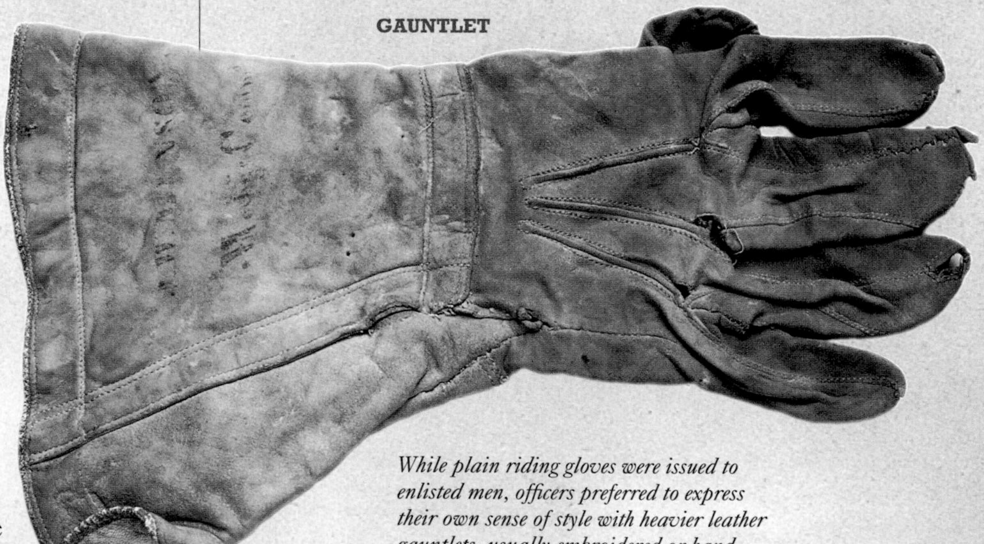

While plain riding gloves were issued to enlisted men, officers preferred to express their own sense of style with heavier leather gauntlets, usually embroidered or hand decorated in some way. This white leather example was worn by J. W. Munson, one of Mosby's Rangers.

At their camp in Falmouth, Virginia, George Custer (left), here still a captain, and General Alfred Pleasonton stand their mounts in McClellan saddles like the one shown here. Designed by Union General George McClellan shortly before the war, it was popular for its strength and simplicity and was widely used on both sides. Spurs were a showy but necessary part of the cavalryman's uniform.

SADDLE

SPURS

Illinois music teacher who hated horses (having been kicked in the head by one as a child) and was assigned to the cavalry against his will by his state's governor. Ulysses Grant, who had gotten a harsh lesson from Forrest, delivered some poetic justice by sending Grierson on a cavalry raid the length of Mississippi, which was instrumental in helping Grant finally conquer Vicksburg. Riding 1,600 miles in 16 days, Grierson's Brigade wrecked John Pemberton's supply and communications lines and kept the city's defender preoccupied while Grant's army crossed the Mississippi River unmolested.

By the summer of 1863, the Union cavalry was up to speed. New Army commander Joseph Hooker reorganized his cavalry into a single corps with more arms and mounts than Jeb Stuart's. In the biggest cavalry battle of the war, at Brandy Station, Virginia, the Union for once held their own, and the Federal cavalry distinguished itself further at Gettysburg, when George Custer and David Gregg tied up Stuart three miles east of the main battle.

When Philip Sheridan came east to take over the Union cavalry in early 1864, he did so with every intention of vanquishing Jeb Stuart, and succeeded at the Battle of Yellow Tavern, where Stuart was killed. After the fall of Atlanta, Grant used Sheridan's cavalry to lay waste to the Shenandoah Valley, which had so richly supplied Rebel armies. Sheridan cemented his legacy in October of 1864 with what went down in history as "Sheridan's Ride," his fearless push from Winchester to Cedar Creek to reverse what the Rebels had thought was a victorious surprise attack.

The Union's superior manpower and supplies eventually prevailed in the cavalry as in every other aspect of the war. The North simply had more men, more horses, and more equipment in the last two and a half years, and the leadership to take advantage of it. As one of Jeb Stuart's staff officers commented after the war, "No branch of the [Union army] contributed so much to the overthrow of Lee's army as the cavalry." ∎

REVOLVER

Modeled after the popular Colt 1851 Navy revolver, the Confederate-manufactured Griswold & Gunnison fired six .36-caliber rounds out of a 7.5-inch barrel. All cavalrymen carried at least one sidearm in case they had to dismount and fight on foot.

SABER AND SCABBARD

Though revolvers were more effective and more frequently used, the curved-blade saber was the signature weapon of the cavalry. The 1840 foreign-made model above was carried by an infantryman in the 21st Mississippi. Like most cavalry sabers, it was paired with a metal rather than a leather scabbard, to better withstand repeated contact with the horse.

SHARPS CARBINE

Breech-loading and lightweight, carbines were the ideal rifle for carrying on horseback, and the .52-caliber Sharps model was among the most popular. Around 80,000 were purchased during the war. Confederate troopers had to make do with muzzle loaders or shotguns until the Confederacy produced a small number of knockoffs at their Richmond armory.

CHAPTER 4

1864
REBELS UNDER SIEGE

"GOD HELP MY COUNTRY," MARY CHESNUT OF CHARLESTON WROTE in her diary on New Year's Day 1864. Since the first shot was fired there at Fort Sumter three years earlier, she had seen hopes rise and fall among the city's Confederate elite as victories gave way to bitter setbacks. Now many people she knew were wondering wistfully what might have been. "One more year of Stonewall would have saved us," a guest remarked to her at dinner on New Year's Eve, referring to Jackson's death at Chancellorsville. "Chickamauga is the only battle we have gained since Stonewall went up!" The war was far from over, but some disheartened Southerners were already enshrining their fallen heroes and looking back longingly to the glory days of their seemingly lost cause.

Northerners, for their part, feared the path to victory might prove so long and hard that the public would lose heart before Federal forces reached that goal. Confederates were down but not out, and it would take all the Union's might to pound those resilient Rebels into submission. Manpower and firepower were essential, but they were not enough. President Lincoln needed commanders who would pursue the enemy relentlessly and bleed him dry. In Grant and Sherman, he found generals prepared to do just that. Grant would go after Lee in Virginia, while Sherman would sweep through Georgia like a whirlwind, fulfilling his grim vow to "make this war as severe as possible and show no signs of tiring till the South begs for mercy." ■

Federal gunners attend a monstrous mortar called the Dictator, used in the siege of Petersburg, Virginia, that began when Grant confronted Lee's forces there in June 1864. Transported by rail, the mortar could hurl a 200-pound shell more than two miles and proclaimed the Union's technological prowess.

GRANT AGAINST LEE

O N MARCH 8, 1864, ABRAHAM LINCOLN WELCOMED TO THE WHITE House a man so popular in the North some considered him a political threat to the president—Ulysses Grant. After his triumphs at Vicksburg and Chattanooga, Grant was touted as a candidate to replace Lincoln as the Republican nominee at this year's convention. "The next president must be a military man," wrote James Gordon Bennett, publisher of the *New York Herald*. No military man was more highly regarded by Unionists than Grant, and come Inauguration Day in 1865, Bennett predicted, "he will be in Washington." Lincoln agreed that Grant belonged in Washington, but not as president. Before summoning him to the capital in March to serve as general in chief, Lincoln made sure Grant would not try to unseat him. "When the presidential grub once gets into a man," Lincoln remarked, "it can gnaw deeply." He was not reassured until he saw a letter written by Grant in which he stated flatly, "nothing could induce me to think of being a presidential candidate, particularly so long as there is a possibility of having Mr. Lincoln re-elected."

Grant's visit to the White House was his first meeting with Lincoln, who was holding a reception. As guests crowded around the famous general, one onlooker noted, he "blushed like a schoolgirl." His discomfort increased when he was asked to stand on a sofa so people could get a better look at him (he was much shorter than Lincoln). "It was the only real mob I ever saw in the White House," a reporter wrote. "For once at least the President of the United States was not the chief figure in the picture. The little, scared-looking man who stood on a crimson-covered sofa was the idol of the hour."

The next day, Lincoln promoted Grant to lieutenant general, a rank recently conferred on several Confederate officers but one that no commander in the United States had held since George Washington. With the promotion came vast authority as Grant took control of all Union armies. His predecessor as general in chief, Henry Halleck, who would stay on as army chief of staff under Grant, had concerned himself with administrative details, leaving larger matters to Lincoln and commanders in the field. But Lincoln made it clear to Grant that he was now fully in charge of Federal forces. "In my first interview with Mr. Lincoln alone," Grant wrote, "he stated to me that he had never professed to be a military man or to know how campaigns should be conducted. . . . All he wanted or had ever wanted was

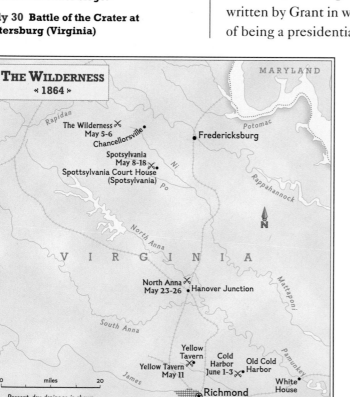

Grant launched his campaign against Lee in early May by crossing the Rapidan River and clashing with Confederates in the Wilderness. Despite heavy losses, Grant continued to push forward, attacking his opponent again at Spotsylvania and Cold Harbor before crossing the James River and besieging Petersburg.

some one who would take the responsibility and act." Having handed that responsibility to Grant, Lincoln promised to stay out of his way and "avoid as far as possible annoying him."

The first test of Grant's powers came when Secretary of War Stanton objected to his plan to send many of the troops guarding Washington to the front lines. "I think I rank you in this matter, Mr. Secretary," Grant told Stanton, who then asked the president to overrule him. "You and I, Mr. Stanton, have been trying to boss this job, and we have not succeeded very well with it," Lincoln responded. Having sent for Grant "to relieve us," he added, "I think we had better leave him alone to do as he pleases." Grant's decision to shift as many troops as possible to the front lines was part of an aggressive strategy to bring overwhelming pressure on Confederates. He believed that the key to victory was not defending Washington or capturing Richmond but destroying the two main enemy forces: Robert E. Lee's Army of Northern Virginia and Joseph Johnston's Army of Tennessee, formerly under Braxton Bragg. Grant himself would lead the campaign in Virginia, while William Sherman would take charge of Union forces west of the Appalachians and advance from Chattanooga into Georgia. As Sherman summed up Grant's strategy: "He was to go for Lee and I was to go for Joe Johnston."

On March 24, Grant left Washington to join George Meade and his Army of the Potomac in camp north of the Rapidan River, which marked the frontier between Federal forces and Lee's Confederates to the south. During the forthcoming campaign, Grant would entrust the execution of his orders to Meade, much as he had done with George Thomas at Chattanooga. The arrangement made sense, for Meade knew the capabilities and officers of this huge army of nearly 120,000 men far better than he did. But Grant was taking a big risk by serving both as general in chief and as field commander. He had never faced an opponent of Lee's caliber, and if Lee got the better of him, he would have no one to blame but himself. Fear of failure was not part of Grant's make-up, however. "The chief characteristic of your nature," Sherman wrote him, "is the simple faith in success you have always manifested, which I can liken to nothing else than the faith a Christian has in the Savior. This faith gave you victory at Shiloh and Vicksburg. When you have completed your preparations, you go into battle without hesitation, as at Chattanooga—no doubts—no reserve." Grant's faith in himself would be severely tested in the months ahead in a campaign so brutal and bloody that Grant, once hailed as the Union's savior, would be denounced by disenchanted Northerners as a butcher.

> **"The chief characteristic of your nature is the simple faith in success you have always manifested."**
>
> GENERAL WILLIAM SHERMAN, *describing Ulysses Grant*

Grant, pictured here in 1864 after his promotion to lieutenant general, was described by one officer serving under him as "stumpy, unmilitary, slouchy . . . very ordinary, in fact." But his men knew he meant business. As one soldier wrote: "We all felt at last that the boss had arrived."

LEE HAD BEEN HERE BEFORE. SINCE TAKING CHARGE OF THE ARMY OF NORTHern Virginia in 1862, he had faced five Union commanders along this front—Pope, McClellan, Burnside, Hooker, and Meade—and rebuffed them all. His army was only half as large as Grant's, and he did not underestimate his opponent. "That man will fight us every day and every hour till the end of this war," warned General Longstreet, who rejoined Lee in late April after campaigning in Tennessee. But Grant would have less room to maneuver here in Virginia against the vigilant Lee than he had out west. Grant's objective was to outflank his opponent—whose army was too well-fortified below the Rapidan to be assaulted frontally—and bring him to battle in circumstances less favorable for the Confederates. If Grant moved west around Lee's left flank, he would leave Washington exposed and lose contact with his maritime supply lines along Chesapeake Bay. If he moved east around Lee's right flank, he would be better able to protect Washington and his supply lines but would have to advance through Fredericksburg or the tangled Wilderness, two places where the Army of the Potomac had been battered by Lee.

On May 2, Lee stood with officers atop Clark's Mountain, overlooking the Rapidan near its junction with the Rappahannock. To the east, he could see two crossings, Germanna Ford and Ely's Ford, used by Hooker's troops on their way to Chancellorsville a year earlier. "Grant will cross by one of those fords," Lee announced. He would not contest the crossing because he felt his best chance of beating the Federals was to catch them in the Wilderness.

> **"That man will fight us every day and every hour till the end of this war."**
>
> CONFEDERATE GENERAL
> JAMES LONGSTREET,
> *on Grant*

[EYEWITNESS]

Private Marcus B. Toney
44TH VIRGINIA INFANTRY, JONES'S BRIGADE

A native of Virginia, Marcus Toney resided with his family in Nashville, Tennessee, at the outbreak of the war. Enlisting in a local regiment, he served in the western theater before transferring to the 44th Virginia Infantry and the Army of Northern Virginia in the winter of 1864. Toney was captured in the fighting at Spotsylvania.

ONE DAY I WAS ON PICKET duty near the Rapidan River, which is a stream a little larger than Duck River; just opposite us were the Yankee pickets. One of them yelled out: "Hello, Johnny Reb! how is sassafras tea today?" I told him the tea was all right, but we had no sugar. I asked him how he was fixed for tobacco, and he said, "Very short"; so we arranged on the morrow to get on duty again. The Federals had their coffee parched, ground,

"Hello, Johnny Reb! how is sassafras tea today?"

and sugar mixed with it, so on the morrow we made the exchange. . . . After making the exchange, he asked me how I would like to have a *New York Herald*? So he tied the *Herald* to a stick and threw it across to me. When I opened it up, I read as follows: "The Rebel Capital Must be Captured at All Hazards; General Grant Has Been Appointed to the Task." ∎

This battle flag of the 42nd Virginia Infantry was captured in the fighting at Spotsylvania Court House.

Grant hoped to avoid battle before his troops made it safely through the Wilderness, but after crossing the Rapidan early on May 4 Federals halted that afternoon to give the wagon train hauling their supplies time to catch up. Men who had fought at Chancellorsville were filled with foreboding as they waited in the Wilderness, littered with the bones of soldiers killed in that struggle. "This is what you are all coming to," one Federal said to his mates as he picked up a disembodied skull, "and some of you will start toward it tomorrow." Meanwhile, Confederates were fast approaching from the west. As one of Lee's men recalled, they knew they were vastly outnumbered but moved eagerly ahead, thinking of nothing else "but victory." That night, Lee drew up orders for an attack. Longstreet's Corps was at least a day's march away to the southwest, but Lee's other two corps, under Richard Ewell and A. P. Hill, were within five miles of the enemy.

At dawn on May 5, Ewell advanced eastward with his corps along the Orange Turnpike toward an intersection near the Wilderness Tavern where Federals were massed. His orders, he remarked, were just the kind he liked: "Go right down the road and strike the enemy wherever I find him." By now, Grant knew that Lee's troops were approaching and decided to challenge them by pivoting his forces westward and probing for the enemy. "If any opportunity presents itself for pitching in to a part of Lee's army, do so," he told Meade, who directed Major General Gouverneur Warren to move out with his corps along the Orange Turnpike and engage the Confederates. Around mid-morning, Ewell ordered his men to halt after being warned by Lee that he was out

When Federals of the Army of the Potomac crossed the Rapidan River on May 4 and entered the Wilderness, they encountered the skeletons of men killed fighting there at Chancellorsville a year earlier (above). This grim reminder foreshadowed the vicious fighting that was soon to follow. Company I of the 57th Massachusetts (at top) went into the Battle of the Wilderness numbering 86 men. Several weeks later, these nine men were all that was left.

Confederates under General Richard Ewell quickly constructed these impressive log fortifications in the Wilderness on May 5 and stymied Federal attacks along the Orange Turnpike. Troops who did not have time to fell trees formed breastworks by piling up dirt, stones, and fallen branches.

"Within one hour, there is a shelter against bullets, high enough to cover a man kneeling, and extending often a mile or two. When our line advances, there is the line of the enemy, nothing showing but the bayonets, and the battle-flags stuck on top of the work."

FEDERAL LIEUTENANT COLONEL THEODORE LYMAN, on Confederate defenses

in front of A. P. Hill's Corps, which was advancing eastward on the Orange Plank Road, a parallel path to the south. Ewell's troops began digging in at the edge of a clearing called Saunders Field. An aide to Meade, Lieutenant Colonel Theodore Lyman, marveled at how quickly the Confederates could dig trenches and raise breastworks: "Within one hour, there is a shelter against bullets, high enough to cover a man kneeling, and extending often a mile or two. When our line advances, there is the line of the enemy, nothing showing but the bayonets, and the battle-flags stuck on top of the work."

Such was the prospect that greeted Warren's Federals as they came up against Ewell's men around midday after struggling through thickets along the turnpike. Entering Saunders Field, they were blasted by Confederates lurking behind the breastworks. When Lieutenant Holman Melcher of the 20th Maine Infantry reached the clearing, many in his brigade had already fallen there and others were approaching the enemy works. "Come on, boys, let us go in and help them," shouted Brigadier General Joseph Bartlett. "And go we did," related Melcher. "Pulling our hats down low over our eyes, we rushed across the field, and overtaking those of our comrades who had survived the fearful crossing of the front line, just as they were breaking over the enemy's lines, we joined with them in this deadly encounter, and there in that thicket of bushes and briers, with the groans of the dying, the shrieks of the wounded, the terrible roar of musketry and the shouts of command and cheers of encouragement, we swept them away before us like a whirlwind."

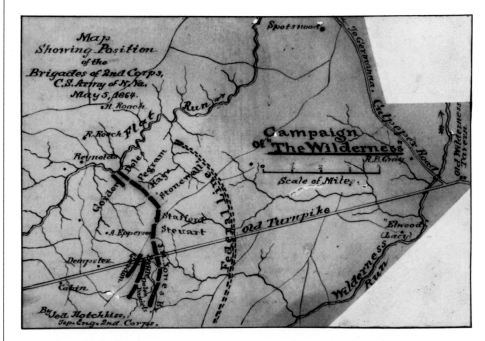

A map drawn by Confederate topographical engineer Jedediah Hotchkiss shows the brigades of Ewell's Corps at left as they confronted Federals along the Orange Turnpike (or Old Turnpike) on May 5. General John Marshall Jones, astride the turnpike, was mortally wounded trying to rally his brigade.

Wounded. escaping from the burning woods of the Wilderness — A. R. Waud.

It was a daring breakthrough, but nothing came of it. Unsupported by Federals on either side of them, who were stopped cold, Bartlett's men were stranded behind enemy lines and had to fall back to avoid being captured. Fighting raged inconclusively around Saunders Field for hours, sparking brush fires that spread quickly through the tinder-dry woods. Some wounded men died in agony as the flames consumed them. Others took their own lives rather than suffer the same fate. One soldier saw a man with shattered legs "lying on the ground with his cocked rifle by his side. . . . I knew he meant to kill himself in case of fire—knew it as surely as though I could read his thoughts."

Soon the smoke and fury of battle had spread to the intersection of the Orange Plank Road and the Brock Road, which would serve as Grant's path out of the Wilderness. "We must hold this point at any risk," said Brigadier General George Getty, who withstood charges by A. P. Hill's troops until reinforcements arrived and the Federals counterattacked. Opposing Getty was a division led by General Henry Heth, who had recovered from a severe head wound suffered at Gettysburg only to find himself in another bind now as General Winfield Scott Hancock brought his corps to Getty's aid. "Usually when infantry meets infantry the clash is brief," wrote an aide to Getty. "Here neither side would give way, and the steady firing rolled and crackled from end to end of the contending lines, as if it would never cease." At Heth's urging, Lee threw in reserves, but they took a beating. "I should have left well enough alone," realized Heth, who was relieved when darkness descended.

Union troops use a blanket suspended from their interlocked muskets as a stretcher to rescue a wounded man from the flaming Wilderness in this battlefield sketch by Alfred Waud. One soldier who fought here said that what he dreaded most was not to be killed outright but "to have a leg broken and then to be burned slowly."

"There in that thicket of bushes and briers, with the groans of the dying, the shrieks of the wounded, the terrible roar of musketry and the shouts of command and cheers of encouragement, we swept them away before us like a whirlwind."

LIEUTENANT HOLMAN MELCHER
20TH MAINE INFANTRY,
in the Wilderness on May 5

Lee, shown here late in the war, was an aggressive commander who had to act defensively against Grant to preserve his much smaller army and shield the Confederate capital. "With the blessing of God," he wrote Jefferson Davis, "I trust we shall be able to prevent General Grant from reaching Richmond."

As one Confederate recalled: "It was a mere slugging match in a dense thicket of small growth, where men but a few yards apart fired through the brushwood for hours, ceasing only when exhaustion and night commanded a rest."

That evening, Grant heavily reinforced Hancock, hoping to overwhelm Lee before Longstreet arrived. Longstreet's Corps was still five miles away when Hancock renewed his assault with irresistible force at dawn on May 6. As Confederates fell back along the Orange Plank Road, they streamed past Lee's headquarters at the Widow Tapp Farm. "My God!" exclaimed Lee when he saw Brigadier General Samuel McGowan retreating with his reserves. "Is this splendid brigade of yours running like a flock of geese?"

"General, these men are not whipped," McGowan replied. "They only want a place to form and they will fight as well as they ever did." But Hancock was so close on their heels that the Confederates had little chance to regroup. "We are driving them, sir," he told an aide to Meade. "Tell General Meade we are driving them most beautifully." As one Rebel recalled: "It looked as if things were past mending." Just then, however, the first of Longstreet's troops—hard-fighting men of the Texas Brigade—reached Lee. "Hurrah for Texas," he shouted, raising his hat. "Texans always move them." Lee was so enthused he began to ride with them into battle, but they grabbed at the reins of his horse. "Go back!" men shouted. "Lee to the rear!" It was a scene repeated in the weeks ahead as Lee tried to lead from the front and was prevented from doing so by his devoted soldiers, one of whom declared tearfully, "I would charge hell itself for that old man."

Soon after the Texans went in, Longstreet rode up and promised Lee to set things right "in an hour if he would permit me to handle the troops." Longstreet had a knack for entering battle at the crucial moment. As a fellow officer put it: "Like a fine lady at a party, Longstreet was often late in his arrival at the ball. But he always made a sensation." At Second Bull Run and then at Chickamauga, he had joined the fight belatedly and routed the Federals. His timely counterattack here averted defeat and stymied Hancock, who served as Grant's trusted warhorse during this campaign much as Longstreet served Lee. As Hancock told Longstreet in later years, "You rolled me up like a wet blanket." Overwhelmed by these fresh corps, Hancock's battle-weary men retreated sullenly to their trenches along the Brock Road. "They were not running, nor pale, nor scared, nor had they thrown away their guns," wrote Theodore Lyman of Meade's staff. "They had fought all they meant to fight for the present, and there was an end of it!" The long-awaited arrival of Ambrose Burnside's Corps—which had gotten lost after being sent to bolster Hancock—helped shore up the Federal line and frustrate the Confederates, who were further disheartened when Longstreet was hit by friendly fire. Unlike Stonewall Jackson, wounded in similar fashion here a year earlier, Longstreet survived.

Fighting continued until nightfall, but neither side could dislodge the other, and the two-day battle ended in a draw. "There lay both armies," one

Union officer recalled, "each behind its breastworks, panting and exhausted, and scowling at each other." Grant's decision to stand and fight had cost him nearly 18,000 casualties, a figure at least 50 percent higher than Lee's losses. Such punishment would have been more than enough to discourage Grant's predecessors, but he gave no thought to retreating. "If you see the President," Grant told reporter Henry Wing, who was returning to Washington, "tell him from me that whatever happens, there will be no turning back." When Wing delivered that message, he cheered the worried commander in chief immeasurably and received a reward he would never forget: "Mr. Lincoln put his great, strong arms about me and, carried away in the exuberance of his gladness, imprinted a kiss upon my forehead."

DEADLOCK AT SPOTSYLVANIA

GLOOM LAY THICK OVER THE ARMY OF THE POTOMAC ON THE MORNING OF MAY 7. "Most of us thought it was another Chancellorsville," one Federal wrote. When told to get ready to march, many assumed they were going to retreat. Not until they set out toward evening did they know otherwise. Shortly after sunset, Grant rode south along the Brock Road, passing troops who hailed him for not backing down. "Men swung their hats, tossed up their arms, and pressed forward to within touch of their chief, clapping their hands, and speaking to him with the familiarity of comrades," recalled Grant's aide, Lieutenant Colonel Horace Porter. "Pine-knots and leaves were set on fire, and lighted the scene with their weird, flickering glare. The night march had become a

Like many of the war's battle sites, Spotsylvania Court House was a quiet place of little strategic significance before opposing armies collided nearby, soon after the Battle of the Wilderness. This was familiar country to Lee and his officers, and their intimate knowledge of the region and its roads helped them reach Spotsylvania and prepare defenses before Grant's troops descended from the north.

"If you see the President, tell him from me that whatever happens, there will be no turning back."

GENERAL GRANT TO REPORTER HENRY WING, *after the Battle of the Wilderness*

triumphal procession for the new commander." The clamor alarmed Grant, who was hoping to make headway before Lee caught on. "This is most unfortunate," he said as cheers echoed through the woods. "The sound will reach the ears of the enemy, and I fear it may reveal our movement."

In fact, Lee had anticipated Grant and was already moving to counter him. Through the night, Longstreet's old corps, commanded now by Major General Richard Anderson, marched southeastward on a path that intersected the Brock Road near Spotsylvania Court House, set amid high ground that Lee was intent on occupying before Grant got there. Confederate cavalry led by Fitzhugh Lee harassed the Federals and slowed their advance, ensuring that Anderson's troops would win the race to Spotsylvania. Grant's forces tried to dislodge them on May 8 but failed. That left Lee in a commanding position, holding a line that extended from west to east across the Brock Road and then protruded northward around a ridge shaped like a mule shoe. This Mule Shoe salient, near the center of the line, was heavily fortified. Grant would have to smash through or find a way around Lee's defenses. As he informed Washington: "Enemy hold our front in very strong force and evince strong determination to interpose between us and Richmond to the last." Maneuvering around Lee's agile army would not be easy and would only postpone the decisive battle Grant was seeking—one he hoped would seal Richmond's fate.

Tempers were short at headquarters after Federals lost the race to Spotsylvania. Meade cast blame on Grant's new cavalry commander, Phil Sheridan, who replied hotly that if Meade would stop interfering with him he would take his corps and whip Jeb Stuart. "Did Sheridan say that?" Grant responded when Meade told him of the quarrel. "Well, he generally knows what he is talking about. Let him start right out and do it." Now Sheridan had to live up to his boast. "In view of my recent representations to Meade," he told his officers, "I shall expect nothing but success." Departing with his corps on May 9, he swung around to the east of Lee's army and advanced toward Richmond, confident that Stuart would follow in pursuit. Stuart was at a disadvantage, for more than half his cavalry corps would remain with Lee at Spotsylvania to guard against a flanking move by Grant's infantry. This was Stuart's biggest challenge yet, and he went out of his way to visit his wife and children on May 10 before riding after Sheridan. One aide was startled to hear the usually buoyant Stuart remark that he did not expect to survive the war—and did not wish to if the Yankees won out. A day later, near a stagecoach inn called Yellow Tavern, his outnumbered cavalrymen were repulsed by Sheridan's troopers. During the battle, Stuart was mortally wounded, a loss that hit Lee hard. "I can scarcely think of him without weeping," he said.

Grant suffered a loss of his own around this time that weighed heavily on the Army of the Potomac. On the morning of May 9, General John Sedgwick, beloved by his corps, was inspecting his lines along the Brock Road when Confederate sharpshooters nearly a half mile away opened fire. Sedgwick chided his men for dodging the bullets and tried to reassure them, saying, "They couldn't hit an elephant at this distance." Moments later, he took a shot beneath the eye and fell dead. "His loss to this army is greater than the loss of a whole division," said Grant, who had few other commanders he trusted as much. He

> **"I can scarcely think of him without weeping."**
>
> GENERAL LEE,
> *on the death of Jeb Stuart*

Confederates at Spotsylvania formed this defensive barrier, known as an abatis, by felling trees and aligning them so that their sharpened points faced the enemy. Using such techniques, Lee's men created a veritable fortress here by the time Grant's forces attacked on May 10.

had doubts about Burnside and Warren, and Sedgwick's successor, Major General Horatio Wright, was unproven. That left Hancock, whose corps had already seen hard duty and would loom large at Spotsylvania.

Early on May 10, fighting erupted west of the Brock Road as Hancock tried to outflank Lee to his left and encountered heavy opposition. Surmising that Lee had weakened his center to strengthen his left, Grant pulled Hancock back and launched fresh attacks on the heart of the enemy line that afternoon. He pinned his hopes on a daring assault organized by Colonel Emory Upton of Wright's Corps, who formed a strike force of 5,000 men to attack the Mule Shoe salient at its apex by charging with bayonets fixed and surging over the breastworks in a human wave. "Colonel Upton was with our regiment and rode on our right," recalled Corporal Clinton Beckwith of the 121st New York Infantry, which joined in the attack. "He instructed us not to fire a shot, cheer or yell, until we struck their works." The suspense for Beckwith was agonizing. "I felt my gorge rise, and my stomach and intestines shrink together in a knot," he wrote. "I looked about in the faces of the boys around me, and they told the tale of expected death."

Many fell to enemy fire as they charged the salient, but Beckwith and others kept going and breached the defenses, only to be forced to retreat for lack of support. The brigade that was supposed to come in after them had attacked prematurely and been repulsed. It was one of several foul-ups that day for the Federals, whose problems began at the top. Lee had a much firmer grip on his army than did Grant, whose orders sometimes went awry as they passed through Meade to officers who lacked the drive of Sherman and other commanders he had relied on in the past. Grant shrugged off the setback and decided to try again, this time with a much larger force under Hancock. The next morning, as Grant prepared that attack, he sent a message to Washington that soon found its way into print: "I propose to fight it out on this line if it takes all summer."

A Confederate soldier lies dead at Spotsylvania after the furious fighting there. Photographer Timothy O'Sullivan captured this scene on a glass negative, which later cracked.

Before dawn on May 12, amid a pelting rain, nearly 20,000 Union troops assembled under Hancock for a sledgehammer blow against the Mule Shoe. Lee had received reports that Grant was about to withdraw from Spotsylvania and had ordered most of the big guns in the salient limbered up and pulled out so his artillery could move quickly in pursuit. One Confederate, Captain William Seymour, recalled the stunning attack: "Just at dawn of day, there burst upon our startled ears a sound like the roaring of a tempestuous sea; the woods before us fairly rang with the hoarse shouts of thousands of men. . . . As far as the eye could reach, the field was covered with the serried ranks of the enemy, marching in close columns to the attack. This was the time for our artillery to open, but not a shot was heard, our guns, unfortunately, not having gotten into position." Some Confederates ran as their foes poured over the breastworks, and many were captured. Others fought the invaders hand to hand. "It was the first time during the war that I had actually seen bayonets crossed in mortal combat," recalled Colonel Nelson Miles of Hancock's Corps.

Lee was quick to respond. Calling on General John Gordon, who had been severely wounded at Antietam but nursed back to health by his wife, he ordered a counterattack and seemed intent on leading it himself until Gordon dissuaded him. "These men behind you are Georgians, Virginians, and Carolinians," he told Lee. "They have never failed you on any field. They will not fail you here." They made good on that promise by pushing the Federals back, but Grant then committed more men and the salient became a seething cauldron, so crowded with soldiers that the battle degenerated into a murderous brawl. "For god's sake," one Union officer implored Hancock, "do not send any more troops in here." Another Federal complained that "there were heaps of our dead lying about and impeding our operations."

Things were no better for the Confederates. "The fighting was horrible," one recalled. "The breastworks were slippery with blood and rain, dead bodies lying underneath half trampled out of sight." Grant hoped that as Lee reinforced the Mule Shoe he might prove vulnerable elsewhere, but fitful efforts by Burnside and Warren to press the Confederates on either flank got nowhere. By late afternoon, Lee had sealed off the ruptured salient with a new defensive line, and the dreadful battle drew to a close. Horace Porter of Grant's staff surveyed the carnage the next morning at the tip of the salient—the so-called Bloody Angle, where the fighting was fiercest. "Below the mass of fast-decaying corpses," he wrote, "the convulsive twitching of limbs and the writhing of bodies showed that there were wounded men still alive and struggling to extricate themselves from their horrid entombment."

The two battles at Spotsylvania cost each side nearly 10,000 casualties and settled nothing. Grant then tried to break the deadlock by maneuvering around Lee's right flank, to the east. As always, his objective was not to elude Lee but to get in a better position to attack him. When Lee shifted troops to his right in response, Grant made one last assault on the Mule Shoe on May 18 but cut the assault short when his troops met with overwhelming resistance. "We found the enemy so strongly entrenched that even Grant thought it useless to knock our heads against a brick wall," wrote Meade. "We shall now try to maneuver again, so as to draw the enemy out of his stronghold."

From Cold Harbor to Petersburg

ON MAY 21, GRANT AND MEADE CONVENED A COUNCIL OF WAR AT MASSAPONAX Baptist Church, east of Spotsylvania. Seated outside on pews, the commanders had much to consider, including setbacks elsewhere in Virginia that affected their campaign. Grant was ever mindful of what Lincoln called the "awful arithmetic" of this conflict, or the fact that the populous Union could afford to engage in a war of attrition, with both sides suffering heavy losses, and outlast the Confederacy. Thus far, Grant and Lee had each lost about one-third of their forces—a toll that Grant was better able to withstand because he had twice as many troops to start with and more reinforcements available. To prevent Lee from being reinforced, Grant had assigned Franz Sigel to keep Confederates pinned down in the Shenandoah Valley while Benjamin Butler

> "I propose to fight it out on this line if it takes all summer."
>
> GENERAL GRANT,
> *in a message to Washington from Spotsylvania*

> "Below the mass of fast-decaying corpses the convulsive twitching of limbs and the writhing of bodies showed that there were wounded men still alive and struggling to extricate themselves from their horrid entombment."
>
> LIEUTENANT COLONEL HORACE PORTER GRANT'S STAFF,
> *after the attack at Spotsylvania on May 12*

moved up the James River with 30,000 troops and preoccupied enemy forces holding Richmond. Both those generals had more political clout than military skill, however, and had stumbled badly. On May 15, Sigel clashed at New Market, Virginia, with John Breckinridge, who was outnumbered nearly two to one and called up cadets as young as 15 from the Virginia Military Institute (VMI). "Put the boys in," Breckinridge said, "and may God forgive me for the order." Nearly one in five cadets fell dead or wounded at New Market, but Breckinridge won the battle. A day later, Butler was attacked at Drewry's Bluff by P. G. T. Beauregard and forced back from Richmond.

Grant foresaw the consequences of those defeats. As he told his staff: "Lee will undoubtedly reinforce his army largely by bringing Beauregard's troops from Richmond, now that Butler has been driven back, and will call in troops from the valley since Sigel's forces have retreated." In response, Grant summoned 16,000 men from Butler's camp, bringing him nearly twice as many reinforcements as Lee received. The arithmetic remained in Grant's favor, and he would keep hammering Lee "until by mere attrition, if in no other way, there should be nothing left to him."

Now as before, Grant hoped to advance quickly around Lee's eastern flank, dislodge his entrenched troops, and bring them to battle before they could dig in again. Lee, for his part, was determined to stay one step ahead of Grant and hit back hard if the opportunity arose. Responding alertly to Grant's maneuver, he withdrew his forces below the North Anna River. He hoped to attack the Federals after they crossed there but fell ill with severe diarrhea. "We must strike them a blow—we must never let them pass us again," he said from his sickbed, but Grant pressed ahead and forced the Confederates back toward Richmond. "Lee's army is really whipped," he concluded prematurely. "A battle with them outside intrenchments cannot be had."

By month's end, the opposing armies were converging on a crossroads called Cold Harbor, 10 miles northeast of Richmond. Grant hoped to hit Lee there before he could entrench, but Hancock's Corps lost its way moving into position on the night of June 1, and the attack was postponed for 24 hours. That allowed Confederates to construct earthworks extending for six miles, with artillery covering every avenue of approach by the Federals, who would have to slog through swamps before making a perilous frontal assault. Grant's men prepared for the worst as battle loomed. Horace Porter noticed that many of them had taken off their coats and appeared to be sewing them up. "This exhibition of tailoring seemed rather peculiar at such a moment," he wrote, "but upon closer examination it was found that the men were calmly writing their names and home addresses on slips of paper, and pinning them on the backs of their coats, so that their dead bodies might be recognized upon the field, and their fate made known to their families at home."

At dawn on June 3, more than 50,000 Federals advanced into a firestorm as intense as any they had ever faced. "To give a description of this terrible

> **"We must strike them a blow—we must never let them pass us again."**
>
> GENERAL LEE, *after being outflanked by Grant at Spotsylvania*

When Grant convened with his top officers on May 21 at Massaponax Baptist Church (above), Timothy O'Sullivan placed his camera in the front window of the second story to take the remarkable photograph at right, showing Grant leaning over one of the pews hauled out into the churchyard to study a map.

charge is simply impossible," related Captain Asa Bartlett of the 12th New Hampshire Infantry. "That dreadful storm of lead and iron seemed more like a volcanic blast than a battle." Some men reached the Confederate works and broke through, only to be cut down or beaten back. The attackers "received the most destructive fire I ever saw," recalled Colonel William Oates of the 15th Alabama Infantry, a veteran of the bruising battle for Little Round Top at Gettysburg. "I could see the dust fog out of a man's clothing in two or three places at once where as many balls would strike him at the same moment." Afterward, he added, Union dead "covered more than five acres of ground about as thickly as they could be laid." Grant hoped to continue the assault, but his men were spent and officers were unwilling to subject them to further punishment. "I will not take my regiment in another such charge if Jesus Christ himself should order it!" declared Captain Thomas Barker of the 12th New Hampshire. "Our loss was very heavy, and to no purpose," concluded Brigadier General Emory Upton, recently promoted for his daring at Spotsylvania. "Our men are brave, but cannot accomplish impossibilities."

In less than an hour, Grant had lost more than 7,000 men, nearly five times as many casualties as Lee suffered. That brought Grant's losses over the past month to a staggering 50,000 men. In Washington, wrote Navy Secretary Gideon Welles, there was "dark talk that Grant, although dogged, was also a butcher who harbored too little regard for human life." Grant's attack at Cold Harbor was no more callous or inhumane, however, than Lee's desperate charge on the last day at Gettysburg or his earlier assault on McClellan's forces at Malvern Hill, which one Confederate general described in the same words Evander Law applied later to Cold Harbor: "It was not war; it was murder." Like Lee, Grant knew that he could not achieve a decisive victory and end the war without exposing his men to murderous punishment. What Horace Porter said of Grant applied equally to his opponent: "He felt that in campaigning the hardest blows bring the quickest relief."

After his dismal failure at Cold Harbor, Grant made a move so sudden and bold it surprised even Lee, who had thus far anticipated his opponent's every step. Convinced now that smashing through Lee's defenses would be too costly, Grant ordered a pontoon bridge laid across the James River east of Richmond and set his sights on Petersburg, 25 miles below the Confederate capital. If the Federals seized Petersburg and the railroads running through it, they would place Richmond in a bind and pinch off the flow of supplies to the city and its defenders. The impact would be much the same as if Lee's army seized Baltimore and isolated Washington. Grant's men would be highly vulnerable to attack as they crossed the James, but he considered the risk well worth taking. If he did not capture Petersburg outright, he would lay siege to it, and Lee could not defend against that without being drawn into the siege. Federals were glad to be leaving Cold Harbor and the swamps around Richmond. "The air was filled with malaria and death," one soldier recalled. "Sickness, as well as battle, was doing fearful work in our ranks."

Before crossing the James, Grant staged diversions to distract enemy cavalry and make it look as if his target was Richmond. Lee was not entirely fooled. "I think the enemy must be preparing to move south of James River," he wrote Jefferson Davis on June 14. What he did not know was that the movement was already under way. That evening engineers completed the bridge, and Grant's forces began crossing. These were agonizing days for Lee, recalled Confederate Major Robert Stiles: "Even Marse Robert, who knew everything knowable, did not appear to know what his old enemy proposed to do, or where he would be most likely to find him." Not until the night of June 17 did Lee conclude that Grant had crossed the James and set out in pursuit.

By then, Grant had nearly 70,000 troops at Petersburg, facing some 20,000 Confederates under General Beauregard. The town's outnumbered defenders were well-fortified, however, and the arrival of Lee's forces on June 18 raised their morale and cheered civilians. "Ladies, old and young," wrote Major Stiles, "met us at their front gates with hearty welcome, cool water, and fresh viands, and did not at all shrink from grasping our rough and dirty hands." Grant's men, for their part, were weary and apprehensive. Their fitful attacks over the past few days had achieved little, and renewed assaults on the 18th failed to break the enemy's grip on Petersburg. "The men went in, but not with spirit," wrote Meade's aide, Colonel Lyman. After this missed opportunity, Grant settled in for a siege, confident that his larger and better-supplied army would eventually wear down the opposition. Lee was not entirely surrounded and still had lines open to the west. But if he pulled back from Petersburg in that direction, Richmond would be doomed. "You will never hear of me farther from Richmond than right now," Grant promised

"The air was filled with malaria and death. Sickness, as well as battle, was doing fearful work in our ranks."
Federal soldier after Cold Harbor

Built by Grant's engineers to carry his forces across the James River in mid-June and circumvent Lee's army, this pontoon bridge extended for 2,100 feet and was the longest such span yet constructed for military purposes.

> "I am just as sure of going into Richmond as I am of any future event. It may take a long summer day, as they say in the rebel papers, but I will do it."
>
> GENERAL GRANT TO ABRAHAM LINCOLN AT PETERSBURG

Lincoln when the president visited him in late June. "I am just as sure of going into Richmond as I am of any future event. It may take a long summer day, as they say in the rebel papers, but I will do it."

CONVULSION IN THE CRATER

MAJOR WALTER TAYLOR HAD HEARD RUMORS THAT OPPOSING FEDERALS WERE tunneling under the Confederate works at Petersburg, but he put no stock in them. "Those scamps in the trenches pass the time circulating these preposterous stories," wrote Taylor on July 22. "Some of our fellows actually heard them digging some fifteen feet deep & about as many yards in front of our lines. . . . At least so they say." Taylor, an aide to Lee, considered these tales no more reliable than recent reports of Grant's death, but they were well-founded. The digging was being done by the 48th Pennsylvania Infantry, made up largely of coal miners. Their commander, Lieutenant Colonel Henry Pleasants, had proposed excavating a tunnel more than 500 feet long and detonating 8,000 pounds of gunpowder below an enemy salient called Fort Elliott. "We could blow that damned fort out of existence," he said. Following the explosion, a division of black troops from Burnside's corps would charge through the gap and advance up nearby Cemetery Hill, a commanding position overlooking Petersburg.

Grant was skeptical of this plan, and with good reason: During the siege of Vicksburg, his engineers had set off explosives below Confederate earthworks, gouging out a crater in which his troops became trapped under enemy fire as they tried to advance. Over the summer, however, Confederate troop strength at Petersburg diminished, and Grant decided to try it. In mid-June, Lee had sent General Jubal Early's Corps off to protect the Shenandoah Valley from Franz Sigel's successor, Major General David Hunter. Early defeated Hunter and went on to threaten Washington. Grant planned to counter that thrust by sending Phil Sheridan against Early. Before doing so, however, he ordered Sheridan's cavalry and Hancock's infantry to menace Richmond and draw more troops away from Petersburg. By late July, Grant thought he had a good chance to break through here and approved the assault on Fort Elliott and Cemetery Hill. "Lee, having sent five divisions to the north of the James, had but three left at Petersburg," one Union officer noted. "Once established on the hill, the city was ours."

Shortly before the attack, Meade overruled Burnside's plan to have black troops lead the charge. Grant backed Meade, explaining later that

Grant's troops mimicked their foes at Petersburg by digging in and creating strongpoints such as Fort Sedgwick, shown here. Named for General John Sedgwick, killed at Spotsylvania, this fearsome compound of trenches, traverses, and bombproof shelters was nicknamed Fort Hell.

he did not want it said "we were shoving these people ahead to get killed because we did not care anything about them." Yet sending in those troops after the initial assault did not greatly reduce the risks, for some Confederates were inclined to kill black soldiers rather than capture them—and could be just as brutal to whites who fought alongside them. Burnside made things worse by drawing lots to decide which of his other three divisions would lead the attack. The honor fell to white troops under Brigadier General James Ledlie, who had a habit of preparing for battle by drinking rum as a "stimulant."

Just before dawn on July 30, the explosives went off, pulverizing Fort Elliott and leaving a gaping crater. "Hell has busted!" yelled one Confederate, who ran from the blast hatless and shoeless. Ledlie's troops failed to capitalize on the shock and confusion among their foes. Without guidance from their commander, who remained holed up behind the lines in a bombproof with a bottle of rum, they advanced to the edge of the Crater and stood dumbfounded. "Little did these men anticipate what they would see upon arriving there," wrote Lieutenant William Powell: "an enormous hole in the ground about 30 feet deep, 60 feet wide, and 170 feet long, filled with dust, great blocks of clay, guns, broken carriages, projecting timbers, and men buried in various ways—some up to their necks, others to their waists, and some with only their feet and legs protruding from the earth." Instead of charging around the Crater toward Cemetery Hill, astonished Federals descended into the pit and began scrounging for souvenirs and pulling survivors from the rubble. They soon came under enemy artillery fire and found it hard to escape from the trap they had stumbled into. The sides of the pit "were so steep that it was almost impossible to climb out after getting in," related Horace Porter.

Amid the confusion, the black troops trained to lead the assault entered battle. Some made headway by moving around the Crater and clashing with Confederates beyond. "The fire upon them was incessant and severe," wrote Lieutenant Powell, "and many acts of personal heroism were done here by

Federals of the 48th Pennsylvania Infantry excavate a mine at Petersburg in July below an enemy strongpoint, Fort Elliott. Thousands of crate loads of soil had to be removed before the mine reached the required length and was packed with explosives.

Men of the 4th U.S. Colored Troops, shown on guard duty at Washington after the war, participated in the Battle of the Crater at Petersburg on July 30 and a subsequent assault in late September on another Confederate bastion there, Fort Harrison, where their hard-fighting regiment suffered 178 casualties.

The mine dug by the Pennsylvanians explodes at dawn on July 30, sending a plume of debris high into the air and signaling the start of an artillery barrage by Federal mortars. Soon after this, Union troops advanced, only to falter in the Crater.

officers and men." One officer who was not cited for heroism afterward was their division commander, Brigadier General Edward Ferrero, who was back in the bombproof with Ledlie. Expecting no mercy from their foes, the black troops fought desperately but were stopped well short of Cemetery Hill. By mid-morning, a Confederate related, the survivors had been forced to retreat into the Crater, which became a killing ground as Rebels poured into the pit "and slaughtered hundreds of whites and blacks." Some of the victims went down fighting, but others died while trying to surrender.

Grant called it "the saddest affair I have ever witnessed in the war." The casualties were bad enough—1,500 for the Confederates and nearly three times as many for the Federals—but the shocking command failures and savage bloodletting made defeat even worse. Unionists were appalled, but those in the North who thought this campaign was mere butchery and would settle nothing were mistaken. Lee understood as well as anyone what his opponent had achieved by pinning him down at Petersburg, where his dwindling forces would be further depleted by sickness, hunger, and hostile fire. As he had said a few months earlier, before Grant boxed him in here: "This army cannot stand a siege. We must end this business on the battlefield, not in a fortified place."

THE SHENANDOAH IN FLAMES

WITH THE UNION CLOSING in on Richmond and Petersburg, Grant devised a new plan to cut off Lee's supply lines by destroying the Shenandoah Valley's railroads and the Rebel supply depot at Lynchburg. Major General David Hunter, whose army was forever being harassed by partisan guerrillas, turned the mission into a vindictive raid that left a swath of destruction from Piedmont to Lexington.

Jubal Early stopped Hunter at Lynchburg in mid-June and proceeded to put a serious scare into the Union. When Hunter retreated from Lynchburg, he moved off into West Virginia rather than back through the valley, for fear of reprisal from partisans. Early seized the chance to lead his army of 15,000 into Maryland on a raid that ended at the outskirts of Washington, D.C. Among the capital's denizens who came under fire was Abraham Lincoln, who went to Fort Stevens, along the city's defensive lines, for a closer look. Not recognizing the lanky civilian, Oliver Wendell Holmes, Jr., shouted "Get down, you damn fool, before you get shot!" The president obeyed, and Early, finding Federal reinforcements too strong, turned back for the valley.

A furious Grant formed a new Army of the Shenandoah and put Philip Sheridan in charge, with orders to follow Early "to the death." From September 1864 to March 1865, "Little Phil" swept through the valley, leaving Early's army in shambles and the Shenandoah in flames.

It began at the Third Battle of Winchester, on September 19,

> **"The people must be left nothing but their eyes to weep with."**
>
> MAJOR GENERAL PHILIP SHERIDAN

Lexington's main street (opposite) returns to normal except for the burned-out ruins of VMI in the background, courtesy of David Hunter's Federals. Hunter was stopped by Jubal Early (top), who was then defeated by Philip Sheridan (bottom).

when Sheridan brought a three-to-one advantage in numbers against Early and sent the Confederates "whirling through Winchester." Three days later at the Battle of Fisher Hill, the formidable bluff to which the Rebels had retreated, Early's outnumbered lines were broken again, forcing them to abandon the upper valley to Union forces.

Wanting to leave nothing to chance, Grant ordered Sheridan to lay waste to the breadbasket of the Confederacy. "[Nothing] should be left to invite the enemy to return," said Grant. "Take all provisions, forage and stock wanted for the use of your command. Such as cannot be consumed, destroy … so that the crows flying over it for the balance of this season will have to carry their provender with them."

Sheridan obliged, reporting to Grant in October that his army had "destroyed over 2,000 barns filled with wheat, hay, and farming implements; over 70 mills filled with flour and wheat; have driven in front of the army over 4,000 head of stock, and have killed and issued to the troops not less than 3,000 sheep."

Jubal Early tried one last counterattack at Cedar Creek, surprising Sheridan's men the morning of October 19, while their commander was in Winchester. Hearing of the rout, Sheridan led a ferocious attack back at Cedar Creek to reverse what the Rebels had already considered a victory. Watching Sheridan inspire hundreds of defeated men to regroup and join him, a veteran of his 6th Corps recalled, "Such a scene as his presence and such emotion as it awoke cannot be realized but once in a century." ∎

DESCENDING ON ATLANTA

THE UNION HAD MORE THAN A HALF MILLION MEN IN UNIFORM, BUT two of them towered above the rest. "We were as brothers," Sherman wrote of Grant, "I the older man in years, he the higher in rank." Serving under the supremely confident Grant, Sherman lost the self-doubt that plagued him early in the war and took the South by storm. Much as Lincoln placed great trust in Grant and left him to manage his campaign against Lee as he saw fit, Grant allowed Sherman wide latitude in conducting his simultaneous offensive against Joseph Johnston, whose Army of Tennessee was camped in April around Dalton, Georgia, 30 miles southeast of Sherman's base at Chattanooga. Sherman's instructions from Grant were broad: "to move against Johnston's army, to break it up, and to go into the interior of the enemy's country as far as he could, inflicting all the damage he could upon their war resources." Johnston was a master of defensive tactics who would yield ground grudgingly rather than see his army battered and broken. In that case, Sherman would press him back toward Atlanta, the second-most important city under Confederate control after Richmond. Seizing Atlanta and its industries would do much to impair the South's war-making capacity.

Unlike Grant, who considered destroying Lee's army far more important than gaining ground, Sherman was keen on seizing territory and wrecking the Southern economy. Grant initiated the policy of consuming everything the enemy might use "to support or supply armies," but Sherman adopted that program enthusiastically and became its chief practitioner. He felt that Confederates deserved such punishment not because they favored slavery—he had dealt cordially with slave owners before the war—but because they were in rebellion. "They have appealed to war and must abide by its rules & laws," he wrote. Southerners could have held onto their slaves by remaining loyal, he added, "but now it is too late, all the powers of Earth cannot restore to them their slaves any more than their dead grandfathers. Next year in all probability their lands will be taken, for in war we can take them & rightfully too, and in another year they may beg in vain for their lives, for sooner or later there must be an end to strife."

Sherman took a hard line with some Unionists as well. He loathed reporters because he had received bad press in the past and felt that war coverage betrayed military secrets to the enemy. Once, when told that "three dirty newspaper scribblers" following his forces were missing and presumed dead, he wrote contemptuously: "We'll have dispatches now from hell before break-

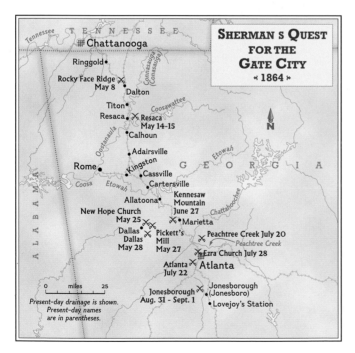

In early May, Sherman advanced from Chattanooga into Georgia, clashing repeatedly with Confederates under Joseph Johnston and pressing them back toward Atlanta. Johnston's successor, John Bell Hood, tried to save the city by launching desperate attacks against the advancing Federals on its outskirts, but Sherman's men severed the railroads feeding Atlanta and forced its surrender.

Sherman, shown here in occupied Atlanta in 1864, made no effort to soften the impact of his bruising campaign on civilians in the South. "War is cruelty," he once remarked. "There is no use trying to reform it; the crueler it is, the sooner it will be over."

"Next year in all probability their lands will be taken, for in war we can take them & rightfully too, and in another year they may beg in vain for their lives, for sooner or later there must be an end to strife."

GENERAL WILLIAM SHERMAN, *on rebellious Southerners*

fast." To supply his army of over 100,000 men during the Georgia campaign, he ordered that railroads under his authority be used for military purposes only and halted civilian traffic and food shipments. Lincoln felt that hungry loyalists in eastern Tennessee deserved a break and asked Sherman to make an exception for "those suffering people," but he refused to back down.

While Sherman prepared for a long, hard campaign, Joseph Johnston sought to bolster an army barely half the size of his opponent's. Johnston might have been denied reinforcements if Grant had become general in chief in time to stop an ill-fated effort by General Nathaniel Banks to move up the Red River in Louisiana and invade Texas, launched in early March at Lincoln's urging. Grant wanted Banks to move instead against the strategic port of Mobile, Alabama, which had not yet been sealed off. That would have prevented Confederates in Alabama from being shifted to Georgia to oppose Sherman, who had sent troops to support Banks. On April 8, Banks was routed at Sabine Crossroads in Louisiana, and Grant ordered him back to New Orleans. "His failure has absorbed ten thousand veteran troops that should now be with General Sherman," Grant fumed, "and thirty thousand of his own that should have been moving towards Mobile."

One consequence of this fiasco for the Federals was that Jefferson Davis was able to send 15,000 troops under Lieutenant General Leonidas Polk from Alabama to Georgia, which would bring Johnston's strength to over 70,000 men. Davis expected Johnston to attack Sherman and was dismayed when he held back. "I can see no other mode of taking the offensive here, than to beat the enemy when he advances, and then move forward," Johnston wrote. His caution contrasted with the zeal of his avid young corps commander, 32-year-old Lieutenant General John Bell Hood, who had lost his right leg at Chickamauga and the use of his left arm at Gettysburg but remained as aggressive as ever. It was time to "drive the enemy beyond the limits of the Confederacy," Hood wrote Davis. "He, the enemy, is at present weak, and we are strong." Davis would not rest easy until his Army of Tennessee was back in Tennessee. If Johnston was not up to that task, Hood was waiting eagerly in the wings.

SHERMAN MOVES SOUTH

SHERMAN CROSSED INTO GEORGIA ON MAY 7, A FEW DAYS AFTER GRANT MOVED against Lee. For the first time, Federal forces on either side of the Appalachians were acting in concert. Leading the way for Sherman was George Thomas, the "Rock of Chickamauga," and his 60,000-man Army of the Cumberland, which moved down the Western & Atlantic Railroad, Johnston's supply line from Atlanta. Two smaller forces—Major General John Schofield's Army of the Ohio and Major General James McPherson's Army of the Tennessee—advanced to the left and right of Thomas, respectively. Sherman greatly admired the 35-year-old McPherson, who had excelled during the Vicksburg Campaign, and tasked him with outflanking Johnston to the west while Confederates massed at Rocky Face Ridge, overlooking the railroad north of Dalton. Sherman staged a convincing demonstration there on May 8 by sending two divisions up the ridge, which was pierced by "narrow crevices, through which but a single man could pass at a time," one Union soldier recalled. "Through these crevices we saw their skirmishers pass, and then their main line opened furiously upon us, and added to our confusion by sending from the top great boulders rolling down the mountain side."

Federals held out long enough on Rocky Face Ridge to preoccupy their opponents while McPherson's 25,000 troops outflanked them to the west. "I've got Joe Johnston dead!" exclaimed Sherman, who expected McPherson to sweep unopposed into Resaca, 15 miles below Dalton, and tear up the tracks there, cutting Johnston off from Atlanta. A few days earlier, however, the first of the Confederate reinforcements from Alabama, a division of 4,000 men, had arrived by train at Resaca, where they put up a good show and held McPherson off. "Well, Mac, you have missed the opportunity of your life," an exasperated Sherman told McPherson as Johnston's entire army hurried south to defend Resaca. By the time Sherman attacked there on May 14, the Confederates were well entrenched along the railroad tracks, with their left flank on the Oostanaula River and their right flank on its tributary, the Conasauga River. Brigadier General Nathaniel McLean reported that his Federals advanced into a "storm of death which was hurled upon them from every quarter," pressing ahead "until they were broken up by a bog and creek into which they plunged more than waist deep. To climb the opposite bank under such a murderous fire was more than they could do."

Late in the day, Hood's troops threatened to outflank Sherman's men along the Conasauga, only to be stymied by Major General Alpheus Williams, a battle-hardened veteran of Antietam who hurried his division from the right of the Union line to the far left to repulse the Confederates. "I astonished the rascals by pushing a brigade from the woods," Williams wrote. "They 'skedaddled' as fast as they had advanced." The next day, McPherson's forces redeemed themselves by crossing the Oostanaula below Resaca and threatening to cut the railroad. Johnston withdrew that night after suffering over 2,600 casualties in the two-day battle. Sherman's losses were somewhat higher, but he was a step closer to Atlanta and gaining momentum.

South of Resaca at Adairsville, the railroad forked and Sherman divided his forces. When Johnston told his men he planned "to give battle," one Confederate recalled, "soldiers threw their caps into the air and shouted themselves hoarse with joy at the thought of going into a fight which they felt in their souls would be successful. It was inspiring to see such enthusiasm in battle-scarred veterans who knew what fighting meant." But confusion and indecision among their commanders thwarted the planned attack. Johnston and Hood blamed each other for failing to strike Sherman before he reunited his forces. "We have run until I am getting out of heart," another Confederate wrote; "we must make a stand soon or the army will be demoralized."

Federals camped in the foreground guard a railroad bridge in Tennessee to protect Sherman's supply line from Nashville to Chattanooga. As Sherman moved into Georgia, he left thousands of troops behind in Tennessee to fend off Confederate raiders and keep supplies flowing to his advancing forces.

Field Music

"I don't believe we can have an army without music."

GENERAL ROBERT E. LEE

THE CIVIL WAR WAS THE WORLD'S LAST MAJOR CON-flict in which bands played on the field of combat. At the outset, both sides called for each regiment to have a regimental brass band. By mid-1862, as the armies grew, it became more practical to organize bands at the brigade level.

Nevertheless, each regiment or company retained their own field musicians—usually fifers, drummers, and buglers. In battle they would use their instruments to transmit commands to the infantry, cavalry, and artillery. Drummers would also "beat the rally" to inspire troops in the midst of fighting. If necessary, musicians, who were trained as infantry, put down their instruments to carry stretchers, act as couriers, or assist field surgeons.

In camp, buglers rousted men from bed by playing reveille, assembled them with "second call" or the "long roll," and announced work details with "fatigue call" or "pioneer's call." Drummers kept the cadence of drills and marches, and "drummed out" cowards or men convicted of crimes with the "rogue's march."

Musicians also provided a welcome distraction for war-weary soldiers. "I have just been listening to some of the most delightful music I have ever heard," wrote Lieutenant Alexander Barclay of the 4th Virginia Infantry after hearing the Stonewall Brigade Band. "Truly 'music hath charms to soothe the savage breast.'"

A remarkable example of music's diplomatic charms came during the Atlanta campaign, when enemies exchanged notes instead of fire. According to Colonel James Nisbet of the 66th Georgia, one Rebel regiment had "the best [coronet player] I ever heard. In the evenings after supper he would come to our salient and play solos." The Yankees applauded him, Nisbet recalled. "They had a good coronet player who would alternate with our man." ■

Regimental drum corps, such as the one shown here attached to the 30th Pennsylvania Infantry, were conducted on the field of battle by flamboyantly dressed drum majors like the unidentified Federal pictured opposite. The field drum at left belonged to the 13th Virginia Infantry, whose roll shows at least one underage drummer among its ranks. Boys as young as 10 enlisted in the drum corps, some dying in battle.

A native of Kentucky who moved to Texas before the war, John Bell Hood led the renowned Texas Brigade before advancing rapidly up the chain of command and replacing the popular Joseph Johnston as head of the Army of Tennessee. "The news thunderstruck the army," wrote one Confederate. Soldiers knew Hood was "loyal, patriotic, and brave," he added, "but doubted his ability to command the army."

After this lost opportunity, Johnston withdrew across the Etowah River and lay in wait at Allatoona Pass, less than 30 miles from Atlanta. Sherman avoided that trap by leaving the tracks, circling to the west. He hoped to rejoin the railroad at Marietta, below Allatoona, and cut Johnston off, but Confederate cavalry detected the move. Johnston responded by forming a new defensive line west of the railroad that extended for several miles from Pickett's Mill and nearby New Hope Church to the town of Dallas. This was rough country, consisting of "old pine forests, half cleared," wrote Major General Oliver Howard, a corps commander under Thomas. The woods, he added, were clotted with "dense underbrush, which the skirmishers had great difficulty in penetrating." Amid these thickets, Johnston's men raised breastworks bolstered with logs. "I wonder that we did not approach those well-chosen Confederate lines with more caution," Howard remarked; "we hoped that by a tremendous onslaught we might gain a great advantage, shorten the battle, and so shorten the war."

Those hopes were soon dashed. After futile assaults on Johnston's entrenched troops at New Hope Church on May 25, Sherman tried again two days later day by sending Howard's Corps against the Confederate right flank, near Pickett's Mill. The "tremendous onslaught" that Howard envisioned fell apart as one brigade after another came up against the crack division of Patrick Cleburne. Sheltered behind rocks and logs, his men awaited the Federals "with calm determination," Cleburne wrote, and "slaughtered them with deliberate aim." Union losses at Pickett's Mill and New Hope Church amounted to about 3,000 men, or nearly three times the Confederate toll. Johnston then attacked on the opposite flank, near Dallas, on May 28, but the Federals had learned their lesson and were well fortified. This time, it was their opponents who came to grief. When ordered to fall back, one Confederate recalled, "we were only too glad to attempt our escape from the death trap into which we had been ordered."

Both sides were weary of this Hell Hole, as the Yankees called it, and Sherman decided to resume his advance along the railroad. Confederates barred his way due east to Marietta, so he had to return to the tracks north of that town, where several mountains occupied by Johnston's forces stood as obstacles in his path. On June 14, Johnston was conferring with Leonidas Polk and other officers atop Pine Mountain when Sherman noticed activity on the summit and ordered his gunners to open fire. While other Confederates ran for cover, Polk walked—he did not want to show fear before the troops—and was hit by an incoming shell. The Fighting Bishop of Louisiana was the second-highest-ranking Confederate to die in action during the war after Albert Sidney Johnston, who fell at Shiloh. "We killed Bishop Polk yesterday," Sherman wired Washington on June 15, "and have made good progress today."

By late June, Joseph Johnston had concentrated his forces on Kennesaw Mountain—the most imposing barrier north of Marietta—and battle loomed. Driving Confederates from that high ground promised to be bloody work. Even John Logan, one of the Union's most combative political generals, worried that the risks were too great and suggested that Sherman find a way around Johnston. Sherman replied that it was "necessary to show that his men could fight as well as Grant's." That sounded harsh and self-serving, but neither Grant nor Sherman could have made much progress without hitting their opponents head on. Frontal assaults wore down the Confederates, who could not replace their losses, and set up flanking moves that succeeded only because the enemy was preoccupied elsewhere.

Such was the case on June 27, when Sherman's troops charged up Kennesaw Mountain in attacks that appeared doomed from the start. Men were slaughtered "like beasts in the shambles," one Federal wrote, and George Thomas concluded, "One or two more such assaults would use up this army." But as Federals faltered on Kennesaw, troops under Schofield were advancing around Johnston's flank to the south. That move, intended by Sherman as a diversion, soon developed into his main thrust. Once more, Johnston had to withdraw toward Atlanta or risk being cut off. For Sherman, that gratifying outcome made the toll at Kennesaw—nearly 3,000 casualties compared to 800 or so for the Confederates—worth paying. As he later wrote his wife: "I begin to regard the death and mangling of a couple thousand men as a small affair, a kind of morning dash, and it may be well that we become so hardened."

In early July, Johnston made a stand along the Chattahoochee River, within sight of Atlanta, but once again Sherman outflanked him, by crossing upstream, and forced him back. Jefferson Davis worried that Johnston would surrender Atlanta without a fight. Hood played to those fears by writing Davis a letter questioning Johnston's resolve. "I regard it as a great misfortune to our country that we have failed to give battle to the enemy many miles north of our present position," Hood declared. On July 17, after Johnston declined to offer any assurances that Atlanta could or would be saved, Davis removed him in favor of Hood. No one doubted that Hood would do all in his power to stop Sherman. But if he attacked recklessly, as some who knew him feared, he risked losing both Atlanta and his army. "Hood is a bold fighter," Robert E. Lee told Davis. "I am doubtful as to other qualities necessary."

STORMING THE GATES

"MINE EYES HAVE BEHELD THE PROMISED LAND!" WROTE MAJOR JAMES Connolly of the 123rd Illinois Infantry outside Atlanta in mid-July. A week earlier, Connolly told his wife, he had been riding up front with his brigade commander "when suddenly we came upon a high bluff overlooking the Chattahoochee, and looking southward across the river, there lay the beautiful 'Gate City' in full view." When troops coming up behind learned that Atlanta—a strategic gateway between the Atlantic Coast and the Southern interior—was in sight, he added, "such a cheer went up as must have been heard even in the entrenchments of the doomed city itself. In a very few

> "I begin to regard the death and mangling of a couple thousand men as a small affair, a kind of morning dash, and it may be well that we become so hardened."
>
> GENERAL SHERMAN, *after the Battle of Kennesaw Mountain*

moments Generals Sherman and Thomas (who are always with the extreme front when a sudden movement is taking place) were with us on the hill top, and the two veterans, for a moment, gazed at the glittering prize in silence."

Sherman knew this prize would not come cheaply once Hood took command. "He'll hit you like hell, now, before you know it," warned General Schofield, a classmate of Hood's at West Point. Sherman's three army commanders—Schofield, McPherson, and Thomas—were descending on Atlanta by separate paths, and Hood hoped to catch Thomas's troops as they crossed Peachtree Creek, north of the city, on July 20. Hood delayed that attack to realign his forces and guard against the risk that McPherson might move in from the east. By the time the battle opened, around 4 p.m., most of Thomas's men were across Peachtree Creek and in position to defend against Hood's bold but ill-coordinated challenge. It looked to one Yankee as if Rebels were "charging by the acre," but those who broke through were forced back under heavy artillery fire. Late in the day, corps commander William Hardee—who was senior to Hood but considered too cautious by Jefferson Davis to command the army—was about to unleash Cleburne's division against Thomas's left flank when Hood grew anxious and sent Cleburne off to the east to block the fast-approaching McPherson. Hood lost over 2,500 men at Peachtree Creek, compared to 1,800 casualties for the Federals. "This was just what we wanted," Sherman wrote, "to fight in open ground, on any thing like equal terms, instead of being forced to run up against prepared entrenchments."

Undeterred, Hood remained on the offensive and launched a stronger attack two days later in a pivotal contest known as the Battle of Atlanta. The stage was set for that showdown on July 21, when Cleburne's troops clashed with McPherson's Federals on Bald Hill, east of Atlanta. McPherson took the hill and placed artillery there but remained vulnerable to attack on his left, to the south. Hood was eager to test that exposed flank, but here as at Peachtree Creek his plan proved hard to implement, delaying the assault. His orders called for Hardee's Corps to march through Atlanta that night, turn McPherson's flank, and strike the Federals from the rear at dawn on July 22 after a grueling march of 15 miles. That was too much to ask of Hardee and his battle-weary troops, who were not in position to attack until noon. By then, McPherson had reinforced his left by calling up a reserve corps under Major General Grenville Dodge over the objections of Sherman, who wanted Dodge—a gifted engineer who would later supervise construction of the Union Pacific Railroad—sent off to tear up tracks around Atlanta. McPherson won his point by visiting headquarters and reasoning with Sherman, who yielded to his promising subordinate. "If he lives," Sherman once said of McPherson, "he'll outdistance Grant and myself."

This was McPherson's finest hour, and his last. When Hardee attacked around midday, his Confederates found a gap between Dodge's Corps on the far left and the main Federal line and poured through. McPherson rode forward with aides to meet the crisis and came up against enemy skirmishers. "I threw up my sword to him as a signal to surrender," recalled Captain Richard Beard of Cleburne's division. "He checked his horse slightly, raised his hat as politely as if he was saluting a lady, wheeled his horse's head directly to the right, and dashed off to the rear in full gallop." Confederates promptly opened fire, and McPherson fell from his horse, mortally wounded. "Who is this man lying here?" Beard asked a Federal officer captured at the same time. "Sir, it is General McPherson. You have killed the best man in our army."

It was a heavy blow for the Federals, but Sherman had other good men he could call on, including John Logan, who replaced the fallen commander and raised a new battle cry: "McPherson and revenge, boys!" Federals closed the gap to their left, only to come under furious assault on their right in midafternoon when a second Confederate corps, led by General Benjamin Cheatham, entered the fray. Sherman responded by calling up batteries from Schofield's army. "The artillery bellowed and thundered," recalled one Union soldier, "and the paths were filled with the dying and the dead. The sound was deafening—the tumult indescribable." Confederates "fought with a fierceness seldom if ever equaled," he added, but could not overcome Sherman's advantage in men and arms. The Battle of Atlanta ended that evening as a major defeat for Hood, who in the past three days had lost over 8,000 men, or more casualties than Johnston suffered in the entire campaign before stepping down. Cleburne's once-splendid division lost nearly half its strength and would never be the same. Ignoring such harsh realities, Hood claimed that the costly battle had infused his army with "new life and fresh hopes."

Sherman's plan now was to deprive Atlanta and its defenders of supplies and reinforcements by severing the last intact rail line feeding the city—the Macon & Western from Savannah, which entered the city from the south at a junction called East Point. As Union troops wheeled around Atlanta in a counterclockwise direction and descended on that junction, Hood sent forces to intercept them at Ezra Church, west of the city, on July 28. The commander who led that attack, 30-year-old Lieutenant General Stephen Lee, emulated Hood by launching furious assaults on Federals lurking behind logs, rails, and pews hauled from the church. "The old-fashioned impression that a soldier should stand up to be shot at had passed away," wrote one Union officer there, "and he had learned to take what advantage he could of his enemy." In a few hours, Confederates lost more than 3,000 men assailing the well-shielded Federals, who suffered only about 600 casualties. Afterward, Hood's army hunkered down within imposing fortifications constructed around Atlanta and extended those defenses to protect the rail junction.

That shift in tactics dismayed Sherman, who hoped the Confederates would continue to attack and "beat their own brains out." Frustrated, he bombarded Atlanta, pouring as many as 5,000 shells a day into the city, where some civilians were killed and others frantically dug shelters. As one resident, Fannie Beers, recalled: "The houses were closed and deserted, in many cases partly demolished by shot and shell, or, having taken fire, charred, smoking, and

> **"If he lives, he'll outdistance Grant and myself."**
>
> GENERAL SHERMAN, *on Major General James McPherson*

General McPherson, slain during the Battle of Atlanta, was the first and only Union army commander killed in action during the war. Sherman wept when he heard the news and wrote later to McPherson's fiancée: "while life lasts I will delight in the memory of that bright particular star which has gone before to prepare the way for us more hardened sinners who must struggle to the end."

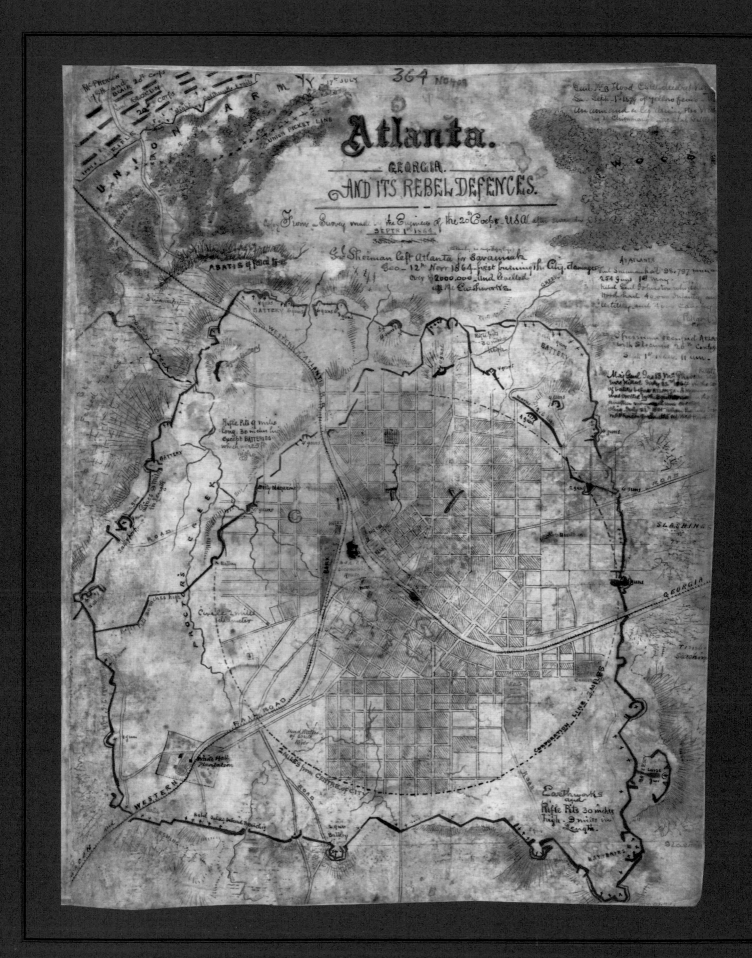

THE DEFENSE OF ATLANTA

As GRANT PUSHED CLOSER TO RICHMOND AND Petersburg, Sherman began his inexorable march toward Atlanta, the city whose size, industry, and position as a railroad hub put it on a strategic par with Richmond.

What the Federals found when they got there were fortified lines completely encircling the city, a perimeter that in Sherman's words "defied a direct assault." This 12-mile cordon of batteries, redoubts, and rifle pits represented a year's worth of labor and a sizeable chunk of the Confederacy's treasury. Slaves had been hired from their owners for $25 a month to dig trenches, construct forts and earthworks, and clear thousands of trees for a variety of barricades: spiked palisades, embedded stakes called fraises, entwined obstacles of trees and branches called abatis, and the thorny chevaux-de-frise that snaked along the lines like spinal cords.

In a way, the fortifications were successful. "I have heard repeatedly that the Yankee gents can't get their men to charge our works," boasted a Texas color-bearer in August. He was right; Sherman had no illusions about storming the city and challenging those defenses. Instead, he rendered them irrelevant by moving his army west and south to sever the Western & Atlantic and Macon & Western railroad lines that supplied the city.

John Bell Hood realized too late what Sherman was up to and made a failed attempt to stop him at Jonesborough, 20 miles south. Hopelessly cut off, Hood evacuated Atlanta the night of September 1, burning supplies and military installations on his way out. Sherman's strategy allowed his army to capture the city's defenses intact. As one Union soldier wrote, "It is astonishing to see what fortifications they had on every side of the city. All in vain for them, but quite convenient for us now." ∎

Robert Knox Sneden's map shows a detailed layout of Atlanta's defenses, including the surrounding batteries and earthworks, and the position of Union forces as of September 1, 1864, the day Hood evacuated the city.

SIEGE WORKS *A redoubt on the northern perimeter stands behind the teeth of a cheval-de-frise, a barrier of spiked logs designed to stop infantry.*

OCCUPYING TIME *The enemy long gone, one Federal reads quietly in the bombproof dugout of a captured earthwork.*

CAPTURED FORT *The heavy artillery in this stronghold on the city's eastern side proved no use once Sherman marched to the south.*

Wallace P. Reed

RESIDENT OF ATLANTA

Wallace Reed, a 14-year-old resident of Atlanta, witnessed the bombardment of his city during the siege by Federal forces in the summer of 1864. Recalling the day of the heaviest shelling, Reed recorded the deaths and injuries of his fellow citizens. After the war, Reed became a writer and reporter for the Atlanta Constitution and penned a history of his home city.

THE FAMOUS ARTILLERY duel! If any one day of the siege was worse than all the others, it was that red day in August, when all the fires of hell, and all the thunders of the universe seemed to be blazing and roaring over Atlanta. It was about the middle of the month, and everything had been comparatively quiet for a few days, when one fine morning, about breakfast time, a big siege gun belched forth a sheet of flame with a sullen boom from a Federal battery on the north side of the city. The Confederates had an immense gun on Peachtree Street, one so large and heavy that it had taken three days to drag it to its position. This monster engine of destruction lost no time in replying to its noisy challenger, and then the duel opened all along the lines on the east, north, and west. Ten Confederate and eleven Federal batteries took part in the engagement. On Peachtree, just where Kimball Street intersects, the big gun of the Confederates put in its best work, but only to draw a hot fire from the enemy. Shot and shell rained in every direction. Great volumes of sulphurous smoke rolled over the town, trailing down to the ground, and through this stifling gloom the sun glared down like a red eye peering through a bronze colored cloud. It was on this day of horrors that the

Solomon Luckie, a free black barber, was mortally wounded by a Federal shell.

"A lady who was ironing some clothes in a house on North Pryor, between the Methodist Church and Wheat Street, was struck by a shell and killed."

destruction of human life was greatest among the citizens. A shell crashed into a house on the corner of Elliott and Rhodes Street, and exploded, killing Mr. Warner, the superintendent of the gas company and his little six year old girl. . . . A lady who was ironing some clothes in a house on North Pryor, between the Methodist Church and Wheat Street, was struck by a shell and killed. Sol Luckie, a well-known barber, was standing on the James's Bank corner, on Whitehall and Alabama, when a shell struck a lamp-post, ricocheted, and exploded. A fragment struck Luckie and knocked him down. Mr. Tom Crusselle and one or two other citizens picked up the unfortunate man and carried him into a store. He was then taken to the Atlanta Medical College, where Dr. D'Alvigney amputated his leg. The poor fellow was put under the influence of morphine, but he never rallied from the shock, and died in a few hours. A young lady who was on her way to the car shed was struck in the back and fatally wounded. On Forsyth Street a Confederate officer was standing in the front yard, taking leave of the lady of the house, when a bursting shell mortally wounded him and the lady's little boy. The two victims were laid side by side on the grass under the trees, and in a few minutes they both bled to death. The sun was sinking behind the western hills when the great artillery duel ended, and the exhausted gunners threw themselves on the ground. From a military standpoint these were no results worthy of mention. Nothing was gained by either side. ■

burnt to the ground. All day frightened women and children cowered and trembled and hungered and thirsted in their underground places of refuge while the earth above them shook with constant explosions." Sherman hoped to make Atlanta "too hot to be endured," but he had yet to sever the last rail line. With Grant's forces stalled at Petersburg, the Union could ill afford another stalemate here as voters prepared to cast judgment on Lincoln and his war effort. Intent on bringing matters to a close, Sherman launched his army in late August on a wide sweep south of Atlanta that skirted the fortifications. At month's end, his troops closed in on the Macon & Western Railroad.

Hood tried to keep that last artery open by sending troops under Hardee to attack Federals dug in along the tracks at Jonesborough, below Atlanta, on August 31, but once again Sherman's men were ready for the Confederates. After a hard fight, Hardee withdrew southward with his exhausted forces on September 1, leaving Atlanta behind. The fate of the city was sealed. Late that night, Hood pulled out after burning all supplies and ammunition that could not be hauled away, including an ordnance train that exploded with volcanic force, shaking Atlanta to its foundations. On September 2, Federals entered the city unopposed and took possession. "Atlanta is ours and fairly won," Sherman wired Washington. Southerners saw nothing fair in his punishing campaign, which ravaged the city and forced its inhabitants into exile, but no one could deny the magnitude of his victory. For an increasingly desperate and depleted Confederacy, it was the beginning of the end.

This wreckage was left by the explosion of a Confederate ordnance train, set afire by Hood's troops as they abandoned Atlanta on the night of September 1. The blasts were heard up to 20 miles away and signaled to Sherman that Hood was pulling out.

"Atlanta is ours and fairly won."

GENERAL SHERMAN, *in a wire to Washington, D.C., on September 3*

CHRONOLOGY

August 31, 1864 **George McClellan nominated by Democrats to challenge the Republican candidate, Abraham Lincoln, in the November election.**

September 22 **John Frémont drops out of the presidential race as nominee of Radical Republicans and endorses Lincoln.**

November 8 **Lincoln wins reelection decisively.**

November 15 **William Sherman launches his devastating march from Atlanta to Savannah, leaving Federals under George Thomas to defend against Confederates advancing northward into Tennessee under John Bell Hood.**

November 30 **Battle of Franklin (Tennessee)**

December 13 **Sherman captures Fort McAllister, below Savannah, and links up with Federal fleet.**

December 15-16 **Battle of Nashville (Tennessee)**

December 21 **Sherman takes Savannah.**

"The Union is the one condition of peace—we ask no more."

GEORGE MCCLELLAN, *after receiving the Democratic presidential nomination*

PATHS TO VICTORY

THE NEWS FROM ATLANTA COULD NOT HAVE COME AT A BETTER TIME for Abraham Lincoln—or a worse time for his political opponent George McClellan. On August 31, McClellan, who had often differed with Lincoln as commander of the Army of the Potomac, was nominated by Democrats in Chicago to challenge the president at the polls in November. Delegates at the convention saddled McClellan with a party platform written by so-called Peace Democrats, urging that "immediate efforts be made for a cessation of hostilities." McClellan was a War Democrat, who wanted to keep fighting until the nation was reunited, but he tried to hold his party together by drafting a letter of acceptance allowing for negotiations with Confederate leaders if they agreed to rejoin the Union. Opposed to emancipation, he appeared willing to compromise with Southerners over slavery. "The Union is the one condition of peace—we ask no more," he wrote.

No sooner had McClellan released this letter than word came that Atlanta had fallen, a victory that thrilled the North and raised hopes that the Confederacy would soon collapse. Many Northerners now saw McClellan's willingness to engage in peace talks as a foolish concession to the faltering Rebels. Critics blasted him for promising war and peace simultaneously and trying to please everyone—including the enemy. "Neither you nor I, nor the Democrats themselves, can tell whether they have a peace platform or a war platform," one Republican charged. "Upon the whole it is both peace and war, that is peace with the rebels and war with their own government." McClellan insisted he was loyal to the Union cause, but the very success of Union forces undermined his campaign and bolstered the president, whose path to victory converged with that of Federals in the field. Lincoln found it encouraging that troops strongly supported his uncompromising efforts to crush the Confederacy. "Who should quail when they do not?" he said. "God bless the soldiers and seamen, with all their brave commanders."

Lincoln had not always been so sure of military and political success. Earlier in the year, widespread doubts about his war effort had exposed him to sniping from Peace Democrats on one flank and Radical Republicans on the other. Radicals wanted Lincoln to be even tougher on Confederates and opposed his promise to pardon Southerners who pledged allegiance to the United States and restore to them all property except their former slaves. Some Radicals broke with Lincoln by staging their own convention in May and nominating John Frémont, who had cracked down on Confederate sympathizers in Missouri. With his party divided and no end to the conflict in sight, Lincoln saw little reason for optimism. "This war is eating my life out," he told an acquaintance. "I have a strong impression that I shall not live to see the end."

Lincoln's one solace was that he finally had commanders who were pre-

ABRAHAM'S DREAM!—
"COMING EVENTS CAST THEIR SHADOWS BEFORE".

Published by Currier & Ives, 152 Nassau St N.Y.

pared to wage total war against Confederates. While he offered Rebels a carrot if they gave up the fight, Grant and Sherman wielded sticks and punished those who remained defiant. By August, that policy was beginning to pay dividends. Although Grant was still deadlocked with Lee at Petersburg, he hit the enemy hard by sending Phil Sheridan to challenge Jubal Early's forces in the Shenandoah Valley and deny Confederates the valley's bounty. "Eat out Virginia clear and clean," Grant told Sheridan. "If the war is to last another year," he added, "we want the Shenandoah Valley to remain a barren waste."

Before Sherman captured Atlanta and Sheridan defeated Early, Lincoln received a boost from Rear Admiral David Farragut, whose efforts, like those of many Union naval officers, had gone largely unnoticed by the public since New Orleans fell in 1862. Although the naval blockade was increasingly effective, blockade-runners continued to reach a few Southern ports, notably Wilmington, North Carolina, and Mobile, Alabama. Before dawn on August 5, Farragut assembled a fleet of four ironclads and 17 wooden ships and prepared to enter Mobile Bay through a narrow inlet flanked by forts and laced with torpedoes or submerged mines. Leading the way was the ironclad *Tecumseh*, which struck a torpedo and foundered, bringing the fleet to a halt under the forts' guns. Farragut then thrust his wooden flagship, *Hartford*, to the fore with a memorable order: "Damn the torpedoes! Full speed ahead!" Most of the

A political cartoon published during the 1864 presidential race portrays Lincoln's worst nightmare—losing the White House to his Democratic opponent, George McClellan, whose commitment to winning the war was questioned by Republicans. The outfit worn by Lincoln as he leaves the White House is one he supposedly put on before traveling in disguise to Washington for his inauguration in 1861.

"This war is eating my life out. I have a strong impression that I shall not live to see the end."
ABRAHAM LINCOLN

Curtis Green

COMPANY K, 6TH GEORGIA CAVALRY—OCTOBER 3, 1864

*Curtis Green served as a scout and spy in a company of the 6th Georgia Cavalry commanded
by Lieutenant J. J. O'Neil. In the fall of 1864, Green was captured in Federal uniform near Rome, Georgia, while
spying on enemy troop movements. He was convicted of espionage and sentenced to death.
On the night before his scheduled execution, Green escaped from his improvised cell
and made his escape into the nearby Oostanaula River.*

WHEN GOT OUT OF the River, I pulled off my hand cuffs by the meanes of sum soap that I had in my pocket and my hands being considerable swivled up in the cold water pulled off my close and rung them. Took up my hand cuffs and started on a march to make good my escape the darkest night that ever was . . . I went so slow and cautious that it consumed the balance of the night to go a short distance from where I got out of the Coosie River . . . I then went up in the mountain and looked back towards Rome and saw a file of Yankees cumming down the road and was satisfied that they was on the hunt of me and I counted them twenty seven in all then I knew that I would have to keep concealde in the mountain untill they went back and I sayed up in the mountain and shivered and chattered my teath for it was coalde and raining and put off the time the best I could untill about 3 oclock . . . and they went back twenty four of them and I knew that would not do twenty seven went down the road and only twenty four went back so I staied conceiled . . . and after a while two more went back and that was not enough . . . I continued in my hiding place for some time and after a

> **"I knew that I would have to keep concealde in the mountain untill they went back and I sayed up in the mountain and chattered my teath for it was coalde and raining."**

while the other one went back and then I felt relieved . . . now I startes an other cautious march traveling slow as my feet was snaged and bleeding as I was capelled to leave my boots in the Calabuce fearing that I would not be able to make the [swim] with them on. I cum in sight of the road at the end of the bluff at the Lamkins place . . . about half an hour after darke, stopt at an olde gentlemans house by the name of Garner who had two sons in the 21st Ga Infantry in Va . . . And I hollard hellow the olde gentleman cum to the dore and said who is that and I said a friend what is your name and I answered Curtis Green and here he cum and in a low tone of voice I hearde the Yanks had you in prison yess I said but I broke prison last night. . . . Cum in we ar ready to eat supper if you are not afraid . . . While I was eating supper his daughter Miss Elminor Garner stood out on the Varanda and lissoned for foot falls horse feet or anything that wood make a noise but she heard nothing. While I was eating supper I give him a detail of my escape . . . and then my cautious traviling and warring out my socks and bloody feet . . . Well says the olde gentleman I have nothing but an olde pare of slippers if you will if you will except of them you may have them . . . Now he said you can stay all night if you are not afraid I tolde him that I was not a feared but would not stay all night bidding the olde gentleman god night with many thanks. Starting for home in the same cautius manner . . . and got home the next day. ■

submerged mines failed to detonate, and Farragut took possession of Mobile Bay after dueling with the Confederate ironclad ram *Tennessee* and forcing its captain, Admiral Franklin Buchanan, to surrender. Mobile itself would not fall to Federal troops until the following April, but the port was sealed off. In Farragut, the Union found a hero who brought the same unflinching resolve to the naval war that Grant, Sherman, and Sheridan did to the land war. "I will attack regardless of the consequences," Farragut vowed, "and never turn back."

Farragut's "brilliant achievement," as Lincoln put it, offered Northerners a ray of hope, but the clouds did not really begin to lift until September, when Sherman's coup at Atlanta was followed a few weeks later by Sheridan's triumph over Early at Winchester, Virginia. "A few more victories such as this and Abe Lincoln will be elected in November," one pundit predicted. On September 22, Frémont acknowledged Lincoln's rising popularity by dropping out and endorsing the president. Some in the South clung to the hope that McClellan would win the race and concede to Confederates in peace talks. But Jefferson Davis, who was serving a six-year term and did not face reelection, gave up on McClellan when he made Unionism a condition for peace. The real issue in the election was not whether the Union as it existed before the war should be restored—Lincoln and McClellan agreed on that —but whether Confederates would be allowed to preserve their old way of life, based on slavery, if they ended their rebellion.

Despite recent victories, many in the North were weary of the war and willing to make concessions to end it. Conscription remained highly unpopular, but Lincoln rejected appeals that he suspend the draft until after the elections. "What is the presidency worth to me if I have no country?" he asked. In the end, the soldiers came through for him. Several states allowed troops to cast ballots in camp, and other men were granted leave to vote at home. When the results were tallied on November 8, Lincoln took nearly 80 percent of the soldiers' votes and 55 percent of the votes overall, sweeping all but a few states. His victory was "worth more to the country than a battle won," wrote Grant. For Sherman in Atlanta, Lincoln's reelection was the signal for him to proceed with his own campaign—one designed to discredit Confederate leaders by showing that they were powerless to stop him.

SHERMAN'S MARCH

"YOU MIGHT AS WELL APPEAL AGAINST THE THUNDER-STORM AS AGAINST THESE terrible hardships of war," Sherman wrote the mayor of Atlanta in September after ordering the evacuation of the city's remaining population to free his forces from having to police civilians. His opponent, General Hood, camped south of the city, was aghast when he received a letter from Sherman seeking his cooperation in relocating the few thousand people who had not already fled Atlanta. "The unprecedented measure you propose transcends, in studied and ingenious cruelty, all acts ever brought to my attention in the dark history of war," Hood replied. "In the name of God and humanity, I protest."

"In the name of common-sense," Sherman fired back, "I ask you not to appeal to a just God in such a sacrilegious manner. You, who in the midst of peace and prosperity, have plunged a nation into war. . . . If we must be ene-

> ## "You might as well appeal against the thunder-storm as against these terrible hardships of war."
>
> SHERMAN TO ATLANTA'S MAYOR, *after ordering the city evacuated*

mies, let us be men, and fight it out as we propose to do, and not deal in such hypocritical appeals to God and humanity." That infuriated Hood, who accused Sherman of "subjugating free white men, women, and children" and placing over them "an inferior race," and pledged defiance to the bitter end: "We will fight you to the death! Better die a thousands deaths than submit to live under you and your government and your Negro allies!"

Hood would have liked nothing better than to settle these differences in blood on a battlefield of his choosing, but Sherman would not give him that satisfaction. In October, Hood headed north toward Tennessee with his 40,000-man army along the Western & Atlantic Railroad, Sherman's supply line, hoping to lure his opponent into a trap. Sherman went after him, clashing with Confederates at Allatoona Pass, but felt he was wasting his time. "Hood can turn and twist like a fox," he complained, "and wear out my army in pursuit." Unwilling to devote all his strength to pursuing Hood, Sherman divided his ample forces, sending troops under General George Thomas—the ever-dependable Rock of Chickamauga—to Tennessee to counter Hood's advance while he himself returned to Atlanta and gathered 62,000 men for a punitive march across Georgia to the sea. "I can make this march, and make Georgia howl!" he assured Grant, who was initially skeptical. "Do you not think it advisable now that Hood has gone so far north to entirely settle with him before starting on your proposed campaign?" Grant wrote Sherman. "With Hood's army destroyed you can go where you please with impunity." But Sherman convinced Grant that the planned march to Savannah would strike a devastating blow to Jefferson Davis and his cause. "If we can march a well-appointed army right through his territory," Sherman argued, "it is a demonstration to the world, foreign and domestic, that we have a power which Davis cannot resist."

On November 16, Sherman left Atlanta, after ordering what was left of the industrial area set ablaze. "Just outside of the old rebel works," Sherman related, he paused with his aides "to look back upon the scenes of our old battles. Behind us lay Atlanta, smouldering and in ruins, the black smoke rising high in the air, and hanging like a pall over the ruined city." Not everything was ruined—many homes remained intact—but Sherman was satisfied that Atlanta would be of little use to anyone for the remainder of the conflict. On their way to Savannah, his men relied largely on foraging, which Sherman encouraged as a way of stripping the country bare. One woman whose farm lay in Sherman's path described what it was like to have ravenous Federals pick her property clean: "To my smoke-house, my dairy, pantry, kitchen, and cellar, like famished wolves they come, breaking locks and whatever is in their way. . . . My eighteen fat turkeys, my hens, chickens, and fowls, my young pigs, are shot down in my yard and hunted as if they were rebels themselves."

"I can make this march, and make Georgia howl!"

GENERAL WILLIAM SHERMAN TO GENERAL GRANT, *before advancing from Atlanta to Savannah*

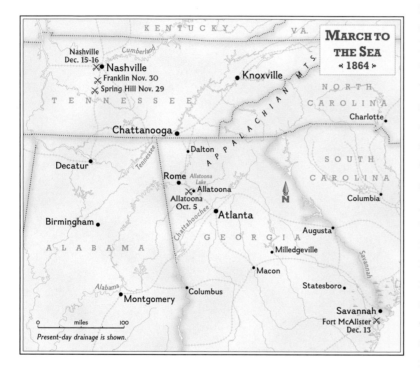

After taking Atlanta, William Sherman had two objectives in the fall of 1864: to finish off Hood's army in Tennessee and to march eastward across Georgia to Savannah, demoralizing the populace and exhausting their resources. Sherman himself led the march to Savannah in mid-November and entrusted the campaign in Tennessee to George Thomas, who settled with Hood at Nashville in December.

Sherman's men seldom assaulted civilians, and Georgians were not too intimidated to protest when soldiers ransacked their homes. "Our men will fight you as long as they live," one woman warned the Federals. "You can kill us, but you can't conquer us," another declared. Diarist Eliza Frances Andrews told of her dismay at witnessing the devastation Sherman's men caused. "The fields were trampled down and the road lined with carcasses of horses, hogs, and cattle that the invaders, unable either to consume or carry away with them, had wantonly shot down to starve out the people and prevent them from making their crops," she wrote. "I almost felt as if I should like to hang a Yankee myself." Many Georgians fled their homes before Sherman's troops arrived, and more than 10,000 fugitive slaves sought refuge with the Federals, trailing behind them as they marched eastward. Sherman felt encumbered by them and defended one of his corps commanders—a general from Kentucky with the unfortunate name of Jefferson C. Davis—after he prevented blacks from following his forces by dismantling a pontoon bridge and stranding them on the far side of a swollen stream called Ebenezer Creek. Fearing that oncoming Confederate cavalry would seize them and return them to slavery, many jumped into the water but were unable to swim across and drowned.

Confederate troopers under General Joseph Wheeler harassed the Federals as they advanced, but Sherman otherwise encountered little resistance. On November 22, at the village of Griswoldville, 3,000 untrained Georgia militiamen made a brave but suicidal attack on a brigade of Federals armed with Spencer repeating rifles. As one Union officer wrote afterward: "Old grey haired and weakly looking men and little boys, not over 15 years old, lay dead or writhing in pain. I hope we shall never have to shoot at such men again." The raw courage of those militiamen was not equaled by state legislators, who

> **"The fields were trampled down and the road lined with carcasses of horses, hogs, and cattle that the invaders, unable either to consume or carry away with them, had wantonly shot down to starve out the people and prevent them from making their crops."**
>
> Eliza Frances Andrews, *on the devastation caused by Sherman's troops*

In this composite view of Sherman's march, liberated slaves follow his army as Union troops devastate Georgia by foraging for livestock, wrecking a bridge, and destroying railroad tracks and telegraph lines. To prevent Confederates from repairing tracks, Federals heated the iron rails over bonfires and twisted them into loops called "Sherman's neckties."

ANDERSONVILLE

"I am afraid God will suffer some terrible retribution to fall upon us for letting such things happen."

Southern woman, after visiting Andersonville

MORE THAN 400,000 SOLDIERS WERE HELD PRISoner over the course of the war. The 150 facilities that served as military prisons were mostly ill-equipped for the unexpected numbers of captured men, leading to ghoulish scenes of emaciated prisoners crowded together in filthy conditions. The death rate in prison was more than twice that on the battlefield.

No prison exemplified this suffering more than the notorious Confederate stockade near Andersonville, Georgia. Officially called Camp Sumter by the Rebels, it was built by slave labor in January of 1864 to accommodate the overflow of Union prisoners from Richmond. The first group arrived by train in February, even before the last pine log was installed in the surrounding fence.

The 16-acre site was designed to accommodate 10,000 prisoners, but by August of 1864, despite being enlarged to 26 acres, Andersonville was bulging with nearly 33,000 men, an average space of 34 square feet per man. There were no barracks or shelters—the tents shown in the photo at right were improvised by the inmates out of blankets and sticks. Malnutrition, exposure, and disease claimed more than 100 lives per day during the hottest days of summer. Others were shot for crossing the "deadline"—a low fence about 20 feet inside the stockade walls.

Andersonville prisoners were moved in September of 1864 as Sherman invaded Georgia, but eventually returned. In its short existence an astonishing 13,000 men died here. It was synonymous with barbarity, and as a result, Captain Henry Wirz, the camp's commander, became the war's only figure executed for war crimes. ■

The Andersonville latrine, in the foreground, was dug alongside the stream from which prisoners drew bathing and drinking water, resulting in a high disease mortality rate.

declared boldly, "Death is to be preferred to loss of liberty," then hastily abandoned their capital, Milledgeville, to the Federals. By month's end, Sherman was nearing Savannah. Some 10,000 Confederate troops awaited him there behind strong fortifications, but he was confident now that the calculated gamble he took by dividing his forces would pay off handsomely. The only army large enough to threaten him was hundreds of miles away in Tennessee under Hood, who was soon to butt heads with the Rock of Chickamauga.

HOOD'S LAST STAND

HE BLAMED EVERYONE BUT HIMSELF. ON NOVEMBER 30, HOOD AWOKE TO FIND that his plan to divide and conquer Federal forces in Tennessee had gone badly awry. The night before, he had been on the verge of cutting off General John Schofield as he hurried northward through the town of Spring Hill with 30,000 troops to link up at Nashville with his commander, George Thomas. This promised to be "the best move in my career as a soldier," he wrote, but his forces failed to block the turnpike overnight and the enemy slipped quietly past them. Hood bore ultimate responsibility for this blunder but faulted his troops, complaining that they seemed "unwilling to accept battle unless under the protection of breastworks." They, in turn, were losing confidence in him. "Not that we doubted his courage," one soldier wrote, "but we clearly saw that his capacities better suited him to command a division."

Hood hurried after Schofield and caught up with him that afternoon at Franklin, less than 20 miles from Nashville. Federals were waiting there behind breastworks that offered them a clear field of fire as Confederates approached. "I do not like the looks of this fight," corps commander Benjamin Cheatham told Hood; "the enemy has an excellent position and is well fortified." Hood decided to attack nonetheless, prompting Brigadier General Daniel Govan to remark to his fellow Arkansan Patrick Cleburne—an esteemed division commander who may have been better suited than Hood to lead this army—that they might not get back to Arkansas.

"Well, Govan, if we are to die," Cleburne replied, "let us die like men." That same fatalistic determination seemed to possess the army as a whole as it entered battle. Smashing exposed Federals led by Major General George Wagner, who ignored warnings to pull back to the main line, Confederates advanced close behind the retreating Yankees and swarmed over the breastworks. It looked briefly as if Hood's desperate gamble might succeed, until Colonel Emerson Opdycke—who had defied his superior, Wagner, and pulled his brigade back within the works—led a counterattack and repulsed the Confederates. As darkness descended, Hood's troops continued their assaults all along the line, taking terrible punishment. As one Federal officer, Colonel Henry Stone, wrote: "It is impossible to exaggerate the fierce energy with which the Confederate soldiers, that short November afternoon, threw themselves against the works, fighting with what seemed the very madness of despair." Patrick Cleburne was among six Confederate generals who perished. Hood's attack failed to prevent Schofield, whose troops suffered around 2,000 casualties, from continuing north and linking up with Thomas. That brought Federal strength at Nashville to over 50,000 troops, whereas Hood had

> **"It is impossible to exaggerate the fierce energy with which the Confederate soldiers, that short November afternoon, threw themselves against the works, fighting with what seemed the very madness of despair."**
>
> UNION COLONEL HENRY STONE,
> *at Franklin, Tennessee*

barely half that number left after losing more than 6,000 men at Franklin.

Hood's troops had demonstrated that they would accept battle under any circumstances—something he should never have doubted. He now had to decide if the circumstances of this campaign justified further sacrifices on their part. Nashville was heavily fortified, and Hood conceded he could not assault the Federals "in their stronghold with any hope of success." Yet he thought that if he coaxed his opponent into leaving his works and attacking, Thomas might prove vulnerable to a counterstroke. It was a faint hope, but Hood acted on it and led his battered army to the outskirts of Nashville. Hood was right about one thing. His presence outside Nashville led Thomas to attack, although not as quickly as Grant and Lincoln wanted. A painstaking general, he spent a week developing his plans, and an ice storm further delayed his offensive. "There is no better man to repel an attack than Thomas, but I fear he is too cautious to take the initiative," concluded Grant, who was about to change commanders when the weather improved and Thomas forged ahead.

On December 15, Federals descended in full force on Hood's troops below Nashville, sweeping around their left flank and forcing them to abandon their first line of defense. Here as at Chattanooga a year earlier, Thomas's troops did not wait for orders to pursue retreating Confederates. "On reaching the enemy's works," wrote Corporal George Herr of the 59th Illinois Infantry, "the men in the advance could plainly see another line of entrenchments further on." Officers ordered the Federals to halt, but they were "bound to have the next line," Herr added, and did not stop until they reached that goal, "capturing many prisoners, two flags and four pieces of artillery."

By evening, the Confederates had fallen back two miles to a new defensive line strung between two hills. Hood still hoped to counterattack, but when fighting resumed the next day, Thomas kept up the pressure and sent troops

Federals who did not go into battle against Hood's Confederates at Nashville on December 15 gathered here on this hillside below the city to watch the contest unfold. The shadowy figure at left moved while this photograph was being taken.

charging up the slopes on either flank. The battle was decided that afternoon on Shy's Hill to the west—so-called for Lieutenant Colonel William
Shy of Tennessee, who fell along with many other Confederates when Federals seized the heights in a rush. "Nothing save annihilation could stop
the onward progress of that line," one Union officer wrote proudly. Their
line shattered, Hood's men retreated in disarray, having suffered another
6,000 casualties at Nashville, twice as many as their foes. The Army of
Tennessee would never fight again, and Hood was through as well. A soldier saw him that night pulling at his hair with his one good hand and "crying like his heart would break."

Meanwhile, Sherman was celebrating a coup of his own that all but
sealed the fate of Savannah. On December 13, his forces had attacked Fort
McAllister, at the mouth of the Ogeechee River, below Savannah, where
Sherman planned to link up with Federal supply ships. As troops led by
Brigadier General William Hazen prepared to storm that bastion, a Fed-
eral ship approached and signaled to Sherman, "Is Fort McAllister taken?"

"Not yet, but it will be in a minute!" he replied. Moments later, he wrote,
"we saw Hazen's troops come out of the dark fringe of woods that encom-
passed the fort, the lines dressed as on parade, with colors flying, and moving forward with a quick steady pace." Advancing relentlessly under heavy
artillery fire across ground sown with land mines, they quickly seized the
fort. "I've got Savannah!" Sherman exulted. Supplied by ship with food,
ammunition, and siege guns, his men could now pound the city into submission. In a letter to General William Hardee, commanding Savannah's
defenses, he demanded its surrender, warning that otherwise he would
make "little effort to restrain my army." Hardee replied firmly that he had
always strictly observed "the rules of civilized warfare" and would "deeply
regret the adoption of any course by you that would force me to deviate
from them in future." He knew that Savannah could not long withstand a
siege, however, and he had to save his forces.

On the night of December 20, Hardee's troops withdrew on a pontoon
bridge across the Savannah River into South Carolina. "They pulled out in
a big hurry," wrote one Federal who entered the city the next day. Left
behind were items such as cotton from nearby plantations. On December
24, Sherman shared his momentous victory with Lincoln by telegram: "I
beg to present you, as a Christmas gift, the city of Savannah, with 150 heavy
guns and plenty of ammunition, and also about 25,000 bales of cotton."

*Minnesotans of General John McArthur's division attack Confederates on Shy's Hill at Nashville on
December 16, advancing into a "fierce storm of shell, canister, and musketry," as one Union officer
put it. When Hood's forces gave way here, another Federal wrote, "the whole Confederate left was
crushed in like an egg-shell."*

THE MEDICAL MIDDLE AGES

"If a fellow has [to go to the] Hospital, you might as well say goodbye."

Union soldier

THE CIVIL WAR WAS FOUGHT WITH MODERN weapons and archaic tactics, the result of which was human slaughter on an appalling and unprecedented scale.

The ranks of both armies were populated with West Pointers trained to attack with infantry units en masse, supported by artillery. The "tactical offensive" had served many Union and Confederate generals well in the Mexican-American War, where the main infantry weapon, the smoothbore musket, had a limited range of accuracy and potency. But with the proliferation of rifled muskets and repeating weapons, the long-range killing power of the infantryman increased dramatically. Charging infantry and cavalry could now be picked off from three or four hundred yards away.

Many officers recognized the need for new tactics, but in the days before field radios, loosening up formations was easier said than done. There was always glory in the charge, too, even as good defense proved to be more valuable than good offense. "It was thought to be a great thing to charge a battery of artillery or an earthwork lined with infantry," wrote D. H. Hill, reflecting on the Seven Days' Battles. "We were very lavish in blood in those days."

To make matters worse, the power to heal was nowhere close to the power to maim. Germ theory and antiseptics were largely unknown to Civil War doctors, who didn't understand the value of sanitation or nutrition, how diseases spread, or how to stop infection. It

Using an instrument kit that resembled a carpenter's tool box more than a modern surgical bag, a Civil War surgeon could remove a damaged limb in 15 minutes. The procedure usually took place on a makeshift table on the field (right) to beat the onset of infection.

was no wonder, then, that Union Surgeon General William Hammond lamented that the war was fought "at the end of the medical middle ages."

SHEER BUTCHERY

THE GRISLY PROCEDURE OF AMPUTATION BECAME EMBLEMatic of Civil War medicine because it was often the only option for saving a wounded soldier's life. The .58-caliber minié balls used in the powerful new rifled muskets often shattered bones, leaving no choice but to remove the damaged limb. Amputation was also the only way surgeons knew to stop the spread of infection or gangrene.

The assembly line fashion with which surgeons removed limbs made them despised for their "sheer butchery," as one wounded man put it. The heat of battle also left little time for decorum. Mary McAllister, a Gettysburg resident pressed into service as a nurse when the Union had to turn a local church into a field hospital, watched as a surgeon "cut off legs and arms and threw them out of the windows." One Yankee soldier described coming upon a field hospital on a farm: "About the building you could see the hogs belonging to the Farm eating [amputated] arms and other portions of the body."

Medical care in the field was crude in general, with tents serving as hospitals and untrained personnel charged with evacuation. "I was wounded Saturday p.m.," wrote a New York private after Second Bull Run. "I laid on the battlefield for 48 hours and then rode in a government wagon for 48 more [before] my wound was dressed for the first time." Jonathan W. Letterman, medical director for the Army of the Potomac, helped improve conditions vastly by organizing field hospitals by division rather than regiment, and giving specific jobs to each doctor, a system that became the model. He was also instrumental in creating a dedicated ambulance corps, which was initiated at Antietam.

Despite the handicaps, Civil War doctors were remarkably effective. Amputation really did save lives. In the end, only 14 percent of Federal soldiers died from their wounds, and 18 percent of Confederates—a high number only by modern standards.

Far more deadly to the soldier than the minié ball was disease, which killed twice as many combatants. Poor sanitation and hygiene were largely to blame, as contaminated water exposed men to diarrhea, dysentery,

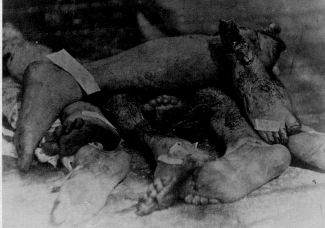

Amputated feet are piled up for disposal. Ideally they were buried; often they had to be tossed aside or left in a heap.

Wounded Federals convalesce on the grounds of a field hospital near the Marye House at Fredericksburg, Virginia, before being transported to general hospitals in Alexandria and Washington, D.C. A Zouave ambulance crew (left) demonstrates the removal of wounded soldiers from the field. The organization of a dedicated ambulance corps by the Union's medical director greatly improved the evacuation of wounded from the battlefield.

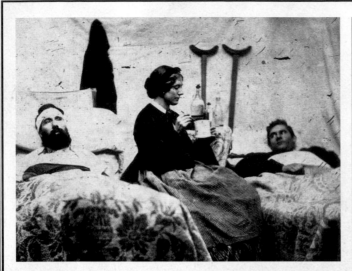

A nurse tends to the wounded in a Federal hospital in Nashville. By Civil War standards, Washington's Armory Square Hospital (right) could be considered luxurious.

and "camp fevers" such as typhoid and typhus. Many rural soldiers had never been exposed to certain contagions, so that soldiers crowded together in tents transmitted childhood diseases like mumps, measles, and even smallpox to one another, . There were also the so-called surgical fevers, which were caused by the use of unsterilized instruments.

In the end, the war's three main killers were diarrhea and dysentery, typhoid, and pneumonia, with malaria fourth. Illness also severely disrupted maneuvers and strategy, as it was not uncommon for entire units to be felled by various maladies. Yet compared to previous wars, disease mortality was low, thanks in part to some gradual improvements in nursing and sanitation, especially on the Union side.

ORGANIZING CARE

NEITHER SIDE WAS PREPARED TO DEAL WITH THE SHOCKing numbers of wounded. The North had only 16 army hospitals at the start of the war; the South had even fewer. By war's end there were 204 and 154, respectively.

Into this gulf flowed tens of thousands of volunteers to help raise money and supplies for army hospitals and to tend to the wounded, including women who defied all expectations of what the "fairer sex" could stomach. Despite Florence Nightingale's much-publicized work in the Crimean War, American women were considered unfit for a military hospital. But such prejudice was soon overwhelmed by the need for both trained nurses and

DOROTHEA DIX

SALLY TOMKINS

MARY ANN "MOTHER" BICKERDYKE

Angels of mercy: Social activist Dorothea Dix was appointed Union superintendent of female nurses. Sally Tomkins was made a Confederate captain so her Richmond infirmary could qualify as an army hospital. Mary Ann "Mother" Bickerdyke was the only woman Sherman allowed in his advance base hospitals.

volunteers, and a number of women became famous in their own right.

On the Union side were Clara Barton and Mary Ann "Mother" Bickerdyke, who was renowned for her ability to find food and clean wounds in the primitive field conditions of the Western Theater. The South had Mobile's Kate Cumming, who defied her family to volunteer at Shiloh, and Sally Louisa Tomkins, whose small infirmary in Richmond was so well-run that Jefferson Davis commissioned her as a captain so the site could qualify as an army hospital. Cumming and another notable volunteer, Louisa May Alcott, both published books after the war vividly documenting their experiences, as did Susie King Taylor, who worked with Clara Barton in South Carolina and became the only African-American woman to publish a Civil War memoir.

Physicians soon came to prefer trained female nurses over their former soldier nurses, who didn't know "castor oil from a gun rod." By 1862 official preference was given to female nurses in recruitment, paving the way for nursing to become a legitimate profession for women after the war.

One of the organizations instrumental in this sea-change was the volunteer Women's Central Association for Relief. Organized just after the fall of Fort Sumter by Elizabeth Blackwell, the first American women to earn a doctor of medicine degree, the initial purpose of the association was to train nurses. But out of the group's lobbying efforts emerged a national organization, sanctioned by the government, that proved hugely important to the Union: The United States Sanitary Commission.

The Sanitary, as it was called, coordinated the efforts of thousands of local volunteer groups. It provided food, supplies, and nurses to Union camps and field hospitals. It outfitted steamers as mobile medical ships and created hospital trains, both for treatment and evacuation. It raised millions of dollars in funds. And it helped instruct soldiers in proper camp procedures, such as drainage, latrine placement, water supply, and cooking—all of which helped reduce instances of disease and sickness among Federal troops. ■

This sampling of cartes de visite are from a catalog assembled by Dr. Reed Brockway Bontecou, a Federal surgeon and director of Washington's Harewood Army Hospital. His documentation of war wounds and their treatment proved valuable for training young physicians.

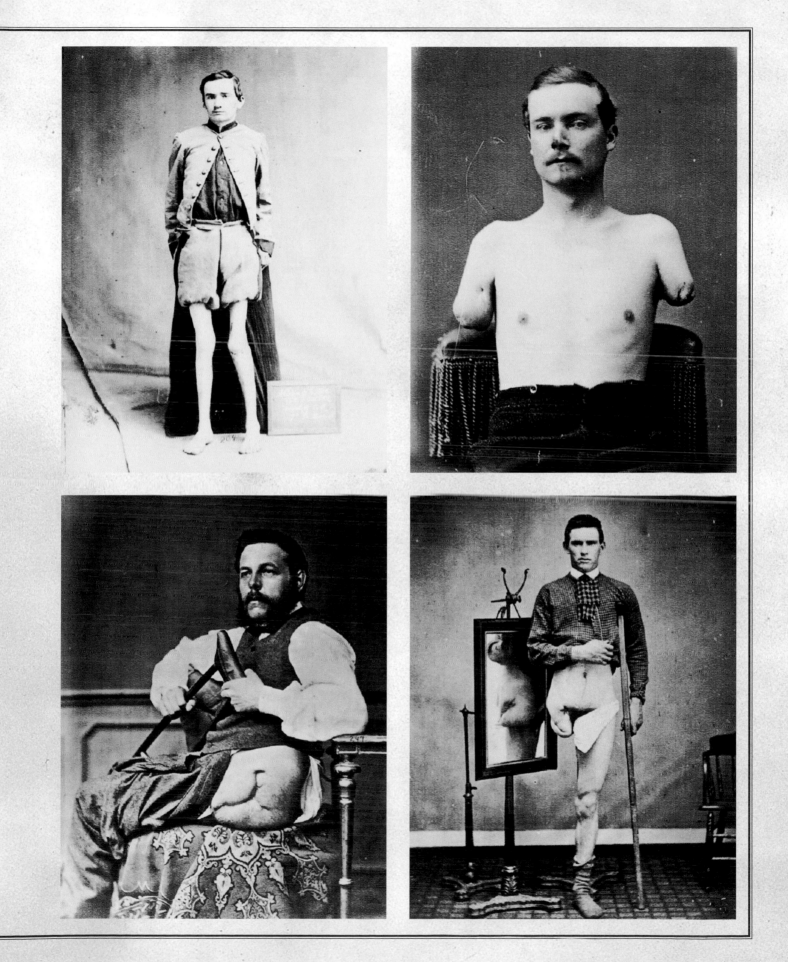

CHAPTER 5

1865
THE FINAL ACT

ON APRIL 7, 1865, NEAR APPOMATTOX COURT HOUSE IN VIRGINIA, Robert E. Lee received a message from Ulysses Grant. "The results of the last week must convince you of the hopelessness of further resistance on the part of the Army of Northern Virginia," wrote Grant, who asked Lee to avoid "any further effusion of blood" by surrendering. The past week—and the past few months—had indeed been calamitous for the Confederacy. After a long and grueling siege, Petersburg had finally fallen to Grant, leading to the abandonment of Richmond, part of which lay in ruins. Farther south, Sherman had resumed his punishing campaign by sweeping northward from Savannah through the Carolinas and repulsing Confederates led by Joseph Johnston. Lee's starving troops were now vastly outnumbered by their opponents. But when he showed Grant's note to James Longstreet, his old warhorse, Longstreet replied firmly, "Not yet."

Longstreet and Lee had suspected for some time that their cause was lost. Yet they felt obliged to play out their parts dutifully in this great national drama called the Civil War, if only for a few more days, until there was no possibility whatsoever of altering the outcome. Soldiers and civilians on both sides continued to fulfill their assigned roles until the curtain came down. There would be no let-up until the final scene of the final act, when the man who saw the Union through to its triumphant finish, Abraham Lincoln, was cut down by an assassin in Ford's Theatre. ∎

Two women in black walk through the ruins of Richmond after Confederates abandoned their capital on the night of April 2, destroying supplies by kindling fires, which spread rapidly. "Women were weeping, children crying," wrote a reporter who entered the city after Federal troops took possession. "Men stood speechless, haggard, woebegone, gazing at the desolation."

CONQUERING THE CAROLINAS

FEW CONFEDERATE OFFICERS HELD A MORE CRITICAL POSITION AS THEIR country tottered on the brink of defeat than Colonel William Lamb, the 29-year-old commander of Fort Fisher, guarding the entrance to the Cape Fear River and the strategic port of Wilmington, North Carolina. This was "the last gateway between the Confederate States and the outside world," wrote Lamb, whose fort kept Federal warships away from Wilmington and shielded blockade runners that delivered goods vital to the Rebel cause. By January 1865, other Southern ports were sealed off and almost everything Confederates imported came through Wilmington. Within the past few months, nearly 70,000 rifles and 500,000 pairs of shoes had been unloaded there, along with tons of meat, much of which found its way to Lee's forces at Petersburg. "General Lee sent me word that Fort Fisher must be held," Lamb remarked, "or he could not subsist his army."

In January 1865, Federals moved to close the port of Wilmington by attacking Fort Fisher while Sherman prepared to march north from Savannah through the interior of the Carolinas, seizing Columbia and forcing the surrender of Charleston. When Sherman repulsed Joseph Johnston's Confederates at Bentonville in March, Lee's army at Petersburg became the last hope for Richmond and the Southern cause.

Seizing Fort Fisher became an urgent matter for the Union when William Sherman reached the coast of Georgia and took Savannah. From there, he planned to proceed northward through the heart of the Carolinas, wrecking railroads, industries, and other Confederate assets along the way. If this campaign succeeded, it would force the surrender of Charleston, South Carolina, the cradle of the rebellion, which was already cut off by sea and would be cut off by land as well. Wilmington would suffer the same fate if Federals captured Fort Fisher and sealed off the port in advance of Sherman's march. Once Wilmington fell, it could serve as a supply depot for his forces.

At dawn on January 13, Colonel Lamb and his men looked out from the fort and beheld a massive armada of 59 warships and dozens of transports, carrying 8,500 troops. Lamb had only about 1,500 soldiers to contend with this huge amphibious expedition, jointly commanded by Rear Admiral David Porter, a veteran of the New Orleans and Vicksburg campaigns, and Major General Alfred Terry. Lamb hoped for reinforcements from Wilmington, where General Braxton Bragg commanded a defense force of over 5,000 men, but Bragg held most of them back. Later that day, Major General W.H.C. Whiting, who had overseen the construction of Fort Fisher, arrived there from Wilmington with alarming news for its commander. "Lamb, my boy, I have come to share your fate," he said. "You and your garrison are to be sacrificed."

Lamb, who had withstood an earlier Federal assault here in December, was

not about to concede defeat. "We shall certainly whip the enemy again," he told Whiting, but he faced a much greater challenge now. In December, Porter's warships had fired indiscriminately at long range, doing little damage to the fort, which was bolstered with timbers, sod, and mounds of sand that blunted the impact of incoming shots. This time, the ships anchored less than a thousand yards from their target—located at the southern tip of a peninsula separating the Atlantic Ocean from the Cape Fear River—and fired with devastating accuracy on the fort's cannon and the men serving them, who were short of ammunition and could return shots only once every half hour. "All day and night on the 13th and 14th of January the navy continued its ceaseless torment," Lamb recalled. "We could scarcely gather up and bury our dead without fresh casualties. At least two hundred had been killed and wounded in the two days since the fighting began."

By January 15, General Terry's troops had landed north of the fort and were preparing to assault the stronghold. Although 20 of its 44 guns faced north to repulse an attack by land, few of them were still in service when the infantry approached. Admiral Porter, who was always hankering for glory, insisted that 2,000 of his sailors and Marines join in the operation. Sailors armed with cutlasses and revolvers were to "board the fort on the run in a seaman-like way," he instructed, while the Marines followed close behind them and provided cover. Storming a fort was nothing like boarding a ship, however, and the seamen had no training for the task. To make matters worse, they struck first, at the northeast corner of the fort, before Terry's troops attacked to the west, along the river. When the sailors rushed the fort in a jumble and charged up the embankment, "a murderous fire greeted them and swept them down," Colonel Lamb related. "Volley after volley was poured into their faltering ranks

Battery Lamb at Fort Fisher, shown here after it fell to the Federals, was named for Colonel William Lamb, who commanded the Confederate garrison there. The fort was built to "withstand the heaviest bombardment," Lamb wrote, but was "extremely difficult to defend against assault after its guns were destroyed. The soldiers in the gun-chambers could not see the approach in front for a hundred feet, and to repel assailants they had to leave all cover and stand upon the open parapet."

"General Lee sent me word that Fort Fisher must be held, or he could not subsist his army."

CONFEDERATE COLONEL WILLIAM LAMB

HEAVY ARTILLERY

"It is probable that never since the invention of gunpowder has such a cannonade taken place."

*Federal officer in charge of
the final bombardment of Petersburg*

THE SHEER SIZE OF HEAVY ARTILLERY—MORTARS, siege and seacoast cannon—mostly confined their firepower to defensive fortifications. But new technology in the form of massive rifled guns capable of accurate long-range fire made these weapons increasingly important in siege operations, beginning with the Federal siege of Charleston in 1863 and especially in the decisive siege of Petersburg at the end of the war.

Among the new rifled cannon were the distinctive Parrott guns, named for their inventor, which came in 100-pounder, 200-pounder, and 300-pounder versions. The most famous of these was the Swamp Angel, a 200-pounder hauled into the marshes of Morris Island to assault Charleston. It saw action for two days before the cannon exploded, a constant hazard with these guns. More reliable were good old-fashioned mortars, like the mighty Dictator (see pages 292-293), used to lob 200-pound shells at the Rebels entrenched at Petersburg.

The choice of heavy artillery and their projectiles depended on the target. Big-bore cannon were intended as breaching guns, for direct fire in smashing down stone and brickwork walls. Mortars, with their extremely high-arcing trajectory, were used for indirect fire into the interior of fortified positions. Direct fire generally called for solid shot or percussion-fuse shells (for mortars) that exploded on impact. To fire on troops, a battery would use shells that burst in midair and scattered shrapnel, or the dreaded case shot and canister, both of which created a shotgun effect. ■

Using 100-pounder Parrott rifles at Battery Rosecrans on Morris Island, the 3rd Rhode Island Heavy Artillery helped reduce Fort Sumter to a rubble pile during the 1863 siege of Charleston.

by cool, determined men, and in half an hour several hundred dead and wounded lay at the foot of the bastion. The bravery of the officers could not restrain their men from panic and retreat."

Confederates cheered their apparent victory, but they could not see beyond the fort's walls and were unaware of the greater threat that loomed to the west as Terry's infantry came on. Lamb had no more warning of that than his men did. "As our shouts of triumph went up," he wrote, "I turned to look at the western salient, and saw to my astonishment, three Federal battle-flags upon our ramparts." Pouring over the walls, Union troops met with fierce resistance and grappled hand to hand with their foes. During the ensuing battle, both Colonel Lamb and General Whiting were severely wounded. Informed by an aide that evening that "it was impossible to hold out much longer," Lamb vowed that "so long as I lived I would not surrender the fort; that Bragg must soon come to the rescue." Bragg was haunted by his earlier defeats in Tennessee, however, and all too aware of the enemy's advantages in men and arms. Given the forces arrayed against Fort Fisher, "it had to fall eventually," he concluded. He would not expend more troops to forestall what he saw as inevitable.

The burden of surrendering the fort fell to Lamb's next-in-command, Major James Reilly, who raised a white flag that night at ten. Porter's fleet sent up rockets in celebration, illuminating the carnage on shore. A sailor who entered the captured fort told of seeing "great heaps of human beings laying just as they fell, one upon the other." It was a bloody day's work, one that left over 500 Confederates and 1,300 Union troops dead or wounded. Yet the Federals not only seized the fort and captured its surviving defenders but went on to take Wilmington, which fell in February. Four years earlier, General Winfield Scott had set the Union blockade in motion by proposing the Anaconda Plan, designed to squeeze the life out of the Confederacy. With the capture of Fort Fisher—which Confederate Vice President Alexander Stephens called "one of the greatest disasters" ever to befall his cause—that Herculean task was accomplished. In the words of Raphael Semmes, a celebrated Confederate raider on the high seas: "The anaconda had, at last, wound his fatal folds around us."

SHERMAN MOVES NORTH

"THE DEVIL HIMSELF COULDN'T RESTRAIN MY MEN," REMARKED SHERMAN AS HE prepared to invade South Carolina, which had launched the rebellion and now faced severe punishment. "I almost tremble at her fate," he wrote, "but feel that she deserves all that seems in store for her." Departing Savannah in late January, his men proceeded northward in two columns toward Columbia, the capital of South Carolina. Sherman's cavalry commander, Brigadier General Judson Kilpatrick, welcomed the opportunity to set this rebellious state ablaze and reportedly spent $5,000 equipping his men with matches. "How shall I let you know where I am?" he asked Sherman before moving out ahead of the infantry. "Oh, just burn a barn or something," Sherman replied. "Make a smoke like the Indians do." Kilpatrick's troopers wreaked such havoc in the town of Barnwell in early February that Federals referred to it afterward as Burnwell.

Rivaling the cavalry in its destructive impact were Sherman's foragers. Some men carried out that task with discipline and restraint under the direction of

"How shall I let you know where I am?"

BRIGADIER GENERAL JUDSON KILPATRICK, *before leading Sherman's cavalry through South Carolina*

"Oh, just burn a barn or something. Make a smoke like the Indians do."

GENERAL SHERMAN, *in response to Kilpatrick*

officers, but others acted as irregulars, wearing civilian dress and flouting military conventions. Known as bummers, they intimidated civilians and sometimes attacked them, provoking violent retribution by Confederates. Near Columbia, a woman was raped, setting off a spate of revenge killings. Some Federals were found with their throats cut and notes pinned to their bodies reading, "Death to all foragers." Sherman did not condone attacks on civilians, but he looked the other way when his troops went beyond the authorized destruction of factories or public buildings and torched homes. "The grudge held against South Carolina and her people by many soldiers was very intense,"

[EYEWITNESS]

Major Thomas A. Huguenin
1ST SOUTH CAROLINA INFANTRY (REGULARS)

Just as he had been the last officer to leave Battery Wagner, Huguenin now assumed the duty of overseeing the evacuation of Fort Sumter. At about 10 p.m. on February 17, after calling the roll and relieving the sentinels, he ordered the 300-man garrison to board two small steam transports. Major Huguenin himself cast off the mooring lines and was the last Confederate to leave Fort Sumter.

THE NEXT MORNing the 17th a new flag was raised, which was never fired upon, and the garrison were informed that we were ordered to evacuate the fort on that night. At sunset the evening gun was fired—and all the preparations for an assault were made as usual. About nine or ten o'clock two small steamers came to the fort and the troops were marched by detachments aboard. When all had been embarked, except the guard, I personally with the Adjt. and Chief Engineer relieved them and ordered them to embark. It was now near 12 o'clock, but singular to say the enemy tho' firing heavily on Sullivans Island did not fire a single shot at us. Under orders received no public property of any description was destroyed except some whiskey which I had emptied into the water for fear the men might get hold of it during the retreat and create a disturbance. My own library of valuable military books I burnt up in the fire-place of my quarters, the official records were sewed up in a pair of my drawers and carried along with us. After visiting every portion of the fort, with a heavy heart I reached the wharf, no one was left behind but many a heart clung to those sacred and battle scarred ramparts, I cannot describe my emotions. I felt as if every tie held dear to me was about to be severed; the pride and glory of Sumter was there, and now in the gloom of darkness we were to abandon her, for whom every one of us would have shed the last drop of his blood. ■

"I felt as if every tie held dear to me was about to be severed; the pride and glory of Sumter was there, and now in the gloom of darkness we were to abandon her."

Two Rebel soldiers pose amid the rubble of Fort Sumter's eastern casemates in this photo by Charleston photographer George S. Cook.

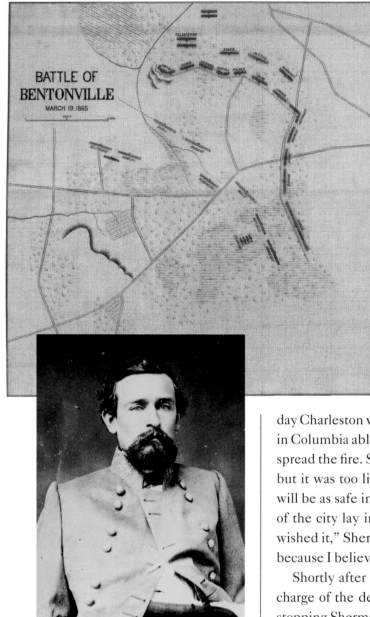

BATTLE OF BENTONVILLE
MARCH 19, 1865

Brigadier General Laurence Baker, wounded earlier in the war and rendered unfit for service, nonetheless returned to duty and led a brigade of underage North Carolina reserves against Sherman's troops at Bentonville. The position of Baker's brigade as the battle began is shown in red on the period map at top, behind the main Confederate line. Among the young Southerners who fought and died at Bentonville was the 16-year-old son of General William Hardee.

wrote Sergeant Rice Bull of 123rd New York Infantry; "many times they ruthlessly destroyed property when they heard it belonged to an active secessionist. They excused their actions by saying that they wished such people to suffer for their responsibility in bringing upon our country the Civil War."

Charleston, where the rebellion began, was fortunate in that it was not occupied by Sherman's vengeful troops when Confederates abandoned the city on February 17, bringing to an end four years of defiance in which troops occupying Fort Sumter and other bastions there withstood repeated Federal assaults by land and by sea. Instead, a black regiment, the 55th Massachusetts Infantry, took possession of Charleston, to the delight of many freed slaves there. "Cheers, blessings, prayers were heard on every side," wrote the regiment's commander, whose men saved much of the city from ruin by putting out fires Confederates had set to destroy military supplies and other assets of value to the enemy. Columbia, occupied by Sherman's men the same day Charleston was abandoned, fared far worse. Confederates set cotton stored in Columbia ablaze before they left, and drunken, disorderly Federals helped spread the fire. Sherman sent out brigades to restore order and fight the blaze, but it was too little too late. "You can sleep tonight satisfied that your town will be as safe in my hands as in yours," he told Columbia's mayor, but much of the city lay in ruins the next day. "Though I never ordered it and never wished it," Sherman wrote later, "I have never shed any tears over this event, because I believed that it hastened what we all fought for, the end of the war."

Shortly after Columbia went up in flames, General Joseph Johnston took charge of the defense of the Carolinas and tried to form an army capable of stopping Sherman. Among the troops he assembled were the soldiers Braxton Bragg and William Hardee had withdrawn recently from Wilmington and Savannah, and several thousand holdovers from the shattered Army of Tennessee. Altogether, he had about 20,000 Confederates to contend with Sherman's army, which had been reinforced over the winter and now numbered about 70,000 men. Johnston's only hope was to catch Sherman's forces while they were still divided and defeat one wing before the other came to its aid. After clashing indecisively in North Carolina with Federals at Kinston and Averasboro, Johnston found the opportunity he was seeking at Bentonville on March 19 and surprised Major General Henry Slocum, commanding Sherman's left wing. A skirmish with Confederate troopers there the day before had given Slocum the false impression he had only cavalry to contend with. Although many of his forces had not yet reached Bentonville, he told Sherman he needed no help. Then around noon, an aide brought him alarming news. A division sent to deal with those enemy troopers had instead encountered Confederate infantry entrenched "along our whole front, and enough of them to give us all the amusement we shall want for the rest of the day." Swallowing his pride, Slocum called for assistance and braced his men for a struggle.

For a few hours that afternoon, Johnston's men fought like the Confederates of old and sent their enemies reeling. After pressing forward for nearly a mile, however, they came up against reinforcements summoned by Slocum. "The enemy fought bravely," he wrote, "but their line had become somewhat broken in advancing through the woods." Forced back under heavy fire, they tried again. "The assaults were repeated over and over until a late hour," Slocum added, "each assault finding us better prepared for resistance." By evening, he had all his forces at hand and felt strong enough to handle anything Johnston threw at him. "That night the whole left wing was in line and well entrenched," wrote Sergeant Rice Bull; "so we had no fears of the morrow." When Sherman's right wing, commanded by General Oliver Howard, reached Bentonville the next day, the odds swung heavily in favor of the Federals, but Sherman was reluctant to risk his superior forces in full battle against Johnston's diehards. On March 21, he launched a reconnaissance in force that outflanked the Confederates and prompted them to withdraw. By the grim standards of earlier contests, casualties at Bentonville were moderate—around 1,600 for the Federals and 2,600 for the Confederates—but that number represented a substantial loss for Johnston and left him with few options. "Sherman's course cannot be hindered by the small force I have," he wrote bleakly. "I can do no more than annoy him."

Some in Sherman's army sensed that their foes were beaten and took pity on those who fell for a lost cause. Sergeant Bull at Bentonville came upon "fifteen unburied Confederate soldiers lying where they had fallen. It was not a pleasant sight to me, even though these men had been our enemies. I thought when I saw them, of the sorrow and grief there would be in fifteen homes somewhere; and for what had these young lives been sacrificed? I hoped if I survived the war never to witness or take part in another." The yearning for peace was even stronger among those Confederates who felt that defeat was now inevitable and longed to return home. Some gave up without a fight, figuring that the war would be over soon and they would spend little time as prisoners before being released. Two of Johnston's men gave themselves up after the Battle of Bentonville to the oldest man in Bull's company. "They seemed to have had all the war they wanted and willingly came in and surrendered to old Joe," Bull wrote; "their excuse for being caught was that they had been left behind, but we thought they seemed very happy to have been captured."

DESPERATION IN RICHMOND

ON MARCH 19, AS FIGHTING RAGED AT BENTONVILLE, AN EXTRAORDINARY SPECtacle unfolded in Richmond—black and white men parading in separate companies down Main Street behind a band playing "Dixie." The white troops were convalescents at a Richmond hospital, and neither they nor the black recruits were in uniform, but they marched together with weapons in hand, signaling that a Confederacy founded to defend slavery was now prepared to accept blacks into its ranks as soldiers, if not as citizens. The enlistment of blacks as Confederate soldiers came at the urging of Robert E. Lee. "We must

> **"Sherman's course cannot be hindered by the small force I have. I can do no more than annoy him."**
>
> JOSEPH JOHNSTON,
> *after the Battle of Bentonville*

decide whether the negroes shall fight for us, or against us," he declared. He proposed granting freedom to slaves who enlisted, but many influential Southerners found that idea abhorrent, stating that the purpose of this war was to uphold slavery and a way of life dependent on it. "If slaves will make good soldiers our whole theory of slavery is wrong," insisted Howell Cobb of Georgia.

Jefferson Davis, who had earlier denounced Lincoln's decision to enlist freed slaves as "the most execrable measure recorded in the history of guilty man," changed his position out of sheer desperation. The Confederacy would soon lose the war if it did not replenish its depleted ranks, he realized, and the pool of able-bodied white men available for service was all but exhausted. In mid-March, with his encouragement, the Confederate Congress called for enlisting black troops but did not guarantee them freedom. The willingness of blacks to fight for the South as many did for the North was never put to the test, for the war ended before any black Confederate regiments were organized. Shifting his stance on this sensitive issue was not the only concession Jefferson Davis made as he tried to ward off defeat. Earlier in the year, at the insistence of Congress, which blamed him for mismanaging Confederate forces, he yielded his powers as commander in chief to Lee. Around the same time, he dropped his longstanding opposition to peace talks with the Union and sent a commission headed by Vice President Stephens to meet Federal representatives at Fort Monroe.

The gulf between the two sides was evident from the start when Lincoln wrote a letter expressing his willingness to enter into talks for the purpose of "securing peace to the people of our common country," and Davis responded by instructing Stephens to negotiate for the purpose of "securing peace to the two countries." Lincoln had never recognized the Confederacy as a separate country and held that stance when he and Secretary of State Seward met with Stephens and his fellow commissioners on February 3. If Rebels laid down their arms and acknowledged the authority of the United States, they would be welcomed back as citizens, he promised. But according to one of the commissioners, he warned "that it would be better for the Rebel States to return at once than to risk the chances of continuing the war" and of increasing the bitterness in Congress. The time might come, he added, "when they would not be considered as an erring people invited back to citizenship, but would be looked upon as enemies to be exterminated or ruined." Lincoln was prepared to offer financial compensation to Southerners whose slaves were freed, but his commitment to emancipation was stronger than ever. On January 31, at his urging, Congress had passed the Thirteenth Amendment, outlawing slavery "within the United States, or any place subject to their jurisdiction."

Lincoln's firm stance left Stephens little room to negotiate, and he returned to Richmond without an agreement. That came as no surprise to Jefferson Davis, who warned that Federals would never grant Confederates peace "on any other basis than our unconditional submission to their rule." The only hope for Southerners, he added, was to keep up the fight and force their enemies to "petition us for peace, on our terms." Realists knew that was no longer possible, but Davis was an incurable idealist, who continued to dream of victory and independence as his armies melted away like snow on a warm spring day.

"If slaves will make good soldiers our whole theory of slavery is wrong."

HOWELL COBB OF GEORGIA, *on plans to enlist slaves as Confederate troops*

Davis would never concede defeat, but Lincoln anticipated that Confederate commanders might soon bow to reality and seek terms from their Federal counterparts. With that in mind, he met on March 28 with Grant, Sherman, and Admiral Porter aboard the presidential steamboat *River Queen*, anchored in the James River at City Point, Grant's headquarters near Petersburg.

As Sherman recalled afterward, Lincoln said more than once during the meeting that there had been enough bloodshed, "and asked us if another battle could not be avoided." His commanders were unable to offer him any assurances. Lee's army at Petersburg remained dangerous and might yet give Grant a hard fight. "What was to be done with the rebel armies when defeated?" Sherman asked the president. Lincoln replied that the Confederates should be allowed to return to their homes and families. As for Jefferson Davis, he implied that he would rather see him flee the country than be imprisoned. "I want no one punished," Lincoln said; "treat them liberally all round. We want those people to return to their allegiance to the Union and submit to the laws." At his insistence, his commanders had been relentless in their assaults on the Rebels, but he urged them to show mercy when the fighting was over. "Of all the men I have met," Sherman wrote of Lincoln, "he seemed to possess more of the elements of greatness, combined with goodness, than any other." It remained to be seen whether the goodness and mercy would prevail when the war reached its shattering climax in April and Lincoln himself was targeted.

Lincoln confers with Sherman, Grant, and Admiral David Porter aboard the steamboat River Queen on March 28. Lincoln's "earnest desire," wrote Sherman, "seemed to be to end the war speedily, without more bloodshed or devastation, and to restore all the men of both sections to their homes."

"Of all the men I have met, he seemed to possess more of the elements of greatness, combined with goodness, than any other."
GENERAL SHERMAN ON ABRAHAM LINCOLN

> ## "You must not be surprised if calamity befalls us."
>
> ROBERT E. LEE,
> *at Petersburg in early 1865*

FROM PETERSBURG TO APPOMATTOX

THERE WAS LITTLE MORE LEE COULD DO. THROUGH A LONG, CRUEL winter he had held out at Petersburg against an army more than twice the size of his own. Without food from the Shenandoah Valley, which had been stripped bare by Sheridan's campaign, or supplies from abroad, which were cut off when Fort Fisher fell, Lee could not maintain his troops much longer. Together, sickness and malnutrition had disabled one-third of his forces and left him with fewer than 40,000 men fit for duty. Two years earlier, in winter camp near Fredericksburg, he had still been able to offer guests small portions of boiled bacon, but a foreigner who dined with him now at Petersburg found him reduced to the meagerest fare. "He had two biscuits," the visitor marveled, "and offered me one." Lee's dispatches to Richmond made it clear that his once-invincible Army of Northern Virginia was fast wearing down and might soon give way before Grant's formidable forces. "You must not be surprised if calamity befalls us," he wrote.

In early March, Lee conferred with his youngest corps commander, 33-year-old Major General John Gordon, who had distinguished himself at Spotsylvania after suffering multiple wounds at Antietam. For the first time, Gordon saw on Lee's face "a look of painful depression," the cause of which became clear when Gordon read the latest reports from Lee's officers, detailing the dismal condition of the troops and their declining morale. "Each report was bad enough," Gordon related; taken together, they foretold "inevitable disintegration." When asked what the army should do under these circumstances, Gordon was reluctant to respond, for he regarded Lee as "almost infallible in such a crisis" and did not feel qualified to advise him. As it turned out, the choices Gordon laid out were the same ones Lee had been pondering. One option was to seek terms from the enemy, but Lee was not prepared to do that without instructions from Richmond. A second option was to leave Petersburg and join forces with Joseph Johnston in North Carolina, but that meant abandoning Richmond as well, and Jefferson Davis remained intent on holding the capital. That left only one choice, Gordon concluded: "We must fight, and without delay." To Gordon as to Lee, it seemed better to go down fighting than to waste away. "They are trying to corner this old army," wrote Lee's aide, Colonel Walter Taylor. "Like a brave old lion brought to bay at last, it is determined to resist to the death and if die it must, to die game."

Before dawn on March 25, Gordon assembled nearly half of Lee's men and launched them against Fort Stedman, east of Petersburg. That Federal fort was targeted because it lay unusually close to the Confederate lines, literally a stone's throw away, but it was shielded by log barricades that had to be cleared away by men wielding axes. "Suddenly there rang out in the stillness the sharp crack of a pistol," one Confederate officer recalled. "Then came the rush and

the rapid sound of axes and the crash of falling timber and the wild cheer from the axemen." The attack surprised the opposing Federals and their commander in chief, who had arrived by boat at nearby City Point the night before to confer with Grant and other officers in the days to come. There was "a little rumpus up the line," Grant told Lincoln, trusting that his officers on the scene would be able to handle anything Lee threw at them.

By midmorning the surging Confederates had captured Fort Stedman and several adjoining batteries, but their attack then bogged down. As Grant's troops had discovered when they tried on several earlier occasions to smash through the Confederate line here, it was nearly impossible for advancing troops to maintain formation in this hellish terrain, riddled with craters, trenches, and other pitfalls. The strongholds they seized became traps when their foes rallied and struck back like wasps defending their hive. By afternoon, the Federals had recaptured Fort Stedman and were advancing in areas where Lee had weakened his defenses to support the attack. Some 2,000 Confederates were captured before the day was out and nearly as many killed or wounded—a heavy blow to an already devastated army. For Grant, who lost fewer than 1,500 men, the battle was a minor distraction that did not prevent him reviewing troops with the president later that day. One astonished Confederate prisoner saw Lincoln and Grant ride by, looking "not the least

Cavalrymen from New York relax at their well-constructed winter camp near Petersburg in March 1865. Not many in Grant's army lived as comfortably as this during the siege, but they were far better supplied than Lee's troops, who went hungry and ragged.

"We must fight, and without delay."

GENERAL JOHN GORDON TO LEE, *before attacking Fort Stedman*

concerned and as if nothing had happened." If the Union's leaders could shrug off an attack that cost his side so much, he concluded, "our cause was lost."

Lee had hoped the attack would force the Federals to abandon part of their line, allowing him to hold Petersburg with fewer troops and send the rest to bolster Joseph Johnston's Confederates against Sherman in North Carolina. Instead, the setback meant that Lee would soon have to abandon his position. "I fear now it will be impossible to prevent a junction between Grant and Sherman," he wrote Jefferson Davis on March 26. The two Federal armies combined would "exceed ours by nearly a hundred thousand," he calculated, and he would then have no hope of defending Petersburg or Richmond. Indeed, Grant's forces alone were capable of routing Lee's army now that Sheridan had secured the Shenandoah Valley and returned with his cavalry. "Feeling that the war was nearing its end," Sheridan wrote, "I desired my cavalry to be in at the death." The question was no longer whether Lee would withdraw from Petersburg but whether he could do so before Grant slipped a noose around his army and forced him to surrender.

A crew including a number of black sailors mans the gunboat Mendota at the mouth of the James River in March 1865. Federal warships like this one and those at right—shown approaching City Point, Grant's headquarters and supply depot at the confluence of the Appomattox and James Rivers—kept Confederate gunboats bottled up near Richmond and protected Grant's maritime supply line.

BREAKTHROUGH AT PETERSBURG

"I WAS AFRAID, EVERY MORNING, THAT I WOULD AWAKE FROM my sleep to hear that Lee had gone, and that nothing was left but his picket line," wrote Grant. "I knew he could move much more lightly and more rapidly than I, and that, if he got the start, he would leave me behind." In that case, the war might be prolonged, and Grant did all he could to avoid that. By late March, most of Lee's escape routes had been closed off. He was hemmed in to the north and east by Grant's army and the Federal fleet, which controlled the James River from its mouth to within a short distance of Richmond, keeping Grant well supplied. Lee still had roads open to the west, but they were muddy and slow in the spring and troops using them might be overtaken by Sheridan's cavalry. His best hope was to join forces with Johnston using the Southside Railroad, which connected Petersburg to southwestern Virginia and North Carolina. That line remained in Confederate hands, but Grant planned to sever it before Lee could organize a withdrawal. With Grant watching his every move, he could not get away without a fight.

Anticipating an attack on the Southside Railroad, Lee sent Major General George Pickett's division—much reduced since its ruinous charge at Gettysburg but still a substantial force of 5,000 men—to defend a crossroads called Five Forks southwest of Petersburg and prevent Grant's troops from reaching the tracks. "Hold Five Forks at all hazards," Lee instructed Pickett. Heavy rain on March 30 raised doubts at Grant's headquarters as to whether the attack should be launched the next day as planned. Sheridan, whose cavalry would figure prominently in the assault, wanted to forge ahead. "I'm ready to strike tomorrow and go to smashing things!" he said. Grant was not one to restrain Sheridan when he was chomping at the bit. The fact that Lee had sent cavalry led by his nephew, General Fitzhugh Lee, to bolster Pickett's

division at Five Forks only encouraged Grant, for it left the Confederates with little in reserve to defend the rest of their line. If Sheridan's troopers, supported by infantry commanded by Major General Gouverneur Warren, could smash the enemy as promised, Grant would launch an all-out attack on Lee's forces. As he told Sheridan, "I feel now like ending the matter."

The fighting on March 31 fell far short of Grant's expectations. Sheridan and Warren did not coordinate their attacks—relations between the two temperamental generals went from bad to worse as the battle progressed—and they made little headway. The only consolation for the Union came late in the day when the beleaguered Warren called on Brigadier General Joshua Chamberlain, a hero at Gettysburg, who launched a spirited counterattack that an opposing Confederate officer called "one of the most gallant things I have ever seen." The continuing rift between Warren and Sheridan might have hurt their chances at Five Forks had not the opposing commanders let down their guard the next day. On the afternoon of April 1, unaware that the Federals were about to renew their assaults, Pickett and Fitzhugh Lee accepted an invitation from Brigadier General Thomas Rosser to attend a shad bake—a spring ritual in Virginia as shad swarmed upriver from Chesapeake Bay. While they were feasting at Rosser's headquarters a few miles away, their forces came under furious attack. Lee was cut off and did not rejoin his cavalry until after the battle. Pickett got through to his troops but found them in disarray. By day's end, he and Fitzhugh Lee had lost over 5,000 men, most of them captured, in a debacle one officer called the "Waterloo of the Confederacy."

Braving enemy fire at close range, attacking Federals raise their flag over the Confederate works at Petersburg on April 2 in this first-hand sketch by Alfred Waud. The fierce battle marked Lee's last stand here and decided the fate of Richmond.

The Federals had prevailed despite the feud between their generals, which grew so bitter that Sheridan, who outranked Warren, relieved him of command that evening, insisting that he had been so lax, "he wasn't in that fight!" In truth, Warren and his infantry had contributed significantly to the victory by sweeping around to the north of Five Forks and blocking the enemy while Sheridan's troopers moved in from the south. Grant's aide, Lieutenant Colonel Horace Porter, who was with Sheridan, criticized him afterward for exposing himself to enemy fire "in a manner hardly justifiable on the part of a commander of such an important movement." Sheridan's reply, Porter added, said much about his success on the field: "I have never in my life taken a command into battle, and had the slightest desire to come out alive unless I won." Much as Grant had nurtured Sheridan, he in turn had encouraged a younger prodigy, 23-year-old Brigadier General George Armstrong Custer, who excelled at Five Forks. Like Sheridan, Custer could be brash and arrogant, but the Union needed commanders as daring as their Confederate counterparts.

Early on Sunday, April 2, following a furious artillery barrage, Federals launched their climactic attack on Petersburg. Grant's troops had long dreaded this moment, but as they surged forward many were glad that the suspense was over and they were finally going to settle things with the Rebels. "It was a great relief," wrote one officer, "a positive lifting of a load of misery to be at last let at them." Enemy resistance was fierce at strongpoints such as Fort Mahone—where the defenders did not yield until the ground "was literally covered with blue-coated corpses," in the words of one Confederate—and Fort Gregg, where soldiers as young as 14 vowed never to give in to the "damned Yankees!" As the fight for Fort Gregg reached its climax, recalled one Union officer, Colonel Rufus Lincoln, "the Stars and Stripes could be seen floating by the side of the Rebel flag. Cheer after cheer rent the air—the Rebels fighting with the desperation of madmen, and shouting to each other, 'Never surrender! Never surrender!' " The oncoming Yankees were just as desperate and determined—one defender likened them to "ravenous beasts"—and seized the stronghold late that afternoon.

By the time Fort Gregg fell, Robert E. Lee was preparing to abandon Petersburg and save what remained of his army. "I see no prospect of doing more than holding our position here till night," he had wired the War Department in Richmond earlier in the day. "I advise that all preparation be made for leaving Richmond tonight." Lee's forces could no longer use the Southside Railroad as an escape route, for it had been severed by Sheridan. Instead, they would have to march west from Petersburg along the Appomattox River, with Union cavalry in pursuit. "This is a bad business, colonel," Lee remarked to an aide. "It has happened as I told them it would at Richmond. The line has been stretched until it has broken."

THE FALL OF RICHMOND

JEFFERSON DAVIS WAS ATTENDING CHURCH IN THE CONFEDERATE CAPITAL THAT Sunday morning when a messenger brought him Lee's message urging abandonment of the city. A fellow worshipper saw him rise and walk out "rather unsteadily." When other officials at the service followed suit, many in attendance suspected that Richmond was lost. Davis and his Cabinet left by train that night for Danville, Virginia, before continuing on to Greensboro, North Carolina. Troops who had been defending Richmond marched south across the James River to link up with the rest of Lee's forces and destroyed the bridge behind them. Warehouses were set ablaze and warships scuttled, causing explosions that shook the city as fires spread and law and order collapsed. "There were said to be 5,000 deserters in the city," one witness wrote, "and you could see the gray jackets here and there sprinkled in the mob that was roaring down the street."

Diarist Judith McGuire went out late that night to see if she could still leave Richmond by train. On her way to the depot, she saw looters hauling away goods: "Women, both white and colored, were walking in multitudes from the commissary offices and burning stores with bags of flour, meal, coffee, sugar, rolls of cotton cloth, etc. Colored men were rolling wheelbarrows filled in the same way." She gave up hope of leaving when she learned Federals had entered the city. "I turned to come home," she wrote, "but what was my horror, when I reached Ninth Street, to see a regiment of Yankee cavalry come dashing up, yelling, shouting, hallooing, screaming! All Bedlam let

"Cheer after cheer rent the air—the Rebels fighting with the desperation of madmen, and shouting to each other, 'Never surrender! Never surrender!'"

UNION COLONEL RUFUS LINCOLN, *at Fort Gregg*

THE SIEGE OF PETERSBURG

For Ulysses S. Grant, the next best thing to capturing Richmond was to capture Petersburg, the key supply center just south of the capital at the junction of five railroads. Grant moved his army across the James River in the middle of June 1864 and began an assault on the city that would last nearly ten months.

General P. G. T. Beauregard commanded the outnumbered Rebel defenders, who dug in behind a sturdy line of fortifications that frustrated repeated Union attacks. Unable to take the city quickly, the Federals dug 30 miles of trench lines along the eastern and southern perimeter [1], forcing Lee to stretch his defenses to the breaking point.

The Union's 41 siege works revolved around Fort Sedgwick [2], which saw so much shelling that it was dubbed Fort Hell by its occupants. The anchor of the Rebel line was Fort Mahone [3], which earned the corresponding nickname Fort Damnation.

The two sides fought numerous battles around the city, none more infamous than the Battle of the Crater. General Ambrose Burnside's Corps mined a 511-foot tunnel under the Confederate lines at Elliot's Salient [4], detonating explosives on July 30 that created a crater some 135 feet wide. Around 300 Confederates were killed by the blast, but Union soldiers, instead of charging around the rim, ran into the crater and were picked off by Rebels firing down on them. More than 5,000 Federals ended up dying in the battle.

Major General Horatio Wright's Corps finally broke through Rebel lines west of the city, cutting off the Boydton Plank Road and the Southside Railroad [5]. By the end of the day on April 2, 1865, Fort Mahone had fallen after massive bombardment by heavy artillery, and Lee had no choice but to evacuate the city. ■

Robert Knox Sneden's map of the investment, or siege, of Petersburg shows the numerous strongholds in the front lines of each side, like knots in a rope. By 1865 the Union siege lines stretched for miles west of the city.

2 FORT SEDGWICK *Wattle cylinders filled with stone and earth line the traverses and parapets of the pivotal earthwork in the Union line.*

3 FORT MAHONE *A Confederate soldier lies dead in the stronghold dubbed Fort Damnation by Union soldiers.*

6 OCCUPATION *The first Federal wagon train, the Army of the James, enters Petersburg after Lee was finally forced to evacuate.*

Warehouses and mills lie in ruins in Richmond after departing Confederates torched the buildings on the night of April 2 to deny oncoming Federals the goods stored here. As the flames spread to other areas, one Union officer wrote, "the few fire engines in order were sought out and placed in the hands of our boys in blue, who worked as earnestly to save the city of Richmond from destruction as if performing a like duty for their native towns."

loose could not have vied with them in diabolical roarings. I stood riveted to the spot; I could not move nor speak. Then I saw the iron gates of our time-honored and beautiful Capitol Square, on the walks and greenswards of which no hoof had been allowed to tread, thrown open and the cavalry dash in. I could see no more; I must go on with a mighty effort, or faint where I stood."

Among the Federals who entered the capital in the early hours of April 3 were black troops, a sight that appalled some diehard Confederates but thrilled those in Richmond who had been held in slavery and saw freedom dawning. "From the colored population of Richmond we received such a reception as could only come from a people who were returning thanks for the deliverance of their race," one Union officer recalled. On April 4, Lincoln himself entered the smoldering city, greeted by blacks so grateful for freedom that some went down on their knees. "Don't kneel to me," he told them. "You must kneel to God only and thank him for your freedom." Later that day, as a reporter looked on, Lincoln responded graciously to another tribute from a freed slave. "May de good Lord bless you," the man said, removing his hat and bowing, "with tears of joy rolling down his cheeks. The president removed his own hat, and bowed in silence. It was a bow which upset the forms, laws, customs and ceremonies of centuries of slavery."

Lincoln had come a long way since his first inaugural address in 1861, when he had endorsed a constitutional amendment protecting slavery in the South if that would save the Union and prevent war. Four years later, in his second inaugural address, delivered on March 4, he condemned slavery as a curse on the land and the Civil War as God's way of ridding the nation of that evil: "Fondly do we hope—fervently do we pray—that this mighty scourge of war may speedily pass away. Yet, if God wills that it continue, until all the wealth piled by the bond-man's two hundred and fifty years of unrequited toil shall be sunk, and until every drop of blood drawn with the lash shall be paid with another drawn by the sword, as was said three thousand years ago, so still it must be said, 'the judgments of the Lord, are true and righteous altogether.'" Yet even as Lincoln pledged to destroy slavery, he held out an olive branch to defiant Southerners, promising to bear "malice toward none" and "bind up the nation's wounds." When the commander of Federal troops occupying Richmond asked him how the populace there should be handled, Lincoln responded much as he had when Sherman inquired how defeated Confederate soldiers should be treated: "If I were in your place, I'd let 'em up easy, let 'em up easy."

"May de good Lord bless you."

Freed slave to Abraham Lincoln in Richmond after Federals occupied the city

---

[EYEWITNESS]

George Lewis
SON OF A FREED SLAVE

Five-year-old George Lewis, the son of a freed slave who lived in the Negro district north of Broad Street, told of his first encounter with Union troops.

"I was frightened and hid behind the kitchen door."

ON THE MORNING OF APRIL 3rd, there was so much noise and excitement that my mother took me out of bed—changed my night clothes, dressed me in my day ones—and started with me out of the house. Just as we left the porch three or four Yankee soldiers with guns on their shoulders stopped us and told my mother that they wanted her to cook breakfast for them. . . . She turned around, took me in her arms and returned to our house. I was frightened and hid behind the kitchen door. After they finished eating the cakes and fish, they got up from the table and took money out of their pockets and paid my mother for the food and for her trouble. These were Negro troops! ■

Former slaves, now freedmen, gather on the towpath of a Richmond canal in the spring of 1865.

LEE'S ARMY HAD BEEN THROUGH MANY ORDEALS, BUT NOTHING LIKE THIS. No Confederate soldier involved in the retreat from Petersburg could "fail to recall it as one of the most trying experiences of his life," wrote Major Robert Stiles. "Trying enough, in the mere fact that the Army of Northern Virginia was flying before its foes, but further trying, incomparably trying, in lack of food and rest and sleep, and because of the audacious pressure of the enemy's cavalry." Sheridan was relentless in pursuit and caught up with the tail of Lee's strung-out army on April 6 at Sayler's Creek, 50 miles west of Petersburg below the Appomattox River. Sheridan now had an infantry commander he trusted, Major General Horatio Wright, and their combined forces trapped Confederates commanded by Lieutenant Generals Richard Anderson and Richard Ewell. Exhausted and outnumbered, the Rebels appeared doomed. As Stiles recalled, Federal officers "evidently expected us to surrender and had their white handkerchiefs in their hands, waving them toward us, as if suggesting this course." But his men were in no mood to give up and staggered their opponents with two deadly volleys before charging them. Stiles knew that a single battalion advancing against heavy opposition stood no chance: "I tried to stop them, but in vain, although I actually got ahead of a good many of them. They simply bore me on with the flood."

Stiles soon regained control of his overeager men and explained that "we would be cut off if we remained long where we were." Then he led them back up the hill they had just charged down: "We were back in the original lines in a few moments—that is, all who were left of us." He had acted respon-

> "There is nothing left me but to go and see General Grant, and I had rather die a thousand deaths."
>
> GENERAL LEE TO HIS AIDES,
> *before surrendering to Grant*

Lee signs the articles of surrender on April 9 as Grant and his aides look on. The ceremony took place at the home of Wilmer McLean, who had moved here to Appomattox Court House with his family from embattled Manassas three years earlier, hoping to escape the war.

sibly, but it did his men little good. They were cut off anyway with other Confederates when Federal infantry and cavalry advanced on them from north and south in a pincer movement like that at Five Forks. "By the time we had well settled into our old position," Stiles related, "we were attacked simultaneously, front and rear, by overwhelming numbers, and quicker than I can tell it the battle degenerated into a butchery. . . . I saw numbers of men kill each other with bayonets and the butts of muskets, and even bite each others' throats and ears and noses, rolling on the ground like wild beasts." Some Confederates held out behind breastworks until Union troopers broke through on horseback. As one Federal recalled: "Many saddles were emptied but on they came, jumping over the works and killing many with the hoofs of the horses."

By day's end, the Confederates had lost nearly 8,000 men, most of them captured. That was nearly as many casualties as Grant sustained in this entire campaign, from Five Forks until hostilities ended, and amounted to one-fourth of Lee's army. "If the thing is pressed, I think Lee will surrender," Sheridan wrote Grant after the battle. Grant sent the message along to Lincoln, who replied promptly: "Let the thing be pressed." Lee's last hope was to obtain food and other supplies awaiting his famished men at Appomattox Station, on the Southside Railroad. But Sheridan's cavalry got there first on April 8 and left the Confederates stranded and starving. Fighting continued nearby until the following morning, but Lee knew that further resistance would be futile. He rejected a suggestion that his troops be dispersed to fight as irregulars, pointing out that guerrilla warfare would have a devastating effect "on the country as a whole." The Confederacy was collapsing, and Lee had to consider the future of the country he could no longer defend and the larger nation it was now compelled to rejoin. "There is nothing left me but to go and see General Grant," he concluded, "and I had rather die a thousand deaths."

Lee met Grant at the village of Appomattox Court House on April 9 after being assured that his opponent—who had once wanted unconditional surrender—was prepared to offer more generous terms now. Grant shared Lincoln's conviction that a vindictive policy toward the Confederates would hinder the task of reconstructing the nation and pledged in writing to allow all officers and men in Lee's army "to return to their homes, not to be disturbed by United States authority so long as they observe their paroles and the laws in force where they may reside." Grant allowed soldiers with horses to retain their animals and arranged for Lee's men to receive food. "It will be a great relief, I assure you," Lee responded, but such concessions did not ease the pain of surrendering. When Confederates gathered around him afterward, his eyes filled with tears. "Men, we have fought through the war together," he told them, his voice trembling. "I have done the best I could for you. My heart is too full to say more."

At war's end, laborers unearthed these skeletal remains of Union soldiers killed at Cold Harbor, near Richmond, for reburial in the North. Mindful of the terrible losses both sides had suffered, Grant instructed Federals not to fire their guns in celebration or exult in other ways when Confederates surrendered. "The war is over," he said. "The Rebels are our countrymen again."

Three days later, his soldiers laid down their arms. During that ceremony, the presiding Union officer, General Joshua Chamberlain, a future governor of Maine, paid tribute to Confederates led by General John Gordon, a future governor of Georgia, by ordering Federals to raise their muskets to their shoulders in salute. Gordon had his men return the compliment and later hailed Chamberlain's gesture as "a token of respect from Americans to Americans, a final and fitting tribute from Northern to Southern chivalry."

"Our people are tired of war, feel themselves whipped, and will not fight."

JOSEPH JOHNSTON TO JEFFERSON DAVIS, *before surrendering to Sherman*

Lee's surrender prompted Joseph Johnston in North Carolina to seek terms from Sherman, much to the dismay of Jefferson Davis, who hoped to carry on the struggle by rounding up deserters and recruiting more troops. Johnston dismissed that as wishful thinking and told Davis bluntly, "Our people are tired of war, feel themselves whipped, and will not fight." On April 17, Johnston met with Sherman, who stunned him by informing him of Lincoln's death by assassination two days earlier. "The perspiration came out in large drops on his forehead," Sherman observed, "and he did not attempt to conceal his distress." Johnston called his death "the greatest possible calamity to the South." That was one point on which he and Davis agreed, for they knew that many in Washington favored far harsher policies toward defeated Confederates than Lincoln had advocated. "I fear it will be disastrous for our people," Davis said of Lincoln's death, "and I regret it deeply." After Johnston surrendered, Davis fled west, hoping to join General Edmund Kirby Smith, whose isolated forces beyond the Mississippi would be last to yield. On May 10, the Confederate president was captured by Federals in Georgia, and his government dissolved.

Jefferson Davis holds a Bible in his prison cell at Fort Monroe, watched over by guards who had orders never to let him out of their sight. Although some Confederate forces did not surrender until after Davis was seized on May 10, his capture brought the Rebellion officially to an end and set the stage for victory celebrations two weeks later in Washington, where Federal forces paraded down Pennsylvania Avenue (opposite).

In Washington, mourning for Lincoln gave way to celebrations as the victorious Army of the Potomac marched down Pennsylvania Avenue on May 23 past joyous crowds and assembled dignitaries, among them Lincoln's successor, Andrew Johnson, a loyalist from Tennessee. The next day, Sherman's men had their parade. They were not quite as rough and ragged as some onlookers expected, having been told by Grant's troops the day before "to wait until Sherman's outlaws marched through if they wanted to see the western savages." After advancing relentlessly across the South, these soldiers were used to being jeered rather than cheered. "Felt kind of queer to get such a welcome," wrote one Ohio man. "Makes us feel like the war is over." It was a stirring moment in the nation's history, and none there wanted it to end. "Even after every veteran had vanished from sight." observed Grant's aide, Horace Porter, "the crowds kept their place for a time, as if still under a spell and unwilling to believe that the marvelous spectacle had actually passed from view. It was not a Roman triumph, designed to gratify the vanity of the victors, exhibit their trophies and parade their enchained captives before the multitude: it was a celebration of the dawn of peace, a declaration of the reestablishment of the Union."

THE ASSASSINATION OF LINCOLN

DEATH WAS NO STRANGER TO Lincoln. His beloved son Willie had died of fever in 1862, throwing a pall over the White House, where the first lady, Mary Todd Lincoln, remained shut up for months, mourning so deeply her husband feared for her sanity. He himself was haunted throughout the war not just by that personal loss but by the Union's grievous losses on the battlefield. Author Harriet Beecher Stowe, who visited him in 1863, wrote of his "dry, weary, patient pain," an anguish that was etched ever deeper into his face as the conflict continued. "Whichever way it ends," he said to her of the war that consumed him, "I have the impression I shan't last long after it's over."

There were some who wanted Lincoln dead. He often received threatening letters, which he kept in a file marked "Assassination." His close friend and guardian, Ward Hill Lamon, insisted that he never go out in public without at least one bodyguard, but Lincoln was fatalistic. "I long ago made up my mind that if anybody wants to kill me, he will do it," he remarked. The welcome news of Lee's surrender at Appomattox did not dispel his premonition that the war's conclusion might signal his own end. Soon afterward, he told Lamon and Mrs. Lincoln of a haunting dream in which he entered the East Room of the White House and saw a shrouded corpse on a catafalque surrounded by soldiers, one of whom informed him that they were guarding the body of the president, who had been slain by an assassin.

As the Lincolns headed to Ford's

> **"I long ago made up my mind that if anybody wants to kill me, he will do it."**
>
> ABRAHAM LINCOLN

Theatre in Washington on Good Friday, April 14, his spirits lifted. "I consider this day, the war has come to a close," he told his wife. "We must both be more cheerful in the future." But one more bloody act would unfold before this tragic conflict ended. As they watched the play that night, Lincoln's bodyguard, an incompetent last-minute substitute, left his post. That allowed John Wilkes Booth, an actor who had performed here often and knew his way around, to enter Lincoln's box unhindered. A Confederate sympathizer from Maryland who had never shed blood for his cause and hoped to make up for it now, Booth was part of a wider conspiracy aimed at assassinating Lincoln, Vice President Andrew Johnson, and Secretary of State William H. Seward. Stepping up behind Lincoln with a derringer in hand, Booth sent a bullet through the president's brain before leaping to the stage below and taking flight. Tracked down, he and others involved in the plot would pay with their lives.

Lincoln never regained consciousness and died early the next morning. Before his body lay in state at the Capitol and went to Springfield, Illinois, for burial, his coffin was placed in the East Room of the White House, attended by many soldiers and dignitaries. One of those present was Ulysses Grant, who had seen thousands killed in battle without displaying emotion but wept openly now. "He was incontestably the greatest man I have ever known," avowed Grant. For millions in mourning, this one great loss seemed to sum up everything their divided nation had suffered and sacrificed on its painful path to reunion. ∎

Lincoln wore this hat to Ford's Theatre on the night he was assassinated. A few months before his death, he sat for the photograph at right. The glass negative cracked, and only a single print was made.

In a series of illustrations published in Frank Leslie's Illustrated Newspaper soon after the event, Booth fires his derringer at Lincoln (above), then leaps to the stage below (near right), where he raises a dagger and shouts, "Sic semper tyrannis!—Thus ever to tyrants!" Booth caught his spur in a flag as he jumped from Lincoln's box and broke a bone in his left leg, but he still managed to get away and seek help from a physician, Dr. Samuel Mudd, later sentenced to life in prison for aiding the assassin.

A poster distributed by the War Department offers hefty rewards for information leading to the arrest of Booth and two of his accomplices, whose names were misspelled: John Surratt, a Confederate courier who was initially skeptical of Booth's plot but joined in; and David Herold, who guided another conspirator to the home of Secretary of State Seward, wounded along with several members of his household in the attack. Surratt fled the country and avoided conviction on a technicality when he was seized two years later and tried in civil court. Herold escaped with Booth to Virginia, where they were cornered by Federals on April 26. Herold surrendered and was convicted in military court. Booth resisted arrest and died after uttering these last words: "Useless, useless."

At left, mourners pack the streets in Chicago as Lincoln's hearse reaches the Cook County courthouse, where his body lay in state before proceeding by train to Springfield for burial. There his coffin was placed in an ornate hearse (top), provided by the mayor of St. Louis. Lincoln's horse, Old Bob—led by Reverend Henry Brown (above, left), a black minister long acquainted with the president—followed the hearse to Oak Ridge Cemetery. On May 4, Lincoln was laid to rest there alongside his son Willie, whose coffin accompanied him home during a journey in which millions of Americans came to bid farewell to the man who had restored their nation.

GEORGE ATZERODT

LEWIS POWELL

MARY SURRATT

DAVID HEROLD

On July 7, 1865, the four condemned conspirators pictured above went to the gallows at Washington's Old Penitentiary, where photographer Alexander Gardner recorded their execution (right). The military court that sentenced them heard strong evidence against David Herold and the two other men here: Lewis Powell, who carried out the attack on Secretary of State Seward; and George Atzerodt, who plotted against Lincoln and undertook to assassinate Vice President Johnson before backing down. Mary Surratt, the mother of escaped conspirator John Surratt and owner of the boardinghouse where the conspirators met, was convicted on suspect testimony by witnesses granted immunity. "Mrs. Surratt is innocent," Lewis Powell said on the scaffold. "She doesn't deserve to die with the rest of us."

"SURELY THERE WILL BE A DAY OF
RECKONING FOR THOSE WHO DEFRAUD
THE LABORER OF HIS HIRE."

JOURDAN ANDERSON,
to the man who once held him in bondage

THE NATION REUNITED

IN AUGUST 1865, JOURDAN ANDERSON, WHO HAD FLED TO OHIO
with his family to escape slavery, wrote to his former master in
Tennessee, Colonel P. H. Anderson. "I got your letter and was
glad to find that you had not forgotten Jourdan," he began, "and
that you wanted me to come back and live with you again, promising to do better for me than anyone else can. . . . Although you
shot at me twice before I left you, I did not want to hear of your
being hurt, and am glad you are still living." He saw little reason
now to return to his master: "I get $25 a month, with victuals and
clothing; have a comfortable home for Mandy (the folks here call
her Mrs. Anderson), and the children." Colonel Anderson owed
him and his wife more than $10,000 for past services, he figured,
but money alone could not compensate them for what they had
been through: "Surely there will be a day of reckoning for those
who defraud the laborer of his hire."

In the tumultuous postwar era known as Reconstruction, white
Southerners like Colonel Anderson hoped to rebuild their old
society and remain masters by controlling former slaves. Republicans in Congress offered a radically different vision—a new
South where blacks and whites would have equal rights and the
last vestiges of slavery and defiance would be rooted out. Party
politics aggravated this struggle, but the core issue was the same
one that underlay the Civil War—the future of African Americans in a land of liberty. ■

*Black laborers on a plantation in South Carolina during Reconstruction haul cotton in a
scene eerily reminiscent of the days when cotton was king and slavery went unchallenged.
One freedman who found himself toiling for the same planter who owned him before the
war remarked on how little his life had changed: "I works for Marse John just the same."*

April 15, 1865 Democrat Andrew Johnson succeeds Abraham Lincoln as president following his assassination.

December 1865 Dominated by Republicans, Congress refuses to seat newly elected representatives from Southern states reorganized by Johnson and launches its own Reconstruction.

May 1868 Impeachment trial in Senate ends with Johnson's acquittal when his opponents fall one vote short.

March 4, 1869 Republican Ulysses Grant succeeds Johnson and supports the Fifteenth Amendment, barring states from denying citizens the right to vote on the basis of race.

March 2, 1877 Republican Rutherford B. Hayes declared winner of disputed presidential election after signaling the end of Reconstruction by pledging to remove federal troops sent to the South by Grant to protect voting rights.

RECONSTRUCTION

MONG THOSE WHO HURRIED TO LINCOLN'S SIDE WHEN THEY LEARNED he had been shot was Senator Charles Sumner of Massachusetts. Sumner knew what it was like to be struck down by a political opponent, having been caned mercilessly on the Senate floor in 1856 for his fiery denunciation of slavery. As a Radical Republican, he had often differed with Lincoln over the years, but they shared the conviction that the Civil War was not just a battle against disunion but a crusade for freedom. As the mortally wounded president lay unconscious on the night of April 14, Sumner took his hand and tried to speak to him. "It's no use, Mr. Sumner—he can't hear you," a physician told him. Yet he remained there until the end, a journalist reported, "sobbing like a woman, with his head bowed down almost on the pillow of the bed on which the President was lying."

Stunned by the assassination, Sumner and other Republican leaders could only pray that Lincoln's successor, Andrew Johnson of Tennessee, was up to the huge task of reconstructing the war-ravaged South and reuniting the nation. As a Southerner and a Democrat, chosen by Lincoln in 1864 to give

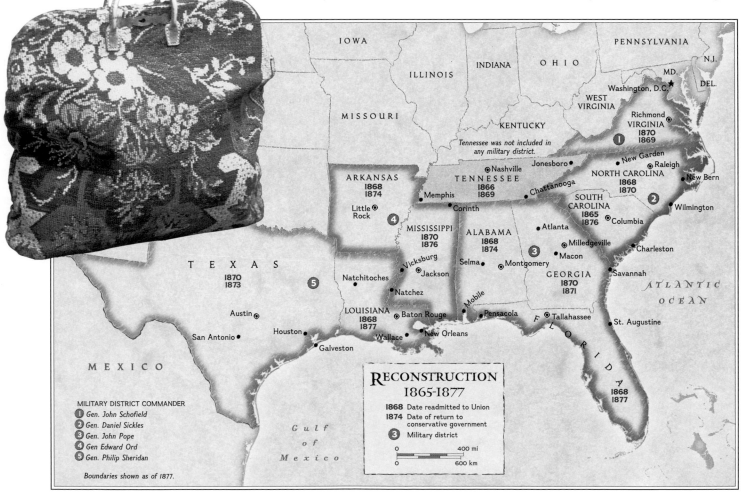

Congress divided the postwar South into five military districts. States were readmitted to the Union under rules favoring Republicans, among them Southern blacks and Northerners known as carpetbaggers for the suitcases some carried (inset). Gradually, conservative Democrats regained control of Southern states.

the ticket bipartisan appeal, Johnson had much to prove to Republicans. He had done himself no favors by drinking whiskey to excess before taking the vice presidential oath before the Senate in March 1865. As one witness put it, he "disgraced himself & the Senate by making a drunken foolish speech." After Lincoln's death, however, President Johnson impressed Sumner and other Republicans who met with him as sober and resolute and left them with the impression that he shared their views on Reconstruction. "There is no difference between us," Johnson assured Sumner.

Republicans who regarded the newly installed president as their political soulmate would have done well to remember that his full name was Andrew Jackson Johnson. Like President Andrew Jackson of Tennessee, he saw himself as the defender of the common man—by which he meant the common white man. "Damn the negroes!" Johnson said during the war. "I am fighting these traitorous aristocrats, their masters." To foil those proud planters and crush their secessionist movement, he accepted the abolition of slavery, but he had no interest in granting blacks equal rights. Furthermore, he opposed a strong, assertive federal government and believed that states should manage their own affairs. That put him on a collision course with Sumner and his fellow Radicals, who felt the war effort would be wasted if they did not impose strict conditions on the rebellious states for readmission to the Union and protect the rights of loyal whites and freedmen, as emancipated blacks were known.

Johnson followed Lincoln's policy of offering amnesty to former Confederates who swore an oath of allegiance. Certain groups, however, had to apply to Johnson for pardons, among them former Confederate officials, high ranking officers, and planters with property valued at more than $20,000. Johnson thought it fitting that such "traitorous aristocrats" should humble themselves by begging his pardon, which he granted to all but a few petitioners. General James Longstreet visited Johnson to appeal for a pardon, only to be informed that he and Robert E. Lee were in the same category as Jefferson Davis. "There are three persons in the South who can never receive amnesty: Mr. Davis, General Lee, and yourself," Johnson told Longstreet. "You have given the Union cause too much trouble." Lee, who hoped to set an example for Southerners by reconciling with his former enemies, was indicted for treason but never brought to trial. Davis also avoided trial but spent two years behind bars before he was released.

Sumner would rather have seen prominent Confederates exiled, but what truly alarmed him and like-minded Republicans was a proclamation by Johnson in late May that allowed whites only to elect delegates to constitutional conventions forming new state governments in the South. "Nothing since Chancellorsville has to my mind been so disastrous to the national cause," declared Sumner, who feared that without black political participation the South would soon be dominated by the very men who had instigated the

"Damn the negroes! I am fighting these traitorous aristocrats, their masters."

ANDREW JOHNSON, *on his stand against the Confederacy*

President Andrew Johnson, Lincoln's successor, incurred the wrath of Republicans in Congress, who suspected that this Democrat from Tennessee wanted to resurrect the old South rather than forge a new South obedient to federal authority. "Is there no way to arrest the insane course of the President?" asked the Radical Republican leader, Congressman Thaddeus Stevens.

Wooden headboards substitute for grave stones at this Confederate cemetery in Richmond, pictured in 1865. Much of the South was in disarray after the war, and federal agencies such as the Freedmen's Bureau provided aid to whites as well as blacks.

Rebellion. Those fears were seemingly realized when former Confederate Vice President Alexander Stephens, who had once declared slavery the "natural and normal condition" of blacks, was elected to the U.S. Senate from Georgia. Moderate Republicans shared the concern of Radicals that Democrats would regain control of the South under Johnson's permissive policy, which he called "restoration." In December 1865, the Republican-dominated Congress refused to seat newly elected representatives from the South and began drawing up its own stringent rules for Reconstruction.

Overriding vetoes by Johnson, Congress passed landmark legislation in 1866 designed to protect the rights of freedmen in the South. One bill strengthened the Freedmen's Bureau—set up by the War Department to aid and educate blacks in occupied territory—by establishing tribunals within the bureau that could override state courts. This provided some legal protection to blacks, who could not serve on juries and were subject to vagrancy laws that allowed unemployed men to be arrested and farmed out to planters. The Freedmen's Bureau was reviled by white Southerners, who called it a "vicious institution" and complained that

After impeaching Johnson, the House named seven Congressmen—including Radicals Benjamin Butler (far left) and Thaddeus Stevens (cane in hand)—to prosecute him in the Senate. Moderate Republicans such as Senator William Fessenden concluded that he could not be convicted simply for "general cussedness."

its agents would not allow for the possibility of "a white man's being right in a contest or difference with a negro." Yet those same agents brought order to the chaotic Southern economy by drawing up contracts between employers and laborers that both sides had to honor. Several thousand black farmers received homesteads on public land from the Freedmen's Bureau, but Congress rejected a proposal by a leading Radical, Congressman Thaddeus Stevens of Pennsylvania, to redistribute the land of wealthy ex-Confederates to freedmen in 40-acre lots. Most blacks who dreamed of "40 acres and a mule" ended up toiling as sharecroppers for white planters and heavily in debt to them. "We soon found out that freedom could make folks proud," said one former slave, "but it didn't make 'em rich."

A President on Trial

"IF MY BLOOD IS TO BE SHED BECAUSE I VINDICATE THE UNION AND the preservation of this government in its original purity and character," Andrew Johnson declared in 1866, "let it be shed." Politically, his Republican foes were indeed out for his blood. Elections that fall strengthened their hand, and in early 1867 they declared invalid state constitutions drawn up under Johnson's rules and called for new constitutional conventions whose delegates would be elected by blacks and by those whites who had not violated previous oaths of allegiance by rebelling. Until Southern states met the conditions imposed by Congress, they would remain under military rule. As commander in chief, Johnson sought to prevent military commanders in the South from coming down hard on local officials, some of whom encouraged assaults on blacks. Recent attacks on freedmen in New Orleans and Memphis, where the police chief urged his men to target blacks, convinced Congress that strict military rule was essential. To that end, they passed laws preventing the president from issuing orders to military governors except through General in Chief Ulysses Grant—a Republican sympathetic to congressional efforts—and from removing Cabinet members without Senate approval, a measure designed to protect Secretary of War Edwin Stanton, an ally of the Radicals.

Johnson considered these measures unconstitutional and defied Congress by first suspending Stanton and then firing him. Grant filled in for Stanton during his suspension but stepped down when Congress disapproved Johnson's action. "He is a bolder man than I thought him," Thaddeus Stevens said of Grant. Stanton's ouster infuriated Republicans. One of Johnson's critics declared that it was pointless for Congress to try any longer "to tie the hands which they should have chopped off years ago." In February 1868, the House impeached Johnson, and he stood trial before the Senate. Several Republicans there agreed with Democrats that the charges against him were politically motivated and voted to acquit Johnson, whose opponents fell one vote short of the two-thirds majority necessary to convict him. It proved to be only a temporary setback for Republicans, who rallied around Grant that fall and elected him president.

> ### "He is a bolder man than I thought him."
>
> CONGRESSMAN THADDEUS STEVENS ON GRANT, *after he defied Andrew Johnson*

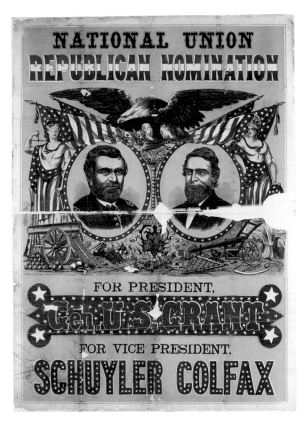

An 1868 election poster for Grant and his running mate, Schuyler Colfax, Speaker of the House, places the Republican nominees under the banner "National Union." Lincoln retitled the Republican Party the National Union Party when he ran for reelection in 1864 in an effort to appear bipartisan and attract votes from Democrats. The label lingered for a while after the war, but Grant's party in 1868 was highly partisan and thoroughly Republican.

At right, two federal officers wear hoods and gowns seized in Alabama in 1868 during a crackdown on the Ku Klux Klan. Klansmen sometimes claimed to be the ghosts of dead Confederates, come back to haunt Yankee carpetbaggers and keep blacks in their place.

> **"All I want is equal rights in the Court House and equal rights when I go to vote."**
>
> *A black politician in Alabama*

Hiram Revels (top) won election to the U.S. Senate from Mississippi in 1870 and took the seat once occupied by Jefferson Davis. A college graduate, Revels was one of many black leaders during Reconstruction educated outside the South, where few freedmen were literate. To remedy that, the Freedmen's Bureau opened hundreds of schools like the one above, and new state constitutions required public education for both races.

Under Grant, Republicans in Congress continued their legislative revolution, which included the Civil Rights Act of 1866, recognizing blacks as American citizens; the Fourteenth Amendment, declaring that no state could "abridge the privileges or immunities" of American citizens or "deprive any person of life, liberty, or property, without due process of law"; and the Fifteenth Amendment, stating that the right of citizens to vote shall not be denied or abridged "on account of race, color, or previous condition of servitude." Those amendments, passed in 1866 and 1869, were ratified by the necessary two-thirds majority of states because Congress insisted that Southern states seeking readmission to the Union adopt them. Many white Southerners resented such coercion and ridiculed the so-called "Black and Tan" state conventions required by Congress, which were dominated by freedmen and white loyalists, including recent immigrants from the North known as carpetbaggers and Southern Republicans known as scalawags. Opponents in Louisiana dismissed the state constitution enacted there as "the work of ignorant Negroes cooperating with a gang of white adventurers."

In fact, most blacks elected as delegates to the conventions in Louisiana and other Southern states were literate and well-informed. In six states, the delegates imposed no voting restrictions on former Confederates, and in other states such restrictions affected a small portion of the white population and were soon removed. Elections held in the South under these constitutions did not fulfill Andrew Johnson's dire prediction that the rules established by Congress would "Africanize" the South. During Reconstruction, two blacks were elected to the U.S. Senate and 15 to the House of Representatives—a relatively small number considering that blacks made up nearly half the population of several Southern states. No blacks served as governors, and most who won elections served as local officials in predominantly black areas. "All I want is equal rights in the Court House and equal rights when I go to vote," said one black politician in Alabama, who insisted that he had "no desire to take away the rights of the white man."

TERROR IN DIXIE

ONE REASON BLACKS DID NOT FARE BETTER IN THE South politically was that many were terrorized by the Ku Klux Klan and other secret societies of whites intent on discouraging blacks from voting, running for office, or otherwise asserting their rights. Founded soon after the war ended, the Ku Klux Klan attracted a number of Confederate veterans, one of whom, General Nathan Bedford Forrest, was reputed to be the Klan's Grand Wizard. "After the order grew to large numbers we found it necessary to have someone of large experience to command," one Klansman later asserted. "We chose General Forrest." Forrest was already under suspicion for his role in a massacre of black troops by Confederates he commanded, who attacked Fort Pillow in Tennessee in 1864. His defense was that the blacks did not surrender but kept fighting and were therefore not entitled to mercy, and that he

AFTER THE WAR

The Civil War launched prominent political careers for some, while others struggled to adjust once the dramatic conflict was over and the nation reunited. The following are postwar biographies for some of war's key military and civilian figures.

Clara Barton The "Angel of the Battlefield" gave lectures about her wartime endeavors and also led a search for missing soldiers. When she went abroad in 1869 to rest, she began to work with the International Red Cross, which led to her eventual establishment of the American Red Cross in 1882.

Benjamin Butler The Union general who had occupied New Orleans and spared little mercy in his handling of its population was a politically influential figure. He was elected to Congress in 1866 on a Republican ticket and became a key figure during the Andrew Johnson impeachment. In 1883 he became governor of Massachusetts, and the following year ran unsuccessfully for president.

George Armstrong Custer With the birth of the 7th Cavalry in 1866, Custer became an Indian fighter, defeating Black Kettle in the Cheyenne battle of the Washita. After his return from a Yellowstone expedition in 1873, he was assigned to Fort Abraham Lincoln, near Bismarck. Before long he and his expedition of 1,200 men discovered gold in the Black Hills, stirring unrest among the Sioux, who considered it their sacred land. In the spring of 1876 Custer set out to quell Sioux and Cheyenne disturbances. Attacking earlier than planned, Custer and his men were surrounded and overwhelmed at the Battle of the Little Big Horn in Montana.

Custer

Jefferson Davis After being captured by Federal cavalry on May 10, 1865, the president of the Confederacy was imprisoned for two years at Fortress Monroe. For the remaining 22 years of his life he endured poor health, lost fortune, and repeated failed business ventures before accepting a home, "Beauvoir," provided for his old age by a bequest of his wife's friend, Sarah Dorsey. There on the Gulf Coast he wrote *The Rise and Fall of the Confederate Government*.

Frederick Douglass During Reconstruction, the freed slave continued to devote his intellect and energies to civil rights, now for freedmen. Enjoying influence in Washington, he served as secretary of the Santo Domingo Commission, recorder of deeds of the District of Columbia, and United States minister to Haiti. Remaining active right up until the day of his death in 1895, Douglass's last function was to attend a woman's suffrage convention.

Nathan Bedford Forrest The cavalry raider who had 29 horses shot from under him returned to his cotton plantations after the surrender. In 1867 he reportedly became a Grand Wizard of the Ku Klux Klan, but resigned two years later. He became president of the Selma, Marion & Memphis Railroad, which failed. In 1877 Forrest died in Memphis from diabetes, and later his remains were re-interred in a park there named for him.

Ulysses S. Grant A national hero after his wartime victories, Grant was elected president in 1868 and again in 1872. But his talent as a general did not carry over into politics. He ran the White House like an army headquarters, had poor judgment selecting the people surrounding him, and allowed financial problems to become rampant. His post-political life was also plagued by financial troubles. He entered into a business that failed, resulting in bankruptcy and embarrassment. Throat cancer was also taking its toll. On his final sickbed he completed his *Personal Memoirs*, which made his family wealthy. His New York City funeral was attended by a million and a half people.

Oliver Wendell Holmes, Jr. The young Union officer returned to Harvard Law School, where he graduated in 1866. In 1881 he wrote *The Common Law* and the following year became a professor at his alma mater. For 20 years Holmes also served on the Massachusetts Supreme Court, part of the time as chief justice. From 1902-1932 he served as an associate justice on the U.S. Supreme Court, where he was known for his strong opinions and for his belief in legislative prerogative.

Joseph E. Johnston The Confederate general who was known for never being defeated during the war became involved in the insurance business in Savannah, Georgia. Moving to Richmond in 1877, he was elected to Congress; by 1885, living in Washington, D.C., he was appointed commissioner of railroads. The previous year Johnston (shown at right meeting with

Lee) had published his *Narrative of Military Operations*. He came down with pneumonia after standing in the cold at Sherman's funeral, and died in Washington in 1891 at age 84.

Robert E. Lee The idolized leader of the Confederate army focused on restoring the crushed South. He became president of Washington College in Lexington, Virginia, later renamed Washington and Lee University in his memory. Indeed, since George Washington, no individual had been so revered by so many as an officer and gentleman. He had a special veranda built onto the college president's house so that his invalid wife could be brought out for a change of scenery. In addition, a barn attached to his house was erected for Traveler, his famous warhorse. When Lee died at the college in 1870, and the entire South went into mourning.

Mary Todd Lincoln After witnessing the assassination of her husband, the bereft former first lady was once again faced with tragedy in 1871. "Tad," the youngest of her four sons, died, leaving only Robert Todd. Mrs. Lincoln's former mental instability now accelerated, and she spent some time in a sanitarium. After being judged sane, and thus able to manage her estate, she traveled abroad for some years. Her final days were spent at the home of a friend in Springfield, Illinois, where she died of paralysis in 1882 at age 63.

Lincoln

James Longstreet Following surrender, Lee's "Old Warhorse," or "Old Pete," as he was commonly called, renewed his West Point friendship with Grant, and became the only senior Confederate officer to join the Republican Party. After running an insurance company and then going into the cotton business in New Orleans, Longstreet was appointed to a series of positions with the federal government, including minister resident to Turkey and United States railroad commissioner. Often criticized in his postwar years by former Confederates, Longstreet published *From Manassas to Appomattox* in 1896 to defend his record as a general.

George McClellan Defeated by Lincoln in the 1864 presidential election, the former Union general spent the next three years abroad. After returning to the United States he briefly became chief engineer of the New York City Department of Docks. From 1878 to 1881 he was governor of New Jersey. Though his efforts during the war had been neither total successes nor failures, he was considered by Lee to be the best commander he had ever fought.

Johnston and Lee

John Mosby The partisan ranger whose guerrilla raids made him an outlaw in the eyes of the Union returned to Virginia to practice law, became a Republican, and served in Ulysses S. Grant's administration. He was appointed consul at Hong Kong until 1885, land agent in Colorado, and assistant attorney for the Department of Justice. A prolific writer, his publications included *Mosby's War Reminiscences* and *Stuart's Cavalry in the Gettysburg Campaign*.

George Pickett Pickett's disastrous charge at Gettysburg made him regretful and bitter for the rest of his life. He ran the Virginia agency of the Washington Life Insurance Company of New York until his death in 1875.

William Seward The highly competent wartime Secretary of State continued his effectiveness during Reconstruction, handling the French diplomatically and securing their evacuation of Mexico. In 1867 he accomplished the cession of Alaska, often referred to as "Seward's Ice Box," and he later recommended the annexation of Hawaii. In spite of a carriage accident in 1865 that left him partially crippled, followed by an attack in his home tied in with the assassination of Lincoln, Seward continued to be active after his term of office came to an end.

William Tecumseh Sherman According to Sherman, his most valuable contribution came not during the war, but soon afterward during his involvement with the Indians, working to rein them in and calm their unrest. Appointed by Grant to go on a mission to Mexico, Sherman succeeded in pressuring France to end its support of Maximilian, the Austrian-born self-proclaimed emperor of Mexico. He became general in chief of the army in 1869 before retiring in 1883 and moving to New York City, where he died in 1891.

Philip Sheridan The cavalry man whose successful engagement at Saylor's Creek, Virginia, brought the war to an end, became administrator of the military division of the Gulf, where he worked to persuade the French to withdraw their support of Maximilian. Before long he became an Indian fighter, eventually forcing several bands to move to reservations. After a series of governmental appointments, he was honored by Congress in 1888 with the highest military rank of general. ■

did what he could to stop the slaughter when the blacks were overwhelmed by his men. Forrest's response to charges that he was responsible for outrages by the Klan was similar. The former cavalry raider denied being the leader of the organization but admitted having influence over Klansmen and claimed he tried to discourage violence. There were "some foolish young men who put masks on their faces and rode over the country, frightening negroes," he testified before Congress in 1871, "but orders have been issued to stop that, and it has ceased."

Forrest may indeed have tried to stop assaults on blacks by Klansman, knowing that such attacks would rouse those he regarded as his true enemies—white Radicals. Elections in the South in the fall of 1868 sparked murderous assaults on hundreds of blacks and some whites allied with them politically. Afterward, the governors of Arkansas and Tennessee declared martial law in many counties and cracked down on the Klan. One Klansman recalled a den meeting at which Forrest spoke defiantly of William Brownlow, Tennessee's governor: "Brownlow says he will bring his militia down here and get us. I say, let him fetch 'em, and you boys be ready to receive 'em." Later, Forrest denounced the governor publicly in Nashville. "Brownlow thinks all Confederate soldiers, and, in fact, the whole Democratic Party in the South, belong to the Ku Klux Klan," he asserted. If the militia targeted suspected Klansmen, Forrest warned, there would be civil war. "I shall not shoot any negroes as long as I can see a white Radical to shoot," he vowed, "for it is the Radicals who will be to blame for bringing on this war."

Despite those fighting words, the militia met with little resistance from the Klan, which disbanded its forces in Tennessee rather than risk a confrontation. Attacks aimed at keeping blacks and their white allies away from the polls continued throughout the South, however. Congress responded by making violations of voting rights a federal offense and authorizing the use of troops to protect those rights. Grant pushed for that legislation and used it to target Klansmen beginning in late 1871. He declared nine counties in South Carolina in a "state of lawlessness" and sent in federal troops. Some suspected Klansmen there were held without trial, for Congress gave Grant authority to suspend the writ of habeas corpus, as Lincoln did during the war. Other suspects in the South were tried, and nearly 1,000 pleaded guilty or were convicted of civil rights violations.

This crackdown served Grant's own interests, for it helped protect his Republican supporters in the South, where he won several states in the 1872 presidential race and secured a second term. Nevertheless, the elections in the region that fall were the freest and most democratic ever held in the South, setting a standard that would not be surpassed there for nearly a century once Reconstruction ended and federal protection for civil rights began to lapse. "We will not find another candidate equal to General Grant," said Frederick Douglass, who realized that

> **"The boss said he would give me a job and pay me $30 a month and more later on."**
> BLACK COWBOY NAT LOVE

Born in Tennessee, Nat Love went West with other adventurous young blacks after the Civil War and proved so adept as a cowboy he later appeared in Wild West shows.

Grant's enormous prestige as the commander who had guided the Union to victory gave him a unique capacity to mobilize support among whites for strenuous efforts to protect the rights of blacks.

RECONSTRUCTION DECONSTRUCTED

DURING GRANT'S SECOND TERM, PUBLIC OPINION TURNED AGAINST FORCEFUL efforts to reconstruct the South and in favor of compromise and reconciliation. There were many reasons for this, including the shared interest of Northerners and Southerners in the West, which became a great realm of opportunity as railroads crossed the continent and lands confiscated from Indians became available for settlement or grazing. Thomas Jefferson had envisioned the West as a place where differences between North and South would be resolved as settlers from both regions intermingled and formed a new society. That hope was seemingly dispelled in the late 1850s—when the furor over slavery made Kansas a battleground—but revived after the Civil War. Union and Confederate veterans labored side by side laying rails across the Plains and extracting wealth from Western mines. Freedmen and former slave owners rounded up cattle together in Texas and drove them hundreds of miles to depots for shipment to Chicago and Kansas City. For black cowboys raised in the South like Nat Love, the West meant freedom. "The boss said he would give me a job and pay me $30 a month and more later on," recalled Love, whose skills earned him the same salary as the whites he rode with.

The West offered opportunity as well for Grant and his fellow Republicans, who faced a political challenge as a result of emancipation. Before the war, each slave counted as three-fifths of a person when determining how many congressional seats and electoral votes a state would receive. Now, however, blacks counted the same as whites for purposes of reapportionment, meaning that the

Seated with other federal negotiators, General William Sherman (third from left) meets with tribal chiefs at Fort Laramie, Wyoming, in 1868 to arrange a treaty. When such peace efforts faltered, Sherman sent troops against rebellious Indians—campaigns many Americans viewed as a more suitable task for the U.S. Army than enforcing federal statutes in the South.

A political cartoon published in Harper's Weekly in January 1875 portrays the danger of removing federal troops from the South—as many in the North were now urging—and leaving blacks to the mercies of the Ku Klan Klan and other hostile forces.

South with its large black population stood to gain politically—a shift that would favor Democrats unless the administration kept troops in the South to protect the rights of blacks, who voted overwhelmingly Republican. If Republicans lost the South, they could still prevail by investing government resources in the West and winning states there. After the Civil War, Westerners demanded federal protection from hostile tribes resisting incursions by ranchers, miners, and homesteaders. Grant sent Sherman and other officers to negotiate treaties with Western tribes and assign them reservations, but those treaties proved fragile and conflict persisted. To suppress defiant Indians and force them back onto reservations, Sherman and Sheridan applied the same punishing tactics they had used against Confederates, burning villages and encouraging white hunters to slaughter buffalo as a way of starving rebellious Sioux and Cheyennes into submission. "Sooner or later," Sherman said, "these Sioux will have to be wiped out or made to stay just where they are put."

Despite George Custer's calamitous defeat in 1876 by Sioux and Cheyennes at Little Big Horn, most Americans supported Grant's campaign to pacify the West and trusted that federal might would prevail over tribal resistance. They were far less supportive of "bayonet rule" in the South to protect blacks. Ruthless intimidation of black voters in Mississippi led that state's governor, Adelbert Ames—a conscientious carpetbagger from Maine—to appeal for federal troops in 1875, but Grant yielded to political pressure and declined to intervene. As his attorney general informed Ames: "The whole public are tired out with these annual autumnal outbreaks in the South, and the great majority are now ready to condemn any interference on the part of the government."

A year later, after whites clashed with black militia in South Carolina, Grant reintroduced federal troops there, but his term was expiring and he was losing his political clout and moral authority. Scandals within his administration had caused many reformers to turn their attention from civil rights to civil service reform, which they hoped would cleanse the political system. People were "sick of carpetbag governments," remarked one Republican leader, who feared that Democrats would link the misdeeds of some Republican carpetbaggers in the South to corruption in Washington.

It had long been clear to those who hailed Reconstruction and those who hated it that the defeated South was being asked to meet higher standards than the rest of the nation. Before the Fifteenth Amendment took effect in 1870, several Northern states had rejected proposals to give blacks there the right to vote. A number of states still had literacy requirements or other restrictions that kept many blacks, Chinese immigrants, and other minorities from voting. No state had yet extended voting rights to women, whose contributions to the Union war effort and emancipation went unrewarded by Republican leaders when they crafted the Fifteenth Amendment and left fully half of America's citizens without that basic right. Powerful men around the country concluded that the crusade for freedom had gone far enough and that white

Southerners should be allowed to "redeem" their states by casting off federal restraints. As one Republican official said of his party's efforts to control the South, "the people will not submit to it any more, nor do I blame them."

Reconstruction came to an end in early 1877 when Grant's Republican successor, Rutherford B. Hayes, a former Union general, emerged as the winner of an agonizingly close and hotly disputed election by making concessions to Democrats that included removing the last federal troops from the South. Reconstruction had been an extension of the war by political means, and not until it ended was the nation reconciled and reunited. But peace came at a terrible price. White politicians in the South found redemption by enacting laws that imposed strict racial segregation, prevented most blacks from voting, and left them without recourse against intimidation and exploitation. "What does it amount to," asked Frederick Douglass, "if the black man, after having been made free by the letter of your law, is unable to exercise that freedom?" The dream of a more perfect Union had been deferred, but the great struggle that began with the Civil War and continued through Reconstruction ensured that this nation conceived in liberty would long endure, in Lincoln's words, and would one day witness a new birth of freedom.

> **"What does it amount to, if the black man, after having been made free by the letter of your law, is unable to exercise that freedom?"**
>
> FREDERICK DOUGLASS
> *as Reconstruction came to an end*

Reunited at Gettysburg on July 3, 1913, Confederate veterans of Pickett's division (right) clasp hands with Union veterans of the Philadelphia Brigade at the stone wall where they collided in battle 50 years earlier. Reenacting Pickett's Charge, some veterans advanced on canes and crutches, one witness observed, before meeting their old foes "in brotherly love and affection."

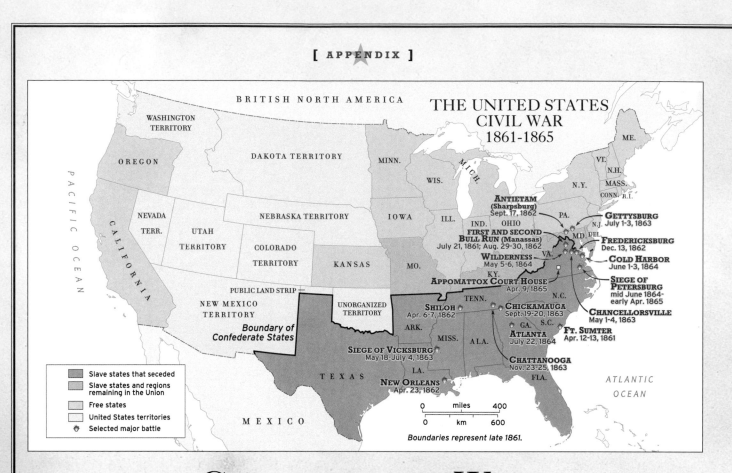

THE UNITED STATES CIVIL WAR 1861-1865

Legend:
- Slave states that seceded
- Slave states and regions remaining in the Union
- Free states
- United States territories
- Selected major battle

Boundaries represent late 1861.

CASUALTIES OF WAR

IN TERMS OF LIVES, THE CIVIL WAR WAS BY FAR THE costliest war in American history. In fact, as many Americans died during the Civil War as in all the nation's wars combined (through Vietnam). The Union lost around 364,000 men, including 37,000 black soldiers. Confederate dead totaled at least 260,000—one-tenth of the South's white males.

Bullets caused the most damage on the battlefield—93 percent of all injuries. Artillery projectiles caused around 6 percent; sabers or bayonets accounted for less than 1 percent. The type of wound usually determined one's chances of survival. Only 13 percent survived abdominal wounds; 37 percent survived chest wounds; 40 percent survived a skull injury; and 67 percent survived a shoulder injury. Amputations increased survival rates, depending on where the injury occurred. The lower the wound was on the limb, the better the chances.

Disease killed even more men.

The map above shows how the United States was not just divided into North and South during the Civil War. Represented are the states that seceded to form the Confederacy, slave states loyal to the Union, free states, and U.S. territories. Selected major battles with dates are denoted by red dots.

Of the more than 620,000 who died, twice as many perished from disease as from combat wounds. In the filthy conditions of camps or of campaigns, tens of thousands died of diarrhea, dysentery, pneumonia, and malaria, while catarrh, bronchitis, scurvy, typhus, typhoid fever, and measles swept away thousands more. Because of a lack of modern medical knowledge, a soldier's chances of recovery from one of these diseases was not greatly increased even if he could be cared for in a hospital. Not to be forgotten were the often disgraceful conditions of prison camps, where thousands more perished.

Weapons had improved over time, but tactics were antiquated. The .58-caliber soft lead bullet, when fired from a rifle at its low muzzle velocity, often shattered bones to bits, requiring amputation. For much of the war, troop movements consisted of massing infantry to compound their firepower, presenting the enemy with easy targets for their powerful new weapons. ■

First Battle of Bull Run (Manassas), Virginia

	Union	Confederate
Killed	418	387
Wounded	1,011	1,582
Missing	1,216	12
Total	2,645	1,981

Battle of Shiloh, Tennessee

	Union	Confederate
Killed	1,754	1,723
Wounded	8,408	8,012
Missing	2,885	959
Total	13,047	10,694

Peninsular Campaign, Virginia

	Union	Confederate
Killed	2,524	4,674
Wounded	11,660	20,507
Missing	6,702	1,351
Total	20,886	26,538

Second Battle of Bull Run (Manassas), Virginia

	Union	Confederate
Killed	1,724	1,481
Wounded	8,372	7,627
Missing	5,958	89
Total	16,054	9,197

Battle of Antietam (Sharpsburg), Maryland

	Union	Confederate
Killed	2,108	1,546
Wounded	9,540	7,752
Missing	753	1,018
Total	12,401	10,316

Battle of Fredericksburg, Virginia

	Union	Confederate
Killed	1,284	608
Wounded	9,600	4,116
Missing	1,769	653
Total	12,653	5,377

Siege of Vicksburg, Mississippi

	Union	Confederate
Killed	763	805
Wounded	3,746	1,938
Missing	162	129
Total	4,671	2,872

(29,491 Confederates surrendered on July 4th)

Battle of Chancellorsville, Virginia

	Union	Confederate
Killed	1,606	1,649
Wounded	9,762	9,106
Missing	5,919	1,708
Total	17,287	12,463

Battle of Gettysburg, Pennsylvania

	Union	Confederate
Killed	3,070	2,592
Wounded	14,497	12,706
Missing	5,434	5,150
Total	23,001	20,448

Battle of Chickamauga, Georgia

	Union	Confederate
Killed	1,657	2,312
Wounded	9,756	14,674
Missing	4,757	1,468
Total	16,170	18,454

Campaign for Chattanooga, Tennessee

	Union	Confederate
Killed	753	361
Wounded	4,722	2,160
Missing	349	4,146
Total	5,824	6,667

The Wilderness, Virginia

	Union	Confederate
Killed	2,246	2,000
Wounded	12,037	6,000
Missing	3,383	3,400
Total	17,666	11,400

(approximately)

Campaign for Atlanta, Georgia

	Union	Confederate
Killed	4,423	3,044
Wounded	22,822	18,952
Missing	4,442	12,983
Total	31,687	34,979

Siege of Petersburg, Virginia

	Union	Confederate
Killed, Wounded	42,000	+28,000
Missing		

(Estimated casualties June 1864-May 1865)

Pre-War	1861	1862

SELECTED MILESTONES

For a nation divided by Civil War, many turning points along the way, whether political, social, economic or war related, helped pave the way for a Union victory.

The South won significant victories in 1861, but in spring 1862, the North gained control of railroad junctions and rivers in the West and launched a campaign against the Confederate capital of Richmond. In late April the Federals took control of the large southern port of New Orleans. The South, however, won a major battle at Bull Run and began to invade Kentucky and Maryland. After a major loss at Antietam, the Confederates were victorious at Fredericksburg.

Early in 1863 the South won the Battle of Chancellorsville, but in July the North beat the Confederates back at Gettysburg and took Vicksburg, thus gaining control of the entire Mississippi River. The war was beginning to turn in favor of the Union.

In late 1864, the capture of Atlanta allowed Sherman to divide the Confederacy. Supply lines in Virginia were also cut when Union forces laid waste to the breadbasket of the Confederacy—the Shenandoah Valley. It was now clear that the Union would be victorious, but the South continued to fight at Petersburg defending Richmond until defeat was inevitable, and they finally surrendered at Appomattox Court House in Virginia, on April 9, 1865.

Pre-War

1820-21 Missouri Compromise enacted.

August 22, 1831 Nat Turner leads a slave rebellion in Virginia.

September 18, 1850 Fugitive Slave Act adopted.

1851-52 Uncle Tom's Cabin published, first in serial form, then in book form.

May 30, 1854 Kansas-Nebraska Act adopted.

May 22, 1856 Senator Charles Sumner attacked by Congressman Preston Brooks.

May 24, 1856 John Brown's raid at Pottawatomie Creek in Kansas.

March 6, 1857 Supreme Court rules against Dred Scott.

October 16, 1859 John Brown's raid at Harpers Ferry, Virginia.

November 6, 1860 Abraham Lincoln elected president.

December 14, 1860 Georgia legislature calls for a convention to consider a confederacy of southern states.

December 20, 1860 South Carolina secedes from the Union.

December 30, 1860 South Carolinians seize Federal arsenal at Charleston.

1861

FORT SUMTER

January 9 Secessionist batteries at Charleston, South Carolina, repulse ship sent to reinforce Fort Sumter.

February 18 Jefferson Davis inaugurated provisional president of the Confederacy.

March 4 Abraham Lincoln inaugurated president of the United States.

April 12 Civil War begins as Confederates open fire on Fort Sumter.

April 14 Fort Sumter falls.

BULL RUN

April 17 Virginia delegates convening in Richmond back secession; Governor John Letcher sends state troops to seize Federal facilities.

April 29 Maryland delegates vote against secession.

May 23 Secession approved by voters in Virginia, which becomes the 11th state to leave the Union.

May 24 Federal troops cross the Potomac River and occupy Arlington and Alexandria, Virginia.

July 21 First Battle of Bull Run (Virginia)

BORDERLANDS

July 3 John Charles Frémont appointed commander of Union's newly created Western Department, which includes the neutral state of Missouri.

August 10 Battle of Wilson's Creek (Missouri).

August 30 Frémont declares martial law in Missouri and names Ulysses S. Grant to command Federal forces along the Mississippi River.

September 3 Confederates under Leonidas Polk occupy Columbus, Kentucky, in defiance of Kentucky's neutrality.

November 2 Frémont relieved of command.

1862

SHILOH

February 6 Battle of Fort Henry (Tennessee)

February 14-15 Battle of Fort Donelson (Tennessee)

April 6-7 Battle of Shiloh (Tennessee)

THE COASTAL WAR

February 10 Battle of Elizabeth City (North Carolina)

March 9 The Virginia and the Monitor clash at Hampton Roads (Virginia).

April 18-28 Federal forces capture New Orleans

RICHMOND

March 17 McClellan's Army of the Potomac begins its campaign against Richmond.

April 16 Battle of Burnt Chimneys (Virginia)

May 3 Confederates withdraw without a battle from Yorktown (Virginia).

May 5 Battle of Williamsburg (Virginia)

May 23 Battle of Front Royal (Virginia)

May 31-June 1 Battle of Seven Pines, or Fair Oaks, near Richmond

June 25-July 1 Seven Days' Battles around Richmond

August 3 Lincoln recalls McClellan's army.

ANTIETAM

August 3 Robert E. Lee launches offensive in northern Virginia.

August 28-30 Second Battle of Bull Run (Virginia)

September 4 Lee invades Maryland.

September 12-15 Battle of Harpers Ferry (western Virginia)

September 17 Battle of Antietam (Maryland)

EMANCIPATION

September 22 Lincoln issues Emancipation Proclamation, to take effect January 1, 1863.

December 13 Battle of Fredericksburg (Virginia).

1863	1864	1865	Post-War
VICKSBURG December 29, 1862 Grant's first campaign against Vicksburg ends with Sherman's defeat at Chickasaw Bluffs (Mississippi). April 16 Grant launches second campaign against Vicksburg (Mississippi). May 16 Battle of Champion's Hill (Mississippi) May 18-July 4 Siege of Vicksburg May 27-July 9 Siege of Port Hudson (Louisiana) **CHANCELLORSVILLE / GETTYSBURG** January 26 Joseph Hooker replaces Ambrose Burnside as commander of the Army of the Potomac. May 1-4 Battle of Chancellorsville (Virginia) June 9 Battle of Brandy Station (Virginia) July 1-3 Battle of Gettysburg (Pennsylvania) November 19 President Lincoln presents the Gettysburg Address to dedicate the Gettysburg National Cemetery. **HOMEFRONT** April 2 Richmond Bread Riot July 13-16 New York City Draft Riots August 21 Confederate raider William Quantrill leads deadly attack on town of Lawrence, Kansas. August 25 Union general Thomas Ewing, Jr., retaliates by ordering inhabitants to evacuate four Missouri counties. **CHATTANOOGA** September 2 Federals seize Knoxville, Tennessee. September 7 Braxton Bragg orders his Confederates to evacuate Chattanooga. September 19-20 Battle of Chickamauga (Georgia) October 23 Ulysses Grant takes command in Chattanooga, where Federals have come under siege. November 23-25 Battle of Chattanooga	**GRANT VS LEE** March 9 Lincoln promotes Ulysses S. Grant to lieutenant general, in command of all Federal forces. May 4 Grant launches campaign against Robert E. Lee in Virginia. May 5-6 Battle of the Wilderness (Virginia) May 8-18 Battles at Spotsylvania (Virginia) June 1-3 Battle of Cold Harbor (Virginia) June 15 Grant's troops reach Petersburg, Virginia, where Confederates soon come under siege. July 18 Battle of the Crater at Petersburg (Virginia) **ATLANTA** May 7 William Sherman launches campaign against Joseph Johnston by advancing into Georgia. June 27 Battle of Kennesaw Mountain (Georgia) July 17 Jefferson Davis replaces Johnston with John Bell Hood. July 20 Battle of Peachtree Creek (Georgia) July 22 Battle of Atlanta August 31-September 1 Battle of Jonesboro (Georgia) September 2 Sherman takes Atlanta. **PATHS TO VICTORY** August 31 George McClellan nominated by Democrats to challenge Abraham Lincoln in the November election. November 8 Lincoln wins reelection decisively. November 15 William Sherman launches his devastating march from Atlanta to Savannah. November 30-December 16 Battles of Franklin and Nashville (Tennessee) December 13 Sherman captures Fort McAllister, below Savannah, and links up with Federal fleet. December 21 Sherman takes Savannah.	**CAROLINAS** January 13-15 Federals capture Fort Fisher and proceed to seal off Wilmington, North Carolina, the last Confederate port open to foreign trade. January 21 William Sherman leaves Savannah to advance through the Carolinas. January 31 U.S. Congress passes Thirteenth Amendment, outlawing slavery. February 3 Peace talks between Union and Confederate leaders at Fort Monroe, on the Virginia coast, conclude without an agreement. February 17 Confederates abandon Charleston, South Carolina; Sherman's troops occupy Columbia, South Carolina. March 19-21 Battle of Bentonville (North Carolina) March 28 President Lincoln lays out plans for peace in a meeting with top commanders near Petersburg, Virginia. **APPOMATTOX** March 31-April 1 Battle of Five Forks (Virginia) April 2 Grant breaks through at Petersburg, forcing Confederates to abandon that city and nearby Richmond overnight. April 6 Battle of Sayler's Creek (Virginia) April 9 Lee surrenders to Grant at Appomattox Court House. April 15 Abraham Lincoln dies after being shot by Confederate sympathizer John Wilkes Booth. April 26 Joseph Johnston surrenders to William Sherman. May 10 Jefferson Davis captured by Federals in Georgia. May 23-24 Victorious Union troops parade through Washington, D.C. May 26 Armed resistance to the Union ends with surrender of Confederate troops west of the Mississippi.	April 15, 1865 Democrat Andrew Johnson succeeds Abraham Lincoln as president following Lincoln's assassination. December 1865 Republican-dominated Congress refuses to seat newly elected representatives from Southern states reorganized under Johnson's proclamation and launches its own program of Reconstruction. May 1868 Impeachment trial in Senate ends with Johnson's acquittal when his opponents fall one vote short of the two-thirds majority needed to convict. March 4, 1869 Republican Ulysses Grant succeeds Johnson and supports the Fifteenth Amendment, barring states from denying citizens the right to vote on the basis of race. March 2, 1877 Republican Rutherford B. Hayes declared winner of disputed presidential election after signaling the end of Reconstruction by pledging to remove the last Federal troops in the South, sent there by Grant to protect voting rights.

VOCABULARY OF WAR

abatis A defensive barrier of fallen trees with branches pointed toward the enemy.

adjutant A staff officer assisting the commanding officer with administrative duties.

battery The basic unit of field artillery, consisting of four to six guns; a position where artillery is mounted.

blockade runner A vessel or captain specializing in evading the Federal naval blockade of Southern ports.

bombproof A shelter from artillery bombardment, usually built with walls and a roof of timbers and packed earth.

bounty A monetary incentive given to induce men to enlist. A bounty jumper was an individual who accepted the enlistment bounty and then deserted to repeat the process.

breastwork A temporary earthwork fortification, about chest high, over which a soldier can fire.

brevet An honorary rank given for exceptional bravery or merit. It granted none of the authority of the official rank.

bummers Union foragers who followed Sherman's campaign through Georgia.

caisson A cart with two large chests for transporting artillery ammunition. Connected to a horse-drawn limber, it carried a spare cannon wheel.

canister A tinned iron can containing lead or iron balls that scattered when fired from a cannon.

cap A percussion cap; a small, copper cup containing a dot of explosive chemical. Placed on the hollow nipple of a firearm, the chemicals exploded when struck by the hammer, igniting the weapon's charge.

carbine A short-barreled shoulder arm used primarily by cavalry.

case shot Case shot properly refers to shrapnel or spherical case; see also shrapnel.

cheval-de-frise A movable defensive barrier made of a log with sharpened stakes.

coffee cooler A shirker or malingerer. One who will resume his march "as soon as his coffee cools."

color company The center company of a regiment in line of a march or battle. It included the color guard—the detachment of men chosen to carry and guard the regimental flags.

Columbiad A large cast-iron, smooth-bore cannon adopted for U.S. sea-coast defenses in 1860.

contraband A slave under the protection of Union forces.

corduroy road A road with a surface of logs laid together transversely.

deadline The wooden fence, placed along the inside of a prison stockade, that marked the line that prisoners could not cross without the risk of being shot. Perhaps the most famous deadline was at Andersonville.

Dutchmen A term for Union soldiers of German descent.

echelon A staggered formation of parallel lines of troops.

elevating screw A mechanism located under the breech of an artillery piece used to raise or lower the elevation of fire.

embrasure An opening in a fort wall through which a cannon was fired.

Enfield rifle Adopted by the British Army in 1853, the North and South imported nearly a million Enfields during the course of the Civil War.

enfilade Gunfire that takes an enemy line lengthwise, or the position allowing such firing.

file closer A soldier marching behind a line of battle to ensure that a formation stayed in order.

flank The right or left end of a military formation.

forage To search for and acquire provisions from the countryside. For many soldiers, it meant stealing.

forlorn hope A unit of soldiers given a desperately difficult or dangerous assignment.

friction primer A tube inserted into the vent of a cannon to discharge the piece. The tube contained combustible material that ignited when a wire friction igniter was withdrawn by pulling a lanyard.

gabion An open-ended, cylindrical basket of brush and stakes filled with dirt or stones and used to reinforce earthworks.

grapeshot Iron balls bound together and fired from a heavy cannon. Resembling a cluster of grapes, the balls broke apart and scattered on impact.

gunboat A shallow-draft vessel, often clad in iron plates, designed mainly for use on rivers.

guidon A small flag used to identify a mounted unit.

gum blanket A waterproof blanket or poncho, coated with rubber or gutta-percha.

hardtack A durable flour and water cracker, or biscuit, normally about three inches square and a half-inch thick.

haversack A shoulder bag for carrying rations or personal items.

housewife A sewing kit containing needles and thread as well as toiletries and other personal items.

howitzer A short-barreled artillery piece that fired its projectile in a relatively high-arcing trajectory.

lanyard A strong cord with a hook to connect to a friction primer inserted into the touchhole on an artillery piece. When the gunner pulled the handle of the lanyard, the primer ignited the powder, firing the weapon.

limber A two-wheeled, horse-drawn vehicle to which a gun carriage or a caisson was attached.

lunette A small field fortification.

masked battery Any concealed or camouflaged artillery battery.

mess A group of soldiers who prepare and eat meals together; the place where meals are prepared and eaten.

Minié ball The standard conical projectile fired from a rifled musket. The bullet's hollow base expanded, forcing its sides into the rifling, causing the bullet to spin and imparting greater accuracy.

monitor A term applied generically to Federal shallow-draft ironclad warships with revolving gun turrets.

mortar A short, thick-walled artillery piece designed to propel heavy projectiles in a steep, high trajectory.

musket A smoothbore, muzzleloading shoulder arm.

Napoleon A smoothbore, bronze muzzleloading artillery piece developed under the direction of the French Emperor Napoleon III. It fired a 12-pound round projectile.

open order A loose open formation in which the men were more widely spaced than in normal line of battle.

orderly A soldier assigned to a superior officer for various duties, including carrying messages.

palisade A fence of strong posts or stakes.

parallel An earthwork for artillery dug parallel to the face of an enemy fortification to cover advancing siege operations.

parapet A defensive elevation raised above a fort's main wall, or rampart.

parole The pledge of a soldier released from captivity that he would not take up arms again until he had been formally exchanged.

Parrott guns Muzzleloading, rifled artillery pieces of various calibers. The cast iron tube has a wrought-iron reinforcing band around the breech. Invented by Union officer Robert Parrott.

picket One or more soldiers on guard to protect the larger unit from surprise attack.

pontoon bridge A portable, temporary bridge resting on floating pontoons.

provost guard Soldiers acting as military police under the direction of an officer, called a provost marshal.

quartermaster An officer in charge of procurement and supply of clothing, tents, and other supplies.

ram A vessel built with a reinforced iron prow for deliberate collision with other ships. The ram was intended to sink enemy vessels by punching through their hull at or below the water line.

rammer An artillerist's tool used to insert the powder charge and projectile down the barrel of a cannon and seat them firmly in the breech.

rampart The main wall of a fort.

ration A specified allotment of food for one person (or animal) per day.

redoubt An enclosed defensive fortification.

revetment Support or bracing used to reinforce the sides of earthen fortifications. Revetments could be constructed of logs, boards, sandbags, or other material.

rifle pit A shallow trench from which soldiers could fire weapons while protected from enemy fire.

round shot A solid, spherical artillery projectile.

salient The part of a trench system or line of defense that jutted out toward the enemy.

section of artillery Part of an artillery battery consisting of two guns.

shelter tent Also called a *tente d'abri*, pup tent, or dog tent, it consisted of two shelter halves buttoned together and hung on tent poles.

shrapnel An artillery projectile used as an antipersonnel weapon. It was a hollow sphere filled with metal balls packed around a small explosive charge. A time fuse detonated the charge in flight, showering the enemy with the smaller projectiles. Also called spherical case.

Sibley tent A conical tent named for its inventor, Confederate general Henry H. Sibley.

skirmisher A soldier advancing in front of the main body of troops to probe the enemy's position.

smoothbore Any firearm or cannon with an unrifled barrel.

solid shot A solid artillery projectile, oblong for rifled pieces and round for smoothbores.

Spencer rifle A repeating carbine with a seven-shot magazine, designed by Christopher M. Spencer.

Spherical case See shrapnel.

sponge A brush-like artillerist's tool that was soaked in water and used to clear a cannon barrel of grime, smoldering cloth, and other detritus between rounds.

Springfield rifle The standard U. S. infantry shoulder arm named for the arsenal at Springfield, Massachusetts; later, any similar weapon regardless of where it was made.

sutler A peddler licensed to sell food, drink, and other supplies to troops in camp or in the field.

torpedo A naval mine that exploded on contact with a ship. Some torpedoes could be fired electrically from a shore station.

traverse A trench or other defensive work constructed obliquely to the enemy to protect against enfilading fire.

volley The simultaneous discharge of a number of firearms.

Zouaves Regiments, both Union and Confederate, that modeled themselves after the original Zouaves of French colonial Algeria.

Bailey, Ronald H., and the eds. of Time-Life Books. *The Bloodiest Day: The Battle of Antietam*. Alexandria, Va.: Time-Life Books, 1984.

Bauer, K. Jack, ed. *Soldiering: The Civil War Diary of Rice C. Bull, 123rd New York Volunteer Infantry*. San Rafael, Calif.: Presidio Press, 1977.

Bedwell, Randall. *War Is All Hell: A Collection of Civil War Quotations*. Nashville: Cumberland House, 1999.

Berry, Mary Clay. *Voices from the Century Before: The Odyssey of a Nineteenth-Century Kentucky Family*. New York: Arcade Publishing, Inc., 1997.

Blaisdell, Bob, ed. *The Civil War: A Book of Quotations*. New York: Dover Publications, 2004.

Butterfield, Roger. *The American Past*. New York: Simon and Schuster, 1957.

Chaffin, Tom. *Pathfinder: John Charles Frémont and the Course of American Empire*. New York: Hill and Wang, 2002.

Chaitin, Peter M., and the eds. of Time-Life Books. *The Coastal War: Chesapeake Bay to Rio Grande*. Alexandria, Va.: Time-Life Books, 1984.

Channing, Steve A., and the eds. of Time-Life Books. *Confederate Ordeal: The Southern Home Front*. Alexandria, Va.: Time-Life Books, 1984.

Clark, Champ, and the eds. of Time-Life Books. *Decoying the Yanks*. Alexandria, Va.: Time-Life Books, 1984.

Clark, Champ, and the eds. of Time-Life Books. *Gettysburg: The Confederate High Tide*. Alexandria, Va.: Time-Life Books, 1985.

Cleaves, Freeman. *Rock of Chickamauga: The Life of General George H. Thomas*. Norman: University of Oklahoma Press, 1948.

Coombe, Jack D. *Gunfire Around the Gulf: The Last Major Naval Campaigns of the Civil War*. New York: Bantam Books, 1999.

Coombe, Jack D. *Gunsmoke Over the Atlantic: First Naval Actions of the Civil War*. New York: Bantam Books, 2002.

Coopersmith, Andrew S. *Fighting Words: An Illustrated History of Newspaper Accounts of the Civil War*. New York: New Press, 2004.

Cozzens, Peter. *This Terrible Sound: The Battle of Chickamauga*. Urbana: University of Illinois Press, 1992.

Culpepper, Marilyn Mayer. *Trials and Triumphs: Women of the American Civil War*. East Lansing: Michigan State University Press, 1991.

Davis, Burke. *Sherman's March*. New York: Random House, 1980.

Davis, George B; Perry, Leslie J.; and Kirkley, Joseph W. *The Official Military Atlas of the Civil War*. New York: The Fairfax Press by Arno Press, Inc. and Crown Publishers, 1983.

Davis, William C. *Battle at Bull Run: A History of the First Major Campaign of the Civil War*. Garden City, N.Y.: Doubleday, 1977.

Davis, William C. and the eds. of Time-Life Books. *Brother Against Brother*. Alexandria, Va.: Time-Life Books, 1983.

Davis, William C. and the eds. of Time-Life Books. *First Blood: Fort Sumter to Bull Run*. Alexandria, Va.; Time-Life Books, 1983.

Davis, William C. and the eds. of Time-Life Books. *Death in the Trenches: Grant at Petersburg*. Alexandria, Va.: Time-Life Books, 1986.

Davis, William C. *Jefferson Davis: The Man and his Hour*. New York: HarperCollins, 1991.

Donald, David. *Charles Sumner and the Coming of the Civil War*. New York: Alfred A. Knopf, 1960.

Ferrell, Claudine L. *Reconstruction*. Westport, Conn.: Greenwood Press, 2003.

Fitzhugh, George. *Cannibals All! Or Slaves Without Masters*. Cambridge, Mass.: Harvard University Press, 1960.

Foote, Shelby, and the eds. of Time-Life Books. Shelby Foote, *The Civil War: A Narrative. 14 vols.* Text copyright 1958 by Shelby Foote. Copyright renewed 1986 by Shelby Foote. Alexandria, Virginia: Time-Life Books, 1998-2000.

Fowler, William M., Jr. *Under Two Flags: The American Navy in the Civil War*. New York: W.W. Norton and Company, 1990.

Goolrick, William K., and the eds. of Time-Life Books. *Rebels Resurgent: Fredericksburg to Chancellorsville*. Alexandria, Va.: Time-Life Books, 1985.

Gordon, John B. *Reminiscences of the Civil War*. New York: Charles Scribner's Sons, 1903.

Grimsley, Mark. *And Keep Moving On: The Virginia Campaign, May-June 1864*. Lincoln: University of Nebraska Press, 2002.

Harsh, Joseph L. *Confederate Tide Rising: Robert E. Lee and the Making of Southern Strategy, 1861-1862*. Kent, Oh.: Kent State University Press, 1998.

Hearn, Chester G. *When the Devil Came Down to Dixie: Ben Butler in New Orleans*. Baton Rouge: Louisiana State University Press, 1997.

Horn, Stanley F., ed. *The Robert E. Lee Reader*. New York: Bobbs-Merrill, 1949.

Jaynes, Gregory, and the eds. of Time-Life Books. *The Killing Ground: Wilderness to Cold Harbor*. Alexandria, Va.: Time-Life Books, 1986.

Johnson, Allen, and Malone, Dumas,eds. *Dictionary of American Biography*. New York: Charles Scribner's Sons, 1958.

Johnson, Robert Underwood, and Buel, Clarence Clough, eds. *Battles and Leaders of the Civil War*, 4 vols. New York: Thomas Yoseloff, 1958.

Josephy, Alvin M., Jr., and the eds. of Time-Life Books. *War on the Frontier: The Trans-Mississippi West*. Alexandria, Va.: Time-Life Books, 1986.

Kagan, Neil, ed. *Great Battles of the Civil War*. Birmingham, Ala.: Oxmoor House, 2002.

Kagan, Neil, ed. *Great Photographs of the Civil War*. Birmingham, Ala.: Oxmoor House, 2003.

Katcher, Philip. *The Civil War Source Book*. New York: Facts on File Inc., 1982. First published by Arms and Armour Press, a Cassell Imprint.

Kennett, Lee. *Sherman: A Soldier's Life*. New York: HarperCollins, 2001.

Kirchberger, Joe H. *An Eyewitness The Civil War and Reconstruction History*. New York: Facts on File, 1991.

Klein, Mary. *Days of Defiance: Sumter, Secession, and the Coming of the Civil War*. New York: Vintage Books, 1997.

Klingaman, William K. *Abraham Lincoln and the Road to Emancipation, 1861-1865*. New York: Viking, 2001.

Korn, Jerry, and the eds. of Time-Life Books. *The Fight for Chattanooga: Chickamauga to Missionary Ridge*. Alexandria, Va.: Time-Life Books, 1985.

Korn, Jerry, and the eds. of Time-Life Books. *Pursuit to Appomattox: The Last Battles*. Alexandria, Va.: Time-Life Books, 1987.

Korn, Jerry, and the eds. of Time-Life Books. *War on the Mississippi: Grant's Vicksburg Campaign*. Alexandria, Va.: Time-Life Books, 1985.

Lepa, Jack H. Breaking the Confederacy: *The Georgia and Tennessee Campaigns of 1864*. Jefferson, N.C.: McFarland & Company, 2005.

Logsdon, David R., ed. *Eyewitnesses at the Battle of Fort Donelson*. Nashville: Kettle Mills Press, 1998.

Logsdon, David R., ed. *Eyewitnesses at the Battle of Shiloh*. Nashville: Kettle Mills Press, 1994.

Long, E. B., with Barbara Long. *The Civil War Day by Day: An Almanac 1861-1865*. New York: Doubleday & Company, Inc., 1971.

Lossing, Benson J., *Mathew Brady's Illustrated History of the Civil War*. Avenel, N.J.: Portland House, 1912.

MacDonald, John. *Great Battles of the Civil War*. London: Marshall Editions Limited, 1989. Macmillan, U.S.A.

Martin, Isabella D., and Avery, Myrta Lockett, eds. *Mary Chestnut: A Diary from Dixie*. New York: Grammercy Books, a division of Random Value Publishing, Inc., 1997.

Marvel, William. *Burnside*. Chapel Hill: University of North Carolina Press, 1991.

McClellan, George B. *McClellan's Own Story*. New York: Charles L. Webster, 1887.

McDonough, James Lee. *Stones River—Bloody Winter in Tennessee*. Knoxville: University of Tennessee Press, 1980.

McMurry, Richard M. *Atlanta 1864: Last Chance for the Confederacy*. Lincoln: University of Nebraska Press, 2000.

McPherson, James M. *The Battle Cry of Freedom*. New York: Ballantine Books, 1989.

McPherson, James M. *Crossroads of Freedom: Antietam*. New York: Oxford University Press, 2002.

McPherson, James M. *Ordeal by Fire: Civil War and Reconstruction*. New York: Alfred Knopf, 1982.

McWhiney, Grady. *Braxton Bragg and Confederate Defeat*. New York: Columbia University Press, 1969.

Miller, William J., and Pohanka, Brian C. *An Illustrated History of the Civil War: Images of an American Tragedy*. Alexandria, Va.: Time-Life Books, 2000.

Nevin, David, and the eds. of Time-Life Books. *The Road to Shiloh: Early Battles in the West*. Alexandria, Va.: Time-Life Books, 1983.

Nevin, David, and the eds. of Time-Life Books. *Sherman's March: Atlanta to the Sea*. Alexandria, Va.: Time-Life Books, 1986.

Nevins, Alan. *The War for the Union, vol. 1*. New York: Charles Scribner's Sons, 1959.

Oates, Stephen B. *With Malice Toward None: A Life of Abraham Lincoln*. New York: HarperPerennial, 1994.

Piston, William Garrett, and Hatcher, Richard W., III. *Wilson's Creek: The Second Battle of the Civil War and the Men Who Fought It*. Chapel Hill: University of North Carolina Press, 2000.

Porter, Horace. *Campaigning With Grant*. New York: The Century Co., 1897.

Quarles, Benjamin. *The Negro in the Civil War*. Boston: Little, Brown and Company, 1953.

Reynolds, David S. *John Brown, Abolitionist: The Man Who Killed Slavery, Sparked the Civil War, and Seeded Civil Rights*. New York: Alfred A. Knopf, 2005.

Robertson, James I., Jr., and the eds. of Time-Life Books. *Tenting Tonight: The Soldier's Life*. Alexandria, Va.: Time-Life Books, 1984.

Robinson, Armstead L. *Bitter Fruits of Bondage: The Demise of Slavery and the Collapse of the Confederacy, 1861-1865*. Charlottesville: University of Virginia Press, 2005.

Roland, Charles P. *Albert Sidney Johnston: Soldier of Three Republics*. Lexington: University Press of Kentucky, 2001.

Sandburg, Carl. *Abraham Lincoln*. New York: Harcourt, 1982.

Sauers, Richard A. *A Succession of Honorable Victories: The Burnside Expedition in North Carolina*. Dayton Oh.: Morningside House, 1996.

Schneider, Dorothy, and Schneider, Carl J. *Slavery in America*. New York: Checkmark Books, 2000.

Schultz, Duane. *Quantrill's War: The Life and Times of William Clarke Quantrill, 1837-1865*. New York: St. Martin's Press, 1996.

Sears, Stephen W. *Chancellorsville*. Boston: Houghton Mifflin Company, 1996.

Sears, Stephen W. *George B. McClellan: The Young Napoleon*. New York: Ticknor & Fields, 1988.

Sears, Stephen W. *Gettysburg*. Boston: Houghton Mifflin Company, 2003.

Sears, Stephen W. *Landscape Turned Red: The Battle of Antietam*. Boston: Houghton Mifflin Company, 1983.

Sears, Stephen W. *To the Gates of Richmond: The Peninsula Campaign*. Boston: Houghton Mifflin Company, 1992.

Shea, William L., and Winschel, Terrence J. *Vicksburg Is the Key: The Struggle for the Mississippi River*. Lincoln: University of Nebraska Press, 2003.

Smith, Jean Edward. *Grant*. New York: Simon & Schuster, 2001.

Stone, Edward, ed. *Incident at Harper's Ferry*. Englewood Cliffs, N.J.: Prentice-Hall, 1956.

Stiles, Robert. *Four Years Under Marse Robert*. New York: Neale Publishing Company, 1903.

Street, James, Jr., and the eds. of Time-Life Books. *The Struggle for Tennessee: Tupelo to Stones River*. Alexandria, Va.: Time-Life Books, 1985.

Strother, David Hunter. *A Virginia Yankee in the Civil War: The Diaries of David Hunter Strother*, Cecil D. Eby, Jr., ed. Chapel Hill: University of North Carolina Press, 1961.

Sword, Wiley. *Mountains Touched With Fire: Chattanooga Besieged, 1863*. New York: St. Martin's Press, 1995.

Thomas, Emory M. *Robert E. Lee*. New York: W.W. Norton, 1995.

Thomsen, Brian M., ed. *The Civil War Memoirs of Ulysses S. Grant*. New York: Tom Doherty Associates, 2002.

Time-Life Books, eds. *African Americans Voices of Triumph: Perseverance*. Alexandria, Va.: Time-Life Books, 1993.

Time-Life Books, eds. *The American Story: War Between Brothers*. Alexandria, Va.: Time-Life Books, 1996.

Time-Life Books, eds. *The Civil War, 28 vols*. Alexandria, Va.: Time-Life Books, 1983-1987.

Time-Life Books, eds. *Echoes of Glory, 3 vols*. Alexandria, Va.: Time-Life Books, 1991.

Time-Life Books, eds. *Voices of the Civil War. 18 vols*. Alexandria, Va.: Time-Life Books, 1998-2000.

Trudeau, Noah Andre. *Out of the Storm: The End of the Civil War. April-June 1865*. Boston: Little, Brown and Co., 1993.

Walsh, George. *"Whip the Rebellion": Ulysses S. Grant's Rise to Command*. New York: Tom Doherty Associates, 2005.

Walther, Eric H. *The Fire-Eaters*. Baton Rouge: Louisiana State University Press, 1992.

The War of the Rebellion: A Compilation of the Official Records of the Union and Confederate Armies. Washington, D.C.: Government Printing Office, 1880; Harrisburg, Pa.: National Historical Society, 1971 (rpt.).

Ward, Geoffrey C. with Ric Burns and Ken Burns. *The Civil War*. New York: Alfred A. Knopf, 2002.

Wheeler, Richard. *On Fields of Fury, From the Wilderness To the Crater: An Eyewitness History*. New York: HarperCollins, 1991.

Wheeler, Richard. *The Siege of Vicksburg*. New York: Thomas Y. Crowell, 1978.

Wheeler, Richard. *Witness to Appomattox*. New York: Harper & Row, 1989.

Wills, Brian Steel. *A Battle From the Start: The Life of Nathan Bedford Forrest*. New York: HarperCollins, 1992.

Winkle, Kenneth J., and Woodworth, Steven E. *Atlas of the Civil War*. Oxford: Oxford University Press, 2004.

Winther, Oscar Osburn. *With Sherman to the Sea: The Civil War Diaries, Letters, and Reminiscences of Theodore F. Upson*. Baton Rouge: Louisiana State University Press, 1943.

Woodward, C. Vann, ed. *Mary Chesnut's Civil War*. New Haven: Yale University Press, 1981.

NOTES:

The C. Paul Loane Collection was photographed by Robert J. Laramie. The David Wynn Vaughan Collection was photographed by Jack Melton.

FRONT MATTER

1 (t), MOC, Photography by Katherine Wetzel; 1 (b) National Park Service, Historic Graphic Collection, Harpers Ferry Center; 2 (l) David Wynn Vaughan Collection; 2 (lc) David Wynn Vaughan Collection; 2 (rc) MOC; 2 (r) David Wynn Vaughan Collection; 3 (l), David Wynn Vaughan Collection; 3 (lc), David Wynn Vaughan Collection; 3 (rc), C. Paul Loane Collection; 3 (r), C. Paul Loane Collection; 4, LOC, LC-DIG-cwpb-04339; 9, C. Paul Loane Collection; 10 (t), LOC, LC-DIG-cwpb-00193; 10(b), USAMHI; 11, LOC, LC-DIG-cwpbh-03243; 12 (t), LOC, LC-DIG-cwpb-00074; 12 (b), LOC, LC-USZC4-1041; 13, LOC, LC-USZC4-4998; 14(t), VHS; 14 (b), VHS; 15, MOC, Photography by Katherine Wetzel.

PROLOGUE: A NATION DIVIDED

16-17, Robin Stanford; 19, USAMHI; 20, NARA; 21, NYHS; 22, LOC, LC-B8171-152-A; 23, MOC; 25 (tl) LOC, LC-USZ62-119343; 25 (tr) NARA; 25 (bl) NARA; 25 (br) LOC, LC-USZ62-11212; 26, Ohio Historical Society; 27, Courtesy of Smithsonian Images; 29, Kansas State Historical Society; 30 (t) LOC, LC-USZ62-2472; 30 (b) LOC, LC-USZ62-126970; 31, CHS, ICHi-11126; 32, LOC, LC-USZ61-440; 33, LOC; 34, LOC, LC-USZ62-79305; 36, LOC, LC-USZC2-331; 37, CHS, ICHi-11472; 38, Louisiana State Museum; 39, LOC; 40 (t), Maggie Steber; 40 (b), Hulton-Deutsch/CORBIS; 41, LOC; 42, NARA; 43, NYHS; 44, Louisiana State Museum; 45 (t), MPI/Getty Images; 45 (b), LOC, LC-USZ62-39380; 46-47, Valentine Richmond History Center.

CHAPTER 1, 1861: FIRST BLOOD

49, LOC, LC-DIG-cwpb-05637; 50, LOC, rbpe 17301000; 51, LOC, LC-USZC4-690; 52, Boston Atheneum; 53, LOC, LC-USZ62-5962; 54, LOC, LC-DIG-cwpb-06563; 55, LOC, LC-USZ62-48564; 56-57, LOC, LC-USZC4-528; 58, Courtesy of National Portrait Gallery, Smithsonian Institution; 60 (t), VHS; 60 (b), NARA; 61 (t), Tulane University, New Orleans; 61 (c), Tulane University, New Orleans; 61 (b), NARA; 63 (t), NARA; 63 (b), LOC; 64-65, Courtesy of Picture History; 66 (l), David Wynn Vaughan Collection; 66 (c), David Wynn Vaughan Collection; 66 (r), C. Paul Loane Collection; 67 (tl), C. Paul Loane Collection; 67 (tc), C. Paul Loane Collection; 67 (tr), David Wynn Vaughan Collection; 67 (cl), David Wynn Vaughan Collection; 67 (c), David Wynn Vaughan Collection; 67 (cr), C.

Paul Loane Collection; 67 (bl), David Wynn Vaughan Collection; 67 (bc), David Wynn Vaughan Collection; 67 (br), David Wynn Vaughan Collection; 68 (t), David Wynn Vaughan Collection; 68 (b), C. Paul Loane Collection; 69, LOC, LC-DIG-cwpb-04768; 70, LOC, LC-DIG-cwpb-01005; 71, LOC, LC-USZC4-5178; 72, MOLLUS-MASS and USAMHI; 73, LOC, LC-USZ62-3131; 74 (l), NARA; 74 (r), NARA; 75, NARA; 76, LOC, LC-DIG-cwpb-00972; 77, Courtesy Stonewall Jackson Foundation, Lexington, VA; 78 (t), LOC, LC-DIG-cwpb-01547; 78 (c), LOC, LC-DIG-cwpb-00954; 78 (b), LOC, LC-DIG-cwpb-00964; 79, VHS; 80, LOC, LC-DIG-ppmsca-09313; 81, Bettmann/CORBIS; 83, State Historical Society of Missouri, Columbia; 84, General Sweeney's Museum; 86-87, WRHS; 88, LOC, LC-USZ62-90934; 89, LOC, LC-DIG-cwpb-06714; 90 (all), MOC, Photography by Katherine Wetzel; 91 (tl), David Wynn Vaughan Collection; 91 (all others), MOC, Photography by Katherine Wetzel; 92 (all) MOC, Photography by Katherine Wetzel; 92-93, MOC, Photography by Katherine Wetzel; 93 (c), David Wynn Vaughan Collection; 93 (all others) MOC, Photography by Katherine Wetzel; 94 (all) C. Paul Loane Collection; 95 (all), C. Paul Loane Collection; 96 (all), C. Paul Loane Collection; 96-97, Courtesy of Smithsonian Images; 97 (all), C. Paul Loane Collection.

CHAPTER 2, 1862: TOTAL WAR

98-99, LOC, LC-DIG-cwpb-01097; 101, LOC, LC-USZ62-36385; 102-103, NARA; 104, LOC, LC-USZC2-1985; 105, LOC, LC-DIG-ppmsca-08352; 106, NYHS; 108, MOLLUS-MASS and USAMHI; 109, David Wynn Vaughan Collection; 111, State Historical Society of Missouri, Columbia; 112 (t), MOLLUS-MASS and USAMHI; 112 (c), LOC, LC-USZ62-3580; 112 (b), LOC, LC-USZC4-1910; 113, VHS; 114, MOC, Photography by Katherine Wetzel; 117 (t), LOC, LC-DIG-cwpb-05369; 117 (b), NYHS; 118-119, LOC, LC-USZC2-3066; 120, Courtesy of Picture History; 121, LOC, LC-DIG-cwpb-01058; 122, WRHS; 124, United States Naval Historical Center; 125, LOC, LC-DIG-cwpb-05210; 126, MOC, Copy Photography by Katherine Wetzel; 127, Trudy Pearson; 128, CHS, P&S-1932.0027; 129, VHS; 131, LOC, LC-DIG-cwpb-05665; 132-133, NARA; 135, LOC, LC-DIG-cwpb-01001; 137, LOC, LC-DIG-cwpb-03792; 138, MOC; 139, Greenville County Museum of Art (John I. Smith Charities); 140, Courtesy Smithsonian Images; 141, LOC, LC-DIG-cwpb-00159; 142, MOC, Photography by Dementi Studios; 144, LOC, LC-DIG-cwpb-07546; 145, FMTW; 146, LOC, LC-DIG-cwpb-04402; 147, LOC, LC-DIG-cwpb-00202; 149, LOC, LC-DIG-cwpb-06341; 150, LOC, LC-DIG-cwpb-00218; 153, LOC, LC-DIG-cwpb-00260; 154, LOC, LC-DIG-cwpb-04017; 156, LOC, LC-USZC2-3813; 157, Tulane University, New Orleans; 158, LOC, LC-DIG-cwpb-04106; 159, LOC, LC-DIG-cwpb-00262; 160, LOC, LC-USZ62-19319; 161, LOC, LC-DIG-cwpb-00255; 163, LOC, LC-DIG-cwpb-00240; 164 (t), LOC, LC-DIG-cwpb-01099; 164 (c), LOC, LC-DIG-cwpb-01108; 164 (b), LOC, LC-DIG-cwpb-00664; 165, VHS; 166-167, LOC, LC-DIG-cwpb-04352; 168, LOC, LC-DIG-cwpb-01098; 169, LOC, LC-DIG-cwpb-01109; 171, WRHS; 172, C. Paul Loane Collection; 175, LOC, LC-DIG-cwpb-01436; 177, NARA; 179, MOLLUS-MASS and USAMHI; 180, C. Paul Loane Collection; 181, LOC, LC-DIG-cwpb-01680; 182 (t), Collection of James C. Frasca; 182 (c), C. Paul Loane Collection; 182 (b), Rutherford B. Hayes Presidential Center; 183 (t), LOC, LC-DIG-cwpb-01010; 183 (b), C. Paul Loane Collection; 184, LOC, LC-DIG-cwpb-01663; 185 (t), From the collections of the Rochester Museum and Science Center, Rochester, NY; 185 (c), MOC, Photography by Katherine Wetzel; 185 (b), LOC,

LC-DIG-cwpb-00367; 186 (t), LOC, LC-DIG-cwpb-03882; 186 (c), C. Paul Loane Collection; 186 (b) LOC, LC-DIG-cwpb-02637; 187, LOC, LC-DIG-cwpb-06588.

CHAPTER 3, 1863: VICTORY OR DEATH
188-189, NARA; 190, LOC, LC-DIG-cwpb-06577; 191, Bettmann/CORBIS; 192, LOC, LC-USZ62-5473; 193, LOC, LC-DIG-cwpb-01012; 194, LOC, LC-USZC4-7984; 195, Ohio Historical Society, AL01904; 196-197, LOC, LC-USZ62-12777; 198, FMTW; 200, CHS, ICHi-39489; 202, LOC, LC-USZC2-1917; 203, MOLLUS-MASS and USAMHI; 204 (t), LOC, LC-DIG-cwpb-07384; 204 (b), Andrew D. Lytle Collection, Louisiana and Lower Mississippi Valley Collections, LSU Libraries, Baton Rouge, LA; 206-207, LOC, LC-DIG-cwpb-00943; 208, Vicksburg National Military Park; 209, CHS; 210, LOC, LC-USZ62-100070; 211, FMTW; 212 (t), VHS; 212 (b), Old Courthouse Museum; 213 (t); LOC, LC-USZC2-499; 213 (c), LOC, LC-USZ62-5558; 213 (b), Albert Shaw Collection; 215, Courtesy West Point Museum, United States Military Academy, West Point, NY; 216, LOC, LC-DIG-cwpb-06980; 217, WRHS; 219, LOC, LC-USZC4-4781; 220, Courtesy Georgia Archives, Vanishing Georgia Collection, GOR 517; 221, LOC, LC-USZ62-72090; 222 (t), NARA; 222 (b), MOLLUS-MASS and USAMHI; 223, Stonewall Jackson Foundation, Lexington, VA; 224, VHS; 225 (t) VHS; 225 (c), NARA; 225 (b), WRHS; 227, USAMHI; 229, Wadsworth Atheneum Museum of Art, Hartford, CT, The Ella Gallup Sumner and Mary Caitlin Sumner Collection Fund; 231, Courtesy Gettysburg National Military Park; 232 (t), LOC, LC-DIG-cwpb-07584; 232 (b), CHS, ICHi-24775; 233, Courtesy Wisconsin Veterans Museum; 234, Courtesy Wisconsin Veterans Museum; 235, LOC, LC-DIG-cwpb-04001; 236, NARA; 237, LOC, LC-DIG-cwpb-04337; 238-239, LOC, LC-DIG-cwpb-00859; 240 (t), LOC, LC-USZ62-55424; 240 (b), LOC, LC-DIG-cwpb-07523; 241, State Museum of Pennsylvania, Pennsylvania Historical and Museum Commission; 242 (t), VHS; 242 (b), LOC, LC-DIG-cwpb-01659; 243 (t), LOC, LC-DIG-cwpb-01640; 243 (c), LOC, LC-DIG-cwpb-00915; 243 (b), LOC, LC-DIG-cwpb-01450; 244, LOC, LC-USZ62-13016; 245, Time Life Pictures/Getty Images; 247 (t), LOC, LC-USZ62-88856; 247 (b), Courtesy Historical Society of Delware; 248, FMTW; 249, LOC, LC-USZ62-126179; 250, The Library of Virginia; 251, The Library of Virginia; 252, Robin Stanford; 253, CHS, ICHi-22172; 254, Getty Images; 255, USAMHI; 257 (tl), Courtesy of Picture History; 257 (tr), LOC, LC-USZ62-3855; 257 (bl), State Historical Society of Missouri; 257 (br), State Historical Society of Missouri; 258, LOC, LC-USZ62-134452; 259, LOC, LC-DIG-cwpbh-01176; 261, William L. Clemons Library, University of Michigan; 262, Kansas State Historical Library; 262-263, CORBIS; 265, NARA; 266, C. Paul Loane Collection; 267 (t), LOC, LC-USZ62-107446; 267 (b), LOC, LC-USZC4-2540; 268, Austin History Center, Austin Public Library, Texas; 271, LOC, LC-DIG-cwpbh-03123; 272-273, Army Art Museum; 273, Michael McAfee; 274, Old State House, Little Rock, Arkansas; 275, CORBIS; 276, LOC, LC-USZ62-90928; 277 (t), FMTW; 277 (b), FMTW; 278, Courtesy of Picture History; 280 (t), VHS; 280 (b), State Historical Society of Wisconsin, Madison; 281 (t), NYHS; 281 (CTR) MOLLUS-MASS and USAMHI; 281 (b), LOC, LC-USZC4-5681; 283, Richard F. Carlile Collection; 284, LOC, LC-DIG-cwpbh-03110; 285 (l), LOC, LC-DIG-cwpbh-03240; 285 (t), Courtesy of National Museum of American History, Smithsonian Institution; 285 (b), C. Paul Loane Collection; 286, MOC, Photography by Katherine Wetzel; 286-287, USAMHI; 287, Courtesy of National Museum of American History, Smithsonian Institution; 288 (all), MOC; 289 (t), LOC, LC-DIG-cwpb-04041; 289 (l), MOC, Photography by Katherine Wetzel; 289 (r), MOC; 290 (t), LOC, LC-B8184-10164; 290 (b), MOC; 290-291, MOC; 291 (t), MOC; 291 (b), David Wynn Vaughan Collection.

CHAPTER 4, 1864: REBELS UNDER SIEGE
292-293, LOC, LC-DIG-cwpb-03851; 295, LOC, LC-DIG-cwpb-04407; 296, MOC, Photography by Katherine Wetzel. 297 (t), Courtesy of Picture History; 297 (b), MOLLUS-MASS and USAMHI; 298 (t), MOLLUS-MASS and USAMHI; 298 (b), LOC, g3884w cwh00166; 299, LOC, LC-USZC4-1308; 300, MOLLUS-MASS and USAMHI; 301, LOC, LC-DIG-cwpb-04406; 302, LOC, LC-USZ62-53692; 304, LOC, LC-DIG-cwpb-01187; 306, LOC, LC-DIG-cwpb-00354; 307, LOC, LC-DIG-cwpb-01191; 309, LOC, LC-DIG-cwpb-01897; 310-311, LOC, LC-DIG-cwpb-01334; 312 (t), FMTW; 312 (b), Getty Images; 313, Getty Images; 314 (t), Valentine Richmond History Center; 314 (b), LOC, LC-DIG-cwpbh-01010; 315, Special Collections, The Leyburn Library, Washington and Lee University, Lexington, VA; 317, LOC, LC-DIG-cwpb-03628; 319, NARA; 320, Michael McAfee; 321 (t), Pick-Up; 321 (b), MOC; 322, NARA; 325, LOC, LC-DIG-cwpb-07052; 326, VHS; 327 (t) NARA; 327 (c), Medford Historical Society/CORBIS; 327 (b), LOC, LC-DIG-cwpb-03400; 328, Atlanta History Center; 329, NARA; 331, LOC, LC-USZC2-1913; 332, David Wynn Vaughan Collection; 335, LOC, LC-DIG-ppmsca-09326; 336-337, NARA; 339, LOC, LC-DIG-cwpb-02085; 340-341, Minnesota Historical Society; 342, MOC, Photography by Dennis McWaters; 342-343, NARA; 344, Stanley B. Burns, M.D. and the Burns Archive; 344-345, NARA; 345, LOC, LC-DIG-cwpb-04095; 346, MOLLUS-MASS and USAMHI; 346-347, NARA; 347 (t), LOC, LC-USZ62 9797; 347 (c), Valentine Richmond History Center; 347 (b), LOC, LC-USZ62-79788; 348, LOC, LC-DIG-ppmsca-10105; 349 (top photos), LOC, LC-DIG-ppmsca-10105; 349 (bottom photos), LOC, LC-DIG-ppmsca-10106.

CHAPTER 5, 1865: THE FINAL ACT
350-351, LOC, LC-USZC4-4593; 353, LOC, LC-DIG-cwpb-04367; 354-355, LC-DIG-cwpb-04734; 357, LOC, LC-USZ62-116996; 358 (t), LOC, g3904b cw030900a; 358 (b), Valentine Richmond History Center; 361, Painting by George Peter Alexander, The White House Collections; 363, LOC, LC-DIG-cwpb-03713; 364, NARA; 365, LOC, LC-DIG-cwpb-02060; 366, LOC, LC-USZ62-15123; 368, VHS; 369 (t), Medford Historical Society/CORBIS; 369 (c), LOC, LC-DIG-cwpb-02548; 369 (b), LOC, LC-DIG-cwpb-01287; 370, LOC; 371, LOC, LC-DIG-cwpb-00468; 372, Painting by Tom Lovell, National Geographic Society; 373, LOC, LC-DIG-cwpb-04324; 374, LOC, LC-USZC4-1157; 375, LOC, LC-DIG-cwpb-02941; 376, Courtesy of Smithsonian Images; 377, LOC, LC-USZ62-8812; 378 (t), FMTW; 378 (l), FMTW; 378 (r), FMTW; 379, LOC, LC-USZC4-5341; 380-381, CHS, ICHi-11252; 381 (t), Courtesy of Picture History; 381 (b) Abraham Lincoln Presidential Library and Museum; 382 (tl), LOC, LC-DIG-cwpb-04216; 382 (tr), LOC, LC-DIG-cwpb-04208; 382 (bl), Getty Images; 382 (br), LOC, LC-DIG-cwpb-04218; 382-383, LOC, LC-DIG-cwpb-04230.

EPILOGUE: THE NATION REUNITED
384-385, NYHS; 386, From the Collection of The Children's Museum of Indianapolis; 387, LOC; 388 (t), LOC; 388 (b), LOC. LC-USZ62-31933; 389, LOC, LC-USZC2-206; 390 (t), LOC, LC-DIG-cwpbh-00554; 390 (b), USAMHI; 391, Rutherford B. Hayes Presidential Center; 392, LOC, LC-USZC2-2161; 393(t), LOC, LC-DIG-cwpbh-01025; 393 (b), MOC; 394, LOC, LC-USZ62-46841; 395, Photo Courtesy of Edward E. Ayer Collection, The Newberry Library, Chicago; 396, LOC, LC-USZ61-1421; 397, Courtesy Gettysburg National Military Park.

EDITOR

NEIL KAGAN heads Kagan & Associates Inc., a firm specializing in innovative illustrated books. Over his 30-year career, the former Publisher/Managing Editor and Director of New Product Development for Time-Life Books was the guiding spirit behind numerous book series, including the award-winning Voices of the Civil War and Our American Century. Recently he edited *Great Battles of the Civil War*, *Great Photographs of the Civil War*, and National Geographic's *Concise History of the World*.

AUTHOR

STEPHEN G. HYSLOP has written books on American and world history, including the *National Geographic Almanac of World History* (with Patricia S. Daniels) and *Bound for Santa Fe: The Road to New Mexico and the American Conquest, 1806-1848*. Formerly at Time-Life Books, he served as a writer and editor for many volumes on the Civil War and the American West. He is a regular contributor to the History Channel Magazine, and his work has taken him to historical sites and battlefields throughout the country.

BOARD OF ADVISERS

HARRIS J. ANDREWS is a military historian who has done extensive research and writing on the Civil War over the past 25 years. A native Virginian and descendant of several Confederate soldiers, he had toured every battlefield on the East Coast by the age of 12. Andrews was a major contributor to all of the Time-Life Books Civil War projects, and he developed and edited the definitive Civil War volumes on arms and equipment, Echoes of Glory. He also played a major role assembling the comprehensive collection of Civil War letters, diary entries, and first-person accounts that appeared in Time-Life Books' Voices of the Civil War. He was a contributing editor to National Geographic's *Fields of Honor: Pivotal Battles of the Civil War* by Edwin C. Bearss.

C. PAUL LOANE has had a lifelong interest in the American Civil War with a special focus on the culture, experiences and gear of the common soldier. Descended from six veterans of the Union army, the Cherry Hill, New Jersey, resident is co-author of the acclaimed *U.S. Army Headgear 1812-1872*, and items from his exhaustive collection of memorabilia have illustrated the pages of dozens of publications. A member of the Company of Military Historians, Loane also serves as Chair of the Collections Committee of Philadelphia's renowned Civil War and Underground Railroad Museum. Retired from the administration of Rutgers University, he continues working on several new publications about the life, uniforms, and equipment of the war's rank and file.

BOB ZELLER is the author of the first narrative history of Civil War photography ever published, *The Blue and Gray in Black and White: A History of Civil War Photography*. He pioneered the modern presentation of Civil War stereoscopic photographs with his books *The Civil War in Depth, History in 3-D, Vols I and II*. He is a founder and the president of the nonprofit Center for Civil War Photography, Inc.

[LIST OF MAPS]

EYEWITNESS TO THE CIVIL WAR: THE COMPLETE HISTORY FROM
SECESSION TO RECONSTRUCTION
Edited by Neil Kagan
Narrative by Stephen G. Hyslop
Introduction by Harris J. Andrews

PUBLISHED BY THE NATIONAL GEOGRAPHIC SOCIETY

John M. Fahey, Jr.	*President and Chief Executive Officer*
Gilbert M. Grosvenor	*Chairman of the Board*
Nina D. Hoffman	*Executive Vice President, President, Books Publishing Group*

PREPARED BY THE BOOK DIVISION

Kevin Mulroy	*Senior Vice President and Publisher*
Leah Bendavid-Val	*Director of Photography Publishing and Illustrations*
Marianne R. Koszorus	*Director of Design*
Barbara Brownell Grogan	*Executive Editor*
Elizabeth Newhouse	*Director of Travel Publishing*
Carl Mehler	*Director of Maps*

CREATED BY KAGAN & ASSOCIATES, INC.,
FALLS CHURCH, VIRGINIA

Neil Kagan	*President and Editor-in-Chief*
Sharyn Kagan	*Vice President and Director of Administration*

STAFF FOR THIS BOOK

Stephen G. Hyslop	*Author*
Neil Kagan	*Illustrations Editor*
Carol Farrar Norton	*Art Director*
Barry Wolverton	*Contributing Author, Essays, Sidebars, Mapping the War*
Trudy Walker Pearson	*Researcher/Writer, Eyewitness Accounts, Maps, Chronologies, Appendix*
Harris J. Andrews	*Editor, Eyewitness Accounts*
Mary Beth Oelkers-Keegan	*Associate Editor / Copy Editor*

NATIONAL GEOGRAPHIC STAFF FOR THIS BOOK

Lisa Thomas	*Project Manager*
Matt Chwastyk	*Map Research and Production*
Steve D. Gardner	
Nicholas P. Rosenbach	
Gregory Ugiansky	
Gary Colbert	*Production Director*
Mike Horenstein	*Production Project Manager*
Meredith Wilcox	*Administrative Director, Illustrations*
Abby Lepold	*Illustrations Specialist*
Rebecca Hinds	*Managing Editor*

MANUFACTURING AND QUALITY MANAGEMENT

Christopher A. Liedel	*Chief Financial Officer*
Phillip L. Schlosser	*Vice President*
John T. Dunn	*Technical Director*
Vincent P. Ryan	*Director*
Chris Brown	*Director*
Maryclare Tracy	*Manager*

One of the world's largest nonprofit scientific and educational organizations, the National Geographic Society was founded in 1888 "for the increase and diffusion of geographic knowledge." Fulfilling this mission, the Society educates and inspires millions every day through its magazines, books, television programs, videos, maps and atlases, research grants, the National Geographic Bee, teacher workshops, and innovative classroom materials. The Society is supported through membership dues, charitable gifts, and income from the sale of its educational products. This support is vital to National Geographic's mission to increase global understanding and promote conservation of our planet through exploration, research, and education.

For more information, please call 1-800-NGS LINE (647-5463) or write to the following address:

National Geographic Society
1145 17th Street N.W.
Washington, D.C. 20036-4688 U.S.A.

Visit the Society's Web site at www.nationalgeographic.com.

This 2013 edition printed for Barnes & Noble, Inc. by the National Geographic Society.

ISBN: 978-1-4351-5046-1 (B&N ed.)

LIBRARY OF CONGRESS CATALOGING-IN-PUBLICATION DATA

Eyewitness to the Civil War: the complete history from secession to Reconstruction / edited by Neil Kagan; narrative by Stephen G. Hyslop; introduction by Harris J. Andrews.
    p. cm.
    Includes bibliographical references and index.
    ISBN-10: 0-7922-6206-9
    ISBN-13: 978-0-7922-6206-0
    Deluxe ISBN-10: 0-7922-5280-2
    Deluxe ISBN-13: 978-07922-5280-1
    1. United States—History—Civil War, 1861-1865—Personal narratives.
2. United States—History—Civil War, 1861-1865—Pictorial works.
I. Kagan, Neil. II. Hyslop, Stephen G. (Stephen Garrison), 1950-
    E464.E93 2006
    973.7—dc22

2006019672

Printed in China
13/PPS/1

ACKNOWLEDGMENTS

To create a unique book on the Civil War one needs a unique group of contributors. There are many people to thank—Lisa Thomas and Kevin Mulroy of the National Geographic Book Division for their support and guidance; author Stephen G. Hyslop for his compelling narrative packed with first-person anecdotes; art director Carol Norton for her elegant and imaginative design; Barry Wolverton for the wonderful essays; Carl Mehler for his care in putting together the maps; Mary Beth Oelkers-Keegan for striving to make the copy perfect; Abby Lepold and Meredith Wilcox for the countless hours they spent gathering hundreds of rare illustrations; Stan Simpson, from Quad Graphics, for his skillful correction of the sharpness and color of our images; Trudy Walker Pearson for her tireless search for eyewitness letters and accounts; and her husband, Robert W. Pearson, for all his help; and Walton Rawls, for proofing the text. I would also like to thank our Board of Advisers—Harris J. Andrews for sharing his endless knowledge of Civil War stories and facts; C. Paul Loane for opening up his amazing collection of Civil War relics, photographs, and memorabilia; and Bob Zeller for his knowledge of private collectors and for leading us to David Wynn Vaughan, who shared his unique collection of ambrotypes and tintypes, many of which grace our cover and title page. And finally, I would like to thank my family, Sharyn, Josh, Lisa, and Lewis who give me the encouragement and support to continue creating one-of-a-kind illustrated books.   *—Neil Kagan*